DICTIONARY OF BANKING

INFORMATION AT YOUR FINGERTIPS

*Up-to-date and comprehensive, Pitman
Dictionaries are indispensable reference
books, providing clear, crisp explanations
of specialist terminologies in an
easy-to-use format.*

*Accounting Terms Dictionary
A Dictionary of Economics and Commerce
Dictionary of Advertising
Dictionary of Business Studies
Dictionary of Banking and Finance
Dictionary of Law
Dictionary of Purchasing Supply Management
Dictionary of Insurance
Dictionary of Human Resources Management*

DICTIONARY OF BANKING

GERALD KLEIN FCIB, CERT ED

Visiting Lecturer, Royal Holloway and
Bedford New College, University of London

Visiting Lecturer, University of Exeter

PITMAN
PUBLISHING

Pitman Publishing
128 Long Acre, London WC2E 9AN

A Division of Longman Group Limited

First published in 1992
Reprinted 1994

© Longman Group UK Limited 1992

British Library Cataloguing in Publication Data
A CIP catalogue record for this book can be obtained from the British Library

ISBN 0 273 03788 9

Printed and bound by Bell and Bain Ltd., Glasgow

Dedicated to my grandson
Gabriel Ian Spiers

PREFACE

When Pat Bond of Pitman Publishing asked me to consider rewriting this dictionary, I questioned this request since it seemed no time at all since I revised Fred Perry's original publication. Looking at my records, it was 1987 when I wrote my manuscript and publication was in 1988.

On investigation, I can well see why it was necessary to rewrite the dictionary. So much has happened in banking that major changes seem absolutely vital in order to keep bankers and other users up to date.

This edition, while having banking and other students in mind, has also been written for use in bank branches, offices and departments and for the various subsidiaries of banks. I trust that they will find it useful and refer to it from time to time.

This book could not have been written without help and consultation with a variety of persons, so that I would first like to acknowledge my thanks to various members of the Bank of England for their notes and advice. To various employees of Barclays Bank plc and National Westminster Bank plc I would like to thank them for their patience and tolerance and responding to my questions speedily and enthusiastically. To the Serious Fraud Office, Standard & Poors, British Bankers' Association, Pauline Hedges Banking Information Service, APACS, The Stock Exchange, LIFFE, The European Bank for Reconstruction and Development, Chartered Institute of Bankers for providing me with up-dated material. To Simon Rubinsohn of Capel-Cure Myer Capital Management Ltd I would like to express my thanks for giving up his time for his researches on my behalf. To Adrian Coleman FCA, who without fuss responded to the many questions put to him at any time of day. To Suzanne Dempsey of Pitman Publishing for her assistance and patience. To my son Laurence Klein for his guidance from time to time and keeping me up to date on investment matters. To my wife Anne who has been my constant support. Should I have inadvertently omitted to mention any person or organisation, please accept my apologies.

Finally, readers should be aware that this dictionary was written during the 1992 parliamentary election campaign, with the party in power producing its own budget in March 1992, while the opposition party publicising the budget it would adopt if it received the country's mandate. While every attempt has been made to be as accurate as possible, there may be variations by the time the book is published.

Gerald Klein
18th March 1992

A

ab initio. From the start. At the beginning.

abandonment. The occasion when an option is allowed to expire without being exercised.

absolute title. The highest and safest title which can be given by obtaining a registered title to land. No other person can contest his/her right to the property. The owner of leasehold land can be given absolute title only if the freehold title is already registered and therefore he/she has the right to grant a head lease or after ten years during which the proprietor/s have been in possession.

absorption. The taking over of a small company by a large company which results in the smaller company almost entirely disappearing into the organisation of the larger company.

absorption costing. A costing principle whereby fixed and variable costs are included in the costs of production. *See also* MARGINAL COST.

abstract of title. A summary showing the chain of title from the good root title of property – at least 15 years old – until point of sale by a vendor.

ABT. *See* ASSOCIATION OF BANKING TEACHERS.

acceleration. This is a provision in a swap agreement for early repayment of the amount due. The reason for the acceleration provision is to cover defaults, non-payment of annual fees, or the failure to meet the obligations of the agreement.

acceptance. The signing across the face of the bill by the drawee of his acceptance to pay the bill on its due date. Often the signature will be accompanied by the word 'accepted' and the date of the acceptance. Where the presented bill is accompanied with other commercial documents, the acceptance of the bill and the delivery of the accompanying documents signifies that the goods have been accepted by the buyer. *See* QUALIFIED ACCEPTANCE.

acceptance credit. It is used primarily for the financing of trade. An arrangement is made by the importer to draw a term bill on a bank/acceptance house who, after acceptance will return it to the importer who will then discount it in the market and on receipt of funds remit the amount due to the overseas seller. It also refers to a term bill of exchange drawn by a beneficiary of a documentary credit on the bank. *See also* DOCUMENTARY CREDIT.

acceptance for honour. In the case of a bill of exchange having been noted or protested for dishonour for non-acceptance and is not overdue, any person who is not already a party to the bill may with the consent of the holder accept the bill supra protest for the honour of the party liable on the bill or for whose account the bill is drawn. To be valid the bill (*i*) must indicate on the face of it that it is an acceptance for honour; (*ii*) signed by the acceptor for honour. If the bill does not indicate in any way for whom the acceptance in honour has been made, it is deemed to be accepted on behalf of the drawer. Where a bill is payable after sight, its maturity is calculated from the date of the protesting for non acceptance and not from the date of acceptance for honour.

acceptance house. A bank usually a merchant bank, who among its many functions specialises in accepting bills drawn by customers. By lending its name, the holder is able to discount the bill at the best possible rates.

acceptor. The endorsement of the drawee on the face of a term bill of exchange, usually with the word 'acceptance' added. The drawee is then liable on the bill.

ACCESS. The name given to a credit card company jointly owned by three clearing banks, namely, Lloyds, Midland and National Westminster. *See also* CREDIT CARD.

accommodation bill A bill of exchange that is accepted by a drawee who merely lends his or her name to the bill and has not received any consideration. When the bill falls due the drawee looks to the drawer to provide funds to make payment.

account. The recording in the ledger of the financial transactions that have taken place: the account will show the receipts, the expenditure and the outstanding balance. In commerce, a statement showing the amount owing for goods, services, etc; on the Stock Exchange, the time elapsing between one Settlement Day and the next; in banking, the current, deposit account either in sterling or currency maintained by the bank for a customer. A *current account* is one running from day to day on which cheques are paid and into which credits are paid. No interest is usually paid, except in special circumstances. Overdrafts may be taken by arrangement. *Deposit accounts* are usually in credit. The balance or part of the balance is repayable after notice of seven days or other agreed times, or at the end of the fixed time for which the deposit has been made.

accountancy. The profession of a practising accountant.

accountant. A professionally qualified person who is able to record financial transactions of a business. A member of either the Institute of Chartered Accountants (ICA) or the Chartered Association of Certified Accountants (ACCA) may act as auditors for companies. The title of *accountant* is often given to a senior bank official in a branch who is responsible for the flow of work within that branch and its daily agreement.

accountants' opinion. *See* AUDITORS' REPORT.

accounting bases. The methods developed for applying fundamental accounting concepts to financial transactions for the purpose of financial accounts.

accounting concepts or principles. Basic assumptions underlying the financial accounts of an organisation.

accounting period. That period of time for which the books of account have been balanced, and final accounts, balance sheet and other statements have been prepared for the period stated.

accounting policies. The specific accounting bases selected by management as being most appropriate to the circumstances of enterprise.

Accounting Standards Committee. A committee set up in the 1970s to set up accounting standards which were to guide the members of the major accountancy bodies in setting up good standards of accounting practice. The rules are comprehensive and precise and any accountant that does not conform to these standards may be asked to justify his behaviour. These rules are known as SSAPS (Statements of Standard Accounting Practice).

account payee. The insertion of these words in the crossing of a cheque has no legal recognition but it is an instruction to the collecting banker to ensure that the account of the payee is credited with the amount on the cheque. A bank will collect a cheque with these words for a customer who is not the payee, providing he or she is of undoubted integrity.

account sales. An invoice sent by an agent (consignee) to his principal (consignor) showing the details of goods sold and the price obtained less expenses. Where goods are sold at a public auction, the agent will send his principal an account of goods sold.

account stated. An account between two parties which consists of items which have been expressly or impliedly agreed between the parties as entries which have properly appeared on the account. Any balance showing is likewise agreed as correct.

accruals concept. Revenue and costs recognised as they are earned or incurred, not as money is received or paid.

accumulated dividend. The dividend due, usually to preference shareholders, but not yet paid. The amount is carried forward as a liability, until such time as it is paid.

acid test. Often known as the liquidity ratio. This is ascertained by adding the amount of the debtors to the cash and bank balances and showing the figure as a ratio to the current liabilities. It is called the 'acid test', because the ratio reveals whether the entity can pay its debts as soon as they fall due.

acquisition. The act of one company taking control over another company.

act of bankruptcy. Under the Insolvency Act 1986 the act of bankruptcy is merely a petition presented on the basis of the debtor being unable or unwilling to pay an unsecured debt of £750 or more owed to a creditor(s).

act of God. Natural catastrophes which are caused by tempests, earthquakes, lightning, gale force winds, etc. They cause exceptional damage. Many insurance policies do not cover such events.

acting in concert. See CONCERT PARTY.

actuary. An employee of an insurance company or similar institution who is qualified by the Institute of Actuaries, and deals with life expectancy, and the average proportion of losses by time and other accidents.

ademption. The revocation of a bequest or grant. A removal. The destruction of an item subject to a specific request between the time the will was executed and the death of the testator.

adjudication order. An order by a court stating that a debtor is bankrupt. The estate of the debtor is transferred to a trustee who will then proceed to wind it up and dispose of assets in favour of the creditors.

administrative receiver. This person is appointed by the court and the powers conferred on him are as specified in Schedule 1 of the Insolvency Act 1986. He is appointed to manage the whole of a company's property on behalf of the holders of any debentures of the company secured by a charge on the assets of the company.

administration order. An application to a court either by the directors of a company or an unsecured creditor of a company to appoint an administrator to either continue the company as a going concern – if advantageous – or make proposals which would be beneficial to the creditors.

administrator. The appointment of a person or persons by the court, to wind up the affairs of an individual who has died intestate. Before a bank will allow a person to take over the assets of a deceased customer, letters of

administration must be exhibited. Under the Insolvency Act 1986 an administrator can be appointed by the court to take over the affairs of a company. The administrator has the power, if thought fit, to continue the business and restore it to a solvent position rather than sell the assets for the benefit of the creditors. To justify the appointment of an administrator the court must be satisfied that one of the following objectives will be reached: (a) the survival of the company as a going concern; (b) the approval of a voluntary arrangement; (c) a compromise agreement between the company and its creditors per s. 425 Companies Act 1985; (d) a more advantageous realisation of the company's assets if winding up is effected.

ad valorum. According to value. VAT is an example of an *ad valorem* tax.

advance. A loan by one person, corporate or not, to another, corporate or not. A prepayment for services or work undertaken, e.g. an advance on salary. A general word indicating that a loan or overdraft has been given.

advice of fate. Where a bank or its customer requires notification of final payment of a cheque or bill of exchange, it is usual to make a special presentation of the instrument with a request by the presenting banker that *fate* should be notified to him or her. Frequently the presenting banker would telephone the paying banker to obtain the result of the presentation. When an enquiry is made as to the possibility of a cheque being paid on presentation, the paying bank would normally answer in terms such as 'If in our hands now and in order it will be paid'.

ADR. See AMERICAN DEPOSIT RECEIPT.

advice note. A note informing the addressee that a transaction is being or had been completed, e.g. a delivery of goods.

advisory funds. Funds that have been deposited with a bank by a customer for investment purposes, but such funds may only be invested after consultation with that customer.

affidavit. A written statement to a person, such as a solicitor or notary, given under oath. It may be used as evidence in a court of law.

after acquired property. Property coming to the bankrupt after the date of the adjudication order. This property should be reported to the trustee.

age admitted. A statement in a policy of life insurance showing the birth date and/or age of the insured. Where it has in the first instance been omitted, it is then added by way of an endorsement. Its importance rests with the fact that the premiums are calculated from that particular date and any mistake deliberate or otherwise could invalidate the policy or an adjustment to the premium or proceeds may be made. When a banker takes a policy as security, he must ascertain that the age has been admitted.

agency. The relationship that exists between two persons, called the principal and the agent, which empowers the agent to act on behalf of the principal for the purpose of binding the principal in law. In banking, the principal is usually the customer while the agent is the bank.

agent. A person who acts on behalf of another. He/she is contracted or employed to act on a principal's behalf and providing he contracts within his powers, then the responsibility is with the principal. *See also* DEL CREDERE AGENT; ESTATE AGENT; EXPORT AGENT; FORWARDING AGENT; GENERAL AGENT; IMPORT AGENT; INSURANCE AGENT; MERCANTILE AGENT; SPECIAL AGENT; TRAVEL AGENT.

aggregate. To bring together, to collect, a sum total of items, a total number of persons in a group.

aggregate monetary demand. Total demand for consumer and capital goods backed by money.

aging schedule. The list of debtors prepared by an accountant showing (*a*) the amounts outstanding; (*b*) the number of days the debts are overdue; (*c*) the percentage of the total debts outstanding:

e.g. up to one month £25 000 50 per cent
1–2 months £15 000 30 per cent
2–4 months £6000 12 per cent
4–6 months £4000 8 per cent
Total £50 000 100 per cent

This schedule assists in the preparation of the provision for doubtful debts.

agio. The act of changing different forms and types of money. The difference in value between one currency and another. The difference in value can be quoted either as a percentage between nominal and par value.

AGM. *See* ANNUAL GENERAL MEETING.

agricultural charge. A fixed and/or a floating charge on the assets of a farmer whether he is an owner or tenant. The charge will be given a security to a bank for providing an advance. These charges must be registered within seven days with the Agricultural Credits Superintendent at the Land Registry, but can be invalid if the farmer goes into liquidation within three months of the date of the charge being given.

Agricultural Credit Corporation (ACC). Formed in 1965 to give guarantees to banks who provide finance to farmers who require funds either for working capital or fixed capital. It is sponsored by the government.

Agricultural Mortgage Corporation (AMC). The AMC was established by the Bank of England in 1928 for the purpose of providing long term funds at favourable rates to farmers. Provided the farmers could show some success in their work and offer freehold land as security then loans of up to 40 years were available.

air bill all risks. An insurance policy/certificate that covers goods despatched by air. It covers a wide range of risks, but not necessarily those appertaining to war, strikes, civil commotion or perishing of goods.

air consignment note. *See below.*

airway bill. Made out by the consignor of goods to be transported by air. Often called *air consignment note.*

air pocket stock. When there is an announcement of bad or unfavourable news, shares are likely to fall sharply. Shareholders will rush to sell, but no buyers are available, consequently the price of shares will plunge sharply rather like an aeroplane entering an air pocket.

all in cost. The overall value or cost of a swap. It can be used as a quotation expressing the absolute value on a semi annual basis, or as a basis point spread to the semi annual or equivalent of the US Treasury yield for interest swaps, LIBOR, etc.

all moneys debenture. A mortgage debenture that secures any funds owed to a bank at any time and on any account. It covers a fixed and floating charge on the assets of the company.

allonge. An attachment to a bill of exchange, when the back of the bill is full of endorsements and further written space has to be provided. The allonge is an integral part of the bill.

allotment. The issue of shares to persons who have applied for the purchase. The amount allotted may be in full, but if the issue is oversubscribed, only part of the number may be allotted.

allotment letter. A letter advising an applicant for shares in a company that he has been successful in obtaining a stated number of shares and advising him/her whether any further instalments are due and when payment must be made. The letter also allows the person to renounce the allocation or sell the rights to another via a stockbroker.

alteration of a bill. Where a bill of exchange has been materially altered, e.g. the date, the sum payable, time of payment or the acceptance without the knowledge or approval of the parties to that bill, it is avoided except against the party who authorised or made that alteration and all subsequent indorsers. However, where the bill has been altered in such a way as not to be apparent and the bill is in the hands of a holder in due course, then that person may avail himself to the bill as if it had not been altered and may enforce it according to its original tenor.

alternative payee. A bill of exchange, including a cheque, may be made payable to two or more persons in the alternative.

American deposit receipt (ADR). Issued by non US companies to represent their shares in the US markets, this encourages both US citizens and other nationals to purchase the shares of non-US companies. ADRs can be traded in the London market. *See* AMERICAN-TYPE SHARE CERTIFICATE.

American Express card. This plastic card issued by the American Express Company is often classified as a leisure card or debit card, but because there is usually no arrangement for long term credit, it cannot be defined as a credit card. Through its various offices in the UK and extensive advertising the American Express Company has increased the number of users of its card. Holders of the card have no limit placed on the sum they can spend, but all outstanding debts must be settled by a given date.

American-type share certificate. Often called an *American desposit receipt.* A certificate which has many of the characteristics of a *bearer bond,* but which is not a negotiable instrument because it does not give to a new owner any better title than the previous owner had. The name of the registered holder appears on the face of the document and a blank form of transfer is printed on the back. Usually the registered holder signs the form of transfer and this allows the certificate to pass from hand to hand like a bearer bond, delivery transferring title. Unlike a bearer bond, however, there are no coupons and the dividend is sent to the registered holder, from whom the owner must claim it. The owner can be registered by completing the back of the form and will then receive dividends, notices, etc. sent direct, but the certificate will have lost its readily negotiable characteristic. *See also* MARKING NAMES.

amortisation. 1. Payment into a sinking fund so that money is available to pay or redeem by annual instalments, bonds with interest that is still outstanding. 2. The transferring of land in perpetuity to a charitable body or ecclesiastical authority 'in mortain'.

ancillary credit business. Any business that is for the purposes of the Consumer Credit Act 1974 involved in credit brokerage, debt adjusting, debt counselling, debt collection or acting as a credit reference agency.

annual general meeting (AGM). The meeting of shareholders and directors of a company that must take place at least every 12 months when the report of the directors is given, and there is an opportunity to discuss the past year's activities and future prospects. At this meeting directors are elected or re-elected, auditors are appointed and proposed dividends are made.

annual percentage rate (APR). The total charge for credit in a consumer credit agreement, which, in accordance with the Consumer Credit Act 1974, must show the annual compound rate of interest to be charged.

annual report and accounts. These are documents that are prepared annually by the directors of a company who report on the activities of that company. This will include a flow of funds statement and the future prospects of the company. The audited profit and loss account and balance sheet will also be presented.

annual return. Under the Companies Act, every company that has a share capital must make a return, to the Registrar of Companies, at least once a year showing: (*i*) the address of the registered office; (*ii*) an up to date copy of the shareholders register; (*iii*) a copy of the list of debenture holders; (*iv*) the share capital and debentur particulars; (*v*) the list of directors; (*vi*) a copy of the final accounts and balance sheet.

annuitant. A person in receipt of an annuity.

annuity. A payment made by an insurance company to a person who has paid in a lump sum or has in some other way purchased an annuity so that he/she may receive at regular intervals a sum of money.

answer on a cheque. It is a rule of the Committee of London and Scottish Clearing Banks that any cheque presented to the paying banker for payment and not paid shall have the reason for non-payment written on the face of the cheque, usually at the top. The answers can be classified into two groups. The first being for technical reasons, e.g. post dated. The second reason is usually due to lack of funds. In this instance, the bank must be extremely careful in checking the appropriateness of the answer so that there is little or no damage to the customer's reputation. It is usual to answer 'refer to drawer' which has for many years been considered a safe reply.

antedate. The placing of the date on a document prior to that on which it is signed. A bill of exchange is not invalid by reason of it being antedated.

antedated cheque. A banker receiving a cheque antedated by six months or more for payment would regard it as *stale*, and would return it unpaid unless confirmation could be obtained from the drawer to pay it. A cheque can also be *stale* for purposes of negotiation. No time has been set by statute for this, but is is thought that a period of ten to twelve days after the date of the cheque will be enough to make it stale. A holder taking a cheque in negotiation cannot claim to be a holder in due course if the cheque is stale but has to take the bill 'complete and regular on the face of it'. A cheque which is stale is not *regular*.

APACS. *See* ASSOCIATION FOR PAYMENT CLEARING SERVICES.

applicant. The person who makes an application. In international trade it is the person who requests a bank to open a documentary credit on his or her behalf in favour of a named beneficiary. The applicant is usually the importer.

appropriation. The putting aside funds for a specific or general purpose. The allocation of money from a special fund to be used for a special purpose.

appropriation account. The account which shows the net profit earned in the year, plus any balance carried down from previous years, will then show how these funds are divided between the reserves and the distribution of dividends.

appropriation of goods. Linking goods with the appropriate contract.

appropriation of payments. The act of a customer who, when paying in a credit to his or her account, specifies the debit against which it is to be set. If the customer does not so appropriate, the banker is free to do so, and may appropriate the credit in discharge or partial discharge of the customer's indebtedness to the bank. For appropriation under the rule in *Clayton's case, see* CLAYTON'S CASE.

APR. *See* ANNUAL PERCENTAGE RATE.

arbitrage. A term used to describe the switching of funds from one centre to another or from one account to another. Dealers in the foreign exchange market and other markets will deal with a view to making a profit due to rates differing between one centre and another. It is also used when bank customers are with present day technology able to switch funds from an account with one institution to an account with another institution, so that they can use their funds profitably.

arithmetic mean. An average, calculated by the division of the total of items by the number of items.

arrangement fee. A fee frequently charged by a bank over and above the interest payable on any accommodation taken. It first made its appearance in connection with bridging loans, where the time of the facility, often up to four months, did not allow very much profit to the bank, when one took into account the time and cost involved in setting up the loan. Often banks leave the matter of an arrangement fee to the discretion of their branch manager and, on occasions, no charge is made at all.

arrangement with creditors or members. The directors of a company may make a proposal to the shareholders of the company and its creditors for a composition of its debts or a scheme of arrangements of its affairs. The implementation of the arrangement must be under the supervision of a nominee who must be an insolvency practitioner. It may also be made by an administrator when an administration order is in force, or if the company is being wound up, by the liquidator.

arrear. Being unpaid or unsatisfied. Owing or behind with payments.

arrestment. By order of a court property is seized and held on behalf of a creditor until such time that money owed is paid. *See also* ATTACHMENT.

articles of association. The document that sets out the internal rules governing a limited company. It deals with such procedures as voting rights, elections of directors, their duties, calling a general meeting, etc.

articles of partnership. The agreement between persons who have become trading partners as defined in the Partnership Act of 1890. It states the rights, duties and obligations of the partners. All partners still retain their personal liability to outstanding debts.

Asian dollar market. The Eurocurrency markets of Singapore, Hong Kong and Tokyo.

asked. The price demanded by the seller.

assent. 1. An agreement or acknowledgment. 2. A document executed by an executor or personal representative of a deceased person, which vests the legal estate in the beneficiary so named in the document. No assent is necessary when the land is sold by the executor. A conveyance is then executed in favour of the purchaser. 3. An agreement of a holder of stocks or bonds to change some of the conditions of the terms of issue.

assented bonds. The agreement by bondholders for an adjusted repayment of the bond or some plan for a financial reorganisation of the bonds.

assessment of tax. The stated amount of tax requested for payment from the Inland Revenue by the individual. This amount is assessed from the annual return made by the individual taking into consideration his earned and unearned income less the allowances permitted. There are four basic schedules. *Sch. A* covers income from property and rents; *Sch. B* from woodlands; *Sch. D* from interest received but untaxed at source i.e. from trades, businesses and professions; *Sch. E* from earnings and pensions. Where there is incomplete knowledge of a persons income or no return has been made, then an assessment of tax payable is made based on the previous year. This can be adjusted at a later period.

asset. An item of property or value. In accounting terms it is any item – real or fictitious – that can be given a monetary value.

asset liability management. The control of a bank's deposit and lending policies to ensure safety, liquidity and profitability.

asset stripping. The buying of a company for the purpose of making a profit by selling its assets due to under valuation. Such an opportunity will arise when a company is trading at a loss, or making poor profits although its *asset values* are high.

asset value. What the assets will actually realise when they are sold. *See also* BOOK VALUE; BREAK-UP VALUE.

assignation. 1. A legal authority to pay, i.e. a writ or subpoena. 2. An order whereby the debtor or holder of a bill of exchange is authorised to remit to an assignee, for the account of the assignor either funds or a document of title. 3. A deed of convenyance in favour of an assignee.

assignee. The person to whom *assignment* of any right or personal property is made.

assignment. The act of assigning allotment, legal transfer of a right or property; the instrument by which such transfer is effected; the right of property transferred. The writing of a cheque is not, except in Scotland, an assignment of funds. There, however, a credit balance on a current account which is insufficient to meet a cheque drawn on that account must be put on a *suspense account* towards the eventual payment of the debt.

assignment notice. The formal notice that a call/put option must be bought/sold at the exercise price so that the obligation must be met.

assignment of life policy. The transfer by the assignor (the assured person) to the assignee (e.g. a bank) of the right to receive the proceeds under a life assurance policy. This assignment must be in writing to the insurance company, who must acknowledge this notice in writing. The policy will be indorsed to this effect and any transfer is subject to equity.

assignor. The person making an *assignment* of any right or personal property to another.

assigns. The plural of assignee. Persons to whom a transfer or assignment of any right or property is made.

associate. A partner or colleague; a member of an association or institution. For the purposes of the Consumer Credit Act 1974 *associate* shall be construed in accordance with s. 184 of the act. The Insolvency Act 1986 s. 435 gives a wide interpretation of the meaning of *associate.* Broadly, any person related to another, or a person in a partnership with another and the husband/wife, a trustee with a trust, an employeee, or a company that has control of another company and a director of a company is an associate of that company.

associated company. 1. Whereby one company has a financial interest in another, and consequently is likely to have an influence on its activities by having a representation on its board of directors. 2. A mutual interest of two companies forming a partnership in a joint venture.

Association of Banking Teachers (ABT). An organisation formed in 1978 to bring together full time and part time teachers in banking subjects as set forth in the syllabus of the Chartered Institute of Bankers. Its aims and objects are: (*a*) to foster and promote the study and development of banking and related subjects; (*b*) to guide and aid the professional development of both full time and part time teachers of banking subjects; (*c*) to act as a consultative body on the tuition needs of bankers in cooperation with the Chartered Institute of Bankers and any other bodies concerned with banking education; (*d*) to cooperate with universities, colleges and other teaching institutions in furtherance of banking education; (*e*) to foster and promote cooperation with banks and bankers and with their educational and professional organisations. The association provides a wide range of courses and conferences throughout each year and regular *Bulletins* containing informative and up to date articles, reports, letters, etc. An effective relationship between the association and the Chartered Institute of Bankers has created a most efficient link between the administrators of banking education and the practitioners.

Association of British Factors (ABF). An association that was established in 1977 consisting of eight members representing those companies which provide full factoring services as their main business as opposed to those only interested in invoice discounting (*q.v.*). See FACTORING.

Association of Corporate Treasurers. A professional association composed of persons whose work is concerned with treasureship in companies and financial institutions. Membership is obtainable by examination and through being engaged in the industry for at least two years. Fellows are appointed from members who must have positions of management, engaged in the industry for at least five years, or who are invoived in teaching treasureship.

association clause. The clause in the *memorandum of association* by which the original members agree to take up the number of shares written against their names.

Association of International Bond Dealers. This association was founded in 1969 for the purpose of standardising market practices. Its members are all active in the issuing and secondary markets.

Association of Investment Trust Companies (AITC) This organisation was formed in 1932 for the advancement and protection of the interests of its members, and their shareholders.

Association for Payment Clearing Services (APACS). Its address is Mercury House, Triton Court, 14 Finsbury Square, London EC2A 1BR. It was established in 1985 as a non-statutory umbrella organisation with responsbility for the management, control and orderly development of the nation's principal payment clearing and money transmission systems. Its formation followed a review of the UK payment clearing systems by a committee set up in 1984 under the chairmanship of Denis Child. The recommendations of the committee (usually known as the Child Report) were rapidly implemented and involved the establishment of a new organisational structure featuring an unincorporated umbrella organisation (APACS) and beneath it three individual clearing companies limited by shares and covering the five principal operational clearings. These companies were established as: (*a*) Cheque and Credit Clearing Co. Ltd (bulk paper); (*b*) CHAPS & Town Clearing Co. Ltd (high value same day settlement); (*c*) BACS Ltd (formerly Bankers' Automated Clearing Services Ltd) (bulk electronic). Membership of any clearing company became open to any bank or building society meeting a range of objective criteria. It also became possible for an institution to join a single company, whereas in the past membership of the bankers' clearing house required an operational presence in all clearings. The establishment of APACS removed all responsibility for clearing matters from the Committee of London Clearing Bankers and to reflect its changed role, the body was renamed the Committee of London and Scottish Bankers. However, the Scottish and Northern Irish paper clearings were not affected. Also included in the coverage of APACS were responsbility for UK financial section standards, cheque card and eurocheque and the payment system research work previously carried out by the Inter-Bank Research Organisation (IBRO). Subsequently, APACS has increased its involvement in European payment systems matters. At the moment, APACS has 20 members (whereas in 1984 there had only been ten members of the Clearing House) including three building societies and one former building society. *See also* BACS LTD,; CHAPS & TOWN CLEARING COMPANY LTD; CHEQUE AND CREDIT CLEARING COMPANY LTD.

assurance. *See* INSURANCE.

at a discount. *See* DISCOUNT.

at a premium. *See* PREMIUM.

at call. This describes a deposit by a bank or financial institution with the money market (discount house) on condition that the funds are repayable on demand.

at par. A quotation (*i*) on the London International Stock Exchange where the price of the stock/share is the same as its nominal value; (*ii*) in the foreign exchange market it is when the forward rate is the same as the spot rate.

at short notice. A deposit by a bank or financial institution with a discount house whereby the funds are to be refunded within 14 days.

at sight. *See* SIGHT BILL.

attachment. Where a person has failed to comply with a court order or is in contempt of court, then the seizure of his chattels and money may be made by the order of the court. Alternatively under the Attachment of Earning Act 1971, the court may order that a specific sum is deducted from the wage/salary of a person. A remedy for a creditor who obtained judgment against a defaulting debitor.

attest. The act of putting a person on oath to testify or act as a witness in a court of law.

attestation. A formal witnessing, especially of a signature. *See also* WILL, WITNESS.

attested copy. A true copy of an original document, certified as such by a witness by a declaration to that effect written on the copy and signed by the witness.

at the money. In the traded options market the exercise price is about the same as the current market price for the security.

attorn. To assign or transfer; to recognise a new owner.

attorney. The name given to a lawyer or solicitor or any person who in a legal capacity is acting on behalf of another. *See also* POWER OF ATTORNEY.

attornment. The recognition by a third party that a legal relationship exists between two other parties. Such legal relationships include mortgagor/mortgagee, landlord/tenant, owner/possessor of goods, e.g. warehousekeepor and bank in whose name the goods are stored.

auction. A sale of goods whereby the goods are sold to the highest bidder, providing the price offered has reached or past the reserve price stated by the seller. Auctions are binding on the buyer and seller and parties are urged to read the conditions of sale as advertised. On completion of an individual sale it is customary to close that sale by the fall of a gavel on the table or lectern. *See also* DUTCH AUCTION; GILT AUCTION.

audit. The examination of the books of account, vouchers, invoices, etc., by an auditor, to ensure that the final accounts represent a 'true and fair view'. Should the auditor discover any fraud or inaccuracy, then his report must be qualified to that extent.

auditing standards. A series of standards approved by the various accounting bodies which lay down the various principles and practices to be followed. *See also* STATEMENT OF STANDARD ACCOUNTING PRACTICE (SSAP).

auditor. A person who is appointed to carry out an audit. That person dealing with a company must have the appropriate professional qualification and must carry out the report on behalf of the shareholders. For the audit of a non-profit organisation, it is usual to appoint an honorary auditor, not necessarily a professional accountant, but a person who understands accounts.

auditors' report. Any report written by an auditor on a matter on which an opinion has been sought and within the scope and terms of the auditor's appointment. To comply with the Companies Act 1985 s. 236 a report on the financial statements of a company must be made.

authorised capital. The sum mentioned in the *memorandum of association* of a limited company as being the amount which the company is authorised to raise.

authorised institutions. Those institutions now recognised by the Bank of England under the Banking Act 1987 to act as banks and accept deposits.

authorised insurers. Financial Services Act s. 22: a body which is authorised under s. 3 and s. 4 of the Insurance Companies Act 1982 to carry on an insurance business which is an investment business in the UK and is authorised in respect of: (*a*) any insurance business which is an investment business and (*b*) any other investment business which that body may carry on without contravening s. 16 of that Act.

authorised person. Under s. 27 of the Financial Services Act, a person corporate or not, authorised by the Secretary of State to carry on an investment business, having regard that the applicant is a fit and proper person to carry on such a business and is able to provide the services described in the application.

automated teller machine. Commonly known as ATM. This machine permits the holder of the appropriate magnetic encoded card to obtain funds anytime of the day or night. Additionally the balance of the account may be obtained and cheque books and statements may be ordered. The machines are often called cash dispensers, although each bank has its own name for this service. UK banks now have the facility to permit customers to use encoded cards to obtain cash while in some European countries there is the possibility of this service being extended.

automatic data processing. See DATA PROCESSING.

aval. The guarantee that a bill of exchange will be paid on presentation. Usually given by bankers at the request of their customers. The *avalisation* of the bill by indorsement on the back of the bill. The *aval* is not recognised in English law and banks do not indorse bills in this manner unless they are asked to do so by customers of the highest integrity and with a suitable indemnity.

AVCO. See AVERAGE COST.

average. In insurance terminology this word means loss, e.g. particular average, meaning partial losses. In the more general sense it refers to an intermediate of several different numbers or quantities; prevailing rate or degree; ordinary; normal. *See also* GENERAL AVERAGE; PARTICULAR AVERAGE

average adjuster. A person who has the professional skill to calculate the proportions which are the responsibility of the owner of a vessel and the owners of the cargo in cases which result from any sacrifices which have to be made for safety of the ship and/or other cargo.

average balance. In banking where an account is balanced daily, that balance is recorded then totalled and divided by the number of days in a specified period to show the average balance in that period.

average bond. Where a consignee of goods has received goods which have incurred some loss, then a bond is given to the master of the vessel on delivery of that cargo in which he agrees to pay a proportion of that loss under a general average as soon as the loss is ascertained.

average clause. A clause in a marine insurance policy stipulating that certain articles shall be free from average, unless general, and that others shall be free from average, unless general, under a certain percentage. The clause is also being used in fire policies.

average cleared credit balance. The average balance on a credit account, adjusted for uncleared effects, used as the basis of an allowance made against the cost of keeping a current account before the commission charge is ascertained.

average cost. The total cost of production incurred by a company or firm in a given time, divided by the number of units of output.

average life. Maturity of a total borrowing after taking into account purchases by the borrower's sinking fund.

averaging. A system on a Stock Exchange whereby a speculator increases his or her purchases or sales as a result of a price movement of the stocks or shares, in order to average out the purchase or sale prices. Thus a *bull* averages by purchasing more stock if the price falls, a *bear* selling more stock if the price rises. *See also* BEAR; BULL.

B

back bond. An acknowledgment by a person that he/she is holding a deed in trust for a specific purpose.

back dating. Giving value to a credit or debit entry earlier than the date on which the entry is made. This is often done at either the request of the beneficiary or debtor or the bank making the payment.

back freight. The freight charged for the return journey of goods not accepted at the port of discharge.

backlog. Work or orders which due to pressure have not yet been completed. This will often refer, for example, to orders for the purchase/sale of securities, which due to heavy demand, cannot be dealt with in the normal day and therefore requires late working or additional staff to complete the backlog of work.

back-to-back credit. The issue of two credits which are almost similar in details except that the second one is usually for a lesser amount, shorter maturity date and shipping date. A second credit is issued to a beneficiary on the strength of the first credit. The beneficiary of the first credit is a middleman or merchant who is seeking financial assistance; by having a credit available in his favour, he can ask his bank or the advising bank to issue another credit (second credit) in favour of a named beneficiary. This second credit relies on the strength of the first credit. It is absolutely necessary to ensure that the documents under the second credit can satisfy the terms and conditions of the first credit. When the documents of the second credit are presented, the invoices are exchanged and used for presentation under the first credit. Thereby the beneficiary of the first credit who is the applicant of the second credit receives his reward which is the difference between the amount of the first credit and the second credit.

back-to-back loan. A procedure to avoid exchange risks. Assuming there are no exchange control regulations it would involve two companies in different countries funding the other parties' operations. For example, where a UK company needs French francs and a French company needs sterling, then one company will provide the other with the funds required providing that exchange rates and interest rates differences can be overcome.

backup line. Where there has been an issue of commercial paper which is due to mature and in the event of new notes not being successfully marketed it is useful to have a bank line of credit to cover the outstanding maturities.

backwardation. A consideration paid by a seller of stock, often a 'bear', on the Stock Exchange for the right to postpone delivery for a time. On the *London Metal Exchange*, the amount by which the price of cash metal exceeds that for a forward delivery.

BACS Limited. BACS Ltd was first established as Bankers Automated Clearing Services Ltd in 1971. The company was renamed as BACS Ltd in 1986 after becoming part of the APACS structure. BACS provides an automated clearing house service in the UK for transactions originated by either the settlement members themselves or others sponsored by them to use the service. Currently there are some 50 000 of these sponsored service providers. The main types of payment processed by BACS are direct debits, standing orders and automated credits. Input media can be magnetic tapes, disks or by telecom lines (BACSTEL). Output is by magnetic tape to each settlement member. In 1989 BACS processed 1416 million transactions for a value of £526 billion. Settlement, at the end of the three-day clearing cycle, takes place across the settlement members' account at the Bank of Englan'l. BACS currently has 18 settlement members: Abbey National plc; Bank of England; Bank of Scotland; Barclays Bank plc; Clydesdale Bank plc; Cooperative Bank plc; Coutts & Co; Girobank plc; Halifax Building Society; Lloyds Bank plc; Midland Bank plc; National & Provincial Building Society; National Westminster Bank plc; Nationwide Anglia Building Society; Northern Bank Ltd; TSB Bank plc; The Royal Bank of Scotland plc; Yorkshire Bank plc.

bad and doubtful debt. Debts which are bad and those which are not recoverable. Accordingly they are written off as losses. *Doubtful debts* are those of which the recovery, in full or in part, is uncertain. These are provided for by sums being set aside out of profits. Balance sheets will show an amount credited to provision for bad and doubtful debts as a deduction from the debtors.

bail bond. When a vessel is under arrest for causing damage to another ship or to the harbour, a warrant is nailed to its mast, so that the vessel cannot sail out of the harbour. In order to secure its release, a bond is delivered to the court by the ship owners so that the vessel can be released. A bond is given by one or more persons to obtain the release of another on condition that he surrenders to custody. In considering the suitability of a proposed surety, regard is made to his character, financial resources, proximity to that accused. Bail Act 1976 s. 8.

bailee. One to whom goods are entrusted for safe keeping or for a specific purpose. A banker as a bailee, has no lien on the property kept in safe custody for his or her customer.

bailment. The relationship between a bailor and bailee. Where a person leaves goods in the custody of another on the agreement that should he require its return he will receive it promptly. In the meantime the bailee is responsible for its safe keeping. The delivery of goods to a person who will retain them and only return them when the purpose of bailment has been concluded.

bailor. The person who leaves his property with another for safe keeping.

balance. The difference between the total credit entries and the total debit entries made in an account since it was last balanced. When the credit entries are larger than the debits there is a *credit balance.* When the debits are larger than the credits there is a *debit balance.* A debit balance in the current account of a customer of a bank is often called an 'overdraft'.

balance certificate. A share certificate issued to a holder after he has presented a share certificate for more shares than he has sold, representing the balance of shares unsold.

balance of payments. The balance of all financial exchanges between one country and the rest of the world, made up of visible and invisible trade (the current account) and capital movements (capital account).

balance of trade. The difference between visible imports and exports.

balance sheet. A statement showing the capital, assets and liabilities of a business entity on a certain date.

balance sheet ratios. The various ratios that enable a banker and others, to interpret the balance sheet of the business. Basically the ratios are divided into three groups: (*a*) profitability; (*b*) liquidity; (*c*) capital/solvency.

ballot. Applied to issues of new shares. When an offer has been over-subscribed shares are alloted to applicants on a random basis.

baltic exchange. The London exchange for shipping cargo and other commodities.

bank. A body corporate or not, that has been recognised by the Bank of England under the Banking Act 1987, to accept deposits as defined by that act. Other than this recognition, there is no statutory definition of a bank. As a verb, *to bank,* this term indicates that a customer has paid in for the credit of his or her account a sum of money, cheques or other financial documents. *See also* BANKER.

bank account. An account held by a bank or banker recording the deposits and withdrawals of a customer from that account. The account may be either a current or deposit account. A statement is sent by the bank to its customer at agreed or regular intervals.

bank balance. The balance of a customer's account as advised by the bank, either in a statement, by telephone or as indicated via an automated teller machine (ATM)

bank bill. A bill of exchange drawn by a bank or accepted by a bank.

bank charge. A charge made by a bank to a customer. This may be directly relevant for the service of keeping the account, plus the interest if any, on accommodation enjoyed by the customer, but could cover a charge for any other specific services, e.g. transmission of funds.

bank credit. The amount of money created by banks by sanctioning loans and overdrafts.

banker. A person conducting a banking business. The term is commonly thought to imply that the person is an individual rather than an incorporated company for which the term 'bank' is used. The term banker is used in statutes, e.g. Bills of Exchange Act, but for the general public, the term 'bank' or 'banker' are synonymous.

bankers automated clearing services. *See* BACS LIMITED.

bankers' draft. A draft drawn by a branch of a bank on its head office or main office. As this is usually paid on presentation, it is acceptable as the equivalent to cash. Such a draft does not satisfy the definition of a bill of exchange because it is not 'drawn by one person on another'. However, there is statutory protection for the paying banker under the Cheques Act 1957 and the Bills of Exchange Act 1882.

banker's lien. A right of a banker to hold any property of a debtor customer that is in his hands through the normal business relationship. Such property includes bills of exchange, promissory notes, coupons, etc. The most common form of property is cheques which the bank acts as agent for collection. The lien is implied in the banker/customer relationship, so a bank has the right of sale after giving reasonable notice to the customer. Where the bank is given some property for a specific purpose, e.g. items handed in for safe custody, then there is no lien.

banker's opinions. *See* STATUS ENQUIRY.

banker's order. A written order from customer to banker authorising the banker to make a series of periodic payments on the customer's behalf.

banker's payment. Any order or draft drawn upon any bank in the UK by a branch of that bank in favour of another bank and used for the purpose of settling some account between the two banks, e.g. a special presentation.

banker's references. *See* STATUS ENQUIRY.

Bank for International Settlements (BIS). The BIS is an international institution with its headquarters in Basle, Switzerland. The bank was established in May 1930, as a result of a conference in the Hague in January of that year to facilitate the reparations to the creditors of Germany's First World War debts, and to promote cooperation among central banks and to provide facilities for international financial operations. The BIS is often referred to as the 'central banks' bank'. It is a complex organisation as it is on the one hand a financial institution limited by shares, and on the other, an international organisation governed by international law with privileges and immunities to enable it to carry out its functions. Some of the issued capital is held by private individuals who have no voting rights, but of the 21 institutions that have voting rights, 18 are central banks of Western Europe, six from Eastern Europe and the other five outside Europe (USA, Canada, Japan, Australia and South Africa). Its functions include: 1. It is an agent for the European Monetary Cooperation Fund (EMCF), responsible for booking and settling the balances which arise from exchange market interventions carried out by EC central banks participating in the EMS. It concludes swap operations on behalf of EMCF. As agent for EMCF it has responsibility for the technical administration of the EC system of reciprocal short term monetary support and of transfer payments in connections with borrowings. Since 1986 it is also the agent for the private ECU clearing and settlement system. 2. Assists central banks in managing and investing its monetary reserves. More than ten per cent of world foreign exchange reserves are managed in Basle. It makes funds available to central banks. With the critical debt situation it will make loans to the central banks of the lesser developed counries. International monetary cooperation: 1. It provides for regular board meetings when the governors of the central banks can meet to discuss international affairs. 2. It has set up a committee on banking regulations and supervision practices. 3. It also organises regular meetings of central bank experts to discuss such matters as gold and foreign exchange markets, economic problems, legal problems relevant to central banks, etc.

bank giro. It is merely a name given for the transfer of credits between banks. It covers the transfers of such items as HP debts, rent payments, etc. Such items are passed through the credit clearing system and balances are settled between banks in the usual way.

bank holiday. A day which is normally a working day, declared as a holiday when banks are closed for that day. Such closures are either by statute or by proclamation.

Banking Act. Prior to 1979 there was no formal system of supervision of the banking sector. It was possible for anyone to take deposits, provide banking services and call themselves a 'bank'. Any supervision of these activities was undertaken informally by the Bank of England as part of its role as the 'central bank'. The Banking Act 1979 provided a statutory framework for supervision of the banking sector by the Bank of England. While this act on the whole worked well, it was felt necessary to abolish this act and introduce the Banking Act 1987. This act replaced the 1979 act and became law on 1 May 1987, but some of its provisions did not come into force until 1 January 1988. The supervision of banks is by a board of banking supervision, which meets monthly and consists of the governor, the deputy governor, the executive director and six external members. Any institution which takes deposits in the UK must be authorised by the Bank of England. The Bank has the power to investigate any illegal deposit-taking and to order early repayment of deposits. A deposit is a sum of money paid on terms that it will be repaid: (*a*) with or without interest and (*b*) on demand, at an agreed time or on the occurrence of an agreed event. Certain institutions, particularly those controlled by other Acts, e.g. building societies, local authorities, etc. do not have to be authorised. The Act lays down four minimum criteria for authorisation of an institution: 1. Every director, controller and manager must be a fit and proper person to hold his position. 2. The business must be conducted in a prudent manner. This covers *inter alia*, adequate capital, liquidity, provisions for bad debts accounting and other records. 3. The business must be carried on with integrity and the proper professional skills. 4. Paid-up capital and reserves of £1 million (£5 million if called a 'bank'). The Bank must be notified of changes in directors, controllers and managers. Any person who can be classified as a significant shareholder (i.e. holding between 5 and 15 per cent of the voting rights) must notify the Bank. Any person who is proposing to hold more than 15 per cent of the voting rights of an authorised institution must give *advance* notice to the bank. Failure to do so is a criminal offence. It will be a criminal offence to provide false or misleading information to the board of banking supervision, nor must an institution withhold information. Any changes in auditors or their resignation must be notified to the Bank. Auditors should give notice if they intend to qualify their opinion of the institution's accounts and the Bank may require auditors to disclose information obtained in the course of their audit, providing such disclosure is made in good faith and relevant to the bank's supervision. All institutions are covered by the depositors protection scheme and the cover is 75 per cent of the first £20 000 of sterling deposits.

banking education service. A service financed by the major banks and available to all educational establishments, particularly schools and colleges of further education, to provide information about the services of banks and the careers available in banks. This service provides books, notes, wallcharts, floppy disks, to cover a wide variety of banking operations. If required, speakers are available, usually free of charge.

Banking Federation of the European Community. *See* EUROPEAN BANKING FEDERATION.

banking information service. A service set up by the major banks to provide information to the public on all matters regarding the activities of the major banks.

banking ombudsman. The banking ombudsman scheme became operational on Thursday 2 January 1986. The first appointment to this office was Mr Ian Edward-Jones QC. He has now retired and his place has been taken by Mr Laurence Shurman, a leading London solicitor. The constitution of the scheme has been changed to allow any deposit taking business authorised as a bank by the Bank of England to apply for membership subject to the approval of the board. So far the banks listed below are members. It should be noted that quite a number of banks are involved almost totally in the business of dealing with securities and investments, so that any complaints against them must be channelled through the appropriate SRO. *Member banks* Abbey National; Allied Irish Bank; Bank of England; Bank of Cyprus; Bank of Ireland; Bank of Scotland; Barclays Bank; Beneficial Bank; Clydesdale Bank; Cooperative Bank; Coutts & Co; Equatorial Bank; Girobank; Lloyds Bank; Midland Bank; National Westminster Bank; Northern Bank; Standard Chartered Bank; The Royal Bank of Scotland; TSB Bank; Ulster Bank; Yorkshire Bank. *Designated associates* Abbey National Personal Finance; Bank of Scotland Insurance Services; Barclays Bank Trust Company; Barclays Insurance Brokers International; Barclays Insurance Services Company; Clydesdale Bank Insurance Services; Coutts Finance Company; Girobank Insurance Services; Lloyds Bank Financial Services; Lloyds Bank Insurance Services; Midland Bank Insurance Services; Midland Bank Trust Company; National Westminster Bank Home Loans; National Westminster Insurance Services; Northern Bank Executor and Trustee Company; Royal Bank Insurance Services; SIGNET (Joint Credit Card Company); TSB Trustcard; Ulster Bank Trust Company; Unity Trust Bank; Yorkshire

Bank Home Loans. The task of the ombudsman is to consider any eligible complaint from personal bank customers after it has been established that existing procedures for dealing with complaints have been exhausted. The ombudsman has powers to make an award that is binding on a bank with an upper limit of £100 000. If a customer decides not to accept the decision he/she will retain the full right to take legal action. The free service provided by the ombudsman covers most personal banking services, although finance house, travel agent and estate agent subsidiaries of banks will be excluded, as well as commercial lending decisions.

Banking Practice. *See* CODE OF BANKING PRACTICE.

bank interest. The interest allowed on money deposited with a bank; the interest charged on an overdraft, loan or accommodation.

bank interest certificate. A certificate issued by a bank to a customer to show the amount of interest paid by him on his bank loan or the amount paid to him for interest earned on his current/deposit account. This information is required for inclusion in a tax return.

bank notes. Notes issued by a central bank or other bank of issue, payable to bearer.

Bank of England The central bank in the UK. Established in 1694 by Royal Charter, it had a capital of £1 200 000. This charter was renewed periodically and over the course of time, the bank very gradually moved from being a commercial to being a central bank. Under the 1844 Bank Charter Act the Bank of England was divided into departments – the *Banking Department* and the *Issue Department.* Both these departments had to issue a balance sheet each week and still do. The fiduciary issue was raised to £14 000 000 and the Bank of England acquired the note issuing monopoly in England and Wales. Its present functions are (a) banker to the government; (b) bankers' bank; (c) manages the Exchange Equalisation Account; (d) handles the issue of Treasury bills; (e) supervises the banking institutions in the UK; (f) maintains the sterling accounts of other central banks and international organisations; (*g*) lender of last resort; (*h*) the note issuing authority in England and Wales.

bank rate. This term originally indicated the minimum rate that the Bank of England would be prepared to discount an eligible bill. This was superseded by the minimum lending rate which was suspended in August 1981, when it was decided to influence the market by ensuring adequate liquidity in the banking sector and open market operations. The Bank of England now keeps short term interest rates within various bands which are not published.

bank return. In order to comply with the Bank Charter Act 1844, the Bank of England issues a weekly statement showing the financial information of its issue department and its banking department.

bankrupt. An insolvent person who has been adjudicated bankrupt by the court. The bankrupt is then deprived of nearly all legal powers, his or her estate passing into the hands of a trustee in bankruptcy. A debtor can only be made bankrupt if (*a*) domiciled in England and Wales; (*b*) personally present on the day on which the petition is presented; *or (c)* at any time in the period of three years ending with that day he or she (*i*) has been ordinarily resident, or has had a place of residence, in England and Wales *or (ii)* has carried on business in England and Wales. This includes a firm or partnership of which the individual is a member and carrying on a business by an agent or manager for that individual or for that firm or partnership. Section 265 Insolvency Act 1986.

bankruptcy debt. Section 382 Insolvency Act 1986. (*a*) Any debt or liability to which the bankrupt is subject at the commencement of the bankruptcy; (*b*) any debt or liability to which he or she may become subject after the commencement of the bankruptcy by reason of any obligation incurred before the commencement of the bankruptcy; (*c*) any amount specified in pursuance of s. 39(3)(c) of the Powers of Criminal Courts Act 1973 in any criminal bankruptcy order made against him or her before the commencement of the bankruptcy.

bankruptcy level. The amount for which a person can be made bankrupt is £750; but the Secretary of State may by order in a *statutory instrument* substitute any amount specified in the order for that amount or for the amount which by virtue of such an order is for the time being the amount of the bankruptcy level, s. 267(4) Insolvency Act 1986.

bankruptcy order. An order adjudging an individual bankrupt. Insolvency Act 1986 s. 381(2).

bank reconciliation statement. A statement drawn up showing why a balance in the cash book is different from that shown on the bank statement.

bank statement Usually a computerised statement supplied by banks to their customers, showing details of the customer's debit and credit transactions, and the balance.

bank sweep arrangement. A standing arrangement with a bank to move funds from current account to a deposit account, or vice versa, when appropriate, without specific instructions from the customer.

Barclaycard. *See* VISA.

bargain. A contract between persons for the purchase/sale of an item: an item purchased cheaply; a Stock Exchange transaction; the item bought or sold.

barring the entail. A procedure whereby a tenant in tail puts an estate into a fee simple (Fines and Recoveries Act 1833 s. 15). A tenant in tail whose interest is in remainder, may, if of full age, convert entail into fee simple with the consent of the protector of settlement. By the Law of Property Act 1925 this device allows the tenant to dispose of the estate as he wishes.

barter. The exchange of goods for goods; to give (anything but money) in exchange for some other commodity. It is a characteristic of a primitive community, but today barter is accepted on an international scale to facilitate trading with countries of the Eastern bloc and others which are short of hard, convertible currencies. Barter is also called *compensation trading* or *counter-purchase*

base drift. A phenomenon found in connection with the control of money supply by the central bank. All the main industrial countries now set formal targets for monetary growth. In the UK the experience has been that the central bank from time to time overshoots the target; that is, the monetary growth is in excess of what it is supposed to be. This poses the problem of what the base should be for the following year – the base has drifted away from the hoped-for figure. The government has a number of choices. One is politically unacceptable, that is, to admit that control has been less than successful, and to start again for the following year. Another is to scale down the percentage increase allowed in the next year so that the growth over the two years will not exceed the sum of the intended growth in each of the two years. This gives the illusion that the central bank is still in charge of inflation.

base fee. An estate in fee simple into which an estate tail is converted, where the issue in tail is barred, but persons claiming estates by way of remainder or otherwise are not barred.

base market value. The average market price of a portfolio of securities as at a specified date. It is often used for comparative purposes with the Financial Times Stock Exchange Index (FTSE).

base rate. The basic lending rate of a bank or financial institution, on which its lending rates and deposit rates are founded. Each bank is free to fix its own base rate as it thinks best but, in practice, there is often no variation. From a bank's point of view, *base rate* represents the marginal cost of borrowing funds.

base year. The selection of a year to be the base year for a series of index numbers, e.g. the General Index of Retail Prices (RPI). The year has a base index number of 100 so that subsequent indices may be compared with the base and represents any rises or falls.

basis price. In a 'futures' market, there will be an agreement to buy or sell a named commodity and the price agreed at the time between the parties is the 'basis' or 'striking price'.

basis of assessment. The period in which various financial transactions take place and are taken into account for the purpose of assessing the tax liability in that period.

Basle Statement. A circular endorsed by the governors of the central banks of the group of ten countries, sent to all financial institutions concerning the principles of money laundering. This circular sets out the principles to be adopted by financial institutions. *See* MONEY LAUNDERING

BCV. Barge carrying vessels.

BE. The abbreviation for Bill of Exchange or Bank of England.

bear. A speculator on the Stock Exchange who anticipates a fall in the value of a certain security and therefore sells stocks which he or she does not possess in the hope of buying them back more cheaply at a later date (frequently in the same account period), thus making a profit.

bearer. A person who has in his possession a bill of exchange, promissory note or cheque which is payable to bearer. A negotiable instrument is payable to the bearer when it is stated on the face of it that it is payable to the bearer, or alternatively when the indorsement is in blank. A bearer instrument can be passed to a transferor. That is, the title passes by mere delivery. *See also* INDORSEMENT IN BLANK.

bearer bill/note. A negotiable instrument, e.g. a cheque, bill of exchange or promissory note which is payable to the bearer or is indorsed in blank.

bearer bond. A bond which is not registered in the books of the company. It is a bond that is transferable by delivery. For the purpose of payment of dividends/interest, coupons are attached, which on the appropriate date are torn off and sent to the address stated, so that payment of the dividend/interest may be made.

bearer cheque. *See* BEARER BILL.

bearer note. *See* BEARER BILL.

bearer scrip. On acceptance of the offer form and cheque for a new issue a temporary document is issued. This document is a negotiable instrument and should be kept in a safe place. When all instalments have been made or when the bond is available, the bearer scrip is then exchanged for a bearer bond.

bed and breakfast. A term used in investment planning. It is a procedure whereby shares are sold on one business day and then re-purchased on the next, in order to establish a capital gain or loss for tax purposes. These transactions tend to occur towards the end of the financial year to reduce tax payable or to take advantage of capital gains exemptions (currently £5000). *See* CAPITAL GAINS TAX.

below par. With regard to the purchase or sale of a security, it indicates that the current price is below the nominal value. For the purchase or sale of a currency, it indicates that the future value is below spot value.

beneficial owner. A person who has the absolute right to any chattel or property which is held in trust by another. Where a vendor as the beneficial owner transfers a title it is implied that (a) the vendor has a right to transfer; (b) the buyer shall have the right of possession; (c) the property is free of any encumbrances; (d) the vendor will ensure that the buyer has a proper title.

beneficiary. One that benefits from the act of another; a person named in a will as a legatee or devisee. A person named in a letter of credit who may draw drafts on the issuing/paying bank.

bequest. A gift or legacy of personal property under a will, especially to a public body or institute.

berth. A space alloted to a vessel for the purpose of loading and discharging its cargo at a wharf or quay.

BES. *See* BUSINESS EXPANSION SCHEME.

bible making. The preparation, collection and checking of the various documents needed for a rights issue, scrip issue or new issue of shares.

bid bond. *See* TENDER BOND.

bidding up. In a rising market an investor that wishes to purchase a considerable number of shares in a company will advise his broker to purchase a limited number of shares at any time at a given price or lower to ensure that the purchases made are at a favourable price. Since prices are moving upwards, he must move his price limit upward to continue purchasing shares. It should be noted that he is contributing to the price rise in the stock he is purchasing.

bid price. A price quoted by a market maker on the Stock Exchange at which he or she will buy stocks or shares on offer. A price quoted by the manage-ment company of a unit trust at which they will buy sub-units of the trust.

Big Bang. This expression refers to the change in method of operations in the Stock Exchange from 27 October, 1986. Organisations on the Stock Exchange are now single capacity operators. Fixed commission agreements have been abandoned. Non members are permitted to have a stake in member firms. With the advent of the international quotations of major companies, it was necessary to improve communications and information technology so from 27 October 1986 trading on the floor of the Stock Exchange for all practical purposes ceased, and deals were carried out through the medium of computers.

big five. This refers to the major clearing banks namely Barclays, Lloyds, Midland, National Westminster Banks and the TSB.

big ticket lease. The leasing of capital equipment for sums in excess of £1m. This form of leasing is often done by a consortium of leasing companies.

bill. This can refer to (a) legislation for discussion in Parliament; (b) a shortened expression for a Bill of Exchange; (c) paper money; (d) a negotiable security document.

bill broker. A merchant who buys and sells bills of exchange. Bill brokers are more commonly termed discount houses. Discount houses are an important part of the short-term money market, one of their important functions being to provide a source of first class bills for bankers. They also tender for Treasury Bills and deal in short-date government stocks.

bill for collection. A collection as defined by the uniform rules for collection means the handling by banks, on instructions received, of documents as defined in order to (a) obtain acceptance and/or, as the case may be, payment or (b) deliver commercial documents against acceptance and/or, as the case may be, against payment. When sending a bill for collection this may be sent on its own (clean) or with commercial documents (documentary) by the exporter via his bank with a request that the bill should be accepted and eventually paid (D/A) or paid on presentation (D/P). The remitting bank will send the bill to its agent/branch in the importer's country for them to present the bill for acceptance/payment and remit the proceeds to them in due course. *See also* UNIFORM RULES FOR COLLECTION.

bill for negotiation. A bill that is being sent for collection may be negotiated by a banker for its customer (exporter). In this case the bank will buy the bill less its commission and interest charges. The bank will be presenting the bill and documents to its agent abroad on its own behalf, but should the bill be dishonoured it will have recourse to its customer.

bill mountain. The number of bills discounted and held by the Bank of England under the present monetary control arrangements. The value of such bills held, at the moment of writing, exeed £16 billion.

bill of exchange. An unconditional order in writing, addressed by one person to another, signed by the person giving it, requiring the person to whom it is addressed to pay on demand, or at a fixed or determinable future time, a sum certain in money to, or to the order of, a specified person or bearer. (Bills of Exchange Act 1882). *See also* ACCOMMODATION BILL; BANK BILL; BEARER BILL; CLEAN BILL; COMMERCIAL BILL; CORPORATION BILL; DOCUMENTARY BILL; ELIGIBLE BILL; FINE BANK BILL; FIRST CLASS BILL; INLAND BILL; LONG BILL; ORDER BILL; ORIGINAL BILL; PREFINANCE BILL; RE-FINANCE BILL; SHORT BILL; SIGHT BILL; SOLA BILL; TERM BILL; TRADE BILL; USANCE BILL.

bill of imprest. An order entitling the bearer to have money paid in advance.

bill of lading. Abbreviated to B/L. A receipt for goods received for carriage to a stated destination, signed by or on behalf of the master of a ship. The bill is also a negotiable document of title to the goods, transferable by indorsement, but is not a negotiable instrument in the true sense. It is furthermore evidence of the contract of carriage. Normally bills of lading are issued in sets of either two or three, while another copy is retained by the ship's master. *See also* CLEAN BILL OF LADING; DIRTY BILL OF LADING; FIRST OF EXCHANGE; ON BOARD BILL OF LADING; RECEIVED FOR SHIPMENT BILL OF LADING; SHIPPED BILL OF LADING; STRAIGHT BILL OF LADING; THROUGH BILL OF LADING.

bill of sale. A document given in respect of a transfer of chattels used in cases where possession is not intended to be given. A bill of sale must be registered within seven days of making with the Central Office of the Supreme Court. It is merely security for a debt or loan. Banks do not accept this type of security, because possession remains with the borrower and there is no control over the security. An absolute bill is governed by the Bills of Sale Act 1878, a conditional bill (e.g. accepted as security) is governed by the Bills of Sale Amendment Act 1882.

bill payable. A bill of exchange which is either payable at sight or has been accepted payable at some fixed or determinable future date. Often abbreviated to B/P. The acceptor of the bill has an outstanding liability.

bill rate. The discount rate on bills of exchange, varying according to the quality of the bill to be discounted.

bill receivable. In contract to a bill payable, this is an asset in the hands of a true owner, or the bank who is an agent for collection. Abbreviated as B/R.

bills discounted. *See* DISCOUNT. *See also* TENDER BILLS.

bills in set. It is customary in many geographical areas to draw a bill of exchange in two or three copies, each copy being an original and for safety sake each copy bill is sent by consecutive air mails, so that should one copy not arrive then payment of the second may be made. To accept or pay, it is only necessary to accept or pay one copy. The copies are identical except the second copy will read 'Pay the second of exchange (first and third copy being unpaid)'. (Bills of Exchange Act 1882 s. 71).

Bills of Exchange Act 1882. This act of codification, sets out the definition of a bill of exchange: its form, the responsibilities of the parties to the bill, the method of presentation and payment. The process in the event of non acceptance or non payment. It also deals with cheques: the crossings, definition, parties to a cheque, payment, etc. The final part of this act deals with the issue and payment of promissory notes.

BIS. *See* BANK FOR INTERNATIONAL SETTLE-MENTS.

B/L. *See* BILL OF LADING.

Black Monday. 19 October 1987 was so named as on that day the market value of all equities on the major international stock exchanges fell sharply due to the US financial, economic and political situations.

blank cheque. An inchoate instrument. This cheque need not have any details other than the signature of the drawer. *See also* INCHOATE INSTRUMENT.

blanket recommendation. A general circular sent either by post, fax, telephone, etc. to clients of a broker, recommending that they buy/sell a particular stock.

blank indorsement. *See* INDORSEMENT IN BLANK.

blank transfer. A transfer of stock or shares with the name of the transferee left blank, sometimes used when shares are mortgaged as security for a debt. If repayment is not forthcoming the lender may then fill in his or her own name as transferee, date the transfer, have it stamped, and send it to the company for registration of the shares in the lender's own name as owner. This procedure should not be used where a transfer has to be under seal, because such a transfer is a deed and takes effect from the date of its delivery. If on that day the deed is not complete, the blanks can only be filled in subsequently by the transferor, or by the transferor's authority which itself must be under seal. A further point is that stamping must be done within 30 days after execution; late stamping attracts a penalty.

block discounting. A service offered by a factoring house whereby the factor will purchase from retailers the existing instalment contracts for a cash payment.

blue chip. Originally 'blue chip' was a gambling term, chips with the highest value being coloured blue. Over the years, however, the term has been accepted as denoting the ordinary shares of the highest class of company.

board room. A room in the registered office of a company or corporation set aside for the purpose of the directors in which they hold their meetings.

bona fide. In good faith. A term used in banking meaning to act in good faith and without negligence. An act can be in good faith yet there can be negligence.

bona vacantia. Goods which are not claimed. On the death of an individual leaving no relative who can inherit his possessions, then estate passes to the Crown.

bond. An agreement under seal whereby one person binds himself to another by either performing or refraining from performing an action. A legal contract to pay a sum of money or perform a certain condition. A certificate of ownership. A certificate of money lent, e.g. a local authority, the government, etc. A surety requested by the customs authority from entities holding dutiable goods on which duty has still to be paid. *See also* ASSENTED BONDS; BAIL BOND; CONVERTIBLE BOND; DRAWN BOND; FLOATING RATE BOND; FOREIGN BOND; INCOME BOND; LOCAL AUTHORITY BONDS; MORTGAGE BOND; NON-ASSENTED BONDS; STRAIGHT BONDS.

bond broker. A person who trades on the floor of an exchange, e.g. LIFFE, Futures Exchange, etc.

bond creditor. A creditor secured by bond.

bonded. Placed in bond, mortgaged.

bonded goods. Goods stored, under the care of customs house officers, in warehouses until duty is paid.

bonded warehouse. A customs store for bonded goods.

bond holder. A person holding a bond granted by a private person, company or a government.

bond washing. An illegal activity in the UK. A tax avoidance procedure whereby a person will sell securities cum div at a higher price and re-purchase them at a later date, at a lower price, ex div.

bonus. Something given as an extra. A payment of money over and above a wage or salary. A gratuitous payment.

bonus certificate. A document notifying the holder of an insurance policy that a percentage of the profits of the company has been transferred to his/her name and will be paid on maturity of the policy.

bonus issue. The additional issue of shares to a shareholder in proportion to the shares already held. When a company considers it necessary to capitalise its reserves, it will issue additional capital to its shareholders. No additional funds are raised, but it does improve the marketability of the shares although the value of the shares will in the short term fall. Often called a scrip issue.

book debts. Funds owed by trade debtors.

book entry. An accounting entry passed in a set of ledgers.

book entry securities. The ownership of securities that is not represented by the possession of a certificate. This method (TAURUS) is now in the pilot stage with the London International Stock Exchange. It reduces paper work, costs and the anxiety of possible loss of certificates.

books of account. Documents and ledgers which must be prepared and kept by a business entity, including the profit and loss account and balance sheet.

book value. The value of the assets of a business concern as shown in the balance sheet.

borrowing powers. This normally refers to the borrowing powers of a company whose borrowing powers are stated in its memorandum of association. It is usual that these powers are exercised by the directors or by the shareholders in a general or extraordinary general meeting. Any limits imposed on the directors will be found in the articles of association. For unincorporated organisations, which have no personal identification, there is no power to borrow. Persons acting as trustees or personal representatives have only the power to borrow as stated in the trust instrument. The borrowing powers of an agent are limited to the authority given to him/her by the principal. Borrowing powers of building societies, local authorities, etc. will be found in statutes.

börse or bourse. A stock exchange.

bottom. A term that denotes the lowest point of a trade/economic cycle. When prices are going lower it is said 'The bottom has dropped out of the market', or when the market has reached its lowest point, it can be said that the market has 'bottomed out'.

bought day ledger. Often referred to as the bought ledger or bought day book.

It is a book/ledger that lists all items purchased by the business for resale.

bouncing. The common term used when a cheque is being dishonoured for lack of funds.

bracket. Banks participating in a Eurobond syndicated loan will be grouped in 'brackets' with the lead manager/s first, then the co-manager/s., followed by underwriters and other participants. In each group the banks are listed in alphabetical order.

branch clearing. The operation within a large bank whereby the collection of cheques between the branches of the bank is organised through a department in the head office of the bank.

branch credit. A credit paid in for a customer of another branch of the same bank.

breach of trust. The result of an improper act or the omission to act in a proper manner by a trustee. Any loss caused by not acting within the powers given will result in a liability to the trustees.

breach of warranty of authority. The result of an agent acting in such a way as to imply that he/she is acting within the authority given by the principal and will render that person liable to be sued by the third party for breach of warranty of authority.

break even analysis chart. The presentation of information either by a chart or statement of figures showing the management at what point the amount or volume of sales need to be in order to equal the sum of the fixed and variable costs. That is the point where neither a loss nor a profit is made on trading.

breaking an account. The stopping of the use of an account by closing it and transferring the balance to another account. This is done to prevent the operation of the *Rule in Clayton's case*, e.g. when a partnership account is overdrawn and one of the partners dies, the partnership account is broken to retain recourse to the estate of the deceased partner.

breaking bulk. Opening a container, package or case of goods in order to sample the contents or for selling part of the consignment.

break-up value. When a company or business is going into liquidation the assets are valued on a 'gone concern' basis.

Bretton Woods Conference. A meeting under the auspices of the United Nations at Bretton Woods, New Hampshire, USA, in 1944, to set up some degree of cooperation in matters of international trade and payments and to devise a satisfactory international monetary system to be operated after the end of the Second World War. The particular objectives hoped to be achieved were stable exchange rates and free convertibility of currencies for the development of multilateral trade. Two important results of this conference were the establishment of the International Monetary Fund and the World Bank (International Bank for Reconstruction and Development).

bridging advance. An advance given for the purpose of assisting a person when selling one asset and buying another. This usually occurs when a person is purchasing one house and selling another. The money is lent to provide the funds for the house being purchased on the assurance that contracts have been exchanged for the sale of the other house. Providing this has occurred and the bank has received an undertaking from the vendor's solicitor that the proceeds of the sale will be remitted to the bank, then the loan will be sanctioned. Banks do not like to lend on an 'open ended' bridging loan, i.e. when the customer wishes to buy one house but has not sold the one he owns already.

British Bankers' Association. An association formed in 1919, for the benefit of British banks whose principal business and head offices were in the UK, and British banks whose principal business was outside the UK and who were at that time members of the British Overseas Banks Association. The membership was widened in 1972 to include all recognised banks operating in the UK, whether British or foreign, including the discount houses. This step was inspired in part by the forthcoming British entry into the European Economic Community and the need to facilitate liaison with the banking industries of other member states, whose representative associations were organised on a similar basis. The association is the British member of the European Banking Federation. At home, it has formed a series of committees which keep all aspects of money-market activity under review.

British Export Houses Association. An association whose members offer finance to manufacturers by providing them with funds against evidence that goods have been shipped to an importer, thus credit is given to the importer. Confirming houses may be members of this association whose aim it is to look after the interests of its members.

British Overseas and Commonwealth Banks' Association. Originally this was the Overseas Bankers' Association, but as British overseas banks were absorbed or amalgamated, the association changed to include the various Commonwealth banks in London.

British overseas banks. These banks were originally established in the nineteenth century as the British Empire grew and banking was needed by expatriates in the colonies. The banking system was based on London practice, but all funds in these colonies were remitted to the various head offices in London. Since the end of the Second World War, many countries obtained their independence so the banking systems changed and adapted to suit local conditions. Many banks have amalgamated and few remain in London today.

Britannia. A British gold bullion coin issued in October 1987. They are minted in one ounce, half ounce, quarter ounce and one-tenth ounce series. The coins are available not only in the UK but world-wide. Britannias' contain 22 carat gold, i.e. 91.66 per cent gold content. The sale of these coins attract value added tax.

broker. An agent, a factor, a middleman, a person employed in the negotiation of commercial transactions between other parties in the interests of one of them. *See also* BILL BROKER; DEPOSIT BROKER; FOREIGN EXCHANGE BROKER; INSURANCE BROKER; PRODUCE BROKER; STOCKBROKER.

brokerage. The commission charged by a broker for carrying out the instructions of a client, e.g. to buy or sell shares.

bronze coins. These are coins of the lowest value. They are made of 95 parts of pure copper, four parts tin and one part zinc. These are legal tender up to 20p.

budget. 1. The annual statement made by the Chancellor of the Exchequer, usually in March, before the end of the fiscal year. The speech made in the House of Commons reports on the past year's activities, assesses the future spending of government and then announces any changes in the revenue and expenditure that will take place. It is then presented as a Bill to Parliament and when passed becomes an Act. 2. The estimated revenue and expenditure of a business entity. While there are many kinds of budgets, there is for example, a cash budget that will show the cash flow. A capital budget will show the anticipated expenditure on capital items.

budget account. This is an account which will facilitate a person in controlling his/her expenditure, by compiling a list of all the major items of expenditure, e.g. mortgage repayments, community tax, gas, electricity, etc., the bank will add all the amounts together plus its own commission, then divide the total by twelve, so that each month one twelfth of the expenditure is transferred from current account to the budget account. This way the customer can pay his bills as and when they fall due.

budgetary control. The assessment of the future financial expenditure of a business. The accounts department will regularly check that expenditure compares with the assessment made and if there is any variance then this is reported to the directors who will make a decision regarding efficacy of the budget control system.

building agreement. An agreement between a building contractor and the owner of land whereby the builder will agree to build houses or flats to meet certain standards and the owner of the land will undertake to grant a lease to the purchaser of the house/flat.

building lease. Whereby the owner of land will grant a lease, usually 99 years, to a builder who having built houses on that land will then sell the houses to buyers and at the same time sublease the land to the house buyers or others, e.g. a finance company at an increased ground rent.

building societies. Societies existing to provide long-term loans for the acquisition of homes on the security of the houses and land so bought. In this capacity they are non-profit making bodies and their interest rates are loosely linked with money rates. To gather the funds which they need the societies must offer a rate sufficient to bring them in. If money is difficult to get, interest rates offered will have to be raised and this in turn will mean that mortgage rates will also have to go up. The present building societies maintain a variety of different accounts. Each building society gives the accounts offered by them an attractive name, but in broad detail they are basically, share accounts, deposit accounts and subscription accounts. All building societies are registered as friendly societies with the Registrar of Building Societies and the vast majority are members of the Building Societies Association. They are regulated by the Building Societies Act of 1986 which has expanded the role and activities of building societies in as much as they can now offer unsecured loans up to £5,000, offer standing orders, direct debits, ATMs, cash cards, cheque books, etc. They are also able to offer estate agency services, insurance, conveyancing, etc. They are now able to raise deposits on the wholesale money markets. While the services of building societies are growing, the number of societies offering these services is diminishing due to mergers.

bull. A speculator on the Stock Exchange who anticipates a rise in the value of a certain security and therefore buys such stocks, not intending to pay for the purchase, but hoping to sell them later, at a profit, before the settlement date.

bulldog bonds. Another name for a sterling loan, in the UK market, to an overseas borrower.

bullet. A straight debt issue without a sinking fund.

bullion. Gold or silver in bars or in specie. The term is also used to describe quantities of gold, silver or copper coins when measured by weight.

buoyancy. A tendency for all prices to rise during periods of inflation. Wages and salaries increase, taxation increases and consequently the prices of stocks and shares also increase.

bureau de change. An office or place where currencies can be exchanged. Banks which have a great deal of business in exchanging foreign currency will designate a counter or department with this name. In touristy large towns, bureaux des changes offer their services.

business cycle. The peaks and troughs of activity in a business entity or in industry. A business cycle can be seasonal, e.g. over a period of a year or can owing to economic circumstances be much longer. During a peak period or a trough, such factors as investment, cash flow, profits are affected.

business day. While many businesses are open for business at varying times, it is usually accepted that the normal business day is between 9 a.m. and 5 p.m.

business development loan. As the name implies, this refers to funds loaned to a business entity for the purchase of fixed assets, e.g. land, premises, plant, etc. The loan may be up to five years, but it is possible to arrange for such a loan to be up to 15 years although the life of the asset purchased is considered in relation to the length of the loan. Repayment is made by regular monthly repayments.

Business Expansion Scheme. With government encouragement, this scheme was started in 1981 to encourage investment in small unquoted trading companies. In order to encourage risk capital in these ventures, tax relief is available for invested amounts up to £40 000 per annum at the highest marginal rate if held for five years. The first year's disposal is exempt from CGT. The scheme does not apply to quoted companies or those on the USM, nor can employees, directors of the company, or the investor own more than 30 per cent of the capital. This scheme will finish at the end of 1993.

business liability. Under the Unfair Contract Terms Act 1977, this refers to a liability for breach of obligations or duties arising from anything done or to be done by any person in course of business activity.

business names. In the case of a business entity (sole trader, partnership, limited company) using a name different from their own they are using a business name. When this happens, then the bank account must be opened in the business name.

business start-up scheme. *See* BUSINESS EXPANSION SCHEME.

buyer. A person who purchases goods. It is also the name given to the employee or agent of a firm who will purchase goods on behalf of the firm.

buyer credit. An arrangement whereby an exporter negotiates a contract with an overseas buyer on a cash basis, the latter finding up to 20 per cent of the contract price and negotiating a separate loan from a UK bank for the balance owing to the exporter. The UK bank obtains an unconditional guarantee from the Export Credits Guarantee Department in respect of the principal and interest due from the buyer. These facilities are usually found for larger contracts (over £2 million), for which the repayment period is normally five years but can be as long as ten years. The buyer has the advantage of long-term credit, while the seller is virtually in the position of having cash payment, providing cover from ECGD has been obtained and they have approved the buyer credit finance.

buyer's market. A situation where there is a plentiful supply of goods and the buyer can dictate the terms or conditions of sale.

buying in. In the Stock Exchange this refers to a situation whereby the seller has not delivered the securities to the buyer and the broker must 'buy in' in order to deliver to the buyer. The charge or loss of such a procedure must be paid for by the seller. In the option market it is where the writer buys an identical option (with a different price) and the second of these options offsets the first and the profit or loss is the difference in premiums.

buy-out. An arrangement whereby the directors and shareholders are willing to sell the company to the staff and management of that company. The purchase price is raised partly from the staff and management and partly from financial institutions that consider that the management have the 'know-how' and skill to make a success of the venture. It is also known as leveraged buy-out.

C

CA. This abbreviation has three meanings. 1 Court of Appeal. 2. Companies Act. 3. The designation of a member of the Institute of Chartered Accountants.

cabinet bid. A method whereby on the options market of the Stock Exchange, the investor instead of allowing his 'out-of-the-money' option to expire, is allowed to sell his contract at 1p so that he may gain a contract note that will assist him in reducing his tax liability. *See also* TRADED OPTIONS.

cable transfer. *See* TELEGRAPHIC TRANSFER.

C & F. *See* COST AND FREIGHT.

CAD. *See* CASH AGAINST DOCUMENT.

call. A request to a shareholder of an instalment in payment of the shares issued. Shares in privatised companies have, in order to attract public subscription, been floated and payment requested in two/three instalments. When a company is in the need of funds and there is an amount of authorised capital not yet issued, it may be issued or called. In banking this may refer to a demand for the repayment of a loan when the borrower has failed to meet his obligations under a loan agreement.

callable fixture. Funds loaned to discount houses by the banks for a short period of time. Money at call or at short notice between banks and the discount houses is arranged each day because the bank need to place their funds in a secure but interest-bearing deposit, while for the discount houses these funds are used for the purchase of bills and short-term bonds. While this method of depositing suits all parties, the discount houses are the buffer between the banks and the Bank of England for the purposes of monetary control. Callable fixture is funds lent for a stated period of between three

days and three months at a given rate of interest, but can be withdrawn by banks on request.

call money. The borrowing by bill brokers from banks for overnight or very short-term funds which are repayable 'at call'.

call option. *See* OPTION.

CAMIFA. *See* CAMPAIGN FOR INDEPENDENT FINANCIAL ADVICE.

Campaign for independent financial advice (CAMIFA). This campaign was formed by a group of life companies to inform the public that their members will provide the best financial advice on life assurance, pensions, unit trusts, etc.

cancellable agreement. Under the Consumer Credit Act 1974, it refers to a regulated agreement which may be cancelled by the debtor/hirer when the agreement was not signed on the premises of the creditor.

cancellation. The making of an agreement void. The payment of a cheque by the drawee bank by a clerk who will cancel the signature of the drawer of the cheque. The discharge of a bill of exchange by the drawee. The mutilation, defacing or revocation of a document. *See also* REVOCATION OF A WILL.

canvassing. For the purposes of the Consumer Credit Act 1974, s. 48 and s. 153, it is defined as the soliciting or obtaining contributions, by oral persuasion from another person, the consumer, into a regulated agreement, during a visit by the canvasser to a place which is not the business premises of the creditor, without having been asked to do so.

capacity. The ability or power to incur legal liability. For example, to become a party to a bill of exchange, owing to the fact that the person/s has capacity to contract. A person may also have the capacity to contract by reason of his/her office or position.

cap and collar. An arrangement whereby the interest charged on a loan shall not exceed a stated maximum percentage, nor fall below a stated minimum percentage.

capital. Funds invested by a person or persons in a business or funds invested by shareholders in a company. *See also* AUTHORISED CAPITAL; CIRCULATING CAPITAL; FIXED CAPITAL; FREE CAPITAL; ISSUED CAPITAL; LIQUID CAPITAL; PAID-UP CAPITAL; SHARE CAPITAL; SUBSCRIBED CAPITAL; VENTURE CAPITAL; WORKING CAPITAL.

capital account. In the accounts of a sole trader or partnership, it is the account that records the amount given by the owner/s to the business and used in the business, plus any profits that have been retained in the business. Any losses incurred in any financial period would be deducted from the balance.

capital adequacy. The regulations imposed on banks both nationally and internationally that they should have sufficient capital to support the business and services that they offer, in whatever currency such operations take place. The importance of capital adequacy is the ability of a bank to meet all its obligations, both in the short term and in the long term and absorb any losses that it may incur. The need to maintain adequate capital will differ from bank to bank. In December 1987 the Basle proposals were made as follows: (*i*) there will be a common definition of capital; (*ii*) a common system of weighting risks applicable to off balance sheet and balance sheet items; (*iii*) a minimum level of capital to be held against risk adjusted assets which is expected to be 8 per cent.

capital allowances. Amounts that are allowed for sums spent on purchasing capital items to be used in a business or profession. The amounts must be claimed from the tax authorities.

capital asset. A term often used to denote the value of a fixed asset.

capital clause. This is a clause in the memorandum of association of a limited company which sets out the details of the authorised capital.

capital expenditure. The funds used to acquire fixed assets or to improve the efficiency or extend the life of an existing fixed asset.

capital flight. The transfer of large sums of money from one country to another in order to seek greater security, higher interest rates, or avoid political and economic upheavals.

capital fund planning. The selection of a plan or plans for the purpose of obtaining funds to finance long- term assets or working capital.

capital gain/loss. In the case of a gain this refers to (*a*) where the net realisable value exceeds the original cost of the asset (or in the case of a loss, less than the original cost), (*b*) the difference between the cost price of the asset and the eventual sale of that asset.

Capital Gains Tax (CGT). A tax introduced by the Finance Act 1965 for the purpose of taxing gains made on the disposal of assets. At the moment the tax authorities will allow a minimum of gains to be tax free (at present it is £5,800) and the remainder taxed at the current rate of income tax. Exemptions to this tax are: national savings certificates, national savings yearly plan, friendly society bonds, insurance policies, personal equity plans, gilt-edge stock, national savings childrens bonds, TESSA accounts and the first disposal of the Business Expansion Scheme. All gains made before 31 March 1982 are also exempt. Gains after that date are indexed, so that gains are reduced in line with inflation.

capital market. A market for borrowing and lending funds usual for medium and long-term finance.

capitalisation. 1. Using a rate of interest to convert a series of future interest payments into one sum. 2. The purchase of assets or to improve assets which are not treated as revenue expenditure. 3. To use an economic event to one's own advantage. 4. To convert retained profits into paid-up share capital by the issue of bonus shares.

capitalised value. Using the current annual earnings multiplied by the current rate of interest, should indicate the current value of an asset.

capitalism. A term used to indicate a free market, whereby the investment of capital is used to produce wealth for the owner/s of the entity.

capital redemption reserve. In instances where the redemption of redeemable shares is not made via a new issue of shares, it is an account which is credited with the nominal amount of the shares redeemed.

capital redemption yield. The difference between the purchase price of a stock and the amount that will be received on redemption. It is usually expressed as a percentage by dividing this profit figure by the number of years to redemption.

capital transfer tax. *See* INHERITANCE TAX.

cargo. A noun describing goods placed on a ship or plane. This does not include a passenger's own personal luggage carried on board by him.

carnet. An international document which permits dutiable goods to pass through a country without paying duty until the good arrive at their destination.

carriage. The transportation of goods from one place to another. The cost of carrying the goods. *See also* CARRIAGE FORWARD; CARRIAGE INWARD; CARRIAGE PAID; CARRIAGE OUTWARD.

carriage forward. The cost of carriage to be paid for on arrival at the destination.

carriage inward. The cost of carriage to be paid by the purchaser.

carriage outward. Another way of describing that the cost of carriage of goods will be paid by the seller.

carriage paid. Where the seller has agreed that the cost of carriage will be his responsibility.

carry over. With the advent of the disbanding of the two/three week account period, this will no longer refer to the continuance of a bargain from one period to another. *See* TAURUS.

cartel. An agreement between producers/manufacturers to keep the price of goods at an agreed level, so that the price and amount may be controlled.

case in need. Bills of Exchange Act 1882, s. 15 states: 'The drawer of a bill and any indorser may insert therein the name of a person to whom the holder may resort in case of need, that is to say, in case the bill is dishonoured by non-acceptance or non-payment. Such a person is called the referee in case of need. It is in the option of the holder to resort to the refereee in case of need or not as he may think fit'. Uniform Rules for Collection – ICC Publication No. 322 Article 18 states: 'If the principal nominated a representative to act as case-in-need in the event of non-acceptance and/or non payment the collection order should clearly and fully indicate the powers of such case-in-need. In the absence of such indication banks will not accept any instructions from the case in need.'

case law. The law built up by judges from their case decisions.

cash. Usually such items as banknotes and coin plus demand deposits with banks. With current developments, this definition may include any thing which may be turned into cash or readily acceptable in settlement of debts. Under the Consumer Credit Act 1974, s. 189(1), it includes money in any form.

cash account. An account recording the payments in and out of cash and cheques, and showing the balance on the account as cash in hand.

cash against document (CAD). The delivery by the presenting bank to the importer of commercial documents against immediate payment.

cash analysis. When large sums of money are required by corporate customers of a bank, for the payment of wages, it is usual for that customer to notify the bank of the different denominations of cash required, so that each employee can receive the exact amount due to him/her.

cash at bank. The amount of money that a business will have on deposit with a bank or authorised institution. Amounts on current account can be withdrawn on demand, while amounts in a deposit account may be made available after due notice has been given.

cash basis. The delivery of goods against immediate payment.

cash bonus. 1. A sum of money given over and above the salary/wage in recognition of increased work, greater production, etc. 2. An amount paid by an assurance company to the insured when increased profits have been announced. This amount is added on to the ultimate payment that will be made.

cash book. A book containing a record of all transactions going through the cash and bank accounts. Three column cash books will contain one column for recording discounts received and discounts given.

cash card. Cards issued to customers of banks to enable them to obtain cash at any time of the day or night from a machine called either a cash dispenser or *automated teller machine* (ATM). The card is made of plastic and by introducing the card into the slot provided and by pressing the keys to give the *personal identification number* (PIN), funds up to agreed amount can be obtained, balances notified. The ordering of cheque books and statements can also be done by ATM. Many banks include a cheque card and debit card function in the cash card.

cash discount. An amount deducted from the invoice amount when paying the amount due on or before the stated time. The amount allowed on the settlement of a bill of exchange when paid before it is due.

cash dispenser. A machine (ATM) situated either in the outwall of a bank or available inside the banking hall to enable persons with cash cards to withdraw funds as and when required. Many banks have their own names for these machines, e.g. Servicetill, Autobank, etc. *See* AUTOMATED TELLER MACHINE: CASH CARD.

cash float. An amount of money a bank cashier will keep to enable him to either give change to customers or cash their cheques. *Retailers* will also maintain a cash float, so that cash in small denominations is available when giving change to customers.

cash flow. The pattern of the flow of cash within a business over a period of time. This will be ascertained by calculating the profit of the business, adding the depreciation on assets, plus the receipt of any capital funds, less the outflow of either a capital or revenue nature.

cashier's check. American terminology for a banker's draft. *See* BANKERS' DRAFT.

cash in hand. The amount of money held in the form of notes and coin by a person or business as opposed to 'cash at bank'.

cash limit. The amount of cash that can be spent by a business for a given purpose in a given period. It also refers to the amount that can be drawn by a customer from an *ATM* or the amount given on an *overdraft* or loan.

cash management. A service that was introduced in 1982 to corporate treasurers, but with the advent of 'home banking', has been extended to the ordinary person. The customer can obtain the details of all his accounts with that bank whether those accounts are held in the UK or any overseas branch of that bank. It allows the customer, through his own computer terminal, or by telephone, to link up with the bank's computer which will show the various debits, credits and balances of the appropriate accounts.

cash on delivery (COD). A term used when the purchaser of goods pays the carrier the sum due.

cash ratio. 1. The ratio of cash to current liabilities. 2. The amount of cash held by banks in tills and balances at the Bank of England as a percentage of the total amounts held on current and deposit accounts.

cast/casting. Adding up a set of figures.

caution. 1. A warning. 2. Any person interested in registered land may lodge a notice with the Land Registry, so that any pending action would be subject to that caution.

caveat. A warning, a caution; a *legal process* to stop procedures.

cedel. An agreement between a large number of European banks to settle their clearing differences in various financial transactions, particularly those involved in Eurobonds.

ceiling. In banking this often refers the borrowing limit imposed by a bank on its customer.

central bank. A bank in any country that is involved in (a) the issue of currency, (b) administers monetary policy, (c) supervises the activities of other banks, (d) maintains the accounts of other banks, (e) maintains the country's foreign currency reserves. While in the UK the Bank of England is a nationalised organisation and subject to government control, central banks in other countries, e.g. Germany, have independence from governmental control.

Central Gilts Office (CGO). For many years the Bank of England maintained at the 'Jobbers Counter' a clerical record of running balances of the gilt-edged stock for the main gilt-edged market participants, allowing them to receive and deliver stock without waiting for the underlying transfer of ownership to be recorded on the main register. To ensure reliable and effective settlement for the future, the Bank and The Stock Exchange jointly developed a computerised book-entry transfer system known as the Central Gilts Office (CGO). The CGO was introduced in two distinct phases. The first phase became operational on 2 January 1986 and phase 2 was inaugurated alongside all the other changes on 27 October 1986 (known as 'Big Bang' in the financial markets). The first merely computerised the facilities which had existed previously, whereas the second allowed all the new market participants under the arrangements introduced with the 'Big Bang' to gain access to the CGO and also provided an assured payments system. The system provides a means of transferring stock electronically either in settlement of bargains or for stock lending between members and incorporates an automatic same day payment arrangement. Since December 1987 membership of the service has been open to any participant in the gilt-edged market. The service is on-line real-time computerised book-entry transfer system for gilt-edged stocks and most 'bulldogs' stocks for which the Bank of England is registrar. The membership consists of gilt-edged market makers, inter-dealer brokers, broker/dealers, Stock Exchange money brokers, discount houses, institutional investors, nominee account holders and banks. For security purposes, delivery may be broken down into three steps and acceptance into two. Members may therefore select for each of their operators a level of authority compatible with their office procedures and experience of their staff to ensure appropriate checking of delivery data. Authentication processes are used to protect messages passing across the communications network. The number of direct members of the CGO at May 1991 stands at 105. Many more firms participate indirectly through

the agency of a direct member. In looking to the future and in particular the European Community's financial union, the Bank has recently been considering the possibility of providing settlement facilities for instruments denominated in ECU.

Central Moneymarkets Office (CMO). Until 1 October 1990, transactions in negotiable instruments were settled by messengers delivering paper securities and exchanging them for payments, usually cheques or drafts drawn on banks in the Town Clearing. From the above date a system was inaugurated to enable the settlement and transfer of sterling money market bearer securities to be carried out by electronic book-keeping transfers. The design of the system was undertaken by the Bank of England which became involved following the failure in 1988 of a private sector initiative, by a company called London Clear to provide a settlement service for these securities. At the launch, 44 institutions joined as direct members, but that number has increased to 66 and no doubt will increase further. Each direct member has an account with the CMO and inputs and receives instrument deliveries details via a CMO terminal located in his own premises, for which he is responsible. A direct member must arrange for a settlement bank to make and receive payments on his behalf for instruments transferred from and to any other member of the service. Indirect participation of the service can also be undertaken by a participant having a nominee who is a direct member of the service. The direct member acts on the instructions of the indirect participant. Any charges for the nominee service is a matter of agreement between the two parties. The electronic book-entry transfer system is currently for the following categories of sterling bearer instruments: Treasury Bills, Eligible Bank Bills, Trade Bills, Commercial Paper, Local Authority Bills, Ineligible Bank Bills, Bank Certificates of Deposit, Building Society Certificates of Deposit. All instruments admitted into CMO must be payable at maturity at a CMO member; the physical instruments represented by the book-entry are stored in a safe custody vault at the CMO. Each direct member has a CMO account on which is held an inventory of their instruments. On enquiry this is displayed, sorted according to issue type (e.g. Treasury Bill, Local Authority Bill, etc.) and sub-sorted in order of form held (i.e. outright, held as collateral against a loan, etc.), maturity date and nominal value. Full details of each instrument are available through on-line enquiries. The current status of each instrument is flagged automatically by the system. Authentication and encryption processes are used to protect messages passing to and from each member's terminals. Members must advise the CMO of the number of their staff requiring access to the system. Each operator is recognised within the system by a number which is used in conjunction with a password applicable only to that operator number. As an aid to members, on-line terminal enquiries are available for monitoring their instrument and payment instruction positions. The following reports are produced overnight for each member and are available for collection from the CMO counter the following morning: Issue Details Report, Instrumentss Held Report, Payments Report, Collateral Returns Report, Withdrawal Report, Daily Tariff Report, Lodgements Report, Settled Deliveries Report, Unsettled Deliveries Report, Pledged Out Inventory Report, Maturities Report.

certificate. A formal declaration stating a fact or facts.

certificate of bonds. A certificate issued to the registered holder of bonds stating that the bonds are registered in his name.

certificate of charge. A certificate issued by the Land Registry showing the register of a charge by a lender on the registered land. The original charge, signed by the borrower, is stitched into the certificate. As evidence of title it takes the place of the land certificate during the lifetime of the charge.

certificate of deposit. A debt instrument issued by a bank evidencing that a deposit has been made for a specified amount, for a stated length of time and attracting a given rate of interest. This is a negotiable instrument

and as such can be purchased and sold in the 'secondary' money market. They are usually issued in sterling and US dollars. *See also* STERLING CERTIFICATE OF DEPOSIT; DOLLAR CERTIFICATE OF DEPOSIT.

certificate of existence. Issued by a pension fund or similar organisation to be signed by an independent person that the person named – the beneficiary – on the document is still alive. Frequently a bank official will sign this document on behalf of his customer, or it may be issued to the customer for delivery to the insurance company or pension fund.

certificate of incorporation. A certificate issued by the Registrar of Companies on its approval of the documents presented to it for the formation of a company. Until such a document is issued, no banker should open an account in the name of a company. It is only after the issue of the certificate of incorporation that a company has a legal entity and has the power to open and conduct a bank account. The banker should inspect the certificate and note the details.

certificate of insurance. This document is frequently drawn up by the insured under an overall policy previously opened with the insurance company. This open cover or floating policy is arranged to allow the exporter to draw the certificate covering part of the total amount in accordance with the value and details specified. Such a certificate has no rights of transfer, but merely confirms that a policy covering the goods as stated are covered by a policy. The exception to this are the policies issued by Lloyd's.

certificate of mortgage or sale of ship. Issued by the registrar at the port at which the vessel is registered to enable the owner to sell or mortgage the vessel.

certificate of origin. A document that confirms that the goods have been made or manufactured in a stated country. In the UK the document is issued by Chambers of Commerce or the Department of Trade. With the advent of the 'single market' an EC cerficiate of origin is also available.

certificate of posting. A certificate issued by the Post Office or some other carrier, certifying that the parcel or package has been received.

certificate of protest. *See also* PROTEST CERTIFICATE; HOUSEHOLDER'S PROTEST.

certificate of registration. Issued by the Registrar of Companies to a lender (bank) that a mortgage or charge given by the borrower (a limited company) that needs registration under the Companies Act 1989 has been so registered.

certificate of search. A certificate issued, at the request of a lender, by the Registrar of Charges or Land Register showing the result of a search made in the register in respect of named properties or against the interested party.

certificate to commence business. A document issued by the Registrar of Companies to a public company approving the registration of the company. It is from the date of this certificate that a public company can commence trading.

certified accountant. A member of the Chartered Association of Certified Accountants (ACCA).

certified check. A US term. It is either a cheque issued by a bank (a banker's draft) or a cheque issued by a customer of a bank which has been guaranteed that payment will be made. Since the bank has guaranteed payment it is customary for the bank to withdraw the funds from the customer's account and hold them until payment is requested.

certified transfer. On the occasion when a holder of shares wishes to transfer part of his holding, he delivers his share certificate of transfer to the company registrar. The transfer form is marked 'certificate lodged' and is evidence that the holding has been split and the company registrar may then issue two new certificates.

certiorari. An order from the High Court to an inferior court that a case be brought to a superior court for review.

cestui que trust. The person on whose behalf land is held.

chain of representation. The appointment of a private person as an executor of a will, is based on trust and mutual understanding, it does not necessarily ensure that he will carry

out this duty. In the case of the death of the executor (Y) before the winding up of the estate of the deceased (X), it will be the duty of Y's executor (Z) to wind up both the estate of X and Y, even though X and Z did not know each other. There is a chain of trust between the parties hence the chain of executorship and representation.

chain of title. The successive conveyances of the title to the present owner. *See* GOOD ROOT OF TITLE.

chairman's statement. A report by the chairman of a company which is published in the annual report and accounts of that company, setting out the opinions of that person regarding the past years trading and his or her views on the future prospects of the company.

chamber of commerce. Membership of a chamber of commerce consists of local businessmen for the purpose of promoting trade and industry both at home and abroad. They will provide information to their members. *See* INTERNATIONAL CHAMBER OF COMMERCE.

character. In computer language this refers to a letter, number, space, mark or symbol. In general terminology, this refers to the behaviour and reputation of a person, so that a banker will only open an account for a person who is of good character and is not likely to abuse the services offered.

charge. An encumbrance, a duty, a price to be paid, the giving of a pledge or security by way of a fixed and/or floating charge on property. A formal demand for payment (*Sc. law*).

chargeable assets. An asset upon disposal for a profit will attract capital gains tax according to the Capital Gains Tax Act 1979.

CHAPS & Town Clearing Company Ltd. The CHAPS & Town Clearing Company was established in 1985 as part of the APACS structure. It operates the two high-value same-day clearings in the UK. CHAPS (Clearing House Automated Payment System) provides a same-day guaranteed sterling electronic credit transfer service within the UK. It was launched on 9 February 1984. The system allows for payments of £5000 or more to be transmitted by one bank branch to another via a computer system linked through British

Telecom's Packet Switched Service. The Town Clearing is a largely annual, low volume, same-day value debit paper clearing for cheques and other items of £100 000 or more. Only cheques and certain other items which are drawn on and paid by branches of member banks with a limited area of the City of London are eligible. The aggregate value of transactions through CHAPS and the Town Clearing in 1989 was £21,487 billion. The number of items was less than 9 million giving an average value of just over £2 million. Settlement at the end of the day in both CHAPS and the Town Clearing is effected across Settlement Members' accounts at the Bank of England. The CHAPS & Town Clearing Company currently has 14 members, i.e. Bank of England, Barclays Bank plc, Clydesdale Bank plc, Coutts & Co., Lloyds Bank plc, National Westminster Bank plc, Standard Chartered Bank plc, Bank of Scotland, Citibank N.A., Cooperative Bank plc, Girobank plc, Midland Bank plc, The Royal Bank of Scotland plc, TSB Bank plc.

chargeable gain. *See* CHARGEABLE ASSETS.

charge account. An account held by a customer of a departmental store or large retail organisation. A statement is sent to the customer on a monthly basis, showing the amounts charged, payments made and the outstanding balance.

charges. The amount debited to a customer's account by a bank for services given. In general, a bank will debit its customer either quarterly or half-yearly in accordance with arrangements. A charge can consist of commission and or interest on an overdraft. Specific charges may be made for such additional services as a special presentation, foreign exchange, money transfers, etc. A charge may be created by way of a legal mortgage over property. An obligation to meet a debt.

charge card. A card issued by a large retail organisation to a person (cardholder) who may use the card for the purpose of buying goods – up to the credit limit available – and settling the account on presentation of a statement.

charges register. *See* LAND CERTIFICATE.

charging order. An imposition imposed by the court on behalf of a judgment creditor. (*a*) Charging property of the debtor for the amount of the debt. If the debt is not paid within six months, then the property can be sold in settlement of the debt. (*b*) Charging securities belonging to the debtor. (*c*) Charging money paid into court by the debtor. (*d*) Placing a stop order on funds in court.

charitable company. A company formed without the prime purpose of making a profit. Its function is for the purpose of promoting a cause, e.g. art, religion, science, etc.

charitable trust. A trust set up by an individual or entity under the terms that any income received is applied to a charitable purpose.

charity. Any institution, corporate or not, which is set up for charitable purposes and is subject to the Charities Act 1960.

charter. A written instrument executed between parties, e.g. a deed. An instrument of the Crown granting certain rights and privileges. A constitution. The hiring of a vessel or ship.

chartered accountant. A person who by examination has qualified as a member of the Institute of Chartered Accountants in England and Wales or Scotland or Ireland.

chartered company. A company that has been brought into existence by the granting of a charter by the Sovereign.

Chartered Association of Certified Accountants. A professional body of accountants that practice their profession not only as auditors, but are employed in industry and commerce.

Chartered Institute of Bankers (CIB). 10 Lombard Street London EC3V 9AS and an office in Canterbury. The Chartered Institute of Bankers, founded in 1879, and granted Royal Charter in 1987, is one of the oldest professional bodies and certainly one of the biggest, with about 120 000 members engaged in banking and finance all over the world. The aims of the Institute are two-fold; to provide the educational foundation on which any man or woman can build a banking/financial career; and to keep its members in touch with the latest developments in banking and business generally. Like other professional bodies, the Institute maintains educational standards through qualifications which are awarded to those who are successful in the examinations. The Institute's members are men and women engaged in banking and finance at all levels. They range from full time students, trainees who have just left school or university to chief executives and directors. Membership is individual. Banks as banks are not members. The whole emphasis is on personal development. Associates of the Chartered Institute of Bankers (ACIB) are elected exclusively from those who have passed their Associateship examinations and who have also completed three years' banking or relevant work experience and have been a member of the Institute for at least three years. The Associateship examinations consist of four core subjects plus four options selected from a range of more than a dozen subjects. For those who do not aspire to middle management, a lower level, technician qualification is available in the Banking Certificate. Entrants without A levels, or equivalents, first study three Preliminary subjects before studying the Final section of six subjects. A level holders, and those with more than five years banking experience, may enter the Final section direct. Associates who wish to continue their studies may enter for the Financial Studies Diploma which is now linked to an MBA in the Lombard Scheme. In this scheme, a number of leading business schools will accept Associates who, in the first two stages of the Scheme, will study traditional MBA subjects. In the third stage, students will study a subject called 'Strategic Issues in Banking' with three other banking 'electives'. Successful completion will lead to the award by the Institute of the FSD and students will be entitled to use the designatory letters DipFS. The fourth stage, which will lead to the award of the MBA, will consist of a 15–20,000 word project relating to banking or finance. Fellows (FCIB) are elected by the Council from Associates who have achieved senior professional status. Their function is to give a lead in Institute affairs at both national and local level. Policy is decided by an elected Council, and the central administration is in London. However the membership is so large and so widespread that many of these activities are organised by a network of local centres. These local centres – in the UK and abroad – are organised by the local members, who run seminars debates, group discussions, lectures and industrial visits, all of which make their contribution to professional education. The centres also help bankers to play their role in their local communities by bringing them into social and professional contact with other organisations in the area. The Institute will undertake the production of tuition material to provide students with the necessary resources to study. Thus it will commission its own textbooks to cover specialist subjects and these are sold through Bankers Books, a subsidiary company of the Institute. Recently it has expanded its work in this field to cover: study guides, books on banking history, videos, student-centred workbooks and computerassisted learning courses. Bankers Books also runs a small bookshop in the City and stocks a wide range of titles of interest to the financial community. Its books can be ordered by mail through the CIB Canterbury office. The Library, which is already one of the best in the financial field, is updating and uprating its services. It is proposed to form links with individual librarians, documentalists, etc., in other countries under the auspices of the Federation Internationale de Documentation. In this way information about banking systems and other matters of banking interest can be exchanged between interested bankers in a way not hitherto available. Besides maintaining files on banking subjects, and copies of important journals, newspapers, etc., the Institute can provide access to specialised databases through its computer terminals. At national level, the Institute runs seminars, management courses and study tours. Internationally, the annual International Banking Summer School attracts senior bankers from more than fifty countries to discuss topics of professional importance. This was started in 1948 and is now held all over the world, returning periodically to the United Kingdom. Further information about the Institute and details about its examinations are obtainable from its London headquarters.

Chartered Institute of Bankers in Scotland. This Institute was founded in 1875 and is the oldest Institute of Bankers in the world. It was granted its first Royal Charter in 1976 and a Supplementary Charter was granted by Her Majesty Queen Elizabeth II in September 1991. The Institute's aims are to improve the qualifications of those engaged in banking and to raise their status and influence. This is done mainly through an educational programme which is in three stages. Stage 1 is the Foundation Course. Stage 2 is the Associateship – broadly equivalent to the English Institute's Associateship. Stage 3 is the Members' Education Programme and is designed for bankers who are likely to reach middle and higher levels of management. The designatory letters on the successful completion of Stage 2 are ACIBS and for Stage 3 MCIBS. Fellows (FCIBS) are elected from those members who have made a major contribution to banking and/or to the Institute. The Institute also conducts short courses on specific topics, lectures and meetings arranged through District Centres. It also publishes a quarterly magazine, *The Scottish Banker.*

Chartered Institute of Public Finance and Accountancy (CIPFA). The Institute is one of the six major professional accountancy bodies in the UK. Its members specialise in financial management for public service bodies and membership as professional accountants is by examination. The Institute's activities include promoting the highest standard of professional competence of its members, providing a common group for the discussion of public finance and accountancy through conferences, seminars and meetings, and publishing statistics, a weekly journal, the Financial Information Service, etc. The Institute also has a research arm, the Public Finance Foundation (PFF).

charter party. A contract between the owner of a vessel and a hirer, agreeing the terms and conditions that the vessel is placed at the disposal of the hirer.

charter party bill of lading. The issue of a bill of lading by the hirer of a vessel stating the terms and conditions of the contract of carriage of goods.

chattels. All property other than freehold land.

chattels personal. Any assets that are capable of delivery by delivery, e.g. furniture, motor-cars, goods, etc.

chattels real. Leasehold property.

cheap money. Money borrowed at a low rate of interest.

checking account. A term now being used in the UK e.g. a building society will advertise its cheque account or checking account. It is a US term for a current account.

cheque. By legal definition it is a bill of exchange drawn on a bank payable on demand (Bills of Exchange Act 1882). However, many building societies, not recognised as a bank, are issuing documents which they and the public call cheques and are generally acceptable as cheques. *See also* ANTEDATED CHEQUE; BEARER BILL, BLANK CHEQUE; CROSSED CHEQUE; MARKED CHEQUE; OPEN CHEQUE; ORDER CHEQUE; PAYMENT OF CHEQUES; STOPPED CHEQUE; TRAVEL CHEQUE.

cheque as an assignment of funds. This only refers to Scotland where the drawee of a bill has in his/her hands funds available for the payment of it. Where the balance of the account of the drawer at the time of presentation for payment, is insufficient to pay the cheque and it is returned unpaid by the paying bank, the funds are transferred to suspense account so that the funds are attached for eventual payment.

cheque book. A book of cheque forms, usually containing 25 or 30 cheque forms. For the corporate customer, cheque books containing five hundred or more cheques are available. The cheque will normally be of a design of the drawee bank, but with the approval of the bank and providing the paper and details conform to the criteria laid down by the Committee of London and Scottish Clearing Banks, customers can arrange to have their own cheque books printed.

cheque book register. A register kept by a bank, not necessarily at the branch, of cheque books issued to customers.

cheque card. The familiar, standard appearance cheque card which has been in existence since the late 1960s has evolved in many directions after two decades of its life. *Functionality.* Single function cheque guarantee cards, which guaranteed cheques up to £50, are only standard in appearance in the marks panel (Shakespeare hologram and line drawing on the front, right-hand side), paper signature panel and magnetic stripe. The remainder of the space – about 65% in total – is available for use by the issuing institution at their discretion. Multi-functionality was first introduced in 1988 and enables the cheque guarantee function identifiable by an alternative version of the Shakespeare line drawing (£50 cards) or holograms (£100 or £250 cards) to be incorporated on some other card issued by the member institutions. The three variable limits indicated above and for use only within the multi-function concept were first introduced in 1989. The Shakespeare insignia by which cards can be identified as issued by scheme members have resulted in the cards becoming affectionately known as 'Bard Cards'. *Issuers.* Following relaxation in 1985 of the criteria for scheme membership by banks, and financial deregulation in 1987 which opened the way for building societies to operate current account banking, the number of card issuers belonging to the scheme has exploded from less than 20 in 1986 to more than 50 in 1990. This number includes all the 'High Street' banks along with the three most important building societies as well as many other medium size institutions. The number of cards in issue grew between the end of 1986 and the end of 1989 by 11 million to 36 million. It is estimated that approximately 1 billion cheques are issued with the backing of a guarantee card every year, out of a total of more than 3.5 billion cheques issued. *Usage.* The card carries the name of the bank or building society, the name and signature of the customer, and may include the sorting code number of the branch maintaining the account, as well as the card number and expiry date. It is normally renewed biennially. The issuing bank undertakes that any cheque not exceeding the indicated guarantee limit will be honoured as long as the cheque has been signed in the presence of the payee, is drawn on a bank cheque form whose code number agrees with the code number on the card, and is authenticated by a signature which agrees with the specimen signature on the card. The cheque must be drawn before the expiry date of the card, and the card number must also be recorded on the reverse of the cheque by the payee. *See also* UNIFORM EUROCHEQUE SCHEME.

Cheque and Credit Clearing Company Ltd. The Cheque and Credit Clearing Company was established in 1985 as part of the APACS structure. It operates the two bulk paper clearings which are situated in London and cover England and Wales. The two clearings are the Cheque Clearing (known previously as the General Clearing) and the Credit Clearing. Most inter-bank cheques, except the small number of high-value cheques that clear through the Town Clearing, are cleared through the Cheque Clearing. The Credit Clearing operates in a similar way to the Cheque Clearing but handles paper credit items. Cheques and credits drawn in Scotland and Northern Ireland are not cleared in London but are handled by clearings in Edinburgh or Belfast. Neither of these comes under the APACS umbrella. In 1989, 2 231 million cheques and 180 million paper credits passed through the Clearings, for a total value of £1 137 billion. Inter-branch items are dealt with separately by each member. Inter-member settlement for both clearings at the end of the three-day clearing cycle, takes place across the Settlement Members' accounts at the Bank of England. The Cheque and Credit Clearing Company currently has eleven members: Abbey National plc, Bank of England, Bank of Scotland, Barclays Bank plc, Cooperative Bank plc, Girobank plc, Lloyds Bank plc, Midland Bank plc, National Westminster Bank plc, The Royal Bank of Scotland plc, TSB Bank plc.

Cheque Card Policy Committee. The Cheque Card Policy Committee forms an operational grouping under the APACS structure. It administers the cheque card scheme and the uniform eurocheque scheme in the UK. Membership of the domestic cheque card scheme currently total 50 financial institutions. Members issue cheque guarantee cards in standard formats agreed within the scheme. These include using the cheque guarantee symbol to support a cheque guarantee function on a multi-function card. Cheque guarantee limits of £50, £100, and £250 are all supported under the scheme. The eurocheque scheme provides a simple international payment medium for transactions in 40 different countries up to national value limits, equivalent to approximately 300 Swiss francs. The administratation of the eurocheque scheme throughout Europe is the responsibility of the Eurocheque Assembly and Eurocheque International S.A. A total of 20 banks are currently members of the UK eurocheque community.

cheque rate. The commission charged for the issue of a cheque or draft issued in the currency of another country.

Cheques Act 1957. This very important Act protects the paying banker when paying cheques without an endorsement (s. 1). It protects the collecting banker when collecting cheques for a customer who has not endorsed the cheque. Section 4 of the Act protects the banker who in good faith and without negligence collects a cheque either for himself or herself or a customer.

Chicago Mercantile Exchange (CME), (International Monetary Market Division – IMM) and (Index and Option Market Division – IOM). The Chicago Mercantile Exchange is one of the largest futures and options Exchanges in the world. Since the CME introduced its range of options on its already highly successful financial futures contracts in 1983, the volume of trading continues to grow at a truly astonishing rate. The underlying US dollar value of the contracts, when weighted by contract size, makes the CME the world market leader for exchange traded futures and options. The European Representative Office of the CME was opened in London, in 1979 followed by the opening of the Tokyo office in 1987. The IMM division of the Chicago Mercantile Exchange was opened for trading in May 1972. It now lists futures and options contracts on nine currencies; Australian dollar, British pound, Canadian dollar, Deutschemark, Japanese yen, and Swiss francs, it also lists currency cross-rate futures contracts on the British pound/Deutschemark, Deutschemark/Japanese yen, and Deutschemark/Swiss franc. The IMM is used by multinational companies, export and import traders and others faced with the exchange risks caused by floating rates of exchange. In 1976 the IMM listed futures and options contracts in short-term interest rates. These took the form of the 13-week US Treasury Bills, followed by the 90-day Eurodollar Time Deposit and more recently the 1-month LIBOR contract. The IOM was created 1982 to trade futures and options on the Standard & Poor's 500 Index, one of the CME's most successful contracts to date, the Nikkei 225 Stock Average and options on the currencies, interest rate and stock indices contracts. These facilities have attracted a wide range of money managers who wish to guard against yield swings in their interest-bearing paper and the resultant hedges have made these contracts among the fastest expanding in the futures industry.

chief rent. Also known as 'fee farm rent'. It occurs when the vendor of land, in lieu of taking the purchase money, reserves a right to take a rent in perpetuity for himself and his heirs. Should there be a default in payment of the rent, then owner of the chief rent has the right of re-entry.

Chief Registrar of Friendly Societies. Under the Building Societies Act 1962 the Chief Registrar obtains powers to register friendly societies, to receive annual returns and if necessary appoint inspectors to investigate the affairs of any society. The Chief Registrar has powers of responsibility over the conduct of building societies, *inter alia* to investigate a society, approve or withhold approval of any society, etc.

chinese wall. This is an artificial barrier set up by financial institutions that have separate subsidiary companies, so that sensitive and confidential information is not passed from one entity to another. The 'chinese wall' ensures that the various operational activities are kept completely separate and proper safeguards are in force. An example of this is the responsibilities of a unit trust and a trustee company, both subsidiaries of the same bank. The importance of the 'chinese wall' has been increased by the provisions on insider dealing contained in the Companies Act.

chip card. A plastic card incorporating a computer chip which gives it a memory substantially greater than a card with a magnetic strip on the reverse. Also known as a memory card or, more properly integrated circuit (IC) card. In widespread use in France and being trialled in the UK.

chose in action. A right enforceable in a court of law.

chose in possession. A sum of money or a good in the actual possession of the owner.

churning. The excessive trading of a client's account by a broker or trustee, for the purpose of increasing the commission earned.

CIB. *See* CHARTERED INSTITUTE OF BANKERS.

CIF. *See* COST INSURANCE FREIGHT.

circulating asset. An asset that will be used or sold during the normal operations of a business entity. During the operation cycle, the asset will be used/sold, then replaced by a similar asset.

circulating capital. The current assets of a business entity, e.g. stock, debtors, cash at bank/in hand.

circulating medium. Money such as banknotes or any other form used as a means of exchange.

cite. To quote, to allege as an authority; to quote as an instance; to refer to; to summons to appear in court.

cital. A summons, a citation.

city. A collective description of the financial institutions of the City of London.

city code on taker-overs and mergers. The published rules setting out the rules to be observed during any merger or take over by all parties concerned.

claim. A right for the payment or repayment of funds. For example, a right to claim a refund of VAT, income tax, a claim by a bank on another for the settlement of inter-bank indebtedness.

claim form. A form used by a branch of a bank to claim an amount due from a branch of the same bank, e.g. a claim for an unpaid cheque, the transfer of an overdraft balance from one branch to another.

claused bill of lading. A bill of lading that has a clause or notation either in writing, typed, or stamped, stating that either the goods or packaging is in a defective condition.

claw back. A term used originally to describe a refund of tax due to the taxpayer; more recently a recovery by the Inland Revenue of tax relief formerly granted, notably in the case of certain family allowances and in some cases of early surrender or conversion of life policies. Claw back is also instanced in connection with stock relief, where deferred tax becomes payable. The phrase is also used in more general commercial terms for obtaining a recovery of funds paid to a third party.

Clayton's case *Devaynes* v. *Noble* **(1916).** When a bank lends money on current account – fluctuating overdraft, it is the normal practice to agree that the security offered is to be 'continuing security'. If this was not done then *Clayton's case* would apply. When a customer pays in funds, he has the right to allocate these funds to a particular payment/cheque. If he does not exercise this right, then the bank has that right. When neither party exercises this right then the ruling by Sir William Gant MR, who gave the judgment in the case will apply. 'Presumably, it is the sum first paid in that is first drawn out. It is the first item on the debit side of the account that is discharged, or reduced, by the first item on the credit side. The appropriation is made by the very act of setting the two items against each other'. This situation is not likely to arise in modern banking practice, since any money lent on a current account where security is deposited, the appropriate form will contain a 'continuing security' clause.

clean bill. A bill of exchange or any other negotiable instrument which has no commercial documents attached.

clean bill of lading. A bill of lading which has no superimposed clauses which indicate that either the goods or packaging are in any way defective or damaged.

clean credit. A credit opened by a banker which provides for payment by the banker of bills drawn upon him, but such bills having no commercial documents attached.

clean rate. A dealer's term for a rate on a deposit where no certificate of deposit has been issued.

clearance. Completion of the formalities and procedure before a ship or an aircraft may leave; of a *bill or cheque*, the obtaining of money in place of the bill or cheque; *of goods*, the performance of duties and formalities which are necessary before goods can be dispatched or allowed to enter e.g. customs duties.

cleared funds. The balance of an account in which the funds are not likely to be reduced by cheques which may for any reason be return unpaid, i.e. three days have elapsed from the date of the presentation of any cheques credited to the account and payment by the drawee bank is assumed.

clearing. Presenting a cheque, draft or other negotiable instrument, through the banking procedure, that is the presentation for its ultimate payment through the clearing house by the drawee bank. *See also* IN CLEARING; OUT CLEARING.

clearing bank. A bank which, until December 1985, was a member of the Committee of London Clearing Bankers. However, as responsibility for managing the clearings passed to the Association for Payment Clearing Services in December 1985, and that body has an open membership structure embracing building societies, wholesale banks and smaller banks, the expression no longer has a defined meaning. References to the largest banks are tending now to be made to 'The Big Five', or 'High Street Banks'.

clearing house. The Bankers' Clearing House of the Association for Payment Clearing Services is situated in 10 Lombard Street, where it has been since its origin in the 1770s. Representatives of member institutions of the Cheque and Credit and Town Clearings attend there each day to agree the settlement figures in those clearings.

Clearing House Automated Payments System. *See* CHAPS AND TOWN CLEARING COMPANY LTD.

Clearing House Inter-Bank Payments System (CHIPS). CHIPS is an electronic payments system in New York for paying and receiving funds on the same day. It is a highly secure and robust system which handles, *inter alia*, high value payments relating to foreign exchange and international transactions. The aggregate daily total of CHIPS payments has increased rapidly since CHIPS was established in 1970. In 1990 the daily aggregate total was about $1 trillion. Payments are made by one participant in CHIPS to another. Each participant sends a payment from its electronic terminal across the CHIPS central computer system to the terminal of the participant receiving the payment. The instruction to make a payment may have been received by the participant from abroad, and this may well have been communicated to the participant via SWIFT. In CHIPS there are 140 participants, some are domestic banks and some are foreign banks. CHIPS forms part of the New York Clearing House Association, which also runs the New York Automated Clearing House and other payment systems. The Association is owned by 11 member banks: The Bank of New York, The Chase Manhattan Bank, N.A., Citibank N.A., Chemical Bank, Morgan Guarantee Trust Company of New York, Manufacturers Hanover Trust Company, Bankers Trust Company, Marine Midland Bank N.A., United States Trust Company of New York, National Westminster Bank USA, European American Bank and Trust Company. There is an important framework of credit risk containment measures in CHIPS, based on credit limits between each pair of participants. CHIPS closes at 4.30 p.m. The Clearing House then notifies each of the 20 settling banks of their net debit or credit positions and the positions of any participants for whom they settle.

Payments are then made across the Fedwire by the settling banks to settle CHIPS transactions. CHIPS is essentially a New York City system; nationwide transfers in the USA are carried out through Fedwire, which is an electronic system operated and controlled by the 11 Federal Reserve banks.

clients' accounts. Current or deposit accounts in the name of a solicitor at a bank, in the title of which account the word 'client' appears. Under the Solicitors' Act 1974, money held for clients must be kept separate from the solicitor's personal or office accounts. They should not become overdrawn. There is no set-off between clients' accounts and the personal or office accounts. Clients' accounts must also be maintained for estate agents, dealers and investment managers and insurance brokers.

close company. A category of company whether public or private, which has been established by legislation for tax purposes. It is a company which is under the control of five or fewer persons being directors, however many directors there may in fact be; or a company in which a person is considered to hold control by possessing a major portion of the capital or voting rights; or a company in which such a person would, in the event of the company going into liquidation be entitled to more than 50 per cent of the assets. Excepted are companies not resident in the UK, companies controlled by the Crown, and registered industrial and provident societies.

closing purchase. A contract whereby the writer buys an option which has the same terms as the option he has previously sold. He thereby terminates his liability as a writer.

closing rate. In the foreign exchange markets the rates for the purchase/sale of spot currency at the close of that day's business. For balance sheet purposes, a company will use the closing rate of exchange in order to produce balance sheet and profit and loss accounts, in order to calculate its various foreign currency accounts into the notional value of the home currency.

closing sale. A contract whereby the holder sells an option which has the same terms as the one he previously

purchased, thereby extinguishing his rights as a holder.

closing stock. The value of all raw materials, work in progress and finished goods at the end of the trading period.

club. *See* UNINCORPORATED ASSOCIATION.

COD. The abbreviation for 'cash on delivery'.

code number. An integral part of the PAYE system of tax deduction. The net allowances, less any untaxed interest, of any taxpayer are listed on a notice of coding and the net total is given a code number by reference to a list of allowances at various levels. An employer is thereby enabled to look up the appropriate code number for any employee in the tax tables issued to the employer and so to discover the correct amount of tax to be deducted weekly or monthly and subsequently handed over to the Collector of Taxes.

Code of Banking Practice. This code sets out the standards of good banking practice to be observed by banks, building societies, and card issuers when dealing with personal customers in the United Kingdom. Any of those institutions may observe higher standards if they wish.

The code is effective from 16 March 1992 and will be reviewed from time to time. (This will be at least once every two years.)

The code has been prepared by the British Bankers' Association (BBA), and the Association for Payment Clearing Services (APACS).

The Code is written to promote good banking practice. Specific services may have their own terms and conditions which will comply with the principles contained in the Code.

The Code is in two parts:

Part A – Customers, their banks and building societies – is addressed to banks and building societies who adopt the Code and offer personal customers ('customers' for short throughout the Code) banking services such as current accounts, deposit and other savings accounts, overdrafts and loans, and various services delivered by use of plastic cards.

Part B – Customers and their Cards – is addressed to banks, building societies and others who adopt the Code and provide financial services by means of plastic cards.

All such providers are called card issuers in part B of the Code and here.

The governing principles of the code are:

(a) to set out the standards of good banking practice which banks, building societies and card issuers will follow in their dealings with their customers;

(b) that banks, building societies and card issuers will act fairly and reasonably in all their dealings with their customers;

(c) that banks, building societies and card issuers will help customers to understand how their accounts operate and will seek to give them a good understanding of banking services;

(d) to maintain confidence in the security and integrity of banking and card payment systems. Banks, building societies and card issuers recognise that their systems and technology need to be reliable to protect their customers and themselves.

The code requires banks, building societies and card issuers to provide certain information to customers. This will usually be at the time when an account is opened. Information will also be available to customers from branches, if any, of the bank, building society or card issuer. Bankers, building societies and card issuers will provide additional information and guidance about specific services at any time on request.

codicil. An additional document varying the terms of a will or revoking part of it. The codicil must be signed by the testator and witnessed in a similar fashion to the execution of a will.

codifying statute. An act which codifies the whole of case and statute law on a particular matter. One of the earliest of such statutes was the Bills of Exchange Act 1882, with the recent Companies Act 1985 having the same effect.

coin. In common usage, it is used to mean to invent a new word or phrase. To acquire wealth/profit very quickly. To make counterfeit money. It is a piece of stamped metal given a value and used as legal tender within a country. *See* COIN OF THE REALM.

coinage. The act of coining the pieces coined; the monetary system in use.

coin of the realm. The coins authorised for circulation in the UK are the penny (1p), two pence (2p), Ten pence (10p), Twenty pence (20p), fifty pence (50p) and the one pound (£1). Under the Coinage Act, 1971, coins have limited legal tender as follows: up to 20p (1p and 2p coins), up to £5 (5p and 10p coins), up to £10 (20p and 50p coins).

collateral. Additional security, security deposited by a third party, as opposed to primary security deposited by the borrower. An American term meaning 'security'.

collecting banker. The banker who collects for his or her customer's account the proceeds of bills, cheques and other instruments which have been paid in to the bank for that purpose. If the customer has a faulty title (as where it has been obtained by fraud) the collecting banker may be sued by the true owner for the tort of conversion. The collecting banker can look to statutory protection against this claim so long as he or she has collected the cheque(s) in question in good faith, without negligence and for a customer. (Cheques Act 1954 s. 4).

collection. The handling by banks of a *financial* document with or without *commercial* documents; or the handling of *commercial* documents with or without a financial document. Uniform *Rules for Collection* define the dealing with the presentation, acceptance, payment and other matters regarding all collections whether documentary or clean.

collection order. The written instructions from a customer (the principal) instructing the bank (the agent) on the presentation and ultimate payment of the specified documents. Instructions should also be received in the event of non-acceptance or non-payment of the draft/documents.

collective bargaining. The negotiations between employers and employees (usually trade union representatives) which relate to the terms and conditions of employment. The result of this is a collective agreement and is the result of such bargaining.

collector of taxes. An official of the Inland Revenue whose job it is to collect the taxes as notified by the Inspector of Taxes.

co-manager. Bank ranking next after the lead manager in the marketing of a new issue, or syndicated loan.

combine. An association of two or more business entities, either temporary or permanently for the purposes of a joint venture or to form an amalgamation of their activities. Such associations may be vertical or horizontal. It may be a cartel or trust.

combined transport. The carriage of goods by at least two modes of transport.

combined transport bill of lading. Often known as a 'through bill of lading'. It is issued when the journey will involve two or more carriers. The goods may be transshipped from one vessel to another or be transshipped to a railway truck. Such a bill will show the port of loading and where the goods are to be delivered.

comfort letter. The security deposited by a third party comfort letter. *See* LETTER OF COMFORT

commercial bank. A bank licensed under the Banking Act 1987. This term is often used to refer to those banks involved in international trade and corporate banking.

commercial bill. A bill of exchange drawn against a commercial transaction. The expression is also used to cover all bills other than Treasury Bills.

commercial court. The court that hears actions arising from disputes between merchants, traders and others. It will also deal with the interpretation of mercantile and commercial documents, export and import, banking, insurance and other mercantile phraseology that has led to a legal action.

commercial documents. Amongst the most common documents are Invoices, Documents of Movement, Insurance Documents, Certificates of Origin, or any other documents that are likely to be given to a bank for the purpose of a collection.

commercial intelligence department. This department is often linked to or part of the Economic Department or Economic Intelligence Department of bank. It provides or keeps records of the trading conditions in the UK and other countries. Issues reports, and responds to status enquiries from banks abroad.

commercial invoice. A commercial document which describes the goods, unit and/or total price, shipping terms, buyer's and seller's references, etc.

commercial loan. Usually a short-term loan to finance the working capital of a business.

commercial paper. A US and UK term for unsecured promissory notes issued by, generally large US and UK corporations. Commercial paper represents a major source of short-term funds for a company although only financially strong, highly rated borrowers have access to the market. Most commercial paper carries an initial maturity of sixty days or less and to ensure payment at maturity, issuers often maintain back up lines of credit at banks. Investors in commercial paper tend to be large institutions such as insurance companies and bank trust departments; because of its relatively low risk and short maturity, commercial paper can be regarded as a close substitute for Treasury Bills, certificates of deposit and other money market instruments.

commission. An allowance made to a factor or agent; a percentage, a charge.

commission agent. A person who buys and sells goods for another, receiving a percentage for the contracts so arranged.

commissioner for oaths. A solicitor legally authorised to administer oaths.

commission on current account. An agreed charge for maintaining a current account with a bank. A charge imposed by a bank on a customer who does not maintain a sufficient balance to warrant the services given. The major banks do not as a general rule charge private customers, providing the account is in credit.

Commissioners of Inland Revenue. Officers of the Inland Revenue appointed to hear appeals by the taxpayer/s. The General Commissioners are lay persons and unpaid. Special Commissioners and full-time civil servants who are specialists in the law of taxation.

committee. A group of persons elected annually to run a business or organisation within the constitution of that organisation. They must attend meetings regularly at which topics are discussed and decisions are made. It is usual to have officers of a committee appointed. They would be the chairperson, treasurer and secretary.

committee of inspection. Under the Insolvency Act 1986, this is no longer used. However, under Sections 26 and 68, 'Where a meeting of creditors summone . . . the meeting may, if it thinks fit, establish a committee (the creditors' committee) to exercise the function conferred on it by or under this Act! If such a committee is established, the committee may on giving not less than 7 days notice require the receiver to attend before it at any reasonable time to furnish it with such information in relation to the carrying out by him of his function as it may reasonably require.

Committee of London and Scottish Bankers (CLSB). A constituent body of the British Bankers Association, it was formed on 1 December 1985, to take over the lobbying and representative functions of the Committee of London Clearing Bankers, following the transference of the money transmission and standards responsibilities to the Association for Payment Clearing Services (APACS). It constitutes a forum for discussion of matters of common interest, which acts as a medium for the circulation downwards to the banks of governmental directives and instructions, and which also communicates upwards to Treasury any requests, - suggestions or recommendations which the committee members, as representatives of their banking organisations, may wish to make.

commitment fee. A fee charged by a bank for committing itself to have funds available when required by the borrower. See NEGOTIATION FEE.

common carrier. A transport organisation obliged by law to carry any goods offered to them at a reasonable charge for delivery to any destination served by the carrier. The goods have to be delivered in an undamaged state; if they are damaged the negligence of the carrier is assumed.

common law. The common-sense attitude of the community has prevailed since the 'early days'. Often referred to as the law of custom which has been in existence since the 13th century when the phrase came into being.

common market. A term used to describe the European Community (EC) This was established under the Treaty of Rome in 1947, and has the task of promoting harmonious relationships between its members. See EUROPEAN ECONOMIC COMMUNITY.

common ownership enterprise. An entity which has no share capital but is limited by guarantee and is a bona-fide society registered under the Industrial Provident Societies Act 1965–75. Its control is vested in the people working in it.

common stock. A USA term which is the equivalent of equity stock in the UK.

company. An association of persons formed to pursue the business of that entity. A company can be formed by charter, Act of Parliament or more usually under the Companies Act 1989. Under this Act, companies can be either formed by guarantee or by the issue of shares and be either a public limited company or a private company. A company exists in its own right in law, and its shareholders have limited liability. See also CLOSE COMPANY; COMPANY LIMITED BY GUARANTEE; HOLDING COMPANY; LIMITED COMPANY; LISTED COMPANY; ONE-MAN COMPANY; PARENT COMPANY; PRIVATE COMPANY; PUBLIC COMPANY; STATUTORY COMPANY; SUBSIDIARY COMPANY; TRADING COMPANY; UNLIMITED COMPANY; UNREGISTERED COMPANY.

company accounts. Accounts prepared under the Companies Act 1989. The accounts and balance sheet must be audited, signed by the auditor/s as showing a true and fair view. Should this not be the case then the accounts must be qualified appropriately. The accounts are available for public inspection and are circulated to the members of the company.

company limited by guarantee. It is usually a company which has been formed for charitable or educational purposes. It has no share capital and in the event of being wound up the members are liable to the extent of the guarantee given.

company insolvency. *See* INSOLVENCY.

company limited by shares. A limited company in the which the members liability is limited to the nominal amount of shares allotted to that member.

company meetings. *See* ANNUAL GENERAL MEETING; EXTRAORDINARY GENERAL MEETING; STATUTORY MEETING.

compensating errors. An error in the book-keeping system whereby both sides agree, but an error or errors on one side, conceals the possibility or an error or errors on the other side, e.g. errors of £60 and £40 on the debit side, equal errors of £70 and £30 on the credit side.

compensation trading. Another name for barter. *See* BARTER.

compensatory damages. Damages awarded to compensate a plaintiff for his loss.

completion. The final stages in a contract. The delivery of land with a good title by one party and the payment of the agreed price and the acceptance of the title by the second party.

compliance cost. A phrase used to describe sums paid to the revenue on account of value added tax. (*q.v.*).

compliance officer. An officer appointed with the approval of the Securities Association or some other regulating body, to ensure that the financial institution complies with the rules laid down by that body.

composition. A sum of money accepted by creditors in satisfaction of debts. The adjustment of a debt as agreed between the debtor and creditor/s.

composite rate of tax. A rate of tax charged on banks and building societies in respect of interest paid to depositors. It is normally lower than the basic rate of tax as it is calculated on the approximate average rate of tax payable by all depositors. The depositors who receive such interest on their deposits can regard that tax has been deducted at the basic rate. Higher rate taxpayers will have to pay an additional charge, while non tax payers cannot under this system claim a refund.

compound arbitrage. Dealing in foreign currencies involving more than one centre when a free market exists in foreign exchange.

compounded annual return (CAR). The net percentage available to an investor after adding the interim interest payable, less tax at the appropriate band rate.

compound interest. Interest earned on the principal amount, plus interest earned on the earlier interest. For example, if £100 is invested at 10 per cent per annum after one year the investor will have £110, at the end of the second year, the sum of £110 would receive 10 per cent so that the new balance of the invested funds would be £110, plus £11 interest, £121 and so on each year.

comprehensive policy. An insurance policy covering all risks except Acts of God.

compulsory liquidation or winding-up. Under the Insolvency Act 1986, an order for the compulsory liquidation of a company rests in the hands of the Court. The grounds for winding up a company are (s. 122) (*a*) the company has by special resolution resolved that the company be wound up by the court; (*b*) being a public company which was registered as such on its original incorporation, the company has not been issued with a certificate under s. 117 of the Companies Act and more than a year has expired since it was so registered; (*c*) it is an old company, within the meaning of the Consequential Provisions Act; (*d*) the company does not commence its business within a year from its incorporation or suspends its business for a whole year; (*e*) the number of members is reduced below 2; (*f*) the company is unable to pay its debts; (*g*) the court is of the opinion that it is just and equitable that the company should be wound up. Under s. 123, Insolvency Act 1986, a company is deemed unable to pay its debts: (*a*) if a creditor to whom the company is indebted in a sum exceeding £750 then due has served on the company, by leaving it at the company's registered office, a written demand (in the prescribed form) requiring the company to pay the sum so due and the company has for 3 weeks thereafter neglected to pay the sum or to secure or compound for it to the reasonable satisfaction of the creditor, or (*b*) if, in

England and Wales, execution or other process issued on a judgment, decree or order of any court in favour of a creditor of the company is returned unsatisfied in whole or in part, or, (c) if, in Scotland, the *induciae* of a charge for payment on an extract degree, or an extract registered bond, or an extract registered protest, have expired without payment being made, or (d) in Northern Ireland, a certificate of unenforceability has been granted in respect of a judgment against the company or (e) it is proved to the satisfaction of the court that the company is unable to pay its debts as they fall due. A company is also deemed unable to pay its debts if it is proved to the satisfaction of the court that the value of the company's assets is less than the amount of its liabilities, taking into account its contingent and prospective liabilities.

computer. An electronic device designed to store and process large volumes of data at high speed. Input is by paper tape, punched card, magnetic tape, disk or other means. Output is by high speed printer or visual display unit. Most accounts of bank customers are now kept in the memory stores of computers, and are updated daily. Each generation of computers is becoming smaller and yet more powerful. The growth of banking over the last decade has been such that the total volume of work now handled could not possibly be dealt with by any other system.

computer language. The language of a particular computer in which instructions are given to the processing unit.

computer program. A sequence of instructions to a computer to enable it to carry out a particular function or series of functions.

concealment. The suppression of a material fact. The neglect to make known a material fact. The concealment of a security document with a view to obtaining a dishonest profit or cause another person to sustain a loss.

concert party. The law requires a shareholder holding 5 per cent or more of the share capital of a company to notify the company in writing (Companies Act 1985). However, this legal requirement did not extend to a number of investors acting 'in concert' to acquire a stake of 5 per cent or over. The object has been to take over control of a publicly quoted company by stages, and secretly so that it is not necessary to make a general offer to all shareholders. This abuse, as it is seen to be, has been tackled by the Companies Act 1985 where notification to the company is now required where persons acting together have built up a group interest in the target company. Failure to comply with the Act constitutes a criminal offence.

conditional. The declaration of an occurence of an event on which a contract depends. Conditions 'in deed' are actual and expressed. Conditions 'in law' are implied.

conditional acceptance. *See* QUALIFIED ACCEPTANCE.

conditional indorsement. An indorsement where the indorser has attached a condition to his indorsement. Such a condition may be disregarded by the paying banker. As between indorsee and indorsee the condition is valid and if the indorser received the proceeds of the bill without the condition being fulfilled, he or she would have no claim to the money, but would hold it as trustee for the indorser until the condition is fulfilled.

conditional order. Where a condition is placed on a draft, it will not definition be a negotiable instrument unless it is merely the completion of a receipt form on the back of the draft. Thus a banker dealing with such an instrument will lose the statutory protection that covers bills of exchange. On unconditional orders protection is provided for bankers under the Bills of Exchange Act 1882 and the Cheques Act 1957.

condition precedent. A stipulation that some event must occur before a contract becomes fixed and binding.

conditions of sale. The terms and conditions upon which goods are to be sold at public auction.

condition subsequent. The making of a contract conditional upon the happening or the non happening of a specified event at a later date – e.g. the contract between banker and a new customer is made subject to a condition subsequent that a reference satisfactory to the banker shall be obtained; in land law, where a condition is annexed to a conveyance, providing that, in case a particular event does or does not happen, or if the grantor or the grantee does or does not do any particular act, the interest shall be defeated – e.g. a grant of land to X 'on condition that he never sells out of the family'.

confirmation. A formal note verifying the details of a contract between parties, e.g. broker versus client.

confirmation dative. The Scots legal term for LETTERS OF ADMINISTRATION (*q.v.*).

confirmation nominative. The Scots legal term for PROBATE (*q.v.*)

confirmed credit. Article 10(b), Uniform Customs and Practice for Documentary Credits – ICC Publication No. 400 states: 'When an issuing bank authorizes or requires another bank to confirm its irrevocable credit and the latter has added its confirmation, such confirmation constitutes a definite undertaking of such bank (the confirming bank), in addition to that of the issuing bank, provided that the stipulated documents are presented and that the terms and conditions of the credit are complied with: (*i*) if the credit provides for sight payment – to pay or that payment will be made; (*ii*) if the credit provides for deferred payment – to pay, or that payment will be made on the date(s) determinable in accordance with the stipulations of the credit; (*iii*) if the credit provides for acceptance – to accept drafts drawn by the beneficiary if the credit stipulates that they are to be drawn on the confirming bank, or to be responsible for the acceptance and payment at maturity if the credit stipulates that they are to be drawn on the applicant for the credit or any other drawee stipulated in the credit. (*iv*) if the credit provides for negotiation – to negotiate without recourse to drawers and/or bona fide holders, draft(s) drawn by the beneficiary, at sight or at a tenor, on the issuing bank or on the applicant for the credit or on any other drawee stipulated in the credit other than the confirming bank itself.'

confirming house. They act as agents for a foreign importer, in as much they will place an order with a UK exporter/manufacturer, but as principals they confirm that they will pay the exporter on evidence of shipment. This relieves the exporter of the credit risk, but the confirming house will give credit to the overseas buyer as arranged.

conglomerate. This term is used when describing a large group of companies. Frequently, the relationships between companies within the group are complex.

connected lender liability. A liability introduced by the Consumer Credit Act 1974. The liability was stated in s. 75 and laid down that where a lender provided credit for a debtor to purchase goods from a supplier, and the debtor subsequently has any claim against that supplier in respect of misrepresentation or breach of contract, then the debtor shall have a like claim against the creditor, who with the supplier, shall accordingly be jointly and severally liable to the debtor. The credit card companies are liable with the supplier for defective articles (or a cancelled service) and any damage which flows directly from the breach of contract.

connected persons. For the purposes of the Insolvency Act 1986, a connected person is one who is connected with a company: if (*a*) he is a director or shadow director or; (*b*) he is an associate of the company (s. 249). *See also* ASSOCIATE.

connected with a company. For the purposes of the Insolvency Act 1986 s. 249, a connected person is (*a*) a director or shadow director or (*b*) is an associate of the company. *See* ASSOCIATE.

consideration. That which is given or accepted in return for a promise. It is defined in law as 'some right, interest, profit or benefit accruing to one party, or some forbearance, detriment, loss or responsibility given, suffered or undertaken by another' (*Currie* v. *Misa* (1875)).

consign. To send goods or to sell goods to another person. To despatch goods.

consignee. The person to whom goods are consigned.

consignment. The act of consigning; the goods consigned.

consignment note. A document made out by the carrier of the goods, addressed to the consignor, showing the description of the goods, marks, weight, etc., evidencing that the goods will be delivered either carriage paid or carriage forward to the consignee at the address stated.

consistency concept. A fundamental accountancy concept as described in SSAP 2. It states that the treatment of an asset should be the same from one accounting period to another.

consolidate. To put together. To unite. To merge. See CONSOLIDATED ANNUITIES; CONSOLIDATED BALANCE SHEET.

Consolidated Annuities, Consols. British Government irredeemable securities, consolidated into a single stock in 1751, bearing interest at 3 per cent (now 2½ per cent).

consolidated balance sheet. The merging and presentation of the balance sheets of two or more entities as if it was one entity.

Consolidated Fund. A government fund, held at the Bank of England into which revenue is paid and payments are made as authorised by Parliament.

consortium. A grouping of a number of companies in order to promote a common purpose, e.g. a consortium bank can be set up by three or four other banks for the purpose of acting as a lead manager for Euro Currency loans.

constructive delivery. See SYMBOLIC DELIVERY.

constructive trust. A trust imposed by law independently on any person's intention.

consular invoice. An invoice that has been approved by a seal or stamp by the consul of the importer's country that has an office in the exporter's country.

consumer. The one who, or that which, consumes or uses up; the purchaser of an article; for the purpose of Consumer Credit Act 1974, any individual or unincorporated body to whom credit is extended under a regulated agreement.

Consumers' Association. An independent organisation set up to act as a watchdog for complaints by individuals. It regularly issues a magazine called *Which*, available monthly by payment of a subscription.

consumer credit. Credit from banks, usually by way of personal loan, or hire-purchase finance. In the UK, comprehensive safeguards for the credit consumer were provided by the Consumer Credit Act 1974. The Act is principally concerned with credit transactions up to £15 000, in the personal sector only. Bank lending comes within the scope of the Act, as well as hire purchase and credit sale agreements, credit cards, private loans and mortgages. The true cost of a facility must in all cases be disclosed, and written agreements will be required – this does not apply to overdrafts. Certainly many security forms have had to be rewritten.

consumer credit agreement. A personal credit agreement by which the creditor provides the debtor with credit not exceeding £15 000. CCA s. 8.

consumer goods. The goods that are purchased to satisfy the needs of individuals and families. These goods can be classified as durable or non-durable goods.

consumer hire agreement. An agreement made by a person with an individual (the 'hirer') for the bailment of (or in Scotland the hiring of) goods to be hired, being an agreement which 1. is not a hire-purchase agreement, and 2. is capable of subsisting for more than three months, and 3. does not require the hirer to make payments exceeding £15 000.

container bill of lading. A bill of lading issued by a container operator; a document which is not a bill of lading, would be a forwarder's receipt evidencing the dispatch of goods in one container in a groupage shipment.

containerisation. A method of despatching goods both nationally and internationally in standard size containers, that can easily fit on to a lorry, railway wagon, or on to a container ship. For international trade, the container is custom sealed at the despatch depot and not opened until arrival at the destination. In Europe the container ports have special facilities to deal with container trade on a roll-on, roll-off basis (known as RORO). The container trade is generally safer against theft, protects the goods against weather and reduces the formalities at ports.

contango. A Stock Exchange word meaning carry over. A client that wishes to postpone settlement of a debt to his broker may on payment of a fee, have the debt postponed until the next settlement day.

contango day. The first of the Stock Exchange settling days, and the day on which arrangements are made for the carrying over of transactions to the next account. Also known as *carrying over day, continuation day* or *making up day.*

contemnor. One who is held to be in contempt of court.

contemptuous damages. Damages of a trifling amount where a plaintiff's claim, though proved, has little merit; an expression of the court's opinion of the plaintiff's worth.

continental depositary receipt. A bearer document which is equivalent to and may be exchanged into an equity issue within the Euromarket.

contingent. An event that may or may not happen.

contingent account. An account specially raised in order to meet any possible liabilities.

contingent annuity. An annuity which is payable only in the event of the happening of some uncertain event.

contingent interest. An interest, usually in property, that will come into existence on the occurrence of an event.

contingent liability. A liability that may arise on a certain event, e.g. the liability of an endorser should a bill of exchange not be paid. Information regarding any contingent liabilities must accompany the balance sheet of a company.

contingent remainder. A reversionary interest where the passing of the benefit is made to depend upon the happening of an uncertain event, e.g. the attaining by the remainder of his or her twenty-fifth birthday. If death occurs before that day, the benefit passes to some other person.

continuation day. *See* CONTANGO DAY.

continuing security. A phrase used when a bank takes any security for an advance. The words 'continuing security' will appear in the Memorandum of Deposit, so that the rule in *Clayton's case* will not operate against the bank.

The security given by the customer and accepted by the bank will secure the balance on the account for each working day and not the balance on the day the security was given.

contra account. An account which is debited or credited against another account, e.g., an account holding funds as cash cover for a documentary credit will show entries passed to its debit/credit from the current account of a customer. In a trading organisation, a customer can be a supplier at the same time and consequently entries may be passed between the accounts.

contract. A promise or promises enforceable in law. Most contracts are of a simple nature and involve an offer and an acceptance and a consideration (something of value) must pass between the two parties. A contract can be made verbally or in writing. A contract under seal needs no consideration. *See* CONTRACT UNDER SEAL; EXECUTED CONTRACT; EXECUTORY CONTRACT; OPEN CONTRACT; SIMPLE CONTRACT; SPECIALITY CONTRACT; STANDARD CONTRACT; UNILATERAL CONTRACT.

contract note. The confirmation in writing from a broker to his client stating the details of the purchase/sale of stock or shares has taken place.

contract of sale. Sale of Goods Act 1979 s. 61(1) 'Includes an agreement to sell as well as a sale. Such an agreement is usually in writing and there must be some consideration'.

contract guarantee. An agreement between parties whereby one person will guarantee the other that performance will take place, otherwise some form of compensation will be given. These guarantees are usually covered by such documents as tender bonds, performance bonds, etc.

contract under seal. A contract to which the maker's seal is attached and delivered as his or her 'deed'. Such contracts are made when there is no consideration, for example, the conveyancing of land.

contribution. A payment legally imposed on a person or payment to a loss where other persons will make their contribution. The difference between the sales value of a product and the variable costs.

contributory. A person who is liable to contribute to the assets of a company in the event of liquidation.

contributory negligence. Where a person by his own carelessness or negligence does not look after his/her affairs, it may be proved that the injured party failed to take reasonable care of himself or his property thereby contributing to his own injury. Under such circumstances, the claim for damages will be reduced to take into account such contributory negligence. In banking it may be found that a customer by his own negligence, e.g. issuing a blank signed cheque, failed to take care and must be liable for his own financial injury.

contributory pension. The contribution an employee makes towards his pension when he ultimately retires from full-time employment. Such contribution is calculated as a percentage of the gross salary, and deducted from the monthly salary payment. Employers will also make a contribution to such a pension.

control. The authority to maintain order, regulate activities, check/audit operations. In some banks it is the listing of debits and credits as part of the journal/accounting agreement system.

control account. An account which hold the same total debits, credits and balances as the ledger/s it represents and to which the individual items have been posted. In effect the total of all the individual balances of a ledger should equal the balance of the control account.

controller. One who controls; a public functionary appointed to oversee the accounts of others. For the purposes of the Consumer Credit Act 1974, 'controller', in relation to a body corporate, means a person 1. in accordance with whose directions or instructions the directors of the body corporate or of another body corporate which is its controller or any of them are accustomed to act, or 2. who, either alone or with any associate or associates, is entitled to exercise, or control the exercise of, one third or more of the voting power at any general meeting of the body corporate or of another body corporate which is its controller.

controlling interest. Ownership of more than 50 per cent of a business entity. A smaller interest may be held by one individual, but a group of persons acting in concert may as a group hold a controlling interest.

control of the money supply. A system of control that was put into operation by the Bank of England in August 1981. The Bank controls the level of liquidity in the banking system and influences the interest rates almost exclusively by open market operations, rather than by lending to the discount houses. This involves buying and selling eligible bills. To make the market in Treasury bills and commercial bills large enough to allow interest rates to be influenced rather than by operation of the *Minimum Lending Rate*. An eligible bill, is a bill which has been drawn or accepted by one of about 100 banks who have been given 'eligible' status by the Bank of England. All banks are requested to maintain a minimum of 2½ per cent and an average of 5 per cent of their eligible liabilities in the form of bills with the London Discount Market Association. As an additional control, the Bank of England will keep the short term interest rates within an unpublished band which it will change as it thinks desirable. The old reserve asset ratios imposed by *Competition and Credit Control* no longer apply, but liquidity of individual banks will be prescribed by the Bank of England. Banks have to maintain 0.45 per cent of eligible liabilities with the Bank of England as non-interest bearing non operational balances.

control period. The period between two specified dates when comparisons are made between the budgeted amounts and the actual amounts.

convention. A convention is an understanding between persons and parties who agree, from long practice, to a standard of practice, or behaviour in conducting business. A tacit understanding of a conduct of behaviour and an absence of formal rules of conduct.

conversion. An act which constitutes a serious and unjustifiable denial of a person's right to his goods. The tort committed in an innocent manner is no defence. Every day bankers collect cheques and other negotiable instruments for and on behalf of their customers. Should a bank collect a negotiable instrument for a customer who has no title or a defective title, then he has committed the tort of conversion and is thus liable to the true owner. Since a bank is collecting millions of these instruments each working day, the Cheque Act 1947 s. 4 protects a banker in such a situation as follows: Where a banker, in good faith and without negligence: (a) receives payment for a customer of an instrument to which this section applies or, (b) having credited a customer's account with the amount of such an instrument, receives payment thereof for himself, and the customer has no title, or a defective title, to the instrument, the banker does not incur any liability to the true owner of the instrument by reason only of having received payment thereof; 2. This section applies to the following instruments, namely: (a) cheques, (b) any document issued by a customer of a banker which, though not a bill of exchange, is intended to enable a person to obtain payment from that banker of the sum mentioned in the document; (c) any document issued by a public officer which is intended to enable a person to obtain payment from the Paymaster General or the Queen's and Lord Treasurer's Remembrancer of the sum mentioned in the document but is not a bill of exchange; (d) any draft payable on demand drawn by a banker upon himself whether payable at the head office or some other office of his bank. 3. A banker is not to be treated for the purposes of this section as having been negligent by reason only of his failure to concern himself with the absence of, or irregularity in, indorsement of an instrument. In monetary terms it can also refer to a procedure whereby the government or a company repays a stock by the issue of another stock either at a higher rate of interest or at a lower rate of interest with an inducement.

conversion stocks. Government stocks which have been offered to holders of other stocks, due for repayment as an alternative to receiving cash payments.

convertible. Where there is an absence of exchange control regulations, then the currency of one country may be exchanged for the currency of another country without any restriction. The exchange of one security for another at the option of the holder. *See* CONVERTIBLE STOCKS OR SECURITIES.

convertible bond. A bond which, on demand by the bearer, can be exchanged for a holding in shares.

convertible stocks or securities. 1. Securities which may readily be turned into cash; 2. securities having the right to transfer from one form of holding to another, e.g. fixed interest securities that are exchangeable at a later date into ordinary shares on pre-determined terms. Most convertible stocks take the form of unsecured loan stocks; there are also a few convertible debentures and preference shares. Convertibles have to be considered both as fixed interest stocks and as potential equities. The expense of purchasing what is in effect an equity option has to be taken as the difference between the yield on the convertible stock and the yield on any investment which gives a fixed interest but has no option built in. Usually the holder of a convertible stock would do better in terms of yield to invest in a debenture or similar stock, but may think it worthwhile to pay the option cost, and a possible conversion premium at some later date, to keep the two-way 'hedge'.

conveyance. The act of conveying real property from one person to another; the *deed* by which it is transferred.

conveyance on sale. Every instrument, and every decree or order of any court, or of any commissioners, whereby any property, or any estate or interest in any property, upon the sale thereof is transferred to or vested in a purchaser, or any other person on his or her behalf or by his or her direction.

conveyancing. The act or profession of drawing up deeds for the conveyance of real property.

cooling off period. Under CCA 1974, a period during which a debtor may cancel a regulated agreement.

co-ownership. The ownership of property by more than one person. Such co-ownership may be co-parceners, tenants in common or joint tenants.

co-parceners. Co-heirs to whom land devolved where a tenant in a fee simple or a tenant in tail died intestate leaving only female heirs, whereupon the females succeeded jointly to the estate. This method of inheritance was abolished in 1925, and co-parcenary can now arise only in the case of entitled interests.

co-partnership. A system of management by which employees are entitled to a voice in the management of a concern and a share in any profits.

copyhold. A tenure given by the lord of the manor. Under the Law of Property Act (1925) and L.P.A (Amendment) 1926 it was converted into freehold.

copyright. Copyright Act 1956, defined as the exclusive right . . . to do and to authorise other persons to do certain acts. These acts include the publication of works, performances, broadcasting, etc. The exclusive right lasts for the lifetime of the author plus fifty years.

cornering the market. The purchasing of a commodity in such quantities that the buyer has control over its price.

corporation. A body of persons united for a common purpose. The authority of a local borough/county council. A professional body. An association granted corporation status by an Act of Parliament or by the Sovereign.

corporate body. A group of persons having an independent identity with its own rules and objects, e.g. a company formed under the Companies Act.

corporation bill. The issue of bills by local authorities for a term not exceeding one year with the consent of the Treasury.

corporation sole. Consists of one person and his successors, e.g. a bishop.

corporation tax. A tax charged on the income and capital gains of a limited company.

corporeal hereditaments. Real assets. It will include such items as land, houses, goods. The owner may enjoy possession ans has the right to pass these to his/her heirs.

corpus. Latin word for body. Used in trust banking when dealing with such matters as securities and personal property.

correction. The removal of an error from the records. The movement of a

price in the money markets or the commodity markets. When prices have gone too high then there could be a dramatic fall to bring the price to a more realistic amount.

correspondent bank. A bank in one country which acts when so required for a bank in another country. The relationship is one of agency. The choice of the correspondent bank may depend on its position, or on the amount of business which has formerly taken place between the two banks.

corset. The Bank of England having introduced Special Deposits – i.e. funds from the commercial banks had to be deposited in an interest-bearing account with the Bank, in order to reduce their lending ability. It was subsequently found in December 1973 that further constraints were necessary, so that a supplementary Special Reserve (the 'corset') was introduced. Neither the Special Reserve account nor the 'corset' now exists.

cost. In accounting, this refers to the value of an asset, or the amount applied to the use of the asset. A charge for the payment of any expense. *See also* DISTRIBUTION EXPENSE; FACTOR COST; FIXED COST; MARGINAL COST; OPPORTUNITY COST; PRIME COSTS; REAL COST; RETAIL COST; VARIABLE COSTS; WHOLESALE COST.

cost accounting. A branch of accounting that provides information for management of an entity to evaluate the costs of operations, processes, departments, products, etc.

cost allocation. The attributing of items of costs to cost centres or products.

cost and freight (C & F). A shipping term showing that the price quoted by the seller includes the payment of freight charges. Any insurance of the goods up to point of unloading or discharge is the responsibility of the buyer.

cost centre. An area of activity in a business to which costs may be attributed. All costs are identified and a cost centre is allocated or apportioned to it.

cost, insurance freight (CIF). A shipping term showing that the price quoted by the seller includes all charges up to the point of discharge are the responsibility of the seller.

cost of sales. The total cost of either producing or purchasing the goods sold in a stated trading period. It is an important figure in the trading account in a business entity.

cost price. The wholesale, as opposed to the retail price.

cost push inflation. An inflation sequence as follows: When demand exceeds supply – prices go up. When manufacturers pay more for their raw materials they increase their prices to wholesaler/retailer who in turn increase prices to consumers. This inevitably leads to a demand for increased salaries/wages.

costs. The expenses of running a business. The expenses involved in a law suit.

cost apportionment. The division of costs, according to the benefit accrued, between two or more cost centres or products.

cost unit. A particular or convenient amount of a product that can be used to state the costs, e.g. a ton of coal, barrels of beer.

counter. A purpose-built table in a banking hall, with cashiers and their tills able to give a service to customers on the other side of the counter. In general terminology this can refer to an opposite or working against.

counter claim. A statement by a defendant as a claim against the costs of the plaintiff.

counterfeit. To coin, to imitate in base metal; *forged*, made in imitation with intent to be passed off as genuine.

counterfeiting. The forging of a note or coin of the currency of a country. An offence under the Forgery and Counterfeiting Act 1981.

counterfeit coin. An imitation of a coin of legal tender.

counterfeit note. A forged banknote.

counterfoil. A record or slip of paper retained by a person as evidence of a transaction. In banking, a cheque book will have cheques held in the book with a counterfoil attached, so that a record of the cheque issued may be made. A paying-in slip will similarly have a counterfoil, so that when funds are paid in for the credit of an account, it will have to be stamped by the cashier receiving the funds as evidence

of credit. Counterfoils may be attached to bonds, certificates, dividends, etc.

counter-indemnity. An indemnity given by a customer of a bank to the bank when an indemnity is given by the bank to a third party on his/her behalf.

countermand. The revocation of an order.

countermand of payment. An order to a banker from a customer to stop payment of a cheque which the customer has issued. The customer may give this over the telephone but must subsequently confirm in writing. The bank must be told the number of the cheque, and preferably also the date, amount, and name of the payee. An order to stop the payment of a direct debit, the bank would wish to know the name of the creditor, the amount if known, and the date the debit is due to be received by the debtor's bank.

countermark. Used when two or more persons agree to place mark on a box, envelope; place in a bank for safe custody and may only be opened when all parties are present.

counterpart. An additional copy of a document, e.g. a lease.

counter purchase. Another term for barter (*q.v.*).

countersign. To add an additional signature to a document to confirm its correctness. Cheques issued by large organisations will have it signed and then countersigned by another official.

coupon. A detachable part of a bond or certificate which is presented to either the issuer of the bond or his bankers which entitles the holder to the dividend/interest due. Where bearer bonds have been issued, it is usual for them to be held by banks on behalf of the customer. It will then be the duty of the bank to detach the coupon, complete the detail and despatch it to the address stated.

coupon rate. The rate of interest payable on a coupon.

coupon sheet. A series of coupons attached to a bond or certificate.

covenant. A signed undertaking to perform certain acts or refrain from certain acts. To make periodic payments, perhaps to a charity. *See* DEED OF COVENANT; RESTRICTIVE COVENANT.

cover. The amount set aside to meet a particular liability. Maintain sufficient funds to defray a specified cost. A deposit by a customer of a bank to ensure that sufficient funds are available to meet a debt due.

cover for dividend. *See* DIVIDEND COVER.

cover note. A note from an insurance company to the insured to advise him/her that a contract of insurance is in existence. It is evidence of good faith and is held by the insured until a policy has been issued.

covered interest arbitrage. The procedure whereby the borrowing in one currency is subsequently converted into another currency, where it is invested, then selling this second currency for a future delivery against the first currency.

covered option. A situation whereby a person who owns say 300 shares in ABC plc and sells three options in the same company is in a covered position. Should the value of the shares increase, then the option may be exercised, the investor has stock available to give to the buyer.

covered warrants. Warrants issued against a holding of existing shares (or for any asset). For example a bank may buy a number of shares in XYZ plc and issue a two-year call over these shares. The option buyer will acquire an option with a longer lifetime than would be obtainable on the traded options market.

covered writer. This person is a seller of covered options, that is, he owns the stock and sells it to obtain the premium. When writing a call option, he may, if the stock price is stable or drops, hold on to the stock, but if the price rises it will have to be given to the option buyer.

credit. In accounting terms a credit entry increases the liability of the business entity or increases its revenue. Credit given is an indication of trust in that person to pay for the goods given or money lent. Under the Consumer Credit Act 1974 credit covers a loan or any other advance or accommodation given.

credit advice. A note from a banker to his customer advising him/her that funds as detailed have been credited to the account.

credit analyst. A person whose function is to research into the records/affairs of an individual or company to assess whether that person/entity has a degree of creditworthiness.

credit balance. A balance in favour of the customer. A liability to a bank.

credit brokers. They are persons, licensed under the Consumer Credit Act 1974, to introduce persons who wish to obtain credit to those able to give credit or other brokers. For example, a retailer may request a finance house to provide finance for a customer who wishes to purchase some durable goods, or a mortgage broker who will be able to arrange finance from a building society.

credit card. A piece of plastic about 85mm by 54mm, bearing the name and computer number of the holder and the period of availability. The holder must sign it. The best known cards in the UK are the VISA card and ACCESS; the American Express and Diners' Club are leisure or entertainment cards as no credit is permitted. With the credit card, goods can be bought in most retail outlets in the UK and many other parts of the world. The retailer pays in a copy of all credit card transactions to the credit of his or her account at a bank which will then transmit the vouchers to the appropriate credit card company. The credit card company will debit the retailer each month with a sum equal to between 2 and 5 per cent of the turnover. The customer on the other hand will receive a monthly statement which will specify the transactions and the outstanding balance. The person is obliged to pay either 5 per cent or £5 whichever is the greater. Any outstanding balance is charged at a rate of interest, which can vary, but is at the moment 1.2 per cent per month. Under s. 14(1) Consumer Credit Act 1974 a credit card is defined as 'a card, check, voucher, coupon, stamp form, booklet or other document or thing given to an individual by a person carrying on a consumer credit business who undertakes – (*a*) that on production of it he or she will supply, cash, goods and services (or any of them) on credit, or (*b*) that where, on the production of it to a third party (whether or not any other action is also required), the third party supplies cash, goods and services (or any of them), the consumer credit business will pay the third party for them in return for payment to the company by the individual.

credit cardholders. Any credit worthy mature person can be a credit card holder. They do not necessarily have to have an account with the bank whose subsidiary is the issuing credit card company. Before a card is issued, certain details are supplied and references given. On approval a credit card is given to the holder and the cardholder is at the same time notified of the maximum credit available to him/her. The credit card can be used at any retail outlet displaying the credit card company symbol. It is usual for settlement or partial settlement to be made by the credit cardholder within 25 days of receipt of the statement.

credit clearing. The credit clearing is now part of the Cheque and Credit Clearing Co. Ltd. It handles the clearing process of branch and other bank credits paid in over the branch counters. They are sorted and cleared in the same way as cheques and it takes three working days for a credit to be received on the account of the beneficiary.

credit creation. As bankers' know, very little of the funds deposited with them is drawn out at any one time. Consequently they are able to lend or invest over 90 per cent of depositors' funds with other persons or institutions. As each loan creates a deposit, so without regulations the banks would be able to create money/credit. However, the Bank of England under the Banking Act supervises the liquidity of all banks, so that there should be no abuse of the system.

credit crunch. A situation in which financial intermediaries, particularly banks, become reluctant to lend to the private sector.

credit insurance. A means of insuring the payment of commercial debts against the risk of non-payment by the buyer because of insolvency, or for some other reason.

credit note. An advice from a creditor to a debtor informing him that his account has been credited with an amount as stated. This may be due to a refund for returned goods, a cash discount, etc.

creditor. A person to whom a debt is owed. Where a customer of a bank has a balance on his account with that bank, he is a creditor to the bank. The Consumer Credit Act 1974 defines a creditor as 'a person providing credit under a consumer credit agreement or the person to whom his or her rights and duties under the agreement have passed by assignment or operation of law, and in relation to a prospective consumer credit agreement, includes the prospective creditor'.

credit rating. An opinion as to the credit-worthiness of a person, obtained by a party who is considering entering into a business contract with the person or supplying goods to him or her. It is usual to obtain the opinion through the banking system, or a trade reference may be given, or the use of a credit reference agency.

credit reference agency. For the purposes of the CCA 1974, a person carrying on a business comprising the furnishing of persons with information relevant to the financial standing of individuals, being information collected by the agency for that purpose.

credit risk. In general, the risk that a lender will not be able to get the money loaned back from the borrower. To guard against this, the credit risk is assessed either by a lending manager at an interview, or by the submission of a specially prepared form which is designed to score the credit rating.

credit sale agreement. A deferred payment system, whereby a contract between buyer and seller which allows the buyer to pay for the goods by instalment. On sale, the property passes immediately to the buyer.

credit scoring. A method of measuring the risk factor in a personal lending situation. By using this computer method, the bank saves on management time, clerical costs, etc. The procedure only demands the time of a junior clerk to see that the customer completes the form correctly and such data as marital status, address, employment, income, etc. is fed into the computer and the answer is given. Should the answer be unreasonable, then the loan application can be referred to a senior official.

credit slip. *See* PAYING-IN SLIP.

credit squeeze. The name given to an economic situation when banks are directed to lend to certain types of borrowers and restrict advances to others. In order ensure that banks have not got surplus funds, then they may be directed to place funds with the Bank of England on a Special Reserve Account.

credit token. For the purposes of the Consumer Credit Act 1974, a credit token is a card, check, voucher, coupon, stamp, form, booklet or other document or thing given to an individual by a person carrying on a consumer credit business who undertakes 1. that on the production of it he or she will supply cash, goods and services (or any of them) on credit; or 2. that where, on production of it to a third party, the third party supplies cash, goods and services (or any of them) the credit business will pay the third party for them, in return for payment to the company by the individual.

credit token agreement. Under the Consumer Credit Act 1974 it is a regulated agreement for the provison of credit in connection with the use of a credit token.

credit transfer. A broad definition of the procedure for transferring funds through the banking system from one person to another.

credit union. A system, popular in North America, by which people with a common bond – membership of the same club, church, tenants' association or trade union – can collaborate to put their savings into a joint fund. Members can then apply to borrow from the fund and make repayments at an annual rate of interest of 12 per cent. The Credit Union Act 1979 included the following: 1. the Chief Registrar of Friendly Societies supervises all Credit Unions; 2. the minimum membership shall be 21 and the maximum 5000; 3. the maximum savings permitted per person to be £3000; 4. the unions must be non-profit making and the purpose is to provide a service to its members.

creditor days ratio. It is a measurement of the average time taken to pay suppliers and other creditors.

$$\frac{\text{Average trade creditors}}{\text{purchases}} \times 365$$

See DEBTOR DAYS RATIO.

creditor's petition. A creditor's petition must be for a debt or debts owed to a creditor/s (*a*) equal to or exceeding the bankruptcy level – at the moment this is £750, but may be amended by the Secretary of State; (*b*) the debt is unsecured; (*c*) the debtor appears either to be unable to pay or to have no reasonable prospect of being able to pay; (*d*) there is no outstanding application to set aside a statutory demand served (under s. 268 Insolvency Act 1986) in respect of the debt or any other debts. Insolvency Act 1986 s. 267.

cross-border leasing. The arrangement whereby a leasing agreement is agreed for the purchaser in one country to be able to obtain a lease of an asset from the lessor in another country.

crossed cheque. Bills of Exchange Act 1882 s. 76(i) states: 'Where a cheque bears across its face an addition of (*a*) The words "and company" or any abbreviation thereof between two parallel transverse lines, either with or without the words "not negotiable" or (*b*) Two parallel transverse lines simply, either with or without the words "not negotiable";' that addition constitutes a crossing and the cheque is crossed generally. A cheque crossed generally does not in any way affect the transfer by a holder. The crossing is a protection for the drawer as a crossed cheque must be paid into a bank account and therefore can be traced.

cross-firing. In a situation where a person having an account at one bank and an account at another bank, then draws a cheque on the first account and pays it into the second account, then on the day or day before the cheque is presented for payment, a cheque on the second account is drawn to meet the cheque on the first account, thereby a credit balance is shown on both accounts although there are in fact uncleared balances. This practice if allowed to continue could mean an increase in the uncleared balances. Banks should ensure that the practice of drawing against uncleared effects does not continue and if necessary regulate any advances.

cross guarantees. Where a banker gives advances to companies that form part of a group of companies, then it is likely to take a guarantee from the parent company and from other companies in the group. Should a borrowing company or more than one company be wound up, then the bank has a claim from each of the other companies, for the value of the guarantee as well as the original debt from the company. *See* LETTER OF COMFORT.

cross rates. The rates of exchange arrived at by expressing the quotations for any two currencies in terms of a third.

crown. The currency of Norway, Sweden and Denmark. When five shilling pieces were in existence in the UK they were called crowns. The monarch or sovereign.

crownhold. Under the Leashold Reform Act 1967, this refers to land which has been obtained by the Land Commission under a compulsory purchase order and subsequently sold or leased to another.

cum div. The sale of stock with the dividend included.

cum drawing. When the repayment of some bonds are about to take place, then the sale of bonds will include the opportunity of early repayment of that bond and any advantage or profit will accrue to the buyer.

cum rights. The accrual to a purchaser of shares not only of the title to the shares but any rights that have been or are likely to be allotted.

cumulative preference shares. Preference shares that are issued on the understanding that any dividends not paid in one year will be paid in a subsequent year.

cupro-nickel. An amalgam of three-quarters parts of copper to one-quarter part nickel. Post war currency has been cupro-nickel in place of the earlier silver currency, which has now become too expensive to maintain. The intrinsic value of a cupro-nickel coin is minimal.

currency. The present time. Anything that is at the moment in circulation, e.g. banknotes, bills of exchange, cheques, etc. *See* CURRENCY BILLS; CURRENCY BONDS; CURRENCY OF A BILL OF EXCHANGE; CURRENCY NOTE; FOREIGN CURRENCY; HARD CURRENCY.

currency bills. *See* FOREIGN BILL.

currency bonds. Bonds issued in a foreign country and repayable in the currency of that country.

currency clearings. Clearings in eight currencies, including the US dollar, take place each day in London. These clearings are managed by the Currency Clearings Committee, which forms an operational grouping under the APACS structure. The Currency Clearings handle cheques, drafts, bankers payments and mandated currency debits drawn on, or payable at, UK branches of members and participants. Bank-to-bank wholesale payments are excluded. The main currency handled is the US dollar, for which a same-day payment service is available. The other currencies handled are the French franc, deutschmark, Canadian dollar, Italian lira, Dutch guilder, Australian dollar and Japanese yen. The volumes handled in these clearings are very modest and in 1989 totalled about 700 000 items, of which about 450 000 were US dollars; this was equivalent to about £39 billion, of which about £38 billion was for the US dollar items. Settlement for these clearings takes place across accounts held in the domiciles of the currencies concerned. There are seven settlement members of the Currency Clearings: Bank of Scotland, Coutts & Co, Midland Bank plc, The Royal Bank of Scotland plc, Barclays Bank plc, Lloyds Bank plc, National Westminster Bank plc.

currency of a bill of exchange. The period which a bill of exchange has to run before its maturity.

currency note. The banknote of a country in which it is the legal and acceptable medium of exchange, i.e. money.

current account. An account with a bank from which any part of the balance may be withdrawn on demand. Withdrawals may be in the form of cheques payable to the drawer or a third party, by direct debits, standing orders and via an Automated Teller Machine (ATM). Funds in the form of cash, cheques and other financial instruments may be credited to the account. In the UK these accounts may be overdrawn and where necessary charges may be made by the banker.

current assets. *See* LIQUID ASSETS.

current balance. The balance of visible and invisible items in international trade, but not including any movements of capital. In retail banking, this could refer to the balance on an account as at close of business of the previous working day.

current cost accounting. A system of accounting based upon a concept of capital which is represented by the net operating assets of a business. These net operating assets – fixed assets and stocks – are expressed for the purposes of CCA at current price levels. The final accounts and balance sheet are drawn up to give management and shareholders and financial viability of the business. SSAP 16 requires publication of a CCA statement in the following circumstances: (*a*) if turnover exceeds £5 million, (*b*) if the balance sheet total is greater than £2.5 million, (*c*) if the number of employees in the UK exceed 250.

current liabilities. Debts arising in the normal course of a business which are due for payment within the next twelve months, such as debts due to trade and hire purchase creditors, amounts due to the bank, and taxation payable.

current ratio. The ratio between the current assets and the current liabilities. It indicates the liquidity of a business.

custodian trustee. A person or persons responsible for the proeprty left in their trust and whom will be responsible for the receipt of all incomes and discharge any debts. Among those entitled to act as a custodian trustee are the Treasury Solicitor and trust corporations. *See* MANAGING TRUSTEE; UNIT TRUST.

custodier. A term in Scots law meaning one who has the custody or guardianship of anything. *See* BAILEE.

custody. The retention or control of a possession. *See* SAFE CUSTODY.

custom. Fashion, usage, habit, business patronage; long established practice or usage, which may have the force of law; a source of law; toll, tax or tribute.

custom duties. A tax charged by the Customs and Excise authorities on imported goods. It can on some occasions be charged on exported goods.

customer. In general terms this refers to a person who enters into a simple contract when going into a shop to purchase goods or where there is a continual service to a person or business entity. In banking, the situation is slightly different. While there is no statutory definition of a customer, it is understood from case law that a customer is a person who has an account with a banker. That relationship begins as soon as the account is opened. Often the current practice of some banks is to open an account immediately the customer completes the appropriate form and pays in cash or cheques (uncleared funds), there is some doubt whether the banker – customer relationship exists until the funds are cleared and the references are satisfactory. Because of this doubt, some banks will not open an account, but place funds on a suspense account until formalities are correct. Until such time no cheques will be honoured and no relationship exists. For a bank to claim statutory protection from conversion under Section 4, Cheques Act 1957 it must collect for customers in good faith and without negligence.

customs house. The office or place where payment is made of duties on imports and exports.

customs invoice. An invoice specially prepared to comply with the regulations of the customs officials of the importing country.

cy-près doctrine. Cy-prè – so near. Where under the terms of a trust, it is impossible to carry out the wishes of the testator, or for some reason it is impractical, the court may apply the principle of cy-prè so that the scheme may be carried out as near as possible to the original purpose. This is important when dealing with a charitable trust.

D

D/A. *See* DOCUMENTS AGAINST ACCEPTANCE.

daisy chain. Dealings between brokers in a market which gives the appearance of active trading and in consequence the prices rise and buyers are attracted and in turn investors cannot sell as there *are no actual buyers.*

damages. An award by the court as compensation in money for injury or detriment sustained by a plaintiff. Its purpose is to place the person in the same position before the action occurred. Damages may be classified as nominal, where no actual damage has been suffered, or substantial which represents compensation for actual loss suffered. They can also be punitive, given to punish the defendant.

data. Information. Characters representing information used for data processing storage.

data bank. A collection of data or recorded information stored in a computer and may be retrieved and used or updated. A series of data banks would commonly be known as a data library.

data processing. The handling of accounting and other information by a computer.

Data Protection Act 1984. Any organisation which stores information concerning individuals on computerised registers must register as a data user, and must observe the principles laid down in the Act. The seven principles which apply to data users are as follows: 1. The information stored in the personal file must have been obtained lawfully and fairly. 2. It shall be held for lawful purposes only. 3. Personal data for a purpose held shall not be used or disclosed in any manner incompatible with that purpose. 4. The personal data held shall be adequate, relevant and not excessive in relation for that purpose. 5. Personal data shall be accurate, i.e. not misleading, and where necessary kept up to date. 6. Personal data held for any purpose shall not be kept longer than is necessary for that purpose. 7. An individual shall be entitled (*a*) at reasonable intervals and without unreasonable delay or expense (*i*) to be informed by any data user whether he holds personal data of which the individual is the subject and (*ii*) to access to any such data held by a data user; and (*b*) where appropriate to have such data corrected or erased. If such data is already covered by the Consumer Credit Act, e.g. held by credit reference agencies, the data is exempt from this Act's requirements. Refer s. 21 Consumer Credit Act.

date. Refers to the day, month and the year. The date that an agreement becomes effective. A bill of exchange is not necessarily invalid due to it not being dated. Any holder may insert the true date. A deed must be signed, sealed and delivered and is effective from the date of delivery or execution. An expiry date is when an agreement or condition lapses, e.g. the date on a documentary credit.

dated stock. Gilt-edged stock issued by the government having a date by which it will be repaid. Where there are two dates, as in the case of 6¼ per cent Treasury 1995–98, the stock may be redeemed at any time between the dates stated.

dating. The extension of credit beyond the customary period. In markets with seasonal activity, it is possible for normal credit – say 30 days – to be extended to 60 days, so that companies can obtain the advantage of additional short-term finance.

dawn raid. The purchase on the Stock Exchange of a large number of shares in a company, executed very quickly, usually at the commencement of the working day in order to obtain a significant holding of capital with a view of obtaining a controlling interest or pre-empt a bid from another party.

days of grace. No longer applicable to bills of exchange. Often a time given for a person to accept or reject a simple contract. Nowadays this may refer to the renewal of an insurance policy, whereby the insurer will allow a period of time (say 30 days) after the expiry of the insurance contract, to allow the insured to pay the premium for the renewal of the policy. Should payment not be made by the expiry of the days of grace, the policy is then considered void.

day-to-day money. Sums of money lent by banks to the discount houses and stockbrokers overnight. Such loans may be renewed from one day to another if both parties are agreeable.

dead money. Money which can only be borrowed at a high rate of interest.

dead stock. Stock which is in hand and unsaleable.

dead weight. The weight of the vessel plus cargo which brings the total weight of the ship down to the Plimsoll line.

dealer. A trader, a merchant; a dealer in foreign exchange; on the Stock Exchange, or any other money or commodity market.

death of a customer. The authority of a banker to pay cheques, drawn by a customer, and debit the account for direct debits, is countermanded by notice of the death of that customer. On receipt of such notice, either from a newspaper, a solicitor or the next-of-kin, the account must be stopped, and all cheques received after the date of death must be returned with the answer 'drawer deceased'. All mandates, i.e. standing orders, direct debits are cancelled and the account must be stopped. Any credits such as dividends may be credited to a new account, but any pension funds received must be returned to the remitter. However, any contracts in the course of execution, e.g. purchase/sale of stock must be completed. Cheques drawn against a cheque guarantee card must be honoured. Where the account is overdrawn at death, the personal representative must be notified of this fact, while an account in credit may be

withdrawn providing a valid letter of administration is presented or probate proven. In cases where the deceased has left no will and the estate does not exceed £5000 then the bank may hand over the balance of the account to the next-of-kin against a counter indemnity and a simple receipt.

debenture. An acknowledgment of indebtedness, usually given by an incorporated company often under seal, and frequently including a charge on the assets of the company. It may be a registered debenture or one payable to bearer. A debenture holder has a right to a fixed rate of interest regardless of the profits made in the trading period and, in the case of redeemable debentures, the right of repayment of the principal at the agreed date. *See also* ALL MONEYS DEBENTURE; FIXED DEBENTURE; FLOATING DEBENTURE; INCOME DEBENTURE; IRREDEEMABLE DEBENTURE; MORTGAGE DEBENTURE; NAKED DEBENTURE; REDEEMABLE DEBENTURE; SANDWICH DEBENTURE; SECURED DEBENTURE; SIMPLE DEBENTURE.

debenture holder. The holder of a debenture, whether registered or payable to bearer.

debenture stock. A debenture which is expressed as part of a total debt. Certificates of debenture stock may be for any amount.

debit. An entry in the accounting records of an entity. By convention, it is an entry on the left hand side of the account and represents an increase in the value of the asset represented. A debit entry in the account of a liability will reduce the value of that liability. In the accounts of a bank, the payment of a customer's cheque will be debited to the account i.e. if the balance is a credit one, it will reduce the amount due to the customer. If the balance is overdrawn, it will increase the amount due to the bank.

debit balance. Such an entry in a personal account represents money owed to the lender or seller. A debit balance in a nominal account represents an expense which will eventually be a charge to the profits of an entity. A debit balance in a real account represents the book valuation of an asset.

debit card A plastic payment card which when used at a point of sale (by paper or electronic means) draws on a current account balance usually two or three days later. Examples are Visa debit cards (Barclays Connect, Lloyds Payment Card, etc), and cards bearing the Switch logo. All debit cards incorporate additional functions, normally cash withdrawal at ATMs, cheque guarantee (*see* MULTI-FUNCTION CARDS). Some retailers will offer to provide cash as well as goods when a debit card is used. This facility is known as cash back. Debit card transactions are sometimes referred to as 'electronic cheque' transactions.

debit note. A commercial document advising a person or firm that a debit entry has been made in his or her account in the books of the sender. This will arise if an underpayment has been made, or an incorrect price given.

debt. Something owed to another, a liability, an obligation. A chose in action which is capable of being assigned by the creditor to some other person. The assignment must be in writing and must apply to the whole of the debt. The debtor must be notified.

debt adjusting. Defined by the Consumer Credit Act 1974 as 'in relation to debts due under consumer credit agreements or consumer hire agreements: (*a*) negotiating with the creditor or owner, on behalf of the debtor or hirer, terms for the discharge of a debt or (*b*) taking over, in return for payments by the debtor or hirer, his obligation to discharge a debt or (*c*) any similar activity concerned with the liquidation of a debt'.

debt capacity. The extent whereby an entity can raise finance.

debt capital. *See* LOAN CAPITAL.

debt collecting. Consumer Credit Act 1974, 'the taking of steps to procure payment of debts due under consumer credit agreements or consumer hire agreement'.

debt counselling. For the purposes of the Consumer Credit Act 1974, the giving of advice to debtors or hirers about the liquidation of any debt due under consumer credit or consumer hire agreements.

debt/equity ratio. The ratio of the shareholders' equity to total liabilities, sometimes taken as shareholders' equity to long-term debts.

debt/equity swaps. The purchase of a debt instrument in the secondary markets by transnational corporations or domestic investors, who then convert the funds into local currency in order to acquire a stake in existing companies or make a fresh investment.

debt factoring. The procedure whereby a factor will purchase (at a discount) the debts of a company. *See* FACTORING.

debt instrument. Any written evidence of a promise to repay a debt. Such instruments include cheques, bills of exchange, treasury bills, certificates of deposit, etc.

debtor. Often abbreviated to Dr. In business terms is any entity that owes money to another. Defined by the Consumer Credit Act as an individual receiving credit under a consumer credit agreement or a person to whom his/her rights and duties under the agreement have passed by assignment or operation of law.

debtor–creditor agreement. A regulated consumer credit agreement being: 1. a restricted-use credit agreement which falls within s. 11(1)(*b*) of the Consumer Credit Act 1974 but is not made by the creditor under pre-existing arrangements, or in the contemplation of future arrangements, between the creditor and the supplier; or 2. a restricted-use credit agreement which falls within s. 11(1)(*c*) of the Act; or 3. an unrestricted-use credit agreement which is not made by the creditor under pre-existing arrangements between himself/herself and a person (the 'supplier') other than the debtor, in the knowledge that the credit is to be used to finance a transaction between the debtor and the supplier.

debtor–creditor–supplier agreement. A regulated consumer credit agreement being: 1. a restricted-use credit agreement which falls within s. 11(1)(*a*) of the Consumer Credit Act 1974; or 2. a restricted-use credit agreement which falls within s. 11(1)(*b*) of the Act and is made by the creditor under pre-existing arrangements, or in contemplation of future arrangements, between the creditor and the supplier; or 3. an unrestricted-use credit agreement which is made by the creditor under pre-existing arrangements between himself/herself and a person (the supplier) other than the debtor in the knowledge that the credit is to be used to finance a transaction between the debtor and the supplier. *See* CONNECTED LENDER LIABILITY.

debtor days ratio. The average time taken by the debtors to pay the debt due. The formula normally adopted to ascertain this ratio is:

$$\frac{\text{average debtors in the period}}{\text{average value of the credit sales}}$$

debtors age analysis. A spread of debtors showing not only the amounts owed, but listed according to the age of the debt. It assists in the preparation of the provision of doubtful debts. *See* AGING SCHEDULE.

debtor's petition. Under the Insolvency Act 1986 s. 2 that 1. a debtor's petition may be presented to the court only on the grounds that the debtor is unable to pay his or her debts; 2. the petition shall be accompanied by a statement of the debtor's affairs containing: (*a*) such particulars of the debtor's creditors, of the debts and other liabilities and of his or her assets as may be prescribed and (*b*) such other information as may be prescribed.

deceased partner. On the death of a partner, subject to any agreement between them, the partnership will be dissolved. However, many partnerships will carry on trading and the value of the deceased share of the business will be transferred to the personal representatives. For banks it would be necessary in the case of an overdrawn partnership account to stop the account and open another in the name of the surviving partners. This is done to retain the liability of the deceased estate.

deceit. The tort of fraudulent misrepresentation (*q.v.*).

declaration of dividend. The publication by a company of the decision of its board of directors that a dividend of a stated amount will be paid.

declining balance method. *See* REDUCING BALANCE METHOD OF DEPRECIATION.

decree (*Sc Law*). The judgment of the court having been given, and no appeal having been notified, the decree of the court is extracted, i.e. an authenticated copy of the judgment is handed to the successful claimant. *See* JUDGMENT CREDITOR.

deed. An instrument in writing, then signed and sealed. It is thus executed and delivered to the parties concerned. It is effective from the date of delivery.

deed of arrangement. Under the Insolvency Act 1986 s. 260(3) this no longer applies to an approved voluntary arrangement. A voluntary arrangement as summoned under s. 258, will allow the meeting of creditors to propose certain arrangements, but the debtor must consent to each and every proposal and modification.

deed of covenant. An agreement between a donor and a charity that he/she will subscribe a fixed sum of money for a stated number of years (five or seven) to that charity. With the approval of the Inland Revenue, the charity may reclaim any tax paid on the amount of the subscription.

deed of gift. A deed which has the effect of transferring money or property by way of a gift.

deed of partnership. An agreement between two or more persons made under seal setting out the conditions of the partnership. This will include such matters as the division of profits, the capital structure, name and address of the business, termination of the business, etc.

deed of postponement. A deed which has been drawn up so that a company borrowing funds from a financial institution will agree that any previous loan received (from a director) shall not be repaid until the loan given by the financial institution has been repaid. It will also be incumbent of the director to sign a deed of postponement not to accept repayment of the loan he had made to the company.

deed of priorities. When a company has given a bank a floating charge, the document will stipulate that the borrower will not create any additional charge that will rank *pari passu* or ahead of the bank's charge. Should the company wish to borrow from another institution and give the lender a charge over an asset, covered by the bank's floating charge, the permission for this must be obtained. In the event of this being granted, then a deed of priorities will be issued.

deed of settlement. On the occasion of a marriage a deed may be drawn up in favour of the wife and any issue from that marriage which will settle land or other property in trust for a specified time. *See* SETTLED LAND.

deep discount. A large discount on the issue of a redeemable security.

de facto. In fact, actually.

defalcation. The misappropriation of any property by a person to whom the property was entrusted.

defamation. The publication of a statement which tends to lower a person in the estimation of the average member of the public. Defence of defamation may be based on truth, privilege or fair comment. Written defamation is libel, while spoken defamation is slander.

default. Fault, neglect, defect, failure to apear in a law-court when summoned. Failure to account for money held in trust, failure to repay a loan or an overdraft as promised. A person may be convicted or a default order made against him or her if found to contravene; 1. ss. 24 and 713 Companies Act 1985; 2. ss. 41 and 170 Insolvency Act 1986. *See also* JUDGMENT BY DEFAULT.

default notice. A term used under the Consumer Credit Act 1974 in connection with a debtor's breach of the agreement, whereby he must be issued with a default notice in the proper manner should the creditor desire to terminate the agreement and enforce the recovery of the goods or security. Under Section 88(1) the notice must specify: 1. the nature of the breach, 2. the action to remedy the breach; 3. the date by which action must be taken; 4. the sum payable for the breach.

default order. An order by a court requesting an officer of a company to remedy a default in filing the accounts and returns of that company. Companies Act 1985 s. 297.

defeasance. A condition relating to a deed and incorporated in it, which being performed renders the deed void; the act of annulling a contract.

defensive securities. Equities and gilts that are more stable in price, provide a safe and regular return to the investor, and when the market is weak, such investments are not likely to fall as quickly or as far as other investments in the market.

deferred. Put off, postponed.

deferred annuity. An annuity which does not begin to operate until after a certain period.

deferred charges. Prepaid items for a period greater than the current accounting period, so that there is a balance of value to be carried forward to the subsequent accounting period, e.g. where rates are paid in advance, or a railway season ticket purchased for a year instead of for three months.

deferred expenditure. *See* DEFERRED CHARGES.

deferred shares. Shares that are issued under the conditions that they will receive a dividend only if the ordinary share dividend has reached a stated limit. They are rarely issued nowadays. They have in the past been known as 'founder shares'. When the company is trading well the return on these shares can be considerable.

deferred taxation. Tax which is payable in the year after which the profit was earned. Reference to this is in SSAP 15.

deficit. The excess of expenditure over income. Frequently used in the accounts of non-profit organisations, whose aim is to match income and expenditure. An amount of money lost or missing.

deficit net worth. It is a situation where the liabilities exceed the assets.

deflation. A decline in the price of goods and services. It is not necessarily the opposite to inflation as, for example, agreed wages, salaries and pensions need not necessarily be reduced. *See also* DISINFLATION; INFLATION.

defunct company. A company which has ceased to do business, and which has had its name struck off the register of companies.

del credere agent. An agent who guarantees to his or her principal that third parties with whom the agent contracts on the principal's behalf will always meet their obligations to the principal; if they do not, the *del credere* agent will make good the deficiency.

delegated authority. The authority given by a principal to his agent to perform certain acts on his behalf. It is normal for such work to be carried out by the agent himself. However, there may be an expressed or implied authority that the agent may delegate to another.

Such delegation is usual where in order to do the job properly, delegation is necessary or it may be custom to delegate. Delegation may be made by one trustee to another, but a trustee may by law use the services of a bank, solicitor, broker, etc., to transact any necessary business.

delegation. The act of assigning work, a duty, or a completion of an order, to another. The ability to delegate is an essential requisite of successful management.

delisting. The removal of the name of a company from the Stock Exchange list as it failed to maintain the necesary criteria or for breach of a regulation.

delivered at frontier. Terms indicating that the goods will be transported and all expenses paid up to the frontier of the buyer or the frontier of the country named in the contract, further expenses, including import duty should be paid by the buyer.

delivery. The legal transfer of possession or ownership to another. It may be actual or constructive. A bill of exchange is incomplete without delivery taking place.

delivery date. The date when a bill, security or other document of title must be delivered.

delivery note. A note that is usually sent with goods setting out the description of the goods, weight, number, etc., so that the recipient may check them.

delivery of bill or cheque. Defined by the Bills of Exchange Act 1882 s. 2 as 'transfer of possession, actual or constructive, from one person to another. Constructive delivery takes place when the bill is handed to the transferee or his known agent. The delivery is completed by an indorsement unless the bill is payable to bearer'.

delivery of deed. A deed to be effective must be signed, sealed and delivered. The delivery can be executed by the person placing his finger on the seal and saying at the same time 'I deliver this as my act and deed'.

delivery order. An instruction to the possessor of goods by the owner to deliver all or part of the goods to a person named in the order. Such an instruction in banking is usual when goods have in the case of a produce loan been stored in the name of the

bank, who will then request the warehousekeeper to release some part or all the goods to the customer who will take delivery of the goods, sell them and remit the proceeds to the bank and thereby reduce or eliminate the advance.

delivery terms. Within a contract the agreement between buyer and seller as to whom will pay the various charges on the goods. Such terms will be stated as, for example, FOB, CIF etc.

demand. A request to obtain, purchase, or not to take any action. An authoritative statement. The amount that is likely to be required, i.e. the goods are in demand, his services were in demand, funds were deposited 'on demand', repayable at request.

demand and supply. *See* SUPPLY AND DEMAND.

demand bill. *See* DEMAND DRAFT.

demand deposit. An American term meaning that funds are repayable on demand. In the UK this would refer to a current account, cheque account with a bank. Building societies have similar accounts but give them different names. In most cases interest is paid on these accounts.

demand draft. A bill of exchange payable on demand; a cheque; a draft drawn by a bank on itself, its head office, or on a correspondent bank and payable on demand.

demand pull inflation. Demand for goods and services exceeds the supply, causing buyers to bid up the prices for such goods and services.

demise. To transfer or convey by lease or will; a transfer or conveyance by lease or will for a term of years or in fee simple; the granting of a lease.

demise charter. A situation where the charterer of a vessel will make all the arrangements necessary to be ready to sail. The charterer will arrange the employment of the crew, order victuals, fuel, etc.

demonetise. The withdrawal of a unit of currency, e.g. the halfpenny is no longer currency in the UK. The £5 note has been changed and is gradually being withdrawn from circulation.

demurrage. A charge by the port authorities on a vessel or the goods for some infringement of the regulations, e.g. the delay in berthing, a penalty for not removing goods, etc.

Department of National Savings. *See* NATIONAL SAVINGS.

deposit. Funds placed with a financial institution. Securities placed with a bank or financial institution for a specific purpose. Money placed with an entity as evidence of good faith that the contract will be completed, e.g. purchase of land. Defined by the Consumer Credit Act s. 189(1) 'as any sum payable by a debtor or hirer by way of deposit or down payment, or credited to him/her on account of any deposit or down payment, whether the sum is to be or has been paid to the creditor or owner or any other person, or is to be or has been discharged by payment of money or a transfer or delivery of goods or by any other means'.

deposit account. A bank account on which a rate of interest is payable. Such interest will be paid net of tax if the account holder is neither an overseas resident or a corporate customer. Funds are normally repayable at seven or fourteen days' notice. A statement is normally issued to a customer periodically.

deposit broker. Intermediaries who arrange for deposits to be placed with one bank or financial insititution by another.

deposit insurance. In the UK the payment by banks of a sort of premium to a central fund whose resources will be used to repay depositors if they are in danger of losing their money on the failure of a bank. The Banking Act 1987 gave protection to bank depositors by the formation of a deposit protection fund which is managed by the Bank of England. All recognised banks must contribute a total sum of not less than £5m. The maximum contribution, applicable to the big clearers, is £300 000, but for small banks and deposit taking institutions any contribution is related to the deposit base, with a minimum of £5000. The fund will be used to pay a depositor an amount equal to three-quarters of the deposit held if the institution which received this deposit becomes insolvent. This protection will apply for sums up to £20 000 for any depositor.

deposition. A written declaration (signed before a magistrate) by a witness who must later appear to testify in court.

deposit rate. The various rates of interest that is paid by banks on the various types of deposit accounts.

deposit receipt. Where no statement is issued or required by a depositor, then a receipt is issued as evidence of the deposit.

deposit taking business. A business whose main function is to accept deposits. Under the Banking Act 1987, no person, corporate or not, may accept a deposit unless authorised by the Bank of England. The minimum criteria required for a deposit taking business is stated in the Act.

depreciation. Defined by SSAP 12 as 'the measure of the wearing out, consumption or other reduction in the useful economic life of a fixed asset whether arising from use, effluxion of time or obsolescence through technological or market changes'.

depreciation accounting. The allocation of an amount of the fixed asset to a stated accounting period, to be deducted from the profits of that period.

depreciation of a currency. The value of a currency will be determined by the demand and supply. Should investors and international traders lose confidence in the currency, then the rate of exchange will fall and the price of the currency will be lower in the international money markets.

depression. An economic situation when there are falling prices, industrial activity slows down, rising unemployment, public confidence falls and there is fear and caution in commercial and industrial activity.

determination. Termination, conclusion, bringing to an end; settlement by a judicial decision. A debt due to a bank may be determined by a call on a guarantor, and the appointment of a receiver under a debenture, or notice of the death, bankruptcy or liquidation of the customer, etc.

detinue. A legal action taken by a plaintiff for the return of a chattel which he/she alleges has been detained unlawfully. Should judgement be given in his/her favour then he/she may obtain the chattel or its value and damages for its retention.

devaluation. The lowering of a country's currency in relation to the currencies of other countries. It can also mean the rise in the value of other currencies in relation to the home currency.

development land tax. A tax no longer applicable on disposals after March 1985.

devise. The act of bequeathing landed property by will.

devisee. One to whom real property is left by will.

devolution. Transference or delegation of authority (as by Parliament to one of its committees); passage from one person to another; descent by inheritance; descent in natural succession.

diarising. Recording either manually or on a computer action that is needed to be taken at some date in the future. Such banking information as head office returns, customer standing orders, direct debits, bills of exchange maturing and for presentation for payment, etc. One of the office procedures, is to bring to the notice of members of staff, the various items that have appeared in the diary and needing attention that particular day.

dictum. An observation made by a judge on matters arising while hearing a case. *See also* OBITER DICTUM

difference. The amount by which one value does not agree with another. A disagreement between totals. The margin between one price and another.

differential. The difference between the remuneration of one group of persons and another. For example, between clerical staff in one company and those in a similar company but earning a greater salary. Salary/wage differentials are sometimes reduced, due to pressure of one group of workers, then at a later date they may be increased. A differential salary may be paid for members of staff who, due to study have obtained a qualification and therefore an increase in their salary.

differential duties. Variable duties imposed on the same commodity coming from different countries.

differential pricing. This phrase refers to the legislation concerning the ability of retailers to charge customers a different price when settlement is made by a credit card instead of cash. Under the Credit Card (Price Discrimination) Order 1990, which came into force on 28 February 1991, a retailer – with effect from 7 March 1991 is no longer prevented from pricing differentially transactions settled by credit cards from those settled by cash. A retailer is thus able from that date, to surcharge credit card transactions, or alternatively to discount cash payments, should the retailer wish so to do. A retailer is enabled to price differentially under this legislation for credit card transactions, where 'credit card transactions' are those defined by the Order. Where a payment card is 'readily distinguishable' from a credit card; 'readily distinguishable' being defined and prescribed within the Order, the legislation does NOT APPLY to such cards – Switch debit cards, for example. Should a retailer determine to price differentially such credit card transactionsd, he is obliged under the Draft Price Indications (Method of Payment) Regulations and Draft Pricing Marking (Petrol) (Amendment) Order: to place general notices at all public entrances to the premises and at points in the premises where consumers make payment or become bound to purchase (Regulation 4). The differential between the marked price and the price for any other accepted method of payment may be indicated on such notices in percentage or absolute terms (Regulation 3). Under consumer law, non-compliance with the Price Indication Regulations constitutes a criminal offence.

diligence (*Sc. Law*). A legal method by which an unsatisfied creditor may proceed to seize his or her debtor's property in satisfaction of the debt, or to prevent dissipation of the property by the debtor (*see* MAREVA INJUNCTION) either personally or by his or her agent (*see* INTROMISSION); the warrant issued by a court to enforce the attendance of witnesses, or the production of documents. Summary Diligence (*q.v.*) refers to certain cases where the creditor can use any of the appropriate forms of diligence without having to establish the claims by an action in court.

dilution. In circumstances where all warrants, share options conversion of bonds, etc., have been taken up in the form of ordinary shares, the issued capital is greater, therefore the earnings per share are lower, i.e. they have been diluted and in consequence shareholders are likely to receive a lower dividend.

dip. Used when the price of securities, commodities or foreign currencies have after a continuous increase in price for some reason incurred a slight drop. The commodity is for a short time, weak.

direct. Straightforward, immediate, in a straight line.

direct access. The ability to obtain access to a location in a computer system directly without going via another location.

direct arbitrage. Dealings in foreign exchange which are confined to one centre.

direct cost. The cost of production in monetary terms. A cost that can be directly attributed to one or more products.

direct debit. A method in the banking system, whereby the creditor can claim on a debtor. The debtor authorises his banker to accept debits on his account, and on each occasion the creditor initiates the debit to the account. Many personal customers were unhappy at the thought of authorising this procedure and in recognition of this, only organisations that can satisfy the criteria, may employ the debit system of collecting debts. As a safeguard to the customer any incorrect debit is repayable without question by the debtor's bank, who will reclaim funds from the creditor. Any adjustment will be made outside the banking system. This system has been proved very useful for payment of insurance premiums, local tax, gas and electricity instalments, etc.

direct expense. A cost which is a charge to a cost centre or production process. It is a cost other than direct labour or materials.

directive. An instruction from a senior authority that must be implemented in accordance with the instructions. It will also tend, in broad detail, to advise and guide the method to be adopted for the implementation of the instructions. A Bank of England directive, especially on lending, will give an indication on the qualitative and/or quantitative controls to be observed.

directive overhead or cost. An expense which can be identified and related to the production of a product.

direct security. Security given by the person or company that has received the advance.

direct selling. Sales by the producer, manufacturer, or the supplier of a service directly to the consumer bypassing wholesaler, distributor and retailer.

direct tax. A tax levied on the taxpayer, e.g. income tax, as distinct from a tax levied on goods or services.

director. There is no comprehensive definition of a director, but in general it is a person who has been elected or appointed by shareholders to run a company. It is usual for a director to be a shareholder of the company in which he is a director. There are a number of Acts of Parliament which are relevant to the responsibilities of a director, among them are: Companies Act 1985 and 1990, Insolvency Act 1986, Company Directors Disqualification Act 1986, Financial Services Act 1986, Building Societies Act 1986 and the Banking Act 1987. Generally a director must: 1. Have an overriding duty to act at all times with due care, skill and the utmost good faith. 2. Not allow his personal interest to conflict with his duty to the company. 3. Ensure that when he has delegated authority, those persons are capable of carrying out such duties. 4. Ensure that proper books of account are maintained. 5. Prepare and file such annual accounts as required and hold general meetings as are necessary. *See also* SHADOW DIRECTOR; LOANS TO DIRECTORS.

director of savings. An officer appointed under the National Savings Bank Act 1971, under whose control the savings facilities known as the National Savings Bank Investment Account and Ordinary Account are administered. He is also responsible, under the terms of the National Debt Act 1972, for National Savings Capital Bonds, Income Bonds, Savings Certificates, Yearly Plan, Premium Bonds and the National Savings Stock Register.

Director General of Fair Trading. The Fair Trading Act 1973, which created the post of Director-General, is concerned with both competition and consumer protection matters. It charged the Director-General with five overall duties: 1. Keeping under review commercial activities relating to the supply of goods and services to consumers in the United Kingdom; 2. Collecting information about activities which may adversely affect the economic interests of UK consumers; 3. Reviewing any of these matters and making appropriate recommendations to the Secretary of State for Trade and Industry; 4. Keeping a watch on monopolies (defined as a company or group of companies having 25 per cent or more of national or local market) and, where monopoly power may be being abused, referring the matter to the Monopolies and Mergers Commission (MMC); 5. Examining actual or proposed mergers which meet the Act's criteria (total gross assets of the target company exceed £30 million or a merger resulting in 25 per cent of the supply of particular goods or services coming under the control of the merged company) and advising the Secretary of State whether the merger should be referred to the MMC. The Consumer Credit Act 1974 gave the Director-General the duty of administering the licensing provisions of the Act, the power to renew, suspend, vary or revoke credit licenses, to supervise the working of the Act and its subordinate legislation and to make recommendations to the Secretary of State on amendments to the Act. Other statutory powers given to the Director-General include the Restrictive Trade Practices Act 1976, which allows him to investigate restrictive trade agreements (cartels) and, where appropriate, seek orders from the Restrictive Practices Court banning agreements; the Competition Act 1980 which allows the Director-General to investigate anticompetitive practices by individual enterprises and, if necessary refer them for deeper investigation by the MMC; the Estate Agents Act 1979 under which the Director-General has powers to ban individuals from engaging in estate agency work; the Financial Services Act 1986 in which the Director-General must consider the competition implications of the rules of self-regulatory bodies, investment exchanges and clearing houses, and amendments to rules, and give advice on them to the Secretary of State. Finally under the Control of Misleading Advertisements Regulations Act 1988 under which the Director-General acts as a back-up to existing organisations such as the Advertising Standards Authority, the IBA and Trading Standards Officers and has powers to seek injunctions in the High Court banning misleading advertisements.

directors' interest. While the Companies Act 1985, instructs the company shall keep records of the shares and debentures held by directors, the Companies Act 1989, Schedule 4, amends Schedule 6 of the Companies Act 1985 and provides that such information as the emoluments, pensions, benefits and compensation for loss of office of the chairman and directors, is also disclosed.

directors' report. The report that must be attached to the annual final accounts and balance sheet of a company and circulated to the members of the company. The report must give a fair review of the development of the business of the company and its subsidiaries during the financial year of the balance sheet; the recommendations of the directors as to the application of profits; the principal activites of the company and its subsidiaries; and details of any major changes that have occurred and any likely future developments. Companies Act 1985 s. 235 and Sch. 7.

dirty bill of lading. A bill of lading marked or claused to show that the goods or packing were received in a damaged condition.

discharge. The dismissal of a person from employment or a director from his duties or a jury from their obligations. The settlement of a debt or obligation. The release of security given by a customer for a loan or the return of an item in safe custody. The unloading of goods from a ship.

discharged bankrupt. A bankrupt is discharged from bankruptcy when the court is satisfied that all conditions of the court have been satisfied. The person concerned may consider his or her debts as settled and can therefore make a fresh start subject to the conditions imposed by the Insolvency Act 1986 s. 281.

discharged bill. The payment of a bill of exchange either by the drawer, drawee or when the acceptor becomes the holder of the bill. A bill will also be discharged when the holder renounces his right to the debt against the acceptor.

disclaimer. The denial, denunciation or disavowal of a claim, e.g. a beneficiary under a will or a trustee in a bankruptcy may disclaim any asset in the bankrupt's estate which is burdened with onerous clauses (Insolvency Act 1985 s. 315).

disclosure. *See* SECRECY.

discount. 1. A deduction from a stated price allowed by a wholesaler/retailer, i.e. a trade discount. 2. A deduction from the invoice amount which may be deducted if payment is made within a stated period, i.e. cash discount. 3. An amount deducted on the depreciation of an asset or investment. 4. An amount deducted from the face value of a bill of exchange when it is sold (discounted) in the money market. This rate is affected by (*a*) the names on the bill, (*b*) the rate of interest appertaining at the time, (*c*) the length of time to maturity. 5. In the foreign exchange market, it is the margin between two currencies and applicable when the forward rate of one currency is cheaper and the discount is added to the spot rate. 6. As an inducement to buyers, new items may be sold at a discount. *See also* CASH DISCOUNT; TRADE DISCOUNT.

discount broker. *See* BILL BROKER.

discounted cash flow. An evaluation of the future net cash flow using present values, the two methods of calculations are as follows: 1. The yield method – the internal rate of return in the form of a percentage. 2. Net present value in which the discount rate is chosen and the answer is in money form.

discount house. *See* BILL BROKER.

discount market. The chief feature of the UK money market is the existence of a discount market. This is not unique as there are discount markets in Spain and Singapore, but amongst the major economies it is certainly the exception. The discount market is important be-

cause the Bank of England does not normally deal directly with the commercial banks but deals mainly with the nine discount houses. Essentially the houses are active traders in treasury bills, commercial bills, certificates of deposit and commercial paper. They finance themselves by borrowing overnight money from the banking system, including overseas banks in London, and to a lesser but growing extent, from industrial and commercial companies and of course by the houses' own capital. The houses provide a smooth, flexible and continuous market in short-term securities, and are the main operational link in the execution of official monetary policy.

discount rate. This is the rate at which the Federal Reserve bank will lend to its member banks on an overnight basis for the reserve purposes and can be regarded as the Central Bank Rate of the US. The discount rate is an important indicator of official government policy and the Federal Reserve has, on occasions, imposed a surcharge or premium on the discount rate to discourage unwarranted borrowing. In the UK the Bank of England discount rate is the rate at which it will discount first-class bills.

discretion. Prudence, discernment, liberty to act according to one's judgment.

discretionary funds. Funds deposited with a bank by a customer for investment purposes, but unlike advisory funds, the bank may invest at their own discretion.

discretionary income. The balance of a person's income that is left after all expenses have been met.

discretionary limits. *See* MANAGERS' DISCRETIONARY LIMITS

discretionary trust. A trust fund which has been established under which the trustees are allowed discretion to pay or give an income to the beneficiaries. The beneficiary/s have no right to claim any part of the income given to him or applied for his/her benefit.

disentail. To break the entail of (an estate), the act of disentailing. *See also* BARRING THE ENTAIL

disentailing assurance. *See* BARRING THE ENTAIL.

dishonour of a bill. The refusal of a drawee of a bill of exchange to either accept it, or to pay it after acceptance. The drawee of a cheque (a bank) may on occasions refuse to honour a cheque and return it unpaid to the presenter.

disinflation. The curtailing or curbing an inflationary situation by adopting certain measures. These measures may include, increasing interest rates, creating a budget surplus, etc.

disintermediation. The borrowing and lending of funds without the use of a middle person. e.g. a bank, broker, etc.

disk. A circular container for the storage of computer data and programs. They have tracks which gives random accessibility for the speedy retrieval of information.

dispense. To divide out in parts; to administer, as laws; to excuse from, to grant a dispensation from a duty or obligation.

dispensing notice. *See* NOTICE OF DISPENSATION.

disposable income. Income left after all direct taxes have been deducted.

disposition. The transfer, conveyance or disposal of property.

disseize. To deprive of an estate in freehold wrongfully.

disseizin. Unlawful dispossession of freehold land.

dissenting creditor. Under the Insolvency Act 1986, a general meeting of creditors (creditors committee) the actions of this committee being limited (s. 301/2). If any creditor (or bankrupt) is dissatisfied by an act, omission or decision of a trustee of the bankrupt's estate, he or she may apply to the court; and on such an application the court may confirm, reverse or modify any act or decision of the trustee, may give the trustee direction, or may make such other order as it thinks fit. Section 303.

dissolution. The bringing to an end of a relationship, e.g. a partnership, marriage, a committee, a legislative assembly.

dissolution of a company. The termination of a company and its business by winding-up and striking off the register of companies. *See also* COMPULSORY LIQUIDATION OR WINDING-UP. VOLUNTARY LIQUIDATION.

dissolution of a partnership. The termination of a partnership either by the agreement of all partners or by the notice given by a partner, or by legal process, e.g. death, bankruptcy, or by an event which makes it illegal for the partnership to continue. On notice of the dissolution of a partnership the bank holding the account would 'stop' the account in order to retain the liability of each partner at the time of dissolution.

distrain. The seizure of goods to satisfy an outstanding debt.

distraint. The act of seizing goods for a debt.

distress. The act of distraining, goods taken in distraint. *See also* DISTRINGAS

distress borrowing. A situation whereby the borrower is compelled by this trading or way of life to borrow more money, even though interest rates are high and the general policy of government is to discourage borrowing. An increased mortgage for an individual or additional funds for a company forced to keep going is called 'distress borrowing'.

distributable profits. The profits of a limited company that are available for distribution to members as a dividend. They must not contravene current law. For the purposes of the Companies Act 1985 s. 263(3), it is accumulated, realised profits, so far as not previously utilised by distribution or capitalisation, less its accumulated, realised losses, so far as not previously written off in a reduction or reorganisation of capital duly made. For a public company s. 264 of the Act states that a company is further restricted in that its net assets must not be less than the aggregate of its called-up share capital and undistributable reserves at the time of or after a distribution.

distribution. 1. The payment of dividends from the profits of a company to its shareholders. 2. The allocation of income or expenses to various accounts. 3. The capitalisation of reserves by the issue of additional shares to the shareholders.

distribution expense. An expense related to the cost of selling, marketing, storing and despatching goods. This may also be known as a distribution overhead or cost.

District Land Registry. A local registry office set up to deal with and maintain the records of the titles to property in the area. *See* LAND REGISTER.

distringas. An old writ that was abolished in 1883. In its place is the *notice in lieu of distringas. see* NOTICE IN LIEU OF DIS-TRINGAS.

dividend. A distribution of the profits to the shareholders of a company. For the ordinary shareholder the dividend is agreed at the annual general meeting – which can vary from year to year – while the preference dividend, which is at a fixed rate is confirmed, if profits permit. Should the Articles of Association permit, a distribution of dividends may be made by the issue of shares. A dividend is also defined as the distribution of the estate of a bankrupt person or a liquidated company by the official receiver to creditors.

dividend counterfoil. The top or side portion of a dividend warrant, containing the name and address of the shareholder, number of shares held, the gross amount, tax credit and the net amount payable. Where the dividend has been paid direct to a bank for the credit of the shareholders' account, the dividend counterfoil will be used as a credit voucher and should be handed to the customer, with his or her statement, to be used as evidence of income received and tax deducted.

dividend cover. The money needed for a dividend payment divided into the profits (after tax) of the company available for the payment.

dividend equalisation account. An account specifically maintained for the transfer of profits from years of high profit to be used to pay minimum dividends in future years.

dividend in bankruptcy. Should a trustee in bankruptcy have sufficient funds, after dealing with preferential debts as stated in the Insolvency Act 1986 s. 386, the trustee may give notice to declare a dividend. In the trustee's calculation of the amount to be distributed, consideration must be given in his/her provisions to 1. bankruptcy debts due but not yet proven; 2. bankruptcy debts claimed, but not yet determined; 3. disputed claims and proofs – s. 324. Section 330 states: '1. When the trustee has realised all the bankrupt's estate or so much of it as can, in the trustee's opinion, be realised without needlessly protracting the trusteeship, he/she shall give notice in the pres-

cribed manner either (*a*) of the intention to declare a final dividend, or (*b*) that no dividend, or further dividend, will be declared.

dividend limitation. Restriction on any increase in dividend payments as a measure to check inflation.

dividend mandate. 1. An authority by a shareholder to the company to pay the dividend by the issues of shares in lieu of cash. 2. An authority for the dividend to be remitted to the shareholder's bank account.

dividend warrant. An order or warrant issued by a company and drawn on its bankers, authorising them to pay the dividend specified thereon to the stock or shareholder.

dividend yield. The gross dividend on a share divided by the share price.

dock warrant. A certificate issued by a port authority or warehouse company stating that they are holding specified goods that have been unloaded by a named vessel for the consignee to whom they are addressed. Such a warrant may be indorsed by the consignee in favour of the bank and deposited with a memorandum of deposit as security for a produce loan. The more usual method is for the consignee to authorise the warehouse company to transfer the title to goods to the bank.

document. A piece of paper containing details which can be relied on. This can be any plan, map, drawing, photograph, disc, tape, soundtrack, etc. (Civil Evidence Act 1968 s. 10).

documentary bill. While there is no definition of a documentary bill, it would in commercial terms mean either a bill of exchange or promissory note which has attached to it, one or more commercial documents. Under Uniform, Rules for Collection, a documentary bill would include the phrase 'financial documents' which is defined as bills of exchange, promissory notes, cheques, payment receipts or other similar documents used for obtaining payment of money.

documentary credit. A method of financing overseas trade whereby the contracting parties insert in the sales contract a provision that payment shall be made by a banker under the provisions of a documentary credit. Under this system, a banker undertakes to pay the amount stated on the documentary credit or accept a bill of exchange, in return for the delivery to him or her by the exporter of the commercial and shipping documents provided they are in strict conformity with the terms and conditions of the documentary credit. The undertaking on the letter of credit may be irrevocable or revocable. All letters of credit are opened in accordance with the International Chamber of Commerce publication *Uniform Customs and Practice for Documentary Credits, 1984*. *See also* ACCEPTANCE CREDIT; BACK-TO-BACK CREDIT; CONFIRMED CREDIT; IRREVOCABLE CREDIT; NEGOTIATION CREDIT; RE-FINANCE CREDIT; REIMBURSEMENT CREDIT; REVOCABLE CREDIT; REVOLVING CREDIT; RED CLAUSE; SIGHT CREDIT; TERM CREDIT; TRANSFERABLE CREDIT.

documentary evidence. The production of documents with the intention that they shall be made available for inspection, e.g. in a court of law.

document of title. A document which enables the possessor to deal with the property described in it as of he or she were the owner (as indeed may often be the case), e.g. a share certificate, a life insurance policy, a bill of lading.

documents against acceptance (D/A). *See* BILL FOR COLLECTION.

documents against payment (D/P). *See* BILL FOR COLLECTION.

dollar certificate of deposit. A document that certifies that a fixed amount of US dollars has been deposited with a bank for a stated period attracting a given rate of interest. The minimum deposit is $25 000 and issued for periods of 30, 60, 90 days or longer if considered necessary. They were introduced into the UK by US banks in the UK in the early 1960s and were popular to holders of US$. There is a secondary money market for these certificates, so that holders are certain to receive the return of the dollars should they be needed. *See* CERTIFICATE OF DEPOSIT.

domestic banking. Often called retail banking as opposed to wholesale or international banking. This is the usual banker–customer relationship dealing with deposits and withdrawals and the transmission of funds.

domestic credit expansion (DCE). A method used by government to measure and control the growth of the money supply. Such measures as an increase or decrease in interest rates, open market operations, special deposits, may be used to stabilise the economy.

domicile. The place at which a bill of exchange is made payable; the place where a person has a permanent place of residence or home, the place of residence in a particular country with the intention of remaining there.

domiciled bill. When accepting a bill of exchange or promissory note, the acceptor has stated a place where the bill should be presented for payment, e.g. a bank.

donation. A sum of money given by one person to another. An asset given as a gift to another person. Donations given by businesses are not normally justifiable expenses.

dormant. Sleeping, undeveloped, inactive, inoperative, in abeyance.

dormant account. An account that has not been active for about one year. While a bank is not legally bound to contact the customer, it will as a matter of course send a statement at least every six months to the last known address of the customer. Should there be no response to any communication, then the account is considered as dormant and transferred to a dormant ledger either in the branch or to a head office department.

dormant company. A company, under the Companies Act 1985, which for any period has had no significant accounting transaction as defined by s. 221 of the Act. If a private company is dormant then its members can resolve not to appoint auditors for the period in which it has been dormant.

dormant partner. A partner of firm who takes no active part in its operations. Nevertheless he will still share in the profits of the business and be liable for its debts.

double entry bookkeeping. A method of bookkeeping which is so organised that every transaction is recorded both as a debit in one ledger account and as a credit in another ledger account.

double taxation relief. Relief given to a taxpayer so that he or she is not taxed twice on the same income under two separate jurisdictions. For example, a

UK citizen, residing in the UK, receives an income from abroad, then it is quite likely tax has been deducted at source. Providing there is a taxation treaty between the UK and the other country, the taxpayer will receive credit for the overseas tax paid when the UK tax liability on this income is determined.

Dow Jones Index. *See* INDICE DOW JONES.

down payment. A payment in advance or a deposit given as evidence of good faith prior to the receipt of goods.

d/p. An abbreviation for documents against payment. An abbreviation for data processing.

draft. Another term for a bill of exchange. An outline of a plan or policy. A written instruction from one party (drawer) to a third party (the drawee) to pay a sum of money to a payee. *see also* BANKERS' DRAFT; DEMAND DRAFT; FOREIGN DRAFT.

draw. The writing of a cheque, promissory note or bill of exchange. In popular terminology, to sketch or portray a picture.

drawback. A rebate of a tax or duty paid on imported goods.

drawee. The person to whom a negotiable instrument is addressed. When that instrument is payable at some future date, then it must be presented for acceptance. On acceptance by the drawee, then he/she will be the acceptor and consequently engages that the bill will be paid according to its tenor. *See also* ACCEPTANCE.

drawer. The person who signs a negotiable instrument. By so 'drawing' a bill of exchange, promissory note or cheque, he/she engages that it will be paid in accordance to its tenor, should the drawee dishonour the bill, then providing the proper procedure has been adhered to, the holder may present the bill to the drawer and demand payment.

drawing. Money, stock or other items withdrawn from the business by the owner/s.

drawings account. An account to record the withdrawal of funds or stock by the owner/s.

drawing rights. *See* SPECIAL DRAWING RIGHTS.

drawn bond. A bond which has been drawn or selected for repayment upon a certain date.

drive-in bank. A branch office having a cashier so positioned that he/she may pay money to, or receive money from, a customer through the window of the customer's car.

drop lock. A provision whereby a borrower of funds agrees that if an interest rate falls below a certain level, then the interest charged will be maintained at an agreed rate. Banks frequently have this agreement with their customers that they will lend at 3 per cent over base rate, minimum 10 per cent.

dual capacity. Since October 1986, the functions of broker and jobber have merged, so that the market makers are now acting in dual capacity. *See* BIG BANG

dual control. A procedural system whereby two persons will fill a function. For example, two keys will be required to open a safe. Each key will be in the hands of separate persons. The signing of cheques/drafts about a stated amount will be signed by two officers.

dual listing. The listing of a security in more than one exchange.

dual purpose trust. *See* SPLIT CAPITAL TRUST.

due course. *See* PAYMENT IN DUE COURSE.

due date of a bill. The date calculated on term bill when it should be presented for payment. Should the bill be payable at a fixed date the this date is the due date, unless that day falls on a non-business day, then it is usually payable on the next business day. A cheque is usually payable on demand, then it should be presented for payment as soon as possible. A post-dated cheque, is by definition not a cheque until it is due, then it is payable on demand.

dumping. Selling goods in overseas markets at a cheaper rate than in the home market.

Dun and Bradstreet. An organisation, known in banking and financial circles as one that provides information about public quoted companies. Useful to stock exchange investors.

duopoly. A situation where there are only two producers of a particular commodity.

duration of bankruptcy. Insolvency Act 1986 s. 279(1): subject as follows, a bankrupt is discharged from bankruptcy: (*a*) in the case of an individual who was adjudged bankrupt on a petition under s. 264(1)(*d*) – i.e. under the powers of the Criminal Courts Act – or who had been undischarged bankrupt at any time in the period of 15 years ending with the commencement of the bankruptcy, by an order of the court under the section next following and (*b*) in any other case, by the expiration of the relevant period under this section. 2. That period is as follows: (*a*) where a certificate for the summary administration of the bankrupt's estate has been issued and is not revoked before the bankrupt's discharge, the period of two years beginning with the commencement of the bankruptcy and (*b*) in any other case, the period of three years beginning with the commencement of the bankruptcy.

duress. A restraint by force, which could include imprisonment. Violence or the threat of violence. A bill drawn or accepted under duress then the burden of proof is shifted to the holder who may have some right against the transferor should he/she have given value and received it in good faith.

dutch auction. A sale in which property is offered above its value, and the price is gradually lowered until someone accepts an offer. *See also* AUCTION.

duty. A legal or moral obligation to another; a tax on either imports or exports.

duty of care. Taking reasonable care to avoid acts or omissions which could injure a person, e.g., a banker is under duty of care to ensure the safety of a customer's items on safe custody. As agent, a banker must deal promptly and diligently with his or her customer's instructions.

E

E & OE. *See* ERRORS AND OMISSIONS EX-
CEPTED.

Eagle. An American gold coin which
has a range from 0.1 ounce to 1 ounce
in weight.

early withdrawal penalty. Where a person has made a fixed term investment,
then subsequently, before maturity,
wishes to withdraw all or part of the
funds, then a penalty would be in-
flicted for such an early withdrawal.

earmark. The setting aside of an item,
asset for a particular purpose. Such
items would bear some marking to indicate their use. Funds may also be
earmarked for a particular purpose. In
banking it would be the practice to
have such funds in a separate account,
e.g. cover for documentary credits account.

earned income. This is defined in the
Income and Corporation Taxes Act
1970 s. 530. It covers all income that is
chargeable for tax under Schedule E,
A and B. Other incomes from pensions, annuities, social security benefits, etc. are all considered as earned
income and are taxed as such.

earnest. A thing of value or a sum of
money given by a person as evidence
of good faith to bind a contract or bargain. A pledge.

earning assets. *See* RESERVE ASSETS.

earnings. A wage or salary received by
an individual from his/her employment. The net profit of a trading concern before deduction of tax.

earnings related contribution. The
social security contribution (National
Health) which is deducted from a
wage or salary, and increases as the
amount earned is increased. There is a
ceiling to the amount deducted, which
will change in accordance to government policy.

earnings per share. In simplistic terms,
this refers to the profit allocation to
each share after paying tax, preference

dividends and minority interests. Thus
for a company that had made £10 million profit and had 10 million shares,
the earnings per share would be £1
(SSAP 3).

earnings price ratio. The relationship
between the earning per share to the
current market price of the share. Also
known as the *earnings yield.*

easement. A right of way or a privilege a
person has over the estate of another,
e.g. the right to walk across the land of
another.

ECGD. An abbreviation for Export Credits Guarantee Department.

economic growth rate. A measurement
of the rate of change in the growth of
national product.

economic indicators. The statistics, e.g.
rate of employment, inflation, balance
of payments, etc., which shows the direction of the economy.

economic planning. The purposeful utilisation of the factors of production in
order to achieve an economic target.

economics. The study of the production, distribution and consumption of
goods and services.

econometrics. The use of statistical and
mathematical methods in the evaluation
and testing of economic theories.

ECU treasury bills. It was as early as
1985 that the UK authorities commenced issuing Treasury Bills denominated in ECUs. These bills are issued
by tender on a monthly rather than a
weekly basis and have a one month,
three months, and six months maturity. Like the UK sterling treasury
bills they are sold at a discount and a
secondary market has developed in
these instruments. *See* TREASURY BILLS.

ECU. *See* EUROPEAN CURRENCY UNIT.

edict. A proclamation or decree issued
by an authority.

edictal, edictal citation (*Sc. Law*). A citation, *see* CITE, by a proclamation when
personal citation is impossible.

effective date. For the purpose of the provisions of utility services to a company, arrangement may be made by the office holder, i.e. the administrator, administrative receiver, the supervisor of a voluntary arrangement or the liquidator, for the giving of gas, electricity, water, etc. The supply will depend on the date (a) the administration order was made (b) the appointment of the administrative receiver (c) the approval by the meetings of the voluntary arrangement (d) the liquidation of the company (e) the appointment of the provisional liquidator. Insolvency Act 1986 s. 233 refers.

effective rate. The yield on an instrument or bond as calculated from the price paid.

effects not cleared. *See* UNCLEARED EFFECTS.

EFTPOS. *See* ELECTRONIC FUNDS TRANSFER AT POINT OF SALE.

elasticity. The ability of a bank to meet its credit and currency demands when necessary and reduce the availability of credit and currency during periods of over expansion and curtailment.

election. The right to choice. The procedure to choose a member of Parliament or local government. The right to accept a negotiable instrument or reject it. Where a plaintiff has to decide whether to sue a person who is a joint defendant, he can only sue one person and not the other.

Electronic Data Interchange (EDI). EDI enables companies to communicate with their suppliers, customers with their banks, by exchanging messages between computers. The messages are standardised so that all computers are compatible. The sender dials and connects to the network and delivers the message which is then sorted and delivered to a centre station for retrieval. This system is speedy, efficient and secure. The major banks are involved as it widens the services offered to customers.

Electronic Data Processing (EDP). The collection, storage, manipulation and retrieval of data by the use of computers. Most procedures in UK banking, consist of fairly simple but repetitive operations which take place millions of times each working day. It is these operations that are essential for the smooth operations in the banking system that allow customers to transmit funds wherever they wish either by cheque, standing order or direct debit; to draw out funds either at another branch or through any ATM, or request the bank to perform any one or more services on their behalf. Data processing is the means whereby the banks internal management and customers services are recorded, stored and processed.

electronic funds transfer at point of sale (EFTPOS). EFTPOS involves the acceptance electronically, at the point of sale of credit/debit/charge card transactions. The transaction data are delivered for settlement, enabling retailers to be credited and the individual cardholders debited, following the delivery of the cardholder transactions to card issuers. Transactions are performed at the retailer's terminal by the cashier 'swiping' the customer's card through the card reader or entering the card details into the terminal using the keyboard. Identification of the cardholder is achieved through verification of the signature. Depending upon the type of terminal or retail system being used, the transaction data are delivered for processing either (a) at the time the transaction takes place, or (b) daily, when a bank or bureau dials up the terminal or (c) when the retailer delivers a tape or transmits the data to a bank or bureau. Processing of the data enables retailers to be credited, individual cardholders to be debited and produces reconciliation and management information for retailers.

eligibility. For a banker's acceptance to be 'eligible' for re-discount at the Bank of England, the bank must meet the following criteria: (i) It must have a broadly based and substantial acceptance business in the UK. (ii) Its acceptance command the finest rates in the market for ineligible bills. (iii) In the case of foreign banks, British banks enjoy reciprocal opportunities in the foreign owners' domestic market. Banks granted eligible status undertake (a) to maintain 5 per cent of eligible liabilities on a secured basis with the members of the London Discount Market Association and/or money brokers and gilt-edged brokers. (*b*) That the proportion with members of the LDMA would not fall below 2 per cent of eligible liabilities on any one day. The banks that are included in this privileged list include not only the clearing banks, merchant banks but members of the Accepting Houses Committee and American, Japanese, Swiss, German and French banks.

eligible bill. A bank bill payable in the United Kingdom and accepted by a recognised bank in the UK whose name appears on the list of eligible banks published by the Bank of England. This bill is eligible for re-discount at the Bank of England. Under present arrangements, the Bank of England controls the level of liquidity in the banking system and influences interest rates through open market operations rather than by lending directly to the discount market. This involves buying and selling eligible bills. To make the market in Treasury Bills and commercial bills large enough to allow interest rates to be influenced, there are about 100 banks who can be described as 'eligible banks'. *See* ELIGIBILITY.

eligible liabilities. A term used to calculate a bank's liquidity. All sterling funds deposited with a bank are used in this calculation, with the exception of deposits that have a maturity of two years or more, but will include any sterling resources gained by switching foreign currencies into sterling. Items in the course of transmission are also included on the following terms. Sixty per cent of promissory notes, bills of exchange, cheques and other negotiable paper less credit items in the course of collection. Interbank transactions and sterling certificate of deposits (held and issued) are taken into consideration irrespective of the term.

embargo. The suspension of trade between one country and another. Goods will not be allowed to leave a country for a specific destination, nor may goods be received from that named country. This will happen when one country is in conflict with another.

embassy documents. Usually invoices and other specified documents that are required by certain countries.

embezzlement. An offence committed by an employee of a business, whereby goods or money is taken by that person for his/her own use.

emoluments. The total monetary payments for work done or services given. The amount of money so given whether it is for fees, salaries, wages, share of profits, etc is chargeable for tax.

employee share ownership plan (ESOP). A policy of public limited companies to either encourage their employees to purchase shares in the company and/or award shares either for long-term loyalty or on a regular basis as part of a profit-sharing bonus.

Employment Protection Act 1975. This Act was intended to improve the relationship between employer and employee and at the same time establish ACAS. The Act was amended in 1978 and consolidated the Redundancy Acts of 1965 and 1969, the Contracts of Employment Act 1972 and the Trade Union and Labour Relations Acts of 1974 and 1976.

encoding. The imprinting of MICR (Magnetic Ink Character Recognition) characters on cheques, credits and other documents to permit them to be processed by computers.

encumbrance. *See* INCUMBRANCE.

endorsement. *See* INDORSEMENT.

endowment mortgage. A person who wishes to purchase a residential property with a mortgage has the option of obtaining the mortgage and covering the debt with a life assurance policy. Once both contracts have been established the person need only pay the interest due on the mortgage and the premiums on the life policy. At maturity of the policy, sufficient funds should be available to pay the outstanding amount on the mortgage, and possibly with bonuses have a surplus. Should the house owner die before the policy matures, the amount available from the policy should repay the outstanding mortgage, thus the widow or widower has a debt-free property. It should be remembered that the interest due to the building society/bank may increase or decrease, but the premium paid to the insurance company will remain the same throughout the life of the policy.

The disadvantage is that should rates increase, then the houseowner cannot extend the length of the loan, on the other hand when interest rates are reduced, he/she may continue if they wish to repay the same amount, thereby very gradually reducing the outstanding capital debt.

endowment policy. A life assurance policy where for a fixed sum of money (the premium) a person may ensure his/her life for a fixed number of years and at maturity is assured of receiving a stated amount plus a profit, if built into the contract and/or bonuses.

enfranchise. The right to vote at an election. The right of a constituency to return a member of Parliament. The conversion of a copyhold into a freehold.

engage. To contract to do something. To be employed.

enquiry (status or bankers). *See* STATUS ENQUIRY.

entailed interest. *See* ESTATE IN FEE TAIL.

enter. To record an entry in an account. To go on to land belonging to another.

enterprise zones. The government aims in setting up enterprise zones were to restore vigorous private-sector activity to certain areas by removing certain tax burdens and by relaxing or speeding up the application of certain statutory or administrative controls. The enterprise zones are not directly connected with other existing policies such as those for inner cities or derelict land. It is intended that the sites chosen would benefit from whatever aid is available under these policies. The size of the individual zones vary from about 120 acres to just over 1100 acres. The first zones were designated between June 1981 and April 1982 and a further 14 were created between July 1983 and April 1984. The benefits are available for a ten year period from the date on which each zone is designated, to both new and existing industrial and commercial enterprises in the zones. The benefits are as follows: (*i*) Exemption from rates/local tax on industrial and commercial property. (*ii*) 100 per cent allowances for corporation and income tax purposes for capital expenditure on industrial and

commercial buildings. (*iii*) Employers are exempt from industrial training levies and from the requirement to supply information to Industrial Training Boards. (*iv*) A greatly simplified planning regime; developments that conform with the published scheme for each zone do not require individual planning permission. (*v*) Those controls remaining in force are administered more speedily. (*vi*) Applications from firms in Enterprise Zones for certain customs facilities are processed as a matter of priority and certain criterial relaxed. (*vii*) Governmental requests for statistical information are reduced.

entrepôt. A bonded warehouse; an intermediate warehouse for goods in transit. *See also* RE-EXPORT.

entrepreneur. A person who takes the risk of business. With the use of his own and other persons capital he will endeavour to buy and sell goods or services and make a profit.

entry. The particulars made in the ledger account of a business. It is good accountancy practice to make a double entry, i.e. a debit in one account and a credit in another. *See also* DOUBLE ENTRY BOOKKEEPING; SINGLE ENTRY.

Equal Opportunity Act. An Act passed in 1975 to promote equality between men and women and to cover any discrimination based on race, colour, religion and age.

Equal Pay Act 1970. An Act that provides that where men and women are doing work of a similar nature under the same conditions of employment, then women and men should receive equal pay.

equalising the dividend. Where there were insufficient profits to maintain the dividend, then the transfer from reserves is permitted for this purpose.

equilibrium price. 1. When the supply of a commodity matches the demand. 2. When the price of a product produces the maximum profitability.

Equipment Leasing Association. The growth of the business of leasing led to the formation in 1971 of the Equipment Leasing Association, whose aims are to represent to the authorities the views of its members on any proposed or actual legislation which may affect the leasing industry to increase awareness of leasing and its role in helping the economic development of the country, and because leasing in the United kingdom is closely linked to the system of taxation, to keep taxation and monetary policy under special and continuous review. Currently there are about seventy members of this association.

equitable. In accordance with the rules of equity. Fair and just.

equitable assignment. *See* ASSIGNMENT.

equitable charge. *See* EQUITABLE MORTGAGE.

equitable doctrine. A legal principle originating from equity as an alternative from common law.

equitable estate or interest. An estate or charge over land which is not a legal estate and the owner has an interest or right to the estate (Law of Property Act 1925 s. 1(3)).

equitable interest. An interest in law which is not dependent on common law but on the principles of equity.

equitable lien. A lien which comes into being when property is transferred to a buyer before he has made payment. The seller is entitled to the purchase money which may be enforceable by a sale by the courts.

equitable mortgage. A mortgage given when the deeds may be in the possession of the lender, but ownership stays with the borrower.

equity. 1. A system of doctrine and laws which developed with common law and statute law and is administered in the Chancery Division of the courts. 2. Fair, just. 3. The issued capital of a company (*See* ORDINARY SHARES). In banking, it is used to show the value of the property held as collateral and the claim that could be made against it.

equity of a company. *See* ORDINARY SHARES.

equity of redemption. When a mortgage has been created, the mortgagor has a legal right to redeem his/her estate on the date of redemption and an equitable right to redeem when the amount outstanding is for less than the value of the property, providing the amount due is repaid. It also gives the right to the mortgagee to sell the property after default and due notice has been given. Any surplus funds are not allowed to be kept by the mortgagee.

equity share. The right of the holder of these shares to participate in the distribution of the profits, i.e. the ordinary class shareholder.

Equivalent Discount Yield. This compares the true discount on a Treasury Bill or other bill that can be discounted, with the actual yield. For example, a £100 000 Treasury Bill (90 days) with a yield of 10 per cent, discounted at a figure of £97 500 would yield.

$$\frac{2500}{97\,500} \times \frac{365}{90} = 10.40 \text{ per cent}$$

ergonomics. The study of the relationship between a worker's abilities and the work done, with the objective of suiting the worker to the work.

escalation clause. A clause in a contract, usually one for a major project which can take a number of years to complete. As inflation makes it difficult to ascertain the costs throughout the construction period, an escalation clause is inserted which permits the overall price to be increased to allow for the additional labour and material costs.

error. A mistake in a calculation. A discrepancy in the value or condition of an item. An amount shown on a statement, invoice, commercial document or books of account which is not correct.

errors and omissions excepted. This is inserted on an invoice or statement so that if the document contains an error or there is some omission, then a revised invoice or statement could be issued.

escrow. A deed or bond given to an independent third party, for retention until certain conditions have been performed, after which they are delivered and become absolute.

ESOP. *See* EMPLOYEE SHARE OWNERSHIP PLAN.

estate. 1. In land law, the rights of ownership and possession of property. 2. The assets of a person, frequently used when a person is deceased. 3. Referred to in the Capital Transfer Act 1984 s. 5 as 'the aggregate of all the property to which he is beneficially entitled, except that the estate of a person immediately before his death does not include excluded property. When the value of an estate is determined for

Inheritance Tax purposes, then liabilities must be taken into account to determine the tax liability'.

estate agent. An entity that arranges the purchase and sale of houses and other property.

estate contract. A contract made by an estate owner or a person authorised to contract on his/her behalf to convey or create a legal estate. This means that a contract for the sale of a lease for a term of years absolute or to renew a lease. Estate contracts are registrable as land charges in the sub-division C(IV). *See also* LAND CHARGES; LAND CHARGES REGISTER.

estate duty. *See* INHERITANCE TAX.

estate for life. An estate where land is limited to a tenant for his or her own lifetime, or for the lifetime of another person (*pur autre vie*).

estate in fee simple. *See* FEE SIMPLE ABSOLUTE IN POSSESSION.

estate in fee tail. Also known as estate tain or entailed interest. It is the continuation of an estate while the tenant is living or a descendant of the tenant still survives. The right of interest is restricted to that class of heir mentioned in the gift.

estate owner. The legal owner of the land (Law of Property Act 1925 s. 205(1).

estate tail. *See* ESTATE IN FEE TAIL.

estimate. An assessment of a cost or price. The estimate given is not binding but can form part of a contract.

estoppel. The rule of a court which prohibits a person from denying the truth of a statement made or in facts which has induced others to believe. The person making the statement, or acting in a particular manner, must accept the consequences of his/her action.

estovers. The rights of a lessee to obtain timber from an estate for fuel, repairs and the necessaries of life.

et al. Et alii, aliae, alia: and others.

Eurobonds. The Eurobond complements the market in Eurodollars (*see* EUROCURRENCY), out of which it developed, by making longer-term funds available. Most bonds are payable to bearer and all are paid without deduction of tax. They are generally issued by consortia of banks and issuing houses, and are designated in dollars, deutschmarks and some other European currencies, being placed with such investors as nationalised industries, governments, multinational corporations and municipal authorities. A secondary market in the bonds has developed in London and Luxembourg. This market is a supranational market and is not subject to the normal domestic regulation, but is affected by international events.

Eurocard. A credit card issued by the European arm of the Mastercard organisation. It has no direct links at present with the Uniform Eurocheque Scheme. (*See* EUROCHEQUE SCHEME.)

Eurocheque Scheme. A means of accessing one's domestic bank account while travelling in European countries and others bordering the Mediterranean. Eurocheques and the accompanying eurocheque guarantee card differ from the account holder's everyday domestic instruments, but are of standard appearance throughout all 22 issuing countries and banks. Eurocheques are encashed in local currency (or in a specified hard currency where the indigenous currency is weak) and the guarantee limit is loosely linked to Swiss francs 300 (350 in France and Italy), £100 in the UK. Eurocheques are encashed in almost all bank brances – more than 200 000 – in the specified areas and in many countries retail acceptance is strong; many guarantee cards are encoded for ATM usage in 20 000 machines in 14 countries. Eurocheques are cleared by a streamlined pan-European system which functions much like the UK domestic system; when the cheque domiciled to a bank in the UK they are converted into sterling at the current rate of exchange and debited normally with a small commission/handling charge, to the drawer's account.

Euroclear. International clearing system for the settlement of transactions in securities, essentially Eurobonds. It is based in Brussels and is provided under contract by Morgan Guaranty for over a hundred banks which own it.

Eurocurrency. The word 'Eurocurrency' is a misnomer. The prefix 'Euro' merely indicates that this market had its origins in Europe. It is a market, mainly in US dollars, therefore it is sometimes referred to as the Eurodollar market. The currency, is borrowed and lent by institutions outside the country of origin, so that it is quite possible for a merchant in Belgium to borrow US dollars from a financial institution in Germany. In theory, there is no national control over this market, it is market forces that dictate the lending rates, but in practice the rates do not tend to diverge from domestic lending rates other than for very short periods. The main operators in this market are international banks, but other large financial institutions are able to enter the market. Since the market had its origins in London, London is the centre for the Eurodollar market.

Eurodollars. *See* EUROCURRENCY.

European Bank for Reconstruction and Development. The European Bank, with its headquarters in London, was established in May 1990 and inaugurated in April 1991.

It is the first international financial institution of the post-Cold War period. Its purpose is to foster the transition towards open market oriented economies and to promote private and entrepreneurial initiative in the countries of Central and Eastern Europe (Bulgaria, the Czech and Slovak Federal Republic, Hungary, Poland, Romania, the USSR and Yugoslavia). The European Bank will endeavour to help the economies of these countries integrate into the international economy, with particular concern for strengthening democratic institutions, respect for human rights and for environmentally sound policies.

As the Bank develops it intends to become a centre for the accumulation and exchange of knowledge on specific problems of the countries of the region and on the problems of transition to a market economy. It also intends to play a significant role in the co-ordination of projects for these countries.

The Bank has 41 members (39 countries and 2 institutions – the EC and the EIB). Its membership spans all of Europe, the United States, Japan and other countries. Membership is open to European countries as well as non-European countries which

are members of the International Monetary Fund.

The initial subscribed capital is 10 billion ECU, of which 30 per cent will be paid in five equal annual instalments, commencing in 1991. The Bank will also borrow in various currencies on world capital markets.

In fulfilling its purpose, the Bank performs a wide range of functions designed to assist countries with operations to implement structural and sectoral economic reforms, including demonopolisation, decentralisation and privatisation.

It merges the principles and practices of development and merchant banking. It lends for specific projects and investment programmes and co-finances with multilateral institutions, commercial banks and other lenders. Joint ventures will be used as one method of mobilising domestic and foreign capital as well as experienced management. It will also invest in the equity capital of private and state-owned enterprises and facilitate access to domestic and international capital by underwriting securities offerings and providing guarantees, financial advice and other forms of assistance.

The powers of the European Bank are vested in a Board of Governors. Each member appoints one Governor and one Alternate to be represented on the Board of Governors. The Board of Governors has delegated powers to a Board of Directors comprising 23 members, that will hold office for a term of three years. The Board of Directors is in charge of the strategy of the European Bank, including the approval of its budget and of its general operations. The President is elected by the Board of Governors for a term of four years. Vice-Presidents are appointed by the Board of Governors on the recommendation of the President.

The European Bank has the following departments: merchant banking, development banking, finance, personnel and administration, project evaluation, secretary general, chief economist, general counsel, political unit, communications and press, internal audit.

European Banking Federation. An organisation comprising professional banking associations from each member state, attaining within the sphere of banking the European aims laid down by the Treaty of Rome. To this end, the Banking Federation maintains relations with the Commission of the EC, the Economic and Social Committee, the European Parliament and the Council of Ministers of the Community. It seeks to contribute to community policy making and by putting forward the opinion of the banks on any question which directly or indirectly affects their activities. An annual report is published, specifying the topics that have been dealt with in that year. For example, the 1988 and 1989 reports dealt with Consumer Protection in the Financial Services, Banking and Financial Markets Legislation and Relations with Third World Countries. Other matters, such as takeovers and bids, capital adequacy, reciprocity, money laundering, etc., were also reported.

European Currency Unit (ECU). The origins of this monetary unit is to be found in the establishment of the European Monetary System. The value of the ECU is arrived at by a complicated formula, based on a fixed amount of each member country's currency, weighted in proportions reflecting its economic importance to the European Community.

Currency	Amounts	Weight (%)
Belgian franc	3.431	8.1
German mark	0.6242	30.4
Dutch guilder	0.2198	9.5
Danish krone	0.1976	2.5
French franc	1.332	19.3
Italian lira	151.8	9.9
Irish pound	0.008552	1.1
Spanish peso	6.885	5.2
Greek drachma	1.44	0.07
Portuguese escudo	1.393	0.08
British pound	0.878	12.6

The importance of the ECU is growing as it now serves as a means of settlement between central banks, banks, merchants, etc. A number of governments including the British government have recently issued debts in ECUs. There are plans to develop the ECU even further so that by the end of the century it is likely to be the single European currency. *See also* HARD ECU.

European Economic Community. Now known as the European Community. *See* COMMON MARKET.

European Free Trade Association (EFTA). An economic association formed in 1960s with the object of achieving an area of free trade by the reduction of tariff barriers between members. Out of the original members that formed EFTA, UK, Denmark and Portugal have left and are now members of the EC and Austria and Sweden are liekly to follow. EFTA is now looking to establish a closer relationship with the EC but if it is unsuccessful in this, the association may disintegrate.

European Investment Bank (EIB). The EIB was formed in 1958 with its headquarters in Luxembourg and has an office in London. It is administered by a Board of Governors which consists of a Minister (usually the Finance Minister) of each member country, that lays down general directives on credit policy, approves the balance sheet and annual report, decides on capital increases and appoints directors and members of the management and audit committees. The Board of Directors consists of 22 members. Twenty-one are nominated by the member countries who are usually senior officials from banks, the public sector and industry, and one by the Commission of the European Communities. There are 11 Alternates nominated by the member countries and one by the Commission. The Board ensures that the Bank is managed according to the provisions of the Treaty of Rome, the EIB's Statute and general directives from the Governors. The Board has overall responsibility for deciding on loans and guarantees, the raising of funds and setting interest rates. The main executive body responsible for the day-to-day running of the bank is the management committee which consists of the bank's president and six vice-presidents. It recommends decisions to the directors and then ensures they are carried out. The European Investment Bank makes loans or guarantees for a wide range of projects across all economic sectors. The pattern of lending is not tied to any predetermined geographical or sectoral quota but depends on demand, the viability of the projects put forward and their consistency with the Community's policies. Almost all the funds necessary to finance its lending operations are raised by borrowing on capital markets, mainly through public bond issues. It is one of the world's principal supranational borrowers and Moody's and Standard & Poor's, the two leading credit rating agencies, have consistently given the Bank their highest rating (AAA). EIB bonds are quoted on the world's major stock exchanges. As the EIB works without a profit objective, its interest rates, for each currency, follows closely the cost of borrowing on capital markets, taking into account a 0.15 per cent margin to cover operational costs. It thus makes the benefits of its 'AAA' standing available to project promoters. The bank's rates do not vary according to the type of project financed, its location or the status of the borrower. The EIB provides any tailor-made financing arrangements in a single currency, or a combination of currencies, to suit the needs of project promoters. While its traditional product is fixed rate loans, adjustable fixed-rate and variable-rate loans are also available. Maturities range between 4–20 or more years with repayment of principal and interest normally in equal six-monthly instalments. Depending on the borrower's preferences and the EIB's holdings, loans are disbursed in a single currency, such as the ECU, or the borrower's own currency, or in a mix of several currencies. The EIB does not charge commitment, management or other fees. Loans are disbursed at par.

European Monetary System (EMS). The EMS was formed in March 1979 with the specific purpose of stabilising members' currencies, ultimately with the objectives to bring about a convergence of financial and economic policies among member states. In effect, it has created an EC currency in the form of the ECU which is not only a unit of account, but is now a medium of exchange. It is used as a denomina-

tor for the exchange rate mechanism which has the intention of maintaining exchange rates within given margins. Most countries have a margin of 2¼ per cent either side of parity, while the UK and Spain has a margin of 6 per cent either side of parity. When a country has reached 75 per cent of the limit on its margin, intervention must take place in order to conform to the limits imposed. Should any country find that the central rate is unsustainable, then a readjustment must be made by agreement with other member countries. While considerable progress has been made for the convergence of financial and economic policies among member states, it has not yet achieved the final success, its aims are (a) that the movement of capital will be free of controls for all member states and (b) there will be a single market within the EC, which to all intents and purposes is already in place.

European Unit of Account (EUA). Dating from the mid-1970s, the EUA was similar to the Special Drawing Right in that it was calculated as a 'basket' of currencies, but by reference to the various currencies of the member states of the European Economic Community only. As it was based on floating rates it had itself a floating value. *See* SPECIAL DRAWING RIGHTS.

Eurotrack 200. The Eurotrack index was launched in February 1991, and combines the FT-SE 100 index of British shares with the Eurotrack 100 index of the continental markets. The 200 index is a continuous computerised real-time index changing each minute and in line with individual price movements. It will be denominated in European Currency Units. The main purpose of the index is to mirror as far as possible the monthly benchmark indices of the European markets, thereby providing a base for derivative options, futures and warrants business for managers of international portfolios.

evidence. The production of facts and/or documents which clearly demonstrate the truth on the point in issue. Contracts are often unenforceable unless evidenced in writing, e.g. Guarantees. Evidence can be: 1. conclusive –

share certificate, certificate of incorporation; 2. circumstantial – facts that can be ascertained by the conduct of the person.

ex-. Former, out of or from, without.

examination of title. The checking of a person's claim to be the owner of a valuable asset, particularly in a bank, in connection with security. Whereas in some cases the mere production of the certificate or evidence of ownership is enough (as in the case of stock exchange security where an equitable charge is to be taken), in others a more searching check is made (as in the case of land). In this last case the examination of title is done by a solicitor, whether the land is unregistered or registered. Because the bank may need to sell the land, if the advance is not repaid, it must be sure that it has a good title to offer a possible purchaser, this in turn depends upon the title of its borrowing customer. *See* LAND CERTIFICATE (for registered land); *PRIMA FACIE* CHECK OF DOCUMENTS.

excepted perils. Terms used in contracts of carriage, whereby the carrier is not liable for loss or damage to goods due to acts of God, perils of the sea, war, theft, collisions, etc.

excess. A surplus. An amount by which assets are greater than liabilities. Surplus funds.

excess clause. A clause commonly used now in policies of insurance, whereby the insured bears the first stated amount of any loss.

exchange. A reciprocal transfer of one item for another. A place where business transactions take place or a market for persons eligible to participate usually by telephone or some electronic device, e.g. Stock Exchange, Foreign Exchange Market, etc.

exchange arbitrage. A situation whereby dealers can gain a profit from a temporary difference between two currencies in terms of a third currency.

exchange as per indorsement. A clause placed on the reverse side of a bill of exchange by the drawer of the bill which states that the drawee pays an amount in his/her own currency which will be equivalent of the sterling amount of the bill. The banker negotiating the bill must ensure that the correct rate of exchange is used to ensure that the drawer receives the face value of the bill.

exchange broker. A person whose function is to marry buyers and sellers particularly in the foreign exchange market. For this function he/she is entitled to a commission.

exchange clause. A clause written on the reverse side of a foreign bill of exchange, but drawn in sterling, indicating the rate of exchange to be used, or by whom the charges are payable, or any interest that may have to be charged to the drawee. It is used in certain geographical areas to ensure that the UK drawer receives the sterling amount owing to him without any deductions for commissions, expenses or loss due to fluctuations in the rate of exchange.

exchange commission. An amount charged for the purchase/sale of foreign currency.

exchange control. A legal control imposed by government on the ability of persons, business entities and others to hold, receive and transfer foreign currency. The reason for this imposition is owing to the fact that the country has scarce supplies of currencies of other countries and in consequence needs to control and conserve the use of foreign currencies through the central bank. By so doing, the importation of goods is restricted to those that are considered essential to the economy of the country and export trade is encouraged, even though the exporter on receipt of foreign currency must surrender it to the banking authorities. While it is usual for the central bank to operate the exchange control in accordance with the directives of government, it would delegate some of its powers to the commercial banks in such matters as the limited issue of foreign currency and travellers cheques to persons going abroad for a holiday, or to business persons on a short trip abroad. Should any person require additional sums of foreign currency or travellers cheques, then the request must be submitted to the central bank for their approval. Similarly, banks may approve, up to a stated amount, the payment for imports, but any additional sum, must be approved by the central bank. In this situation, it would be quite normal to refuse permission for the purchase of any foreign stocks and shares or for the purchase of property in another country without permission. The holding of foreign stocks, shares and property purchased before the imposition of an exchange control regulation must be registered with the authorities, so that the authorities may if they consider it necessary, demand the sale of these assets and also compulsorily purchase the foreign dividends, rent and interest received. Foreign residents in the country would not be able to receive funds from citizens of the country without permission but would be entitled to receive funds from abroad without restriction and pay their living expenses in the country and remit funds abroad without seeking bank approval. The UK abolished exchange control in 1979, so that UK citizens may now receive and transfer foreign currency without restriction, hold assets abroad, purchase, sell and hold gold without requiring any form of approval from the authorities in the UK.

exchange equalisation account. An account held at the Bank of England for the Treasury that contains the country's foreign currency and gold reserves. This account is used to stabilise the value of sterling against other international currencies, so that if the Bank considers that sterling is drifting too low, it will buy sterling with funds from the account, or if sterling is becoming expensive it will sell sterling and receive foreign currency and replenish the account.

exchange gain. A profit made due to a fluctuation in the rate of exchange, for example should a UK importer buy goods in dollars from the USA at a rate of $1.50 = £1 and the rate increases to $1.75 = £1 then it will cost less in sterling terms, an additional profit has been made.

exchange loss. A loss made should the pound sterling become cheaper, e.g. an importer buys goods in US dollars when the rate is $1.75 = £1, then before payment the rate changes to $1.50 = £1 he must then pay more and consequently suffer an exchange loss.

exchange rate. The price of one currency in terms of another. It is usual in the UK to quote the exchange rate against pound sterling, e.g. £1 = number of currency units.

exchange rate mechanism (ERM). Calculated in terms of a weighted average of all EMS currencies, including sterling.

exchange rates. *See* PARITIES.

exchequer. That government department which is responsible for receiving all national revenues and distributes funds to various departments and authorities.

excise duty. A tax levied on goods produced in the United Kingdom.

exclusion clause. A clause which excludes or modifies a contract that would otherwise be part of that contract by the implication of law. Under the Unfair Contract Terms Act 1977, liability for loss or damage cannot be excluded by reason that the goods or service fails to satisfy a test of reasonableness. Liability for loss or damage due to negligent manufacture cannot be excluded or restricted.

ex coupon. Bonds sold without the benefit of the next instalment of interest to be paid.

ex curia. Out of court.

ex div. Shares sold without the benefit of the current dividend shortly to be paid.

ex drawing. Bonds sold without any benefit there may be from a drawing for repayment due to be made.

executed. Some deed or action which has been done. The signing of a document by all the parties.

executed agreement. This means a document, signed by or on behalf of the parties, embodying the terms of a regulated agreement, or such of them as have been reduced to writing.

executed contract. The performance by one party of his/her part of a contract.

execution creditor. The person in whose favour a writ of execution has been issued.

execution debtor. The person ordered by the court to pay money into that court by order of a writ of execution.

executive. A person or a group of persons responsible for the affairs of a company, club, or some official body, e.g. departments of state, local authorities.

executor. A person appointed under a will to carry out the wishes of the testator. He/she will marshall the assets, pay any outstanding debts and distribute the remainder of the estate to the named beneficiaries.

executor and trustee department/company. In many banks and financial institutions, there will be either a subsidiary or a department dealing with matters relating to personal representatives or trustees. They will agree to carry out the duties of an executor, e.g. obtain probate, pay capital transfer tax, funeral expenses, etc. and generally conform to the wishes of the testator. Should the bank take over the function of an executor, the will must make some provision for this fact, so that the estate may be charged with any fees and expenses. They will when required act as trustees and act for the beneficiaries of the estate.

executor de son tort. A person who without authority intermeddles in the estate of a deceased person.

executor's year. The period, usually one year from the death of the deceased which is considered sufficient for the executor to complete the administration of the deceased estate.

executory contract. One in which all the duties set out in the contract remain to be performed in the future.

exemplary damages. Damages imposed by the court as a punishment of the defendant rather than compensating the plaintiff.

exemplification. An attested copy of any proceedings in a court of record.

exemplification of probate. Should the original document be lost then a duplicate copy can be made available by the court.

exemplify. To show by illustration, act as an example, to prove by an authenticated copy.

exempt agreement. Under the Consumer Credit Act 1974, it is an agreement that is not a regulated agreement as specified under s. 16.

exemption clauses. Clauses in an agreement which seeks to exempt the parties from liability due to negligence, non-compliance, loss, damage, etc. Such clauses will appear in banking documents, for example, in response to status enquiries. Clauses will appear in Uniform Rules for Collection, Article 4 and Uniform Customs and Practice for Documentary Credits, Articles 17, 18 and 19 which forms the basis of agreement between banker and their customers. Such clauses must pass the reasonable test under s. 11 of the Unfair Contract Terms Act and in Schedule 2 of that Act.

exercise notice. In a traded option it is a formal notice to LOCH that the holder of a call/put option wishes to buy/sell the security at the exercise price.

exercise price. The price at which the holder of a put/call option may buy/sell the security.

ex facie. Manifestly, on the face of it.

ex gratia. As a favour (not as a legal right).

exigible. Due for payment.

ex officio By virtue of office, official.

exoneration. Under circumstances where there are funds in the estate of the deceased, it is quite possible that some or all beneficiaries may or may not be able to receive their entitlement. Should this happen, then as stated in the Administration of Estates Act 1925, creditors should be satisfied in full; however, where the testator has indicated that a special fund should be established for payment of debts 'in exoneration of all other funds', then the proceeds of the special fund will be taken first. Again a testator may instruct that a fund is set up 'in exoneration' of the legacies, which might be subject to Capital Transfer Tax.

ex parte. On one side only, one-sided.

expectant heir. A person who has a vested interest in the remainder of the property.

expectation of life. The mathematical assessment made by an insurance company of the possible length of life of a person. It is impossible to state how long a person is likely to live, but tables prepared by actuaries, can show in broad detail how long groups of persons are likely to live and the premiums of life assurance are based on these tables.

expenses. 1. Money spent in the day-to-day operations of a business entity. 2. A payment of money. 3. For tax purposes, a legitimate amount that may be deducted from income before tax is charged. 4. An amount chargeable to profits.

expiry date. The date of maturity of a bill of exchange, a letter of credit, the latest date an option can be exercised.

export. The despatch of goods abroad. *See* INVISIBLE EXPORTS.

export agent. A person or entity that arranges a contract on behalf of his/her principal, to provide goods or services to a foreign importer.

Export Credits Guarantee Department (ECGD). This government department is better known by its initials, ECGD. Its basic service is to provide insurance to exporters to cover non-payment by buyers and government actions that restrict the transfer of funds to the exporter. The most basic of policies is the comprehensive short-term policy that covers not only the insolvency of the buyer, but the buyer's failure to pay within six months and government action that prevents or restricts payment. It covers credit given by the exporter up to a period of six months and is usually for goods of a repetitive nature. For credit given above six months, then a comprehensive supplemental policy of specific policy may be required. For the longer-term export import contract, non-recourse finance is available to the exporter, by requesting ECGD to give a guarantee to his bankers, arranging buyer finance or finance to an overseas financial institution. In order to keep premiums as low as possible, ECGD would like the exporter to insure all his exports, whether they are high risk or low risk. For the specific project, then ECGD would prefer to be advised at the earliest moment so that they can assess both buyer risk and country risk.

Exporters' Yearbook. A source of information of documentary requirements for different countries.

export factoring. *See* FACTORING. As well as covering all the services offered in the domestic market, export factoring offers the following: 1. Clients may invoice their customers in local currency. 2. Exchange risks are covered. 3. Collection of funds from abroad are credited to the client's account in sterling. 4. Any collection or language problems are dealt with by the factor

local correspondent. *See also* ASSOCIATION OF BRITISH FACTORS; BRITISH EXPORT HOUSES ASSOCIATION.

export finance companies. These companies specialise in providing finance frequently on a non-recourse basis for specific projects and manufactured goods. They may require the exporter to take out an ECGD policy or for such a policy to be assigned to themselves as a form of security. The clearing banks, merchant banks and foreign banks may have such companies as subsidiaries or departments dealing in such matters, as the current policy of banks is to offer their customers 'financial packages' and assist them in all their undertakings, without discouraging them to seek their services for 'one off' orders.

export houses. These organisations provide three basic services: 1. They will act as a principal and buy goods from a UK manufacturer and sell them abroad, thereby relieving the UK seller of international risks. 2. Act as an agent for a UK manufacturer. The export house obtains orders, then when goods are produced pays the seller and obtains reimbursement from the buyer. This can be non-recourse finance for the seller. 3. Act as a confirming house, that is the company confirms orders received from a buyer for whom he acts as an agent.

exposure draft. A document issued when some form of legislation or rule is proposed. It is circulated to interested parties for comment and criticism. When all such comments have been received and reviewed the final draft is then prepared.

express trust. A trust created as the result of a settlor's express intention.

ex quay. Goods to be taken under the control of the purchaser as soon as they have been landed.

ex ship. A price quoted for goods on arrival at the port, not including costs of unloading and delivery to the premises of the purchaser.

extended credit. The act of giving the purchaser additional time to pay. This may be under a credit card agreement, or a hire purchase agreement or simply a bank loan or overdraft.

extension. To prolong the life of a contract or financial instrument. For example, a documentary credit can be extended subject to the agreement of the parties. The agreement that a loan or overdraft can be paid off at an agreed later date. The extension of the maturity date on a negotiable instrument.

external account. Sterling accounts of non-resident customers maintained by banks in this country.

external audit. An audit carried out on a business organisation by auditors who are not employed by them and are independent of the managers and directors of the organisation.

external convertibility. While a currency may be subject to some convertibility for residents, it will have complete convertiblity between foreign holders of that currency.

external debt. The amount of debt owed by one country to another.

external loan. A public loan raised from sources abroad.

extraordinary general meeting. Abbreviated as EGM. A general meeting of shareholders which is not the annual general meeting, but one which has been called to discuss particular issues. Such meetings may be called in accordance with the Articles of Association or consititution and only those with voting rights may attend and vote.

extraordinary item. An item or an amount which is or should be stated on a financial statement to draw the attention of the readers. Such an item is reported because its source is outside the normal trading activities of the entity and may be material to the facts disclosed even though it may be a non-recurring factor.

extraordinary resolution. A resolution which has been passed by three-quarters or more votes cast at a meeting of members of which due notice has been given to propose the resolution.

ex **warehouse.** The price to be paid if the purchaser collects the goods personally from the warehouse in which they are stored.

ex **works.** The price to be paid if the purchaser collects the goods personally from the factory.

F

face value. The value of a share certificate or other security as shown on the front or face of the document. The nominal value of any article including coins, banknotes, etc.

facility. In banking this is referred to as an arrangement between banker and customer for the use of a banking service, e.g. documentary collections, documentary credits, etc. Alternatively, it is an understanding that overdraft and loans are available, if required, up to a given amount. In general usage, this means a fluency, an absence of difficulty, easy access.

facility letter. A confirmation from a bank to its customer agreeing to an advance and stating the amount, terms of repayment, interest to be charged and other conditions. Under the Consumer Credit Act 1974, any monies lent under a regulated agreement must be advised to the borrower as specified in the Act.

facsimile. *See* FAX.

facsimile signature. The signature as shown on a rubber stamp. This is frequently used on cheques. The practice is frowned upon by banks unless an indemnity has been given to the bank to cover any irregularity or misuse of the stamp.

factor. An agent who has authority from his principal to buy and sell goods on his behalf. These goods are consigned to the factor and deals with them in his own name (Factors Act 1889). This can also refer to a company that will purchase the book debts of a trading organisation. *See* FACTORING.

factorage. The commission paid to a factor by an employer.

factor cost. The price of goods paid by the consumer, less any tax or duty included in the price.

factoring. The service provided by a financial institution for a trading company for the purchase of its invoices. The advantages of a trading company to factor its debts are as follows: the company will at regular intervals receive the outstanding debts from the factor, as good money. The factor will be responsible for bad debts, so the company need make no provision for bad debts. The factor takes care of sales ledger accounting. Credit control is in the hands of the factor. The company can concentrate on its main activities, production and selling. The factor also has the advantage of receiving a commission for services rendered. Factors have intelligence departments, or use the facilities of their bank holding company, to ensure that there is adequate credit control. By having a large number of clients, the acounting costs are kept low by the utilisation of computers and the economies of scale. Any early payments by debtors, may be placed on the short-term money market, with other funds, to give the factor additional income. Factors will only deal with organisations that are likely to have a turnover above £250 000, but there are factors who will deal with much smaller turnovers. *See also* EXPORT FACTORING; INVOICE DISCOUNTING; RECOURSE FACTORING.

factory cost. Any expense that can be attributed to the cost of producing as opposed to administrative, selling, distributive, financial costs.

fail to deliver. Where a client of a broker has agreed to sell securities, fails to deliver the appropriate certificate/s, the broker in his turn, cannot deliver to the broker/dealer. Consequently the seller will not be paid until delivery has been made. *See* FAIL TO RECEIVE.

fail to receive. A situation where a broker/dealer has agreed to sell securities to a client, has not received those securities from the broker/

dealer who engaged to sell them to him, is unlikely to receive payment from his buyer.

failure. Cessation, deficiency, omission, non-performance, non-occurence, breaking-down; insolvency, suspense of payment, bankruptcy or liquidation.

fair comment. This is a defence for an action for defamation and providing the defendant could show that whatever words were used were stated honestly and without malice, then the alleged defamation could be considered as fair comment.

fair rent. Where a tenant and his landlord cannot agree on what is a fair rent, then the rent officer may decide the issue. Should neither party agree with the rent officer, then the matter may be taken to a rent tribunal for a decision. That decision is final (Rent Act 1947 and 1977).

fair trading. Under the Fair Trading Act 1973, should a firm not give an assurance to the Director of Fair Trading that a practice that is unfair to consumers will cease, then proceedings can be made against the firm in the Restrictive Practices Court.

fair wear and tear. Normal depreciation of an asset over a period, not covered by insurance.

fait accompli. An accomplished fact.

fallen angel. In financial terms this means a company that has had a down-grading.

false accounting. An offence under the Theft Act 1968 s. 1: 'Whereby a person dishonestly, with a view to gain for himself or another or with intent to cause loss to another; (*a*) destroys, defaces, conceals or falsifies any account or any record of document made or required for any accounting purpose; or (*b*) in furnishing information for any purpose produces or makes use of any account, or any such record or document as aforesaid, which to his knowledge is or may be misleading, false or deceptive in a material particular'.

false pretences. This relates to an offence of obtaining property by deception under the Theft Act 1968. In banking such acts refer to goods being purchased with cheques that the drawer knows or should know will not be met by the bank owing to lack of funds. Attempting to obtain a loan or overdraft by trickery, or otherwise obtaining goods or services by pretence or misrepresentation.

family protection policy. *See* MORTGAGE PROTECTION POLICY.

Fannie Mae. *See* FEDERAL NATIONAL MORTGAGE ASSOCIATION.

farmer. As defined in the Agricultural Credits Act a farmer is: 'A person (not being an unincorporated company or society) who, as tenant or owner of an agricultural holding, cultivates the holding for profit, and "agriculture" and cultivation shall be deemed to include horticulture, and the use of land for any purpose of husbandry, inclusive of the keeping or breeding of livestock, poultry, or bees and the growth of fruit, vegetables and the like.' A firm of partners is within the definition, but a limited company, incorporated under the Companies Acts, or a society is not.

farming. Carrying on activities appropriate to land recognisable as farm land. It must include the raising of beasts, the cultivation of land and the growing of crops.

farm land. Land in the UK wholly or mainly occupied for the purposes of husbandry, excluding a dwelling or domestic office and market garden land. Income and Corporation Taxes Act 1970.

FAS. *See* FREE ALONGSIDE SHIP.

fate. The decision whether a cheque or other negotiable instrument when on presentation will be either accepted or paid.

faux pas. A tactless remark or action.

favourable trade balance. A situation which indicates that the value of the country's exports exceeds the country's imports.

favourable variance. A variance which results in increased profits.

fax. A means of transmitting documents, plans, instructions, information, etc. by use of the telephone system. The person wishing to remit a message will simply dial the recipient's number, which providing it is not engaged, will be able to receive the document despatched. The document will be fed through a machine which will simultaneously copy and remit the data, and on receipt an acknowledgment will be signalled. The whole operation will take a matter of seconds. Should the recipient's machine run out of paper, then a memory will carry the message which will then be converted on to paper when the roll has been refilled.

feasibility study. An enquiry into whether a particular project is capable of being done, or is practical, or will be profitable. Such a study may be performed by a bank as a preliminary to seeking a new market, extending its branch structure, introducing a new service, embarking upon a new training system, etc.

Federal Funds. This term traditionally refers to the balances that depository institutions maintain on the books of the Federal Reserve Banks; these funds are considered finally collected and immediately available. There is a broad Federal Funds market in the United States, as depository institutions with excess reserves will sell those funds to institutions requiring reserves. Federal Funds are sold on an overnight (or weekend) basis or for a longer term, referred to as term funds. Federal Funds or Fed Funds which are immediately available differ from Clearing House Funds which are regarded as funds with next-day availability.

federal home loan banks. Created in 1932, the twelve federal home loan banks provide credit on a secured basis and other services to their savings and loan members and certain other institutions involved in home financing. Members must hold stock in their regional bank. The federal home loan banks finance their lending activities through the joint issuance of notes and debt securities.

Federal Housing Administration (FHA). FHA is a division of the Department of Housing and Urban Development, whose function is the insurance of residential mortgage loans made by private lenders.

Federal National Mortgage Association ('FNMA or Fannie Mae'). Fannie Mae is a private corporation sponsored by the United States Government to provide funds for housing. It provides assistance to the secondary market for home mortgages through the purchase of mortgages and the issuance or guarantee of various debt instruments secured by mortgage loans.

Federal Open Market Committee ('FOMC'). This committee meets eleven times a year at the offices of the Board of Governors of the Federal Reserve System and is responsible for the formulation and implementation of the monetary policy in the United States. The FOMC is composed of the seven Governors of the Board and five Federal Reserve Bank Presidents. The Chairman of the Board of Governors serves as Chairman of the FOMC; the president of the Federal Reserve Bank of New York serves as Vice-Chairman. While all 12 Reserve Bank presidents attend FOMC meetings, the presidents of the other eleven Reserve Banks serve in rotation. The Committee has a staff selected from the staffs of the Board of Governors and the Reserve Banks. At its regular meetings the FOMC issues directives to the managers of the domestic and foreign desks at the Federal Reserve Bank of New York who are responsible for carrying out on a daily basis the Committee's instructions. The domestic desk carries out its operations through the purchase or sale of United States Government and Federal agency securities. The Chairman of the Board of Governors reports to the Congress twice a year on the monetary and credit targets set by FOMC; this is referred to as the 'Humphrey Hawkins' report.

Federal Reserve Banks. The twelve Federal Reserve Banks and their branches are privately owned instrumentalities of the United States and are the operational and supervisory arm of the Federal Reserve System. Each Reserve Bank is supervised by the Board of Governors, controlled by a nine-member board of directors, and managed on a day-to-day basis by its president and first vice-president. The directors establish a discount rate at least once every 14 days; these rates are not effective until approved by the Board of Governors. The Bank hold reserves, provide payments services, and provide discount window credit. The staffs of the Reserve Banks also carry out bank supervision for the Board of Governors. These banks also carry out a number of activities on behalf of the United States Treasury, including the conduct of auctions for government securities, as well as the issuance and redemption of such securities.

Federal Reserve System. In the United States, the central bank was designed in 1913 as a system with both central and regional features. The system is now composed of the seven-member Board of Governors of the Federal Reserve System, an independent agency, located in Washington, DC, the twelve Federal Reserve Banks, the Federal Open Market Committee, and the Federal Advisory Council, a group of individuals that meets periodically to advise the Board of Governors. Similar to other central banks and monetary authorities around the world, the system has the following responsibilities: 1. to develop and implement monetary policy, 2. to set and hold the reserves of depository institutions, 3. to furnish currency, 4. to provide payments services to depository institutions, 5. to serve as bank and fiscal agent for the United States Government, 6. to supervise and regulate State member banks, foreign banks with banking offices in the United States, and bank holding companies, and 7. to extend credit to depository institutions and on rare occasions to others (called the 'discount window') and to set the interest rate for that credit (called the 'discount rate'). The three major tools of monetary policy are the purchase and sale of government securities, the discount rate, and the reserve requirement rate.

Fedwire. An electronic payments system linking the 12 Federal Reserve Banks and their branches with depository institutions and others. Fedwire handles wire transfers of funds, delivery of United States Government and certain other securities against payment, and automated clearing house payments. Most depository institutions in the United States, including foreign banks, and a number of central banks and international organisations have access to Fedwire.

fee. An amount paid in return for a service. The indication in land that it can be inherited.

feedbank. The information received or retrieved from a computer or some system or procedure, to enable persons to evaluate the data or performance.

fee farm rent. In some parts of the UK it is customary for a purchaser of a fee simple to enter into a covenant to pay a perpetual annual rentcharge, often called a fee farm rent or a chief rent, instead of paying a lump sum for the purchase. The vendor retains a right of re-entry in the case that the annual payment falls into arrears.

fee simple absolute in possession. The word 'fee' originally meant the granting of a benefit – usually land – to a man and his heirs in exchange for services rendered i.e. the land is capable of being inherited. The word simple merely indicates that the estate could pass to any heir and not just a particular class of heir. 'Absolute possession' indicates that the person who inherits the land does so without conditions or restrictions, and is therefore entitled to receive any profits or rents from the land.

fee tail. *See* ESTATE IN FEE TAIL.

fellow. A person who is a senior member of a professional organisation, university, etc. A person may be elected as a Fellow in the Chartered Institute of Bankers, for his/her contribution to bank education. With other professional bodies, this can be by examination, or practised in the profession for a specified number of years.

feme sole. An unmarried woman, a spinster, a widow, a wife economically independent of her husband.

fiat. A formal demand, an authoritative order; the order or warrant of a judge or other constituted authority sanctioning or allowing certain processes.

fiat money. Paper money made legal tender by governmental decreee.

fiction. Something feigned, invented or imagined. *See also* LEGAL FICTION.

fictitious asset. An item that appears on a balance sheet, but could not be sold. It is usually written out of the balance sheet as soon as possible.

fictitious payee. A payee named in a bill of exchange that does not exist, or the person named in the bill was never intended to have value. Section 7(3) Bills of Exchange Act 1882 states: 'Where the payee is a fictitious or non-existing person, the bill may be treated as payable to bearer'. A fictitious or non-existent person cannot indorse, and therefore any indorsement must be a forgery.

fidelity guarantee insurance. An insurance policy taken out by an employer in case of misappropriation by an employee.

fiduciary. Holding or held in trust.

fiduciary capacity. The capacity descriptive of a trustee.

fiduciary issue. The issue of notes by the Bank of England which has no backing of gold or silver. The public has confidence in the notes that they will be able to purchase goods and services up to the amount stated on the note. The backing of the total fiduciary issue is by government stock.

fiduciary loan. A loan or advance made without the borrower giving any security.

fiduciary relationship. A relationship based on trust, where there is such a relationship, e.g. guardian and ward, then undue influence can be presumed, therefore a high degree of care must be maintained.

fief. An estate formerly held on condition of military service.

field. A section of a computer record on which designated information is stored. It can also be a specific space on a document for encoding details, for example, on a cheque, an amount field is available for a computer operator to encode the amount of the cheque, before it proceeds through branch accountancy system and onward to the paying branch-bank.

fieri facias (fi. fa.). A writ which may be issued on behalf of a judgment creditor, whereby the sheriff is authorised to seize goods of the debtor in satisfaction of a debt.

file. 1. A term used in the Consumer Credit Act 1974, to refer to information retained by a credit reference agency on an individual; 2. an organised method of storing documents; 3. a bundle of documents, letters, etc., recording the correspondence between the firm and its customer/supplier. A folder/binder, box used to keep information. A name given to a particular set of records. Personnel file, computer file, sales file, etc.

filing of accounts. The submission of the accounts of a company to the Reg-

istrar of Companies as required by the Companies Act 1985.

FIMBRA. *See* FINANCIAL INTERMEDIARIES', MANAGERS' AND BROKERS' ASSOCIATION.

final accounts. The statements drawn up at the end of a financial period. These are the Trading, Profit and Loss Accounts, which will show the gross and net profit and the appropriation of the profit or in the case of a club or non-profit-making organisation, the income and expenditure, which will show either a deficit or surplus for the period involved. A balance sheet which shows the capital, liabilities, fixed and current assets. Finally, a statement of the sources and application of funds is normally produced.

final dividend. The dividend paid at the end of the financial year, when an interim dividend has been paid.

finance. The resources available to an entity. Money set aside for a particular purpose. The management of funds used in a project.

Finance Act. That annual act of parliament which imposes the income tax and corporation tax and amends any tax law that might be in existence.

finance bill. A bill put before parliament to approve the amendment of the taxes and on being passed will become the Finance Act. A bill of exchange, often known as an accommodation bill for the purpose of one company giving finance to another.

finance house. A company that finances the purchase of consumer goods, and industrial equipment. This it does by means of hire purchase agreements, credit sales agreements and leasing. *See also* HIRE PURCHASE; CREDIT SALE AGREEMENT; LEASING.

Finance Houses Association. While the major finance houses are owned by the large banks, 47 of these companies are members of the Finance Houses Association, which represents 90 per cent of all finance house business.

finance lease. A leasing contract providing for the lessee to pay the rental for a minimum non-cancellable period of time (the primary period) which suffices in total to amortise the lessor's capital outlay, incurred in the purchase of the asset which is to be leased. These rentals commonly include also an element of interest. The lessee always assumes the liability to maintain the equipment: a service agreement may be offered by the suppliers of the equipment. Where the asset is not fully amortised during the hire period, the lease is called an 'operating lease' or a 'rental contract'. Here the lessor aims to engage one customer, or a series of customers, for a sufficient number of consecutive rental periods to achieve the desired return. Also known as a 'full payout lease'. *See also* LEASING.

finances. The income of a state or person, resources, funds.

financial accounting. The recording of financial transactions in monetary values in books of account and at regular intervals. The accounts are balances and financial statements showing profits/losses and the state of affairs of the organisation in monetary values.

financial document. A document which has a monetary value and can be used in obtaining goods and services, e.g. cheques, bills of exchange, etc.

financial futures. *See* LONDON INTERNATIONAL FINANCIAL FUTURES EXCHANGE.

financial institution. An institution that accepts deposits from the public and places those funds in the money market, and gives advances to the public. These institutions include the various banks, pension funds, unit trusts, building societies, insurance companies, etc. and are either recognised by an Act of Parliament, e.g. Banking Act 1987, or are regulated by a self-regulating organisation.

Financial Intermediaries', Managers' and Brokers' Association (FIMBRA). A self-regulating organisation (SRO) under the Financial Services Act 1986, set up with the purpose of monitoring the activities of its members, providing regulations and standards for its members, and providing adequate investor protection.

financial intermediary. Any organisation that accepts funds from one party and passes these funds to another, making their profit by an interest rate margin. In broad detail they redistribute funds from those that have surplus savings and wish to earn a rate of interest on these balances and provide funds that need short- or long-term finance and are willing to pay interest on the funds borrowed.

financial market. A market, not necessarily with a physical presence, where money is either bought and sold or borrowed and lent. They may deal in financial instruments, e.g. Certificates of Deposit, Treasury Bills, or book entries, e.g. Foreign Exchange Market.

financial savings ratio. That proportion of personal disposable income that flows into financial assets.

Financial Services Act 1986. Until this Act was passed, financial services in the UK were regulated either by a number of government acts or by codes of practice set up by bodies such as the Stock Exchange. It became clear that current measures to protect investors needed reform and additionally, with 'Big Bang' and the internationalisation of markets, some restructuring was necessary. Professor Gower was commissioned to examine the protection that was available for investors. His paper was published in 1984 and from this the government produced a White Paper 'Financial Services in the United Kingdom; a New Framework for Investor Protection'. This paper recommended that a new body should be established to be responsible for overseeing the self regulating bodies and the investment business and markets in which they operate. After due discussion and amendments in Parliament, the Act was passed and phased in throughout 1987/8. The Act primarily dealt with the protection of the investor through the structure of self regulating bodies. Under the Act it is a criminal offence to conduct an investment business without proper authority and those who may deal in investments have to meet stated criteria before authority is granted. The rules of any self regulating body must include not only a compensation fund, and adequate protection for clients' money, but such matters as advertising, conflict of interests within a firm or company, 'cold calling' on persons etc. The Act also defines security instruments such as shares, debentures, stocks, option warrants, unit trusts, futures contracts and some long term insurance contracts. Negotiable instruments are not included, nor are building society accounts, property documents and non-life insurance documents. It should be noted that the investment risk still is with the investor. Should the value of the shares of a company go down, that is the investor's risk. The Act has established the Securities and Investment Board (SIB) which will oversee the whole operation. Although accountable to the Secretary of State for Trade and Industry, it will be financed by the financial services industry itself. Self Regulating Organisations (SROs) will be set up to regulate the activities of its members and provide regulations and standards on dealing with the public. With the need to regulate business on the various exchanges, Recognised Investment Exchanges (RIEs) have been set up so that there is an orderly and regulated market, adequate procedures for recording transactions, clearing arrangements and adequate financial resources.

financial statement. Any statement by a business entity, whether it is a sole trader, partnership or company, listing the capital, assets and liabilities of the organisation. The larger and more comprehensive organisation will have to conform to current legislation as well as having the accounts certified by qualified accountants. The financial statement should show the 'net worth' of the business and is an historical statement.

financial supermarket. A name given to describe the major banks in the UK. Since they are able to provide any financial service to small and large businesses and individuals no matter what the requirements are, they have been compared with supermarkets. It can be seen that a bank may have an interest in: insurance services, travel service, income tax, investment, executor trustee, international trade, estate agency, travel, etc.

Financial Times Actuaries Indices. Equity indices calculated daily and covering 30 sectors of the Stock Market, aggregated in the 500 Index and the All-share Index. There are also gilt and fixed-interest indices. Introduced in April 1987, the world index covers about 24 countries subdivided into geographical areas, with each quoted in sterling, US dollars and local currency. Of the 2400 or so companies,

most are in the USA, Japan and the UK.

Financial Times 30 Index (FT Index). An index of price changes measured hourly, of industrial ordinary shares on the London Stock Exchange, based on thirty publicly quoted companies chosen to represent a wide range of British industry, which in the aggregate form a significant proportion of total equity capitalisation. The index is based on a figure of 100, fixed on 1 July 1935, which acts as a reference point, and is no more than a calculation of the percentage deviation from that point in time.

Financial Times Stock Exchange 100 Index (FTSE). An index of the 100 largest companies' shares, updated every minute throughout the working day. It is an arithmetic average and is weighted according to market capitalisation – representing about 70 per cent of total. Base date is 3 January 1984 at 1000. Commonly known as 'FOOTSIE'.

financial year. The period between the balance sheet date (usually twelve months) and the next balance sheet date) Companies Act 1985 s. 227 and s. 742(1)(c). For company tax purposes the period is from 1 April to 31 March the following year. (Income and Corporation Taxes Act 1970 s. 527), but for fiscal purposes it is from 6 April to 5 April the following year.

fine bank bill. Often referred to as a prime bank bill. This bill is defined as a bill drawn by or accepted by an eligible bank. *See* ELIGIBLE BILL.

fine rate. A very competitive rate charged on the discounting of a fine bank bill or Treasury Bill. This can also refer to a rate of interest charged to a customer of good standing.

fire insurance. A contract of indemnity by which an insurance company undertakes to make good any damage or loss by fire to buildings or property during a specified time.

fire policy. A policy guaranteeing compensation up to a stated limit in case of damage by fire.

firm. A noun describing persons who are trading as partners as defined by the Partnership Act 1890. In popular terms this may describe any business entity. Solid, steady, reliable, secure.

firm name. The name, other than those of the partners, by which a partnership for trading purposes is known.

firm offer. A definite offer to purchase specified property at a stated price.

first class bill. *See* FINE BANK BILL.

first cost. The cost of production in money terms.

first in, first out (FIFO). A method of accounting for stock. It is assumed that the goods are withdrawn from stock in chronological order, i.e. the first goods deposited are the first goods withdrawn.

first mortgage. A mortgage on a property which is not subject to any prior mortgage.

first of exchange. Where it is customary for a bill of exchange to be issued in a set, i.e. two or three original copies, then each copy states as follows: 'Pay this first of exchange, second/third unpaid', or 'pay this second of exchange, first and third unpaid'. *See* BILLS IN SET.

fiscal. Pertaining to the public treasury or revenue.

fiscal drag. The increase in taxes due to inflation and not necessarily to a change in the tax rates.

fiscal policy. The use of taxation in the Budget as a weapon of monetary policy.

fiscal year. The tax year or years of assessment in the UK, ending on 5 April.

fishing expedition. A practice by bank customers making two or more status enquiries in order to find out the financial standing of another person/firm. Banks should not respond to more than one enquiry from the same source unless they have positive proof that it is for genuine business transactions.

fixed. Made firm, made permanent, established, secure, determined.

fixed asset. Any asset of a business which has been purchased for retention and continuing use in the business (Companies Act 1985 Sch. 4). Fixed assets may be divided into the following groups: 1. Intangible; patents, goodwill, trade marks, etc. 2. Tangible; land and buildings, plant and machinery, office equipment, etc. 3. Investment; shares and loans to other companies.

fixed capital. *See* FIXED ASSET.

fixed charge. A regular charge on the profits, e.g. interest on a debenture, interest on a long-term loan, rent. Often described as a fixed cost.

fixed cost. Any cost that does not vary with sales or production.

fixed debenture. A debenture charged on the fixed assets of a company, such as land.

fixed deposit. A deposit which is repayable at a fixed future date. The interest paid may be fixed for short periods, i.e. up to one year, but may be variable if over a longer period. Any early withdrawal may be subject to a penalty.

fixed exchange rate. A set rate of exchange agreed between two or more countries. That rate will not change unless an agreement is agreed between parties. Such a system was adopted after the Bretton Woods conference in 1944. It has now been abolished.

fixed future foreign exchange contract. A legal binding contract to purchase/sell a stated amount of currency at a fixed rate of exchange on a specific date.

fixed loan. A loan where one of the conditions is that it shall be repaid on a future specific date. It is not unusual for the interest rate for the period to be fixed as well.

fixed rate contract. *See* HIRE-PURCHASE AGREEMENT.

fixed-sum credit. For the purposes of the Consumer Credit Act 1974, a facility which is not a running-account credit, but which enables the debtor to receive credit (e.g. a loan).

fixed trust. A unit trust whose trust deed provides for a set list of security holdings for spreading risk over a period ten to twenty years, with severe restrictions on the ability of the management to vary the investments.

fixings. *See* LONDON GOLD MARKET.

fixtures. An item (chattel) that is considered part of the land or building to which it is fixed. It will pass automatically when ownership of the estate is transferred.

flat market. A market which has a very slow activity and its turnover is also very low.

flat (or running) yield. The annual return derived from the interest or dividend on an investment, divided by the price and multiplied by 100.

flexible budget. A budget that can be altered according to the amount of activity in the particular budget centre.

flexible trust. The trust deed of a unit trust that will give discretion to the managers of the trust to vary the holdings.

float 1. An amount of notes and coins that a cashier is likely to have in his till. 2. The amount of money a retailer has at the commencement of his days' business. 3. A sum of money retained in a Petty Cash Account. 4. The setting up of a trading company, i.e. to float a company. 5. A political policy to allow a country's currency to find its own level in the foreign exchange market.

floater. A debt instrument deposited with banks and other financial institutions to secure overnight or call-money lending.

floating asset. Another name for current or circulating or liquid asset. *See* LIQUID ASSET.

floating charge. A charge given over assets of a company but allows the chargee to use the assets as he thinks fit. However, if the lender appoints a licensed insolvency practitioner, then the charge is 'crystallised', and will then for all practical purposes be fixed from the day the practitioner was appointed.

floating currency. *See* FLOATING RATE.

floating debenture. *See* FLOATING CHARGE.

floating debt. A debt that is continuously renewed usually on a short-term basis.

floating money. Money in the hands of bankers and others at a time of excessive liquidity, for which no profitable use can quickly be found.

floating mortgage. *See* FLOATING CHARGE.

floating policy. A marine policy covering goods which may be widely spread over a district or area, or in whatever ship they may be.

floating population. Shifting population whose movements are controlled by the fluctuating demand for labour, especially in sea-ports or industrial areas.

floating pound. The pound sterling left to find its own level on the foreign exchanges through the operation of the laws of supply and demand.

floating rate. A rate of interest charged on a loan or overdraft whereby the lending banker and borrower agree that the rate of interest may be altered as agreed in the loan agreement.

floating rate bond. A bond issued in the money markets which is linked to the rate of interest of the money market (usually LIBOR) and will be changed periodically as interest rates change. *See* FLOATING RATE NOTES.

floating rate notes. These are securities issued in the Euromarket where the interest rate is *floating* rather than fixed. Usually the rate is set at about ½ per cent above six months' LIBOR with a stipulated minimum interest, e.g. 5½ per cent. The rate is adjusted at six-monthly intervals.

floor limit. The maximum amount that can be withdrawn out in cash from an Automatic Teller Machine. The amount authorised in any financial transaction.

floor trader. A member of a commodity exchange, e.g. LIFFE, who trades in the pit or on the floor of that exchange, either for his own account or the company that employs him/her. He/she must abide by the rules of the exchange.

flotation. The act of launching a commercial enterprise, especially a limited liability company; the launching of a new capital issue.

flow chart. A presentation in graphic form showing the procedure to be taken, its link with other procedures and the date of its completion.

fluctuation. The rise and fall in the value of a commodity, e.g. stocks and shares, money, etc. The rise and fall in the economy.

fluctuation limit. A limit imposed in a commodity exchange to avoid any dealer from losing too much money on dealing. If a commodity should reach its upper or lower limit, then trading for the day may be stopped.

FOB. *See* FREE ON BOARD.

folio. A page number in a book or ledger; the number of words (seventy-two or ninety) taken as a unit in computing the total number of words in a document; a page of manuscript.

FOOTSIE. *See* FINANCIAL TIMES STOCK EXCHANGE 100 INDEX.

forecast. A written or spoken prediction of future events. Financial budgets, production budgets, sales budgets, etc.

are essential for all businesses and often required to accompany a borrowing proposition. These forecasts are based on the strengths and weaknesses of the business, costing and selling policies, and general economic conditions.

foreclose. The right of redemption of a mortgage. To deprive a person of the use of the property.

foreclosure. A procedure whereby a mortgagee obtains the property of the mortgagor who has in some way breached the agreement, e.g. failure to pay the interest. An order to foreclose must be given by the court.

foreclosure order. Having applied to the courts for an order for foreclosure, the court will if necessary, issue an order for foreclosure *nisi*, which requests the mortgagor to pay the amount due by a certain date (usually six months) otherwise he/she will lose the property. The order is made absolute and the fee simple absolute is vested in the mortgagee and extinguishes the mortgage.

foreign. A place, a territory which is not governed by domestic law, but the law of another country. Alien.

foreign banks. The collective description given to banks, authorised by the Banking Act 1987, to open offices in the UK, accept deposits and offer banking services. The head office of these banks is in their own country.

foreign bill. The Bills of Exchange Act 1882 s. 4 merely states that 'an inland bill is one' which is or on the face of it purports to be (*a*) both drawn and payable within the British Isles or (*b*) drawn within the British Isles upon some person resident therein. Any other bill is a foreign bill'. Consequently any bill payable abroad, or drawn and payable abroad is a foreign bill. Section 4 of the Act states: 'unless the contrary appear on the face of the bill, the holder may treat it as an inland bill'. For the purposes of the Act the British Isles means any part of the United Kingdom of Great Britain and Ireland and the Channel Isles.

foreign bill for collection. See BILL FOR COLLECTION.

foreign bill for negotiation. See BILL FOR NEGOTIATION.

foreign bond. A security issued by a borrower in the national capital market of another country.

foreign currency. The money of any foreign country.

foreign currency account. A customer account maintained in a bank which is in the currency of a foreign country. The accounts of a UK bank which they have abroad for the purpose of giving services to their customers. These are usually called '*Nostro Accounts*'.

foreign currency securities. Funds invested in companies abroad, therefore interest and dividend warrants are drawn in local currency.

foreign draft. A bankers' cheque or draft drawn on a branch or correspondent abroad, usually in the currency of that country. A bill of exchange payable abroad.

foreign exchange. In general terms this refers to the exchange of one currency for another. In banking a foreign exchange department may deal with the receipt and transmission of funds to and from countries abroad. The purchase and sale of spot and forward deals in foreign currency. The exchange of foreign currency notes by cashiers.

foreign exchange broker. A firm operating in the foreign exchange market, with the approval of the Bank of England, for the purpose of marrying up buyers and sellers of foreign exchange. The market dealers will be banks, government departments, and other major institutions.

foreign exchange risk. Often referred to as exchange risk. This is a risk taken when there is a need to buy or sell foreign currency. Should the exchange rate move against the buyer/ seller of the currency, a loss could very easily be incurred. To avoid such risks, a fixed or forward option contract can be obtained from a bank.

foreign items. Bills of Exchange, cheques, drafts, other negotiable instruments with or without commercial documents attached to be sent abroad for collection or payment.

foreign trade. The importing and exporting of goods and services between different countries.

FOREX. The abbreviation for foreign exchange or foreign exchange market.

forfaiting. The purchase by a bank of medium and long-term bills of exchange which have been accepted by the drawee, usually guaranteed by the drawee's bank without recourse to the seller/drawer.

forfeiture. A punishment depriving the offender of his property.

forfeiture of shares. When a shareholder fails to pay the amount due on a call on the partly paid shares in his/her name, then a resolution of the directors under the company's Articles of Association, may after due warning and time, declare the shares forfeit.

forged banknotes. Copies of banknotes put into circulation other than by the proper authorities. The illegal circulation of counterfeit money.

forged indorsement. The forgery of an indorsement, does not *per se* invalidate a bill of exchange, but when it forms part of a chain of title, then the person who receives the bill from a forger has no real title. However, where a bill is payable to bearer, therefore needs no indorsement, then it may be ignored.

forged share transfer. When a bank accepts a share certificate with a stock transfer form for purposes of a legal charge, then the bank must satisfy itself that the person who is the transferor has been properly identified. The registrar of the company looks to the bank to guarantee the genuineness of the signature on the form. Any forgery will be at the expense of the bank.

forged signature. A forged signature on a cheque or any negotiable instrument is wholly inoperative. Bills of Exchange Act 1882 s. 4 states: 'Subject to the provisions of this Act, where a signature on a bill is forged or placed thereon without the authority of the person whose signature it purports to be, the forged or unauthorised signature is wholly inoperative, and no right to retain the bill or to give a discharge therefor, or to enforce payment thereof against any party thereto can be acquired through or under that signature, unless the party against whom it is sought to retain or enforce payment of the bill is precluded from setting up the forgery or want of authority. Providing that nothing in this section shall affect the ratification of an unauthorised signature not amounting to a

forgery. It should be mentioned that a drawer of a cheque who has facilitated forgery by his/her negligence would in some way be responsible to the paying banker.

forgery. The production of a false instrument, bill or note with a purpose of inducing another to accept it as genuine, to that person's detriment and the giver's advantage.

formal protest. *See* PROTEST.

formation expenses. *See* PRELIMINARY EXPENSES.

for the account. A Stock Exchange phrase referring to transactions which are to be settled or paid for on the next account day or settling day.

forward. Onward in time; to promote, to re-address, to send out or despatch (of goods). *See also* CARRIAGE FORWARD.

forward contract. The purchase/sale of a specific commodity, security, foreign currency or any other financial instrument for delivery and payment at some future date.

forward discount. The difference between the forward and spot rates in the foreign exchange market. A currency quoted at a forward discount will be cheaper. *See* MARGIN.

forward exchange. The purchase/sale of foreign currency at some future specified date (Fixed Forward Contract) or between two specified dates (Option Forward Contract).

forwarding. Despatching merchandise sending goods forward.

forwarding agent. An agent who undertakes the collection, forwarding, documentation and delivery of goods.

forwarding note. A note giving the description of goods, etc., and the name and address of the consignee, which is transmitted with the goods.

forward premium. The difference in the foreign exchange market. A currency quoted at a forward premium will be dearer. *See* MARGIN.

forward rate. The rate quoted for the purchase/sale of foreign currency on a forward foreign exchange contract. *See also* FORWARD DISCOUNT; FORWARD PREMIUM; OPTION FORWARD RATE; SWAP.

founders' shares. *See* DEFERRED SHARES.

franchise. The right to vote in a national or local election. That amount of the insured goods that the insured is expected to cover him/herself. An agreement between a retail outlet and a major distributor of goods or services that the retailer will only sell the goods of the distributor who will be responsible for the quality of the goods, national marketing and advertising etc. Franchising arrangements may be found in clothing stores, restaurants, hotels, etc. Due to the expansion of this method of retailing, many banks have franchising departments.

franchisee. A person or entity who has been granted a franchise.

franchisor. The person or entity granting the franchise.

franco. Free of expense.

frank. To send or cause to be sent under an official privilege; the right to send letters through the post free of charge; the letter thus sent.

franked income. Revenue on which a tax has been paid and which therefore is free of liability to that tax in the hands of the recipient.

franked investment income. An income of a UK company which has had the tax deducted at source and therefore the company is entitled to a tax credit. However, should such income be distributed as a dividend, then the company does not have to pay advance corporation tax, as tax has already been deducted.

franking machine. A machine which stamps or franks envelopes with a symbol indicating that the postage has been paid.

fraud. A deception or an act either by stating what is false or by suppression of the truth in order to deceive another, gain an advantage over another. The Theft Act 1968, makes a fraudulent act a criminal offence to gain a monetary advantage by such methods.

fraudulent. Practising fraud, intended to deceive; in bankruptcy, having the intention to defeat or delay creditors.

fraudulent conveyance. The disposal of property made with the intention of defrauding creditors. A court may declare such a transfer as void. Under the Insolvency Act 1986 s. 357(1): 'The bankrupt is guilty of an offence if he makes or causes to be made, or has in

the period of 5 years ending with the commencement of the bankruptcy made or caused to be made, any gift or transfer of, or any charge on, his property. . . . (3) The bankrupt is guilty of an offence if he conceals or removes, or has at any time before the commencement of the bankruptcy concealed or removed, any part of his property after or within 2 months before, the date on which a judgment or order for the payment of money has been obtained against him, being a judgment or order which was not satisfied before the commencement of the bankruptcy'.

fraudulent misrepresentation. A deceitful act. An act or statement made recklessly, without caring whether it is false or true. Making a statement knowing it to be false. The intention in all cases is that the person shall act, to his/her detriment, on such information. On discovering such misrepresentation the person may rescind the contract.

fraudulent preference. A transfer of money, property or chattels made by a person to another (a creditor) with the aim of giving that creditor preferential treatment. The Insolvency Act 1986 s. 40: 'Where an individual is adjudged bankrupt and he has at a relevant time given a preference to any person, the trustee of the bankrupt's estate may apply to the court for an order under this section. The court shall, on such application, make such order as it thinks fit for restoring the position to what it would have been if that individual had not given that preference. An individual gives a preference to a person if (a) that person is one of the individual's creditors or a surety or guarantor for any of his debts or other liabilities and (b) the individual does anything or suffers anything to be done which (in either case) has the effect of putting that person into a position which, in the event of the individual's bankruptcy, will be better than the position he would have been in if that thing had not been done'.

fraudulent settlement. 1. A settlement made before and in consideration of marriage where the settlor is not at the time of making the settlement able to pay all his or her debts without the aid of the property comprised in the settlement; or 2. any covenant or contract made in consideration of marriage for the future settlement on, or for, the settlor's wife or children of any money or property wherein he had not at the date of his marriage any estate or interest. If the settlor is adjudged bankrupt, or compounds or arranges with creditors, the court may refuse or suspend an order of discharge or refuse to approve a composition or arrangement, if it thinks the transaction was done in order to defeat creditors or was not justifiable, having regard to the state of the debtor's affairs, at the time when it was made.

fraudulent trading. Insolvency Act 1986 s. 213. 1. If in the course of winding-up of a company it appears that any business of the company has been carried on with intent to defraud creditors of the company or creditors of any other person, or for any fraudulent purpose, the following has effect; 2. the court, on the application of the liquidator may declare that any persons who were knowingly parties to the carrying on of the business in the manner above mentioned are to be liable to make such contributions (if any) to the company's assets as the court thinks proper.

free. Not under restraint, not subject to restrictions, duties, etc.; gratutitous, liberal.

free alongside ship (FAS). An INCOTERM indicating that the seller must deliver the goods to the quay or alongside the ocean-going vessel and from this point, the buyer must make arrangements that the goods are taken from the quayside or the barge alongside the vessel, accept all the risks and pay all expenses.

free capital. That part of the capital of a bank or financial institution that would in other types of companies be called the working capital.

free carrier (FCR). An INCOTERM whereby the seller is responsible for the expenses and delivery of the goods to the carrier's depot, and the buyer from that point is responsible for making the arrangements, paying the freight and other costs for delivery of the goods to the destination.

freehold. A term used to denote a legal estate that can be held in perpetuity.

freeholder. The possessor of a freehold estate.

freehold estate. Legally known as an estate in fee simple absolute in possession. In more general terms it is the best type of ownership that a person may have. *See* ESTATE IN FEE SIMPLE; FEE.

free market. A market where persons may buy or sell goods without any cumbersome procedure and supply and demand is the only influence on the price.

free movement. A phrase referred to in the Treaty of Rome, setting up the EEC, and concerning the movement of persons, capital, goods and services.

free of particular average. A clause in a marine insurance policy meaning that claims for particular average cannot be recovered.

free of tax. *See* TAX FREE.

free on board (FOB). An INCOTERM indicating that the seller must load the goods on board the vessel and the buyer accepts the risks, payment of freight once the goods have cleared the ship's rail.

free on rail (FOR). An INCOTERM which indicates that the seller must deliver the goods to the railway depot or siding, place the goods on board a railway wagon. From that point, all risks and costs are for the buyer.

free on truck (FOT). The same liabilities and obligations as in 'free on rail', except the goods go by road and are placed on board a lorry or truck.

free port. A port where ships of all nations may load or unload free of duty.

free ship. A neutral ship, free from liability to capture.

free trade. The policy of unrestricted international trade; the free interchange of commodities without protective tariffs.

freight. The cost of carriage of goods. The goods being transported. The amount paid for hire of all or part of the vessel.

freight car. A railway car used for goods.

freight collect/freight payable at destination. A note or allonge placed on a document of movement, e.g. a bill of lading indicating that payment of freight will be paid for at the destination.

freight forward. The term to indicate that freight on goods is payable at the port of destination.

freight indemnity. A guarantee given by a trading company or its bankers to a shipping company for the payment of freight charges. This is likely to occur when a major company wishes to pay the charges due on a monthly basis, so the shipping company is willing to accept this form of payment subject to the receipt of a guarantee.

freight note. A shipping document specifying the freight charges for a particular cargo.

freight paid. A note either stamped, typed or written on the face of a bill of lading stating that the freight has been paid.

friendly society. A society registered with the Chief Registrar of Friendly Societies under the Friendly Societies Act 1974 and 1981. The objectives of this form of society is to provide benefits for sickness, old age, death, those in need, particularly widows and orphans.

fringe benefit. A benefit given to an employee in addition to a wage or salary. This may include non contributory pensions, private health arrangements, subsidised meals, cars, etc.

front-end finance. A loan made by a UK bank to an overseas buyer to assist him to pay the UK exporter. This type of loan is usually for the large 'one off' type of contract and is frequently covered by a guarantee of the Export Credits Guarantee Department. In these circumstances, it is usual for the buyer to give a deposit of 20 per cent of the purchase price and the remainder borrowed from the bank.

front-end loading. Any loan where from its commencement of the total interest, plus any other charges due is added on to the amount borrowed and the borrower makes periodic payments to cover the whole amount due.

front running This occurs when persons deal in the market, knowing that a large transaction will take place in the near future and that prices are likely to move in their favour.

frozen assets/balances. Funds that are held in banks and other financial institutions which due to government directives or a court order may not be transferred. This happens when one country is in conflict with another, funds held cannot be withdrawn.

frustration of contract. Where an event or circumstances, completely unforeseen, makes it impossible for the contract to be completed, then the contract is frustrated. Funds paid are recoverable and funds due for payment do not have to be paid. Such events as sickness, war, third party interference, legislation will have the effect of frustrating a contract.

full accounts. The Companies Act 1985 s. 239 requires that companies should produce statements relating to profit and loss account or income and expenditure account, the balance sheet, the directors' report, the auditors' report. Should a company have a subsidiary or subsidiaries, then it is obliged to prepare their accounts and the group accounts. For small or medium size companies, modified accounts may be produced if permission is granted by the Registrar of Companies.

full disclosure. The necessity to disclose all material facts that are relevant to a contract.

fully-paid shares. The amount paid for the share capital is equal to the value of the nominal capital issued. Any premium paid for the share should be ignored. Where shares are issued by instalment, once all the instalments have been paid, then the capital is fully paid.

functional. Having a special purpose, pertaining to a duty or office.

fund. A sum of money set aside for a particular purpose. Financial resources or working capital. To fund, to provide or lend money.

fund flow forecast. A statement covering a period of up to a year, showing the possible future receipts and expenditure of funds, usually on a monthly basis, estimating the balance of cash available at the end of each month.

fund flow statement. Often referred to as a statement of Sources and Application of Funds. *See* SOURCES AND APPLICATION OF FUNDS STATEMENT.

funded debenture interest. A payment of the interest due by issuing a further debenture instead of a payment of cash.

funded debt. Government stock which has no maturity date, and therefore will only be repaid when it is considered necessary by the government.

funding. The refinancing of a debt before maturity. Setting aside funds into a reserve account to provide finance for a future expense. Used when a company issues a debenture to fund its operations. Setting aside money for a future project.

fungibles. Any item, e.g. negotiable instruments, goods that are interchangeable with each other. They can be valued against each other.

future goods. Goods to be manufactured or acquired by the seller after the making of the contract of sale.

futures. Commodities that are traded for delivery at a future time.

futures contract. A contract to buy/sell a specific amount of a named commodity or financial paper at an agreed price on a given future date. The method of obtaining a price is usually in open outcry in the market place or commodity exchange.

futures market. A market or commodity exchange where futures contracts are traded. *See* LONDON INTERNATIONAL FINANCIAL FUTURES EXCHANGE (LIFFE).

G

gage. Something given as security against a loan. A pledge.

gain. The increase of resources, due to profitable trading. Where income is greater than expenditure.

garnishee. A person to whom a garnishee order has been addressed. The court has instructed that person (a bank) that funds must be held, so that payment may be made to a third party who is owed a debt.

garnishee order. An order from the court to a garnishee, advising them that the funds that they hold for a third party, the judgment debtor, should be held to the order of the court. The garnishee (bank) must not dispose of any funds. It attaches all accounts. Where the bank holds one account in credit and another account in an overdraft position, then the net credit balance must be attached. Should the situation arise that the net position is an overdraft, then with nothing to attach, the court must be advised of the situation with the consequence that the order will be withdrawn. When the balance has been attached the funds are placed on a suspense account with the bank. The customer can continue his normal business. Later, the garnishee or his solicitor must appear in court to state any reason why the funds should not be taken to satisfy the debt due to the judgment creditor. Should the judgment debtor wish to enter a defence he may do so, but should this fail and the order is made absolute then the garnishee must pay either the creditor or the court the amount due, plus any costs, if the balances held are sufficient to cover these. Building society accounts as well as bank accounts are also subject to this remedy.

garnishee summons. The same procedure as a garnishee order, except that the summons is from a county court.

gazette. *See* LONDON GAZETTE.

gazumping. A colloquial term used where a person has agreed to sell his property 'subject to contract'. The buyer agrees the price, but before contracts can be exchanged, the seller finds another buyer willing to pay a higher price which he then accepts leaving the first buyer to continue his search for a suitable property. It is a term to describe a state of indifference by the seller who has failed to keep his word.

gearing. The proportional relationship in any accounting period between the shareholders funds and the total of the long-term debts. The greater the proportion of borrowed capital the higher the gearing. Whether it is acceptable for a company to be highly geared or low geared depends on its trading ability and economic circumstances. The payment of fixed interest due to lenders is a charge to profits, so that while a company is utilising its borrowed funds efficiently and trading profitably, it may increase its profits and possibly pay an increased dividend to its shareholders. It would then be useful to be high geared. However, during times of recession and lower profits, it could be that the interest due on long-term loans utilises any profits and therefore no dividends may necessarily be paid during this period. A low-geared ratio would then be essential.

general agent. An agent employed to conduct a particular trade or business, having implied or ostensible authority to do whatever is incidental to that trade or business.

General Agreement on Tariffs and Trade. This international agreement was made in 1947, with the purpose of reducing tariffs and other import controls and so aid the expansion of international trade. Although there was at the outset no intention of having a permanent institution, it has become one. The various conferences that have been held have achieved some success especially the one in 1967, known as the 'Kennedy Round', so called because it was at the initiative of the late President Kennedy and put an end to the 'most favoured nation' clauses and discrimination among nations. The organisation has its headquarters in Geneva.

general average. Taken from the word *aeria* (damage). General average refers to a situation where the loss is caused by some sacrifice, thereby the safety of other goods are preserved, for example should the safety of a vessel be in jeopardy, then the captain may decide to jettison some of the cargo in order to save the vessel and the remainder of the cargo. The loss in this situation is shared between the shipowner and the owners of the other cargo, so that all interested parties share some of the loss.

general clearing. *See* CLEARING HOUSE.

general crossing. *See* CROSSED CHEQUE.

general equitable charge. An equitable charge on unregistered land. The lender does not surrender the deeds of the property, but the charge should be registered with the Land Charges Department as charge class C(iii).

General Index of Retail Prices. This is commonly known as the Retail Price Index or RPI and has its origins in a cost of living index which commenced in 1914. At that time it concentrated on basic goods such as bread, potatoes, clothing, lamp oil and candles. Other items which in those days were considered as luxuries were not included. These days, it measures the extent that prices change, not what people actually spend on consumer goods, so that it is strictly not a 'cost of living' index. The index is constructed by the Retail Prices Index Advisory Committee, which has members from the CBI, TUC, experts from universities, economists and statisticians. Since 1946, when the committee was known as the Cost of Living Advisory Committee, they have submitted ten reports to the Secretary of State for Employment, the latest being in September 1986. The index measures 130

000 separate price quotations for 600 items and is collected each month by staff of the Department of Employment making personal visits to shops. The index relates to the prices of goods taken on a single day each month, usually a Tuesday in the middle of the month. The total weighting given is 1000 and the 'basket' is divided into the following groups.

	Weighting
Food	167
Meals purchased outside home	46
Alcohol and tobacco	114
Housing costs fuel and light	218
Household goods	73
Household services	44
Clothing and footwear	74
Personal goods and services	38
Motoring and travel costs	149
Leisure goods and services	77
Total	1,000

The reference date is simply a convenient point to which a continuous series of index values can be related and the latest date is that of 13 January 1987, when the index point of 100 measured all future movements from that date. The index is frequently used as a means of calculating the 'standard of living' and in wage and salary negotiations.

general issue. An issue of certain articles on a large scale; a legal issue which denies the whole declarations or charge, equivalent to a plea of 'not guilty' in contradistinction to a special issue.

general ledger. A part of the organisation of the accountancy system, where the accounts of the entity, other than the creditors, debtors and *cash book* are kept. In some small businesses this may be called the *private ledger*.

general lien. A right to retain possession of the goods belonging to another until outstanding debts are paid. *See* BANKER'S LIEN; LIEN.

general meetings. *See* ANNUAL GENERAL MEETING.

general partner. *See* PARTNER.

general policy. A policy issued by an insurance company to an exporter who wishes to insure all the goods he is likely to export in the forthcoming year. Rather than have an insurance policy issued for every shipment, a small premium is paid to cover the year, then as and when goods are despatched, a certificate is written out by the insurer for the consignment, a copy of which is sent to the insurance company with a further premium. At the end of the year, a financial adjustment is made.

general register of sasines. *See* SASINE.

general reserve. The retention of profits of the company in an account so named, for the purposes of expansion or the financial strengthening of the balance sheet.

genus. A stock, a species, a kind.

gift *inter vivos*. A gift given in the lifetime of the donor. Such a gift would not attract inheritance tax if between husband and wife, but it would attract inheritance tax on a sliding scale if the gift to another is within seven years of the donor's death.

gilt auction. A recent method of selling government stock whereby there is no set price but investments are accepted from the upper price downwards. This is a risky method of purchase for the small investor, who can apply for the 'non competitive bid price' which is calculated at the average price of all institutional bids.

gilt-edged securities (gilts). This is the term used to describe the issue of British government stock. They are called gilts, because the certificates were at one time edged in gold. It is mainly long term, but from time to time short-term issues may be seen. Generally, short-term issues are up to five years, medium-term are five to fifteen years, and long-term fifteen years and longer. All gilts have a fixed interest rate, and most are redeemable at some future date. A few, for example, War Loan has no redeemable date, while some which have a low yield are linked to the retail price index and in consequence, the price of these will increase with inflation. Gilts may be purchased via a broker or via the National Savings Stock Office. Any profits made by selling gilts do not attract capital gains tax.

giro *See* BANK GIRO; GIROBANK.

Girobank. The National Giro as it was called when it was established by the Post Office in 1968. The reasons for its establishment were the need to modernise the remittance services of the Post Offices and substantial increase in recent years of the sort of transactions for which a giro system is particularly appropriate; the payments of rates and bills by instalments, hire purchase and mail-order remittances, and payments for the renting of consumer durables. In 1975 the government agreed to a series of measures, which included a provision of more banking services. In 1978 National Giro changed its name to National Girobank to reflect the wide range of services available. It obtained a listed bank status in 1979 and became a member of the clearing system in 1981 and a full member of the clearing house in 1983. It is a founder member of the Association of Payment Clearing Services (APACS) and in 1985 became a public limited company. All account records are held on computer at Girobank's head office in Bootle and it uses the 20 000 Post Offices as its outlets. It is now a subsidiary of the Alliance & Leicester Building Society.

glamour stock. A stock which has had a steady rising price and there is always a demand to buy. In times of a rising market, these tend to rise faster than the market, and can often have a blue chip category.

globalisation. The integration of the worlds' financial markets into a single homogeneous entity, e.g. 1. A bank in Europe issues a Canadian dollar debt in the Euromarkets and swaps it for a floating rate US $ debt. 2. A UK company issues commercial paper in New York, and swaps it for a fixed rate sterling debt.

godown. An eastern warehouse for the storage of goods.

go-go funds. A unit trust that invests in the more speculative type of stock, with the aim of above average reward. The fund managers take risks in order to make gains but also tend to change investments quickly.

going concern. A business which is in full working order. The only type of business to which a banker will willingly give accommodation. *See also* GONE CONCERN.

going naked. In connection with an options trading market, when operators take option money on stock which they do not own and cannot deliver in the hope that it can be bought back at a lower level.

going public. A phrase used when a private limited company is going to become a public limited company and therefore will obtain through a complicated precedure a quotation on the Stock Exchange. The capital that has been in the hands of private investors will then be increased and the new shares and possibly some of the issued capital will become available in the market. By going public, the company takes the opportunity of obtaining more capital to expand.

gold. A precious metal which historically was used as money, i.e. a medium of exchange, throughout the world. There was a time when currency notes were only issued against a reserve of gold (*see* GOLD BULLION STANDARD; GOLD STANDARD). Nowadays, gold is no longer a medium of exchange, but it is retained by individuals either as ornaments, for personal adornment, coin collections etc. However, gold is still retained by investors, governments, banks and central banks in bullion form. A market exists in London for the purchase and sale of gold bullion. The public may also hold gold bars which are of 24 carat and can weigh 5, 10, 20 and 50 grams. While there is a risk of theft, banks will not only purchase these on behalf of customers, but are willing to hold the bars, issuing a certificate to the owner.

gold bond. A bond issued by some goldmining companies that relate the interest payments to the price of gold, therefore any investor who anticipates that gold prices will rise, may be tempted to purchase such bonds.

gold bullion. Gold bars each weighing 400 ounces (11.3 kilograms), which are normally held by banks, central banks and dealers in the gold market.

gold bullion standard. Up to 1931, paper money was backed by a reserve of gold and any settlement of international debts was settled by the transfer of gold from one country to another. With the collapse of the gold standard in 1931, many countries suspended the movement of gold, but gold still being a precious metal is still quoted each day on the market in fine ounces against the US $.

gold clause. A clause in an agreement which offers the lender repayment in terms of the price of gold equivalent to the currency at the time the loan was made. In times of devaluation, such a clause is a hedge against inflation.

gold coins. Gold coins have been issued in England since 1257, and have over the years had a variety of values and were once the currency of the country. These days, while gold coins are minted and issued, they are of interest only to investors and collectors of coins. In the UK the gold coins of this country and of South Africa, USA and Canada can be bought and sold. The price will fluctuate according to supply and demand and inflation, additionally they are subject to value added tax.

gold credit card. A credit card that indicates that the holder has a greater credit status. That is, he/she is able to obtain more than the usual amount of cash from an ATM, automatic travel insurance, a loan/overdraft without formality or payment of a negotiation fee, etc.

golden handcuffs/hello. An inducement paid by a company to attract an executive to join or remain on its staff. At the same time in order to retain his services, certain conditions are laid down.

golden handshake. Compensation paid by a company or firm to a highly-placed executive for loss of office. Such pay-offs are tax free up to £30 000 but any additional amounts attract the full rate of income tax.

gold exchange standard. Where a country has no gold reserves, but keeps its reserves in the currency of another country. This standard, which no longer exists, was not a good system, because should either the country that adopted this standard or the 'parent' country revalue its currency, then the consequences can be serious for the other country.

gold fixing. The twice daily determination of the price in the London Gold Market and the Zurich Market.

gold market. *See* LONDON GOLD MARKET.

gold points. *See* SPECIE POINTS.

gold reserves. Gold reserves may be held by any country for (*a*) the purpose of settling international debts, (*b*) backing its note issue. In the UK the gold reserve is maintained by the Bank of England. Such balances are held in the Exchange Equalisation Account.

goldsmiths. Those men whose function it was to work in gold. During the seventeenth century many of them became bailees for gold. Then very gradually became the early bankers, accepting deposits in gold and issuing notes backed by the gold available in their vaults. Later they became lenders. However, it was the goldsmiths receipts that became the first banknotes.

gold standard. The backing of the note issue of a country against the reserves held in gold. The price of gold must be fixed to the national currency and consequently there must be a free interchange between the note issue and gold. Internationally, it provided a stable rate of exchange, fixed to the price of gold. While the gold standard had some advantages, i.e. a stable rate of exchange, automatic correction of the rate of exchange, the disadvantages were (a) purchasing power could be increased by the import of gold, (b) the function of the monetary system depended on the flow of gold, (c) the purpose of keeping gold reserves for the note issue was unnecessary. The gold standard was finally removed in 1931.

gone concern. A departure from the normal assumption that a business will continue to operate indefinitely (see GOING CONCERN), the 'gone concern' concept attempts to measure what a business is currently worth at a break-up value in the hands of a liquidator. Where it seems to a banker asked for accommodation that a company customer may be in danger of liquidation, the banker will assess the company's resources as a gone concern. Each asset has to be valued on a forced-sale basis; the estimated proceeds may then be notionally apportioned among the various classes of creditors and a very rough rate of dividend calculated.

good. Right, proper, safe, adequate, honest; commodity.

good and marketable title. A phrase that is used, when bankers take an asset as security, e.g. property, and the report quotes this phrase indicating that which is being taken as security is acceptable.

good consideration. Consideration which is of adequate value to be acceptable in a court of law.

good delivery. The transfer of a negotiable instrument in good order to the transferee. The delivery in good order of a Stock Exchange security.

good faith. These words mean honestly. There is no intention of committing a criminal offence. An act can be in good faith even though it may be done negligently. To take a bill of exchange in good faith is to take it complete and regular on the face of it, without notice of any defect of title.

good for. The entity has the confidence of another party that he/she is able to meet any stated liability. Often a response to a banker's enquiry, e.g. 'good for £3000 in one amount'.

good leasehold title. Under the Land Registration Act 1925, it is a title granted by the Land Registrar for leases with more than 21 years to run. It gives the lessor absolute leasehold title.

good marking names. See MARKING NAMES.

good merchantable condition. Goods up to standard, and having no defect which will in any way affect their sale.

good money. Derived from 'Gresham's Law'. Coins that are not debased will be retained, while mutilated or debased currency will be circulated. Cleared funds on a current account. A draft drawn by a UK bank on itself.

good root of title. A document which will act as the starting point for checking a land title. The document chosen must be at least fifteen years old. It must cover all the essential facts about the land, describing it in terms sufficient to identify it clearly, stating who then had the legal interest in it, saying whether there were any equitable interests, and if so who had them, and generally leaving no doubts or ambiguities about the authenticity of the title at that time. Examples are an asset, a deed of conveyance or a deed of mortgage.

goods. Under the Sale of Goods Act 1979 it covers all personal chattels other than 'choses in action' and money. This phrase includes all growing crops and anything attached to or forming part of land which are agreed to be severed before or after sale.

goods and chattels. Goods, possessions and property, belongings.

goods shed. A shed for the storage of goods at a railway siding or quay.

goodwill. An intangible asset which only arises on the purchase/sale of a business. In accounting terms it refers to the difference between the total business as a going concern and the aggregate value of the individual assets.

government securities. Funded stocks and Treasury Bills.

government stock. *See* NATIONAL DEBT.

grace period. *See* COOLING OFF PERIOD.

grant. The allocation of some right. The transfer of property, privilege. The giving of a gift. The assignment or conveyance of a title.

grantee. The person to whom property, etc., is transferred.

grant-in-aid. A government finance, usually to a local authority to supplement their revenue.

grantor. The person who transfers property.

gratuity. A gift, present or tip given voluntarily in respect of some service; an amount payable under a pension scheme at the time of commencement of the pension payments.

green baize door. *See* CHINESE WALL.

green field project. A new business entity which requires capital. It has no past history, no assets and is for all practical purposes nothing more than an idea of the founders of the entity.

greenmail. A payment made by the management of a company that is threatened to be taken over by a person who owns shares in the company. The purchase price of those shares is sufficiently high for the person threatening to take over, not to pursue his aim.

green paper. The report of a committee appointed by the Government, to be circulated for discussion and comment, possibly as a guide to later legislation. *See* EXPOSURE DRAFT; WHITE PAPER.

green pound. The accounting unit, in which farm import and export prices are calculated in the EC for transactions between the UK and the EC. It is a special rate of exchange which does not necessarily move in line with the normal exchange rate.

Gresham's Law. When coins have been debased, coins of the proper weight and value will circulate side by side with the 'light' coins. When this happens people will tend to hoard the good coins and pass on the bad ones. This tendency for debased coins to drive good coins out of circulation is called Gresham's Law, after Sir Thomas Gresham, Queen Elizabeth I's financial adviser, who was the first official to note the working of this tendency.

gross. Unrefined; total, not net; general, not specific; twelve dozen. *In Gross.* In bulk, wholesale.

gross cash flow. The sum of a company's net profit after tax and director's remuneration, and provision for depreciation as shown in the accounts.

gross dividend. The net dividend amount paid to a shareholder plus the amount of the tax credit.

gross domestic product (GDP). The monetary value of all goods and services produced in a country. This does not include income from abroad.

gross earnings. *See* GROSS RECEIPTS.

gross income. A person's total income from all sources before deduction of tax.

grossing up. When interest on any bank or building society deposit is paid net of tax, the grossing up amount is the measurement of such income for tax purposes. This grossed up figure is necessary so that individuals can state the gross income on their tax returns. It is also of importance for those persons that pay income tax above the standard rate, so that their liability can be calculated.

gross interest. Interest received on an investment before payment of tax.

gross national product. The total value of all goods and services produced in a country plus income from abroad in any given period. It does not include any indirect taxation.

gross profit. Net sales less cost of goods sold.

gross receipts. Total receipts before deduction for expenses.

gross rental. The rent of a property before outgoings such as rates, taxes and repairs are deducted.

gross sales. The total amount of goods sold to customers, without deductions such as returns, discounts, allowances etc.

gross value. The letting value of premises to a landlord, less any costs in maintenance, insurance, repairs carried out by the landlord.

gross weight. The weight of the goods together with the package, case or container in which they are packed.

gross yield. The total return on an investment prior to the deduction of tax.

ground rent. The annual payment of rent to the owner of the land for the duration of the lease.

ground rent receipt. If a bank lends against the security of leasehold property, the borrower must show these receipts to the lending bank. Should the rent not be paid, then the owner of the property has the right of re-entry and terminating the lease. this would obviously mean that the bank has lost its security.

group accounts. Under the Companies Act 1985, it is necessary for a holding company to prepare consolidated final accounts and balance sheet for the whole group, i.e. the holding company and its subsidiaries. The function of a banker lending money to either the holding company or a subsidiary is to ascertain any inter- company debts and investments, so as to be able to ascertain the financial strength of the borrowing company.

groupage documents. Container documents covering more than one consignee's goods.

groupage shipment. Shipments from different exporters handled in one or more containers by one forwarding agent to save freight charges and handling costs. The goods have a common destination.

group of seven. The finance ministers of the largest industrial nations of the world, namely, USA, Canada, France, Great Britain, Italy, Japan and Germany, meet annually to discuss economic and financial matters that affect them and other nations of the world, e.g. US$ budget deficit. Their objectives are to secure stability of their own currencies and give some lead and indication of their views of international financial and economic matters.

group insurance. Members of a company, business organisation or professional organisation, can obtain better terms of insurance – particularly life assurance. This is due to (a) savings in administration costs, (b) life expectancy of certain groups may often be higher than normal.

group of ten. An agreement ten countries, namely, USA, UK, France, Japan, Italy, Germany, Netherlands, Belgium, Sweden and Canada, whereby their central banks would make funds available to the International Monetary Fund should the need arise.

group trading. A method wherby wholesalers and/or retailers, particularly in the grocery trade try to compete with the supermarkets and other major outlets. The small retailer will join an organisation which has made an agreement with a wholesaler or number of wholesalers, whereby bulk purchases are made at a discount or lower prices, which then allows the retailer in turn to cut his prices and so compete with the larger outlets.

growth share. The expansion of the sales of a company's product in a particular market, usually stated in percentage terms of that market.

growth stock. A stock or share which is expected to increase in value in the future. This is owing to such factors as (a) an increase in profits above inflation, (b) the retention of a high percentage of profits over a number of years, (c) good management and expansion in trading. Due to this growth, it would be expected that the price of such a stock/share will increase in value on the Stock Exchange.

guarantee. The taking of responsibility for the payment of a debt, or the performance of an obligation, should the prime debtor or person fail to fulfil his/her obligation. From the point of view of the guarantor, if a business entity will have a contingent liability which should be shown as a note to the final accounts. From a banking point of view, a guarantor need not be a customer of the bank, but whosoever gives a guarantee, must be aware of the responsibility involved. If necessary a banker may require the guarantor to deposit some form of security to cover the amount of the guarantee. All bank guarantee forms also have an indemnity clause inserted.

guaranteed bond. A bond issued by a financial institution usually for five years or longer, guaranteeing that the person to whom the bond has been issued will receive a fixed amount on its maturity. Under present legislation, such interest earned is not of standard rate of income tax. Any high rate taxpayer, will have the amount of tax payable, duly adjusted.

Guaranteed Growth Bond. *See* NATIONAL SAVINGS GUARANTEED GROWTH BOND.

guaranteed stock. An investment usually in government stock, which guarantees a stated rate of interest on the capital. Although such stock will state a future maturity date, they can usually be sold on the Stock Exchange.

guarantee fund. A fund built up with a society or other organisation to replace any defalcations of an employee.

guarantee letter. 1. A letter from a bank to either another bank or a customer, that will guarantee that person against a loss as stated in the letter. 2. A letter from a bank that will guarantee the payment of an excercise price on a put option.

guarantor. A person or entity that has undertaken, in writing, to fulfil a promise or obligation, should the prime debtor fail to so do. Before a guarantor signs the guarantee form, he has been given, or should be given the opportunity of asking the principal debtor/bank official any relevant questions, which must be answered truthfully. Under the Consumer Credit Act 1974, the amount of debt outstanding must be disclosed if requested, should the amount be less than that stated in the guarantee. Should the amount of the advance be greater, then the answer must be 'the guarantee is fully relied on'. Any guarantor that repays the debt in full, may obtain any security that has been deposited against the debt.

guardian. One who has the charge, care or custody of any person or thing; a protector – one who has the charge, custody and supervision of a person not legally capable of managing his own affairs.

guild. A society or corporation belonging to the same class, trade or pursuit, combined for mutual aid and protection of interests.

guinea. A gold coin formerly current in the UK, whose value was fixed as 21s (now 105p) in 1717; a sum of money equivalent to a guinea. It was applicable to professional fees and subscriptions.

H

Hague rules. These rules were drawn up in 1924 relating to carriage of goods at sea. They cover all goods from time of loading to final discharge at the port of destination. It has also been agreed the bills of lading shall be conclusive evidence of ownership when transferred in good faith to a third party.

half a bar. A transaction for half a million pounds.

half sovereign. The sovereign is the standard unit of British coinage. It is a gold coin representing one pound. A half sovereign is a coin whose standard weight is 61.63723 grains troy and eleven-twelfths fine gold. They are rarely minted and are collected as a hedge against inflation or by numismaticians.

hallmark. In general terms it indicates a high standard. It is a mark used by a silversmith or goldsmith to indicate the standard of silver or gold used. He would do this by stamping his mark on the object.

hammered. The fate of a member of the Stock Exchange who is unable to meet debts. Prior to Big Bang, three blows with a mallet were struck on the rostrum of the 'House' by a waiter to attract the attention of the members, after which the name of the defaulter was announced, and the defaulter was expelled from the House. Any loss to that member's clients was then met from the compensation fund, which was guaranteed by all members.

harbour dues. The rental paid for the anchoring or mooring a vessel in a harbour or quay.

hard arbitrage. Borrowing from a bank under an existing overdraft limit and re-lending the money at a profit on the inter-bank market of on some other secondary market. This device is only possible for the company which can borrow at the finest rates – base rate plus 1 or 1½ per cent. The minimum sum invested is usually £1m. The company needs to have undoubted credit standing, and direct lines to banks and brokers. Hard arbitrage (also known as 'round tripping') creates no real wealth nor any jobs. It is inflationary in its effects and bad for the control of the money supply. One way to overcome it would be to relate the overdraft rates of these companies, not to base rate, but to London Inter-Bank Offered Rate (*q.v.*). The difficulty is that all banks would have to decide this together, otherwise the offending companies would merely move their accounts to those banks still offering base-related money. Other markets also offer opportunities for the big company treasurer when the time is right, such as the inter-company loans market (*q.v.*) or the sterling certificates of deposit market (*see under* STERLING CERTIFICATE OF DEPOSIT) or the local authority loans market. Or it is possible, when the interest rate is relatively low, for the company to draw a bill on itself for one, two or three months, pay a bank its fee for an acceptance commission, discount it and still be able to invest the proceeds on the inter-bank market at a profit – another practice frowned upon by the Bank of England.

hard currency. A currency of a country that is in constant demand and whose value fluctuates very litle in the international money markets and is frequently used in international trade.

hard ecu. While each member country of the European Monetary System has its currency linked to the ecu, the ecu is realigned periodically to member countries currencies, depending whether they are re-valued or devalued. There are various schemes being put forward to retain the basic value of the ecu and realign the member currencies against the ecu. Whatever method is accepted by member countries, it will mean a recomposition of the rates at less frequent intervals, a widening of the use of the ecu, perhaps to the private sector, and it is possible the number of ecu instruments issued may change. Presently realignments of members' currencies against the ecu are allowed which resulted in the ecu appreciating against the weaker currencies and depreciating against the stronger currencies. The hard ecu proposals are designed to turn the ecu into a non-depreciating currency. The route by which this will be done has yet to be agreed.

hard sell. A determined, vigorous and often an aggressive method of selling goods or a service.

hardware. When used in reference to computers, this is the collective term for all pieces of equipment which together make up a computer instalation. Subdivision is into 'Central Processing Units' (CPUs) (*q.v.*) and 'Peripherals' (*q.v.*).

haulage. In transportation terms this refers to the cost of moving goods from one place to another either by road, rail, sea, etc. In more popular terms, the act of pulling.

head lease. The execution of the original document by the owner of freehold land on the first granting of a lease to the leaseholder.

head mortgage. On the occasion of a mortgagee wishing to borrow money, he may offer the mortgage to a lender as security. This newly created mortgage is a sub-mortgage, while the original mortgage is known as the head mortgage.

health certificate. *See* ZOOLOGICAL CERTIFICATE.

hedge against inflation. An investment in such assets which are likely to increase in line with the retail price index, so that the investor will be able to retain his/her purchasing power.

hedging. The process whereby a dealer or investor will seek to gain some protection against the possible loss of their investment owing to some sudden movement in the market. Such methods will include options, forward contracts, etc.

heir. A person who is entitled by law to inherit property or rank.

heir apparent. A person who on surviving his ancestor will on the death of that person be the heir to the estate/property.

heirloom. An item of property which has remained in the same family for a number of generations. By custom it is likely to stay in the house. Heirlooms may be sold by the owner/s in order to raise funds, e.g. for payment of inheritance tax.

heir presumptive. A person who is likely to be the heir if the ancestor were to die immediately.

hereditaments. Real property which may be passed to an heir on intestacy. Property which may be shown in the list of chattels for probate purposes.

heritable bond. In Scotland, a bond given by a debtor as security for the repayment of a loan, the security consisting of a conveyance of land in favour of the creditor, which can be implemented upon failure in repayment of capital or interest.

heritable. That which is capable of being transferred by inheritance.

hidden reserve. Such reserves of an entity that are not seen by examination of the balance sheet. This may be due to the way the assets and liabilities have been presented or where the assets have been deliberately understated.

high coupon. A high yield of interest that is payable on a bond.

high flyer. A person whose career is moving rapidly upwards. A share/stock that fluctuates rapidly upwards and downwards and tends to be speculative.

high-geared. *See* GEARING.

high grade bond. A bond that has a good credit rating.

highs. A situation on the Stock Exchange when shares have reached a new high in a given period (e.g. year). Many national newspapers will show the highs and lows of shares.

high street bank. The description of a bank that usually has branches in a large number of towns and cities.

hire. An agreement between two persons to use the services of that person or another person, or to use, for a stated length of time the property of another. Such a contract will involve the payment of an agreed amount by the hirer.

hire purchase. A method of purchasing goods, whereby the hirer will be a stated sum of money for a given length of time and when the contract has been completed the property then becomes the property of the hirer.

hire-purchase agreement. An agreement other than a conditional sale agreement, under which (*a*) goods are bailed (or in Scotland) hired in return for periodical payments by the person whom they are bailed or hired; and (*b*) the property and the goods will pass to that person if the terms of the agreement are complied with and one or more of the following occurs: 1. the exercise of an option to purchase by that person, 2. the doing of any other specified act by any party to the agreement, 3. the happening of any other specified event (Consumer Credit Act 1974 s. 189(1)).

hire purchase company. *See* FINANCE HOUSE.

hirer. The person to whom the goods have been hired under a hire purchase agreement.

historical cost. Showing the value of an asset at its original cost or acquisition.

hive-off. The splitting of a subsidiary company from its parent or holding company or the separation of particular functions from others within the company.

holder. The person whether he/she is the payee or the endorsee of a negotiable instrument and is in possession of it.

holder for value. Bills of Exchange Act 1882 s. 27(2), 'where value has at any time been given for a bill, the holder is deemed to be a holder for value as regards the acceptor and all parties to the bill who have become parties prior to such time'. In simple terms this means that the acceptor, drawer and any other parties to the negotiable instrument, cannot set up a defence that value has not been given. Once consideration for the bill has been given it benefits all subsequent parties. Additionally s. 30(1), 'Every party whose signature appears on a bill is prima facie deemed to have become a party thereto for value. Value is therefore presumed unless the contrary can be proven by the contestant'.

holder in due course. Bills of Exchange Act 1882 s. 29(1) states: 'A holder in due course is a holder who has taken a bill complete and regular on the face of it, under the following conditions: (*a*) That he became a holder of it before it was overdue and without notice that it had been previously dishonoured if such was the fact. (*b*) That he took the bill in good faith and for value, and that at the time the bill was negotiated to him he had no notice of any defect in the title of the person who negotiated it'.

holding. Something owned or possessed. This frequently refers to an interest in stock, shares and property.

holding company. This refers to a company that either (*a*) holds more than half the equity capital of another company or (*b*) controls the composition of the board of directors of the subsidiary company (Companies Act 1986 s. 257(7)).

holding deed. The deed which transferred the ownership of land to the person now holding it.

holding over. Delaying the discussion or making of a decision by a court, committee, board of directors, etc. until the next hearing or meeting or the deferment of payment purchase of stocks or shares until the next settlement day.

home banking. A service provided by many of the larger banks to enable the ordinary customer to transfer funds from one account to another and to remit funds to a named beneficiary. This may be done by the use of a computer terminal in the home of the customer or by telephone using the voice as a means of identification or a personal indentification number (PIN). This service is still in its infancy, but there is a possibility of gradual expansion.

honorarium. A voluntary fee or reward paid to a person for his professional services.

honour. To meet an obligation. To pay a cheque or bill of exchange when presented for payment.

horizontal combination. An amalgamation or merger of two or more companies at a particular point or stage of manufacture in their common industry.

hotchpot. Bringing into account sums already received by a beneficiary under a will during the lifetime of the testator, so that his or her share of the total sum available shall not exceed that of other beneficiaries of equal title under the same will. Especially used in relation to a class of beneficiaries such as children of the testator. Also applicable to intestacy. In the case of wills, usually only applies if the gift is after the date of the will.

hot money. Funds of a speculative nature that are used to buy or sell foreign currency, take advantage of interest differentials, or any funds used in a financial market, that will flow out as quickly as it came in.

hot treasury bills. Treasury Bills allocated on the last day of the tender.

house. A noble family; a school boarding house; the audience at a place of entertainment; a general term in commerce to refer to a large or old-established firm or company, e.g. a discount house; the House of Commons or House of Lords; the Stock Exchange; the Bankers' Clearing House.

house bill. A bill drawn by a company or firm upon itself.

house bill of lading. Strictly speaking, it does not conform to the definition of a bill of lading, as title does not pass to the holder, it is merely a form of receipt issued by a forwarding agent.

house of issue. *See* ISSUING HOUSE.

householder's protest. Bills of Exchange Act 1882 s. 94: 'Where a dishonoured bill or note is authorised or required to be protested and the services of a notary cannot be obtained at the place where the bill is dishonoured, any householder or substantial resident of the place may, in the presence of two witnesses, give a certificate, signed by them, attesting the dishonour of the bill, and the certificate shall in all respects operate as if it were a formal protest of the bill.

housing association. An authority established by Housing Act 1964 and 1974, which is concerned in the assistance and promotion of registered housing

associations and unregistered building societies.

housing trust. A corporation or body of persons whose object is to obtain funds for the provision of houses for those persons who are in need of accommodation.

human resources accounting. The measurement in monetary terms of the value of the persons employed by the business. Whereas historical cost accounting will only consider human beings from the point of view as costs for wages, salaries, insurance, training, it is often considered necessary to value the employees from the point of view of their contribution to present and future profits.

human relations. A general term covering the relationship between workers, who should be regarded as individuals rather than units of production, and management, together with such factors as affect the environment in which workers work, the facilities afforded to them (e.g. free medical attention during working hours), and conditions of remuneration and pension rights. The emergence of staff and personnel departments has paid witness to the increasing recognition of the importance of this subject, which should be based on the recognition of human dignity rather than on the mere expectancy of increased output. The relationship should work both ways; workers and staff who are well treated should feel that they wish to do a good day's work, and ought to feel a part of the organisation which employs them.

hypothec. The security that a creditor has over property owned by his debtor.

hypothecation. In banking terms it gives the banker a charge over goods or the documents to those goods in instances where the goods are either on the high seas, in a bonded warehouse, etc. In maritime law it gives the ship's master, where necessary, the right to assign the ship or its cargo.

I

idle money. Funds which are available, but uninvested.

illiquid assets. Those assets which are not easily convertible to cash. This could include premises, plant, machinery. There are grades of illiquidity depending on a variety of factors.

IMF. *See* INTERNATIONAL MONETARY FUND.

immaterial. Not material to the subject in hand. Of no consequence.

immediate annuity. One which takes effect at once.

immediately available funds. *See* VALUE DATE.

immediate parties. For the purposes of bills of exchange, this refers to those entities that have an immediate relationship on the contact and transfer, payment of the bill, e.g. the drawer/drawee relationship, the payee/indorsee relationship, etc.

impersonal account. Often referred to as a nominal account, dealing with the expenses and gains of a business.

impersonal payee. When a cheque has the words 'Wages' or 'Petty Cash' written instead of the name of a payee, then such an instrument is by definition not a cheque, i.e. a cheque/bill of exchange must be made payable to 'a specified persons or to bearer'. Consequently, a cheque for use in such instances will only be paid to the drawer or his/her known agent.

implement. To instal; to put into use; a proposed service, system or procedure that is installed and actually working in a bank.

implied contract. By the conduct of the parties or a relationship that exists between them, it can be inferred that a contract exists.

implied trust. A trust that arises in law, which has never intentionally been created by the donor.

import. The act of bringing in foreign goods to the home country.

import agent. A person or entity who ac-

ting on behalf of a principal will arrange for the import of goods or services from abroad.

import deposit. A legal obligation to desposit funds with the central bank or their agent, in order to obtain permission to import goods. This restriction was imposed in the 1950s, but is no longer operated in the UK.

import duty. A tax imposed on the importer based on the value of the goods he/she is importing from abroad.

importer. An entity that purchases goods from abroad.

import licence. In order to restrict the import of goods from abroad, or where goods are dangerous to the public, then a licence may be needed from the authorities to import the goods under the appropriate licence.

import quota. A measure to restrict the amount of goods coming into the country. This may be an economic necessity, when a government wishes to defend a new industry and does not wish to receive goods from abroad which may undercut domestic supplies. The import quota will be specified by the appropriate government department.

import restrictions. An imposition on free trade, whether it is by taxation, quotas, licences, etc. it is a restriction. This may be imposed by a government that has a trade deficit or a shortage of foreign exchange, or a desire to restrict certain types of goods from entering the country.

import specie point. *See* SPECIE POINTS.

import surcharge. A tax on imports, either general or particular, with a view to improving a balance of payments deficit.

impost. That which is imposed or levied as a tax, tribute, a duty (especially on imported goods).

impound. To seize and retain goods in custody.

impressed stamp. 1. The pressing of a document between two dies so that an impression (company seal) has been made. 2. A revenue stamp impressed, by a stamping office, on a document evidencing that duty has been paid.

imprest. In book-keeping, the fixed sum of money available for petty expenses; a loan, an advance, especially for carrying on any of the public services.

imprest bill, bill of imprest. An order entitling the bearer to have money paid in advance.

imprinting. The procedure involved in for example the personalisation of cheques, credit slips and other documents. Frequently called encoding. This involves printing the customer's name, account number, cheque number, sorting code number, etc.

improved ground rent. *See* GROUND RENT.

improving lease. In Scots law, a lease granted for a longer period in order to encourage the tenant to make improvements to the property.

inability to pay debts. For the purposes of the Insolvency Act 1986 s. 123, a company is deemed unable to pay its debts (*a*) if the creditor is indebted for an amount exceeding £750, served a written notice on that company and that company has for three weeks neglected to pay the sum or settle the matter to the reasonable satisfaction of the creditor; (*b*) a judgment order in favour of a creditor of the company which is unsatisfied in whole or in part; (*c*) if in Scotland, the *induciae* of a charge for payment on an extract decree, or an extract registered bond have expired without payment being made; (*d*) if in Northern Ireland, a certificate of unenforceability has been granted in respect of a judgment against the company; (*e*) if it is proved to the satisfaction of the court that the company is unable to pay its debts as they fall due. Under s. 268, 1. if a debtor appears to be unable to pay a debt immediately or (*a*) the creditor has served a demand on the debtor in the prescribed form requiring payment or satisfaction of the debt and three weeks have elapsed and the demand has neither been complied with or set aside in accordance with the rules; or (*b*) a judgment order in favour of one or more creditors has been served and

the debt has been returned unsatisfied in whole or part: 2. the debtor appears to have no reasonable prospect of being able to pay the debt immediately or at least three weeks have elapsed since the demand was served and that demand has been neither complied with or set aside in accordance with the rules.

inactive account. *See* DORMANT ACCOUNT.

inactive stock. A security which has few transactions.

in arrears. Unpaid, unsatisfied, behind with instalments of repayment.

in bond. Goods held in a bonded warehouse because customs duty has not yet been paid.

in camera. In secret.

incapacity. The lack of legal power, ability or competence to enter into a legal contract. e.g. an infant, a bankrupt.

in case of need. *See* CASE IN NEED.

incentive shares. Shares issued to the staff of a company often at a price lower than the market price, either as a reward for loyalty, a bonus and/or long service.

inchoate instrument. This refers to cheques and bills of exchange which is some respect incomplete. 'In order that any such instrument when completed may be enforceable against any person who became a party thereto prior to its completion, it must be filled up within a reasonable time, and strictly in accordance with the authority given. Reasonable time for this purpose is a question of fact. Provided that if such instrument after completion is negotiated to a holder in due course, it shall be valid and effectual for all purposes in his hands, and he may enforce it as if it had been filled up within a reasonable time and strictly in accordance with the authority given (Bills of Exchange Act 1882 s. 20(2)).

in clearing. *See* CLEARING HOUSE.

income. The amount of money (usually annual) accruing as payment, profit, interest, etc., from labour, business, professions or property. *See also* REAL INCOME

income and expenditure. The final account of a non-profit-making organisation, e.g. a tennis club or amateur dramatics society, showing the surplus or deficit for a stated financial period.

income bond. A bond for a fixed period obtained in return for a single lump sum payment, where an element of life assurance cover is obtained together with the right to make regular withdrawals. Most income bonds are a combination of two types of life policy, and so high returns are dependent upon the extent to which tax relief is granted on the premiums of the related policies. Also issued by the Department of National Savings for deposits of not less than £2000 on which income is payable monthly. The rate of interest will vary from time to time. This income is subject to income tax.

income debenture. A debenture which states that interest will be payable only out of the company profits.

income gearing. *See* GEARING.

income statement. *See* INCOME AND EXPENDITURE.

income tax. A tax charged on all earned and unearned income on persons resident in the UK whether such income originates from the UK or abroad. The tax is annual and is imposed from the 6 April in one year, until 5 April the following year. The amount of tax paid is based on the total annual income less any personal allowances at a rate announced in the annual budget and passed in the Finance Act of that year. Earned income is based on a Pay as You Earn (PAYE) system.

income yield. The gross interest paid to a stockholder over a period, namely, one year.

incoming partner. A person who joins a firm, will have no liability to creditors of that firm prior to his date of joining. In banking when the partnership changes, it is customary to stop the account and open a new one unless the new partner is willing to accept any liability for any previous debts. For any security held by the bank, should bear the additional signature of the incoming partner.

incomplete records. Accounting records that do not conform to the double entry book-keeping system. It may be that only certain records are kept, e.g. bank and cash accounts and records relevant to fixed assets. It is, however, possible to produce final accounts and a balance sheet.

inconvertible. Not capable of being exchanged.

inconvertible paper money. Paper money that cannot be exchanged for either gold or silver by the central bank.

incorporated company. An entity which has been given a legal status by registration under the Companies Acts.

incorporeal. Immaterial, intangible.

incorporeal hereditaments. Non-tangible interests attached to land, such as rent-charges or rights of way.

incoterms. The interpretation of the various shipping terms published by the International Chamber of Commerce and adopted by all trading nations. It not only defines the shipping terms, but sets out, in each case, the responsibilities of the buyer and those of the seller.

incumbrance. A burden, a hindrance to freedom of action or motion, a liability upon an estate, such as a mortgage.

in curia. In open court.

indefeasible. That which cannot be made void or annulled.

in demand. Much sought after.

indemnifier. A person or entity who guarantees a lender that on the occasion of loss, he/she will pay. He/she has prime liability.

indemnity. A promise to a lender that the indemnifier will reimburse or promise to pay for goods or services supplied to a third party. *See also* COUNTER-INDEMNITY; GUARANTEE; STAND-BY LETTER OF CREDIT.

indenture. A formal legally binding agreement between two persons, this could be between a person wishing to take up an apprenticeship and the employer (master), setting out the terms of the apprenticeship.

index. The measurement of changes in any given activity, e.g. the economy, a financial market, etc. The index is made up of key components and a given number, e.g. 100 would form the base and from a given time any upward or downward movement would be stated as an increase or decrease from the base.

indexation. The taking into account any adjustment from the base figure. Indexation is used to reflect the change in the cost of living for salary, wage increases, or pensions. Tax on capital gains is also subject to indexation, etc.

index number. A percentage figure, used in statistics, to show fluctuations over a period as compared with a fixed standard.

index of retail prices. *See* GENERAL INDEX OF RETAIL PRICES.

indication. An approximation of the interest shown in the purchase/sale of stock. In the privatisation of nationalised organisations, the indication of interest was reflected by the number of applications that were registered to received details of the issue.

Indice. Index number, a number used for statistical comparisons of all kinds. A representative period is chosen as a base, then all other figures are related to and compared with it. *See also* GENERAL INDEX OF RETAIL PRICES.

indice **Dow Jones.** New York Stock Exchange index figure based on the mean prices of a selection of stocks and shares. It is calculated separately on industrial shares, railway shares and public utility shares. It serves in particular to indicate the tendencies of the market according to the theories of Dow. (Dow, Jones & Co. were owners of the *Wall Street Journal.*)

indirect. Oblique, circuitous, not resulting directly or immediately from a cause.

indirect arbitrage. *See* COMPOUND ARBITRAGE.

indirect evidence. Evidence deduced from collateral circumstances.

indirect exchange. Exchange operations between two countries carried out through the medium of a third.

indirect tax. A tax on a commodity which is collected from the manufacturer or supplier, but is ultimately paid by the consumer. e.g. value added tax.

indorse. Often spelt 'endorse'. The writing of one's name on the back of a bill of exchange, cheque or other negotiable instrument. The purpose being to make a transfer of the document to another, e.g. a bill of lading will be indorsed by the exporter before it is sent to the importer. To confirm or approve.

indorsee. The person to whom a negotiable or quaisi negotiable instrument has been delivered by indorsement and delivery.

indorsement. The actual writing of the name of the person/entity on the back of a negotiable or quasi negotiable instrument. The simple signature of the indorsee is sufficient, but in the case of a company then a per procuration signature must be made. *See also* CONDITIONAL INDORSEMENT; QUALIFIED INDORSEMENT; RESTRICTIVE INDORSEMENT; SPECIAL INDORSEMENT; INDORSEMENT IN BLANK.

indorsement in blank. Often referred to as 'blank indorsement'. This merely gives the signature of the payee or indorser, therefore it is not payable to the order of any named person. Such an indorsement makes the instrument payable to bearer.

indorser. The person who signs his name on the back of a negotiable instrument, by so doing he 'incurs the liabilities of an indorser to a holder in due course', s. 56, Bills of Exchange Act 1882. There can be any number of indorsers on a bill of exchange, so that as each indorser in his turn indorses and delivers the bill to another, so that the second, third or fourth person when he/she indorses the bill becomes liable. By indorsing the bill the liabilities are as follows: (*a*) He/she engages that on presentation it will be accepted and paid according to its tenor. (*b*) Should acceptance/payment not take place s/he will compensate the holder or subsequent indorser providing that the procedure for dishonour has been accomplished. (*c*) S/he cannot deny the genuineness and regularity of the drawer's and other indorsers' signatures. (*d*) Cannot deny to the previous indorser that at the time of the indorsement the bill was valid and that he had a good title to it.

inducement. The persuasion either by a threat, promise to a course of action to another person.

Industrial and Commercial Finance Corporation (ICFC). From May 1985 this company is known as Investors in Industry or 3 i's. *See* INVESTORS IN INDUSTRY.

industrial and provident societies. A society registered under the Industrial and Provident Societies Act 1965–78, which confers on the various institutions so registered amongst other things, the right of limited liability, dealings in property and land, carry on such operations as co-operative societies, building societies, and trade unions. *See* FRIENDLY SOCIETY.

industrial life policy. A life policy that is now almost extinct. They are no longer being issued, but there are some policies still in existence. It is a life assurance policy for small amounts, whereby an insurance salesman collected weekly sums from a person. Nowadays with the sum being so small, insurance companies, to save costs, will collect the premiums on an annual basis.

ineligible bill. A bill of exchange which does not bear the signature either as a drawer or acceptor of an eligible bank. By not having this, such a bill cannot be discounted by the Bank of England.

inertia selling. The delivery of goods which have not been ordered on the terms that they may be considered on approval for a specified term, on the expiry of which it is assumed that the receiver has decided to purchase them. An example of this was seen on the introduction of one of the major credit card companies in the UK.

infant. A person under the age of 18 years. May also be described as a minor (Family Law Reform Act 1969). *See* MINOR.

infeft. To invest with heritable property, to place a person in possession of a fee simple.

inflation. A situation whereby the quantity of money is increasing more rapidly than output. That is, the value of money falls in the general level of prices in the economy of the country.

inflation accounting. The presentation of the final accounts of an enterprise which shows the effect of inflation by showing the value of the assets at the current value rather than at cost.

information retrieval. The procedure for the recovery of stored data.

information technology. Often referred as IT. Banks are regularly spending vast sums of money in the continuing pursuance of improved technology. The term applies to the gathering, transmitting, recording and updating of information. *See* DATA PROTECTION ACT.

ingot. A mass of cast metal, especially copper, steel, gold or silver, a bar of gold or silver for assaying.

in gross. In bulk, wholesale.

inherent vice. A particular quality of some product or element which renders it especially liable to cause damage or loss to itself or other goods, particularly during transport. In general, therefore, insurance companies exclude loss so caused from cover.

inherit. To receive by descent, or by will or intestacy, to fall heir to.

inheritance. That which is inherited – property, mental or moral quality, tradition, etc.

inheritance tax. An inheritance tax is payable when the value of the estate of the deceased exceeds an amount specified in the Annual Finance Act which changes from time to time.

inhibition. A writ to prevent a person from burdening heritable property to the prejudice of a creditor; in the law of registered land, a notification to the Land Registrar to protect a minor interest, such as a receiving order where land is affected.

in-house. Within an organisation. Thus if it is said that the credit provided is wholly in-house, it means that the bank has itself found all the funds necessary, without calling upon any other bank or banks to assist.

in-house funds. Funds held by a bank for its customers for investment either on a discretionary or advisory basis. The greater the amount of these funds, the greater is the placing power of the bank.

injunction. An instruction from a court to a person forbidding him/her from doing an act or continuing any act or the omission of any act. Non-compliance with the authority of the court will be treated as contempt of the court. Injunctions are classified as (*a*) a mandatory injunction – compelling a course of action, (*b*) prohibitory injunction – forbidding an action, (*c*) interlocutory injunction – an injunction granted pending a hearing – i.e. retain the status quo, (*d*) perpetual injunction. After a hearing of an action this is granted to one of the parties.

inland. Carried on within a country, interior, domestic.

inland bill. Bills of Exchange Act 1882. A bill of exchange which is both drawn and payable in the United Kingdom. A foreign bill is any other bill.

Inland Revenue. A department of government set up for the purpose of assessing and collecting income tax, capital transfer tax, licences of various kinds. It does not include excise duty.

in locol parentis. In the position of a parent.

innocent misrepresentation. A misrepresentaion is a statement made that misrepresents the facts. It is made to either deceive or to induce another to enter into a contract. A misrepresentation may be done innocently without any intention to deceive. The injured party has a right to damages and/or rescission and it would be for the defendant to prove that the representation made was what he/she believed was true.

input. Coded documents, tapes, punched cards, MICR numbers on cheques and credits, etc., are types of inputs. It is basically any medium which will accept data and transfer this to the computer for storage and retrieval.

input process. In data processing it is the procedure whereby the data is processed into the system.

in re. In the matter of.

in rem. An action '*in rem*' is one against property, usually land.

inscribe. To insert as a permanent record on to a surface. The inscription of a person's name and details into a stock or share register. To mark a book with an inscription. To carve or engrave on to a hard metal or stone.

inscribed stock. No longer issued – stock is now registered.

insider dealing. The purchase and sale of company shares by persons who are in a position of authority and take advantage of their position for personal gain. Where such a person acts in such a manner he/she has committed a criminal offence under the Companies Act 1985 and is liable to imprisonment, a fine or both. Some officers of the Crown are prohibited from using information obtained in their official capacity.

in situ. In its original position.

insolvency. Insolvency Act 1986: 'The inability of a person or entity to pay their debts as they fall due.' To be declared insolvent, debts due to a creditor or creditors should be £750 or more.

insolvency practitioners. In relation to the winding up of a ompany, a person can either be a liquidator, provisional liquidator, administrator, an administrative receiver or a supervisor under a voluntary arrangement. So far as an individual is concerned, an insolvency practitioner can act as 1. a trustee in bankruptcy or interim receiver; 2. as a trustee under a deed which is a deed of arrangement made for the benefit of creditors; 3. as supervisor of a voluntary arrangement; 4. in the case of a deceased individual, an administrator to the estate. A person who is not an individual cannot act as an insolvency practitioner. A person cannot act as an insolvency practitioner if (*a*) the person has been adjudged bankrupt and is not discharged (*b*) he or she is subject to an order under the Company Directors Disqualification Act (*c*) the person is a patient within the meaning of the Mental Health Act 1983. A person must be a member of a professional body as recognised by the Secretary of State, which by its rules allows a person to act if (*a*) they are fit and proper persons to act (*b*) meet acceptable requirements as to education and practical training and experience.

inspect. To view narrowly and critically, to examine officially.

inspection. Careful survey, official examination; the examination of a branch bank by a party of inspectors appointed by the bank for that purpose, to confirm that the proper amount of cash is held and that the business of the branch is generally run in accordance with the bank's regulations. *See also* COMMITTEE OF INSPECTION.

inspection certificate. A certificate issued by a third party certifying that the goods are of a particular standard and/or agree that the goods conform to the contract details.

inspection of company's register. A company's register of members must be open to inspection by members free, and by other people on payment of a small charge, during business hours.

inspection or investigation order. The authority of the Department of Trade to inspect the books, documents and other papers of a company (Companies Act 1980).

inspectectorate. This refers to a department of a bank whose function it is to visit branches and/or departments and perform the function of internal auditors. In many banks, they are referred to as internal auditors.

instalment. Tranches, or parts of a debt repaid either at regular or irregular intervals. The delivery of goods by intervals.

instalment allotment. Where there has been new issue or rights issue of stock, then it may be conditional that payment should be made partially on application and further payments on specified dates in the future. In order to make the privatisation of nationalised industries popular, the payment for the shares has been payable over two/three years.

instalment credit. Hire purchase finance.

instant access accounts. These are building society accounts where immediate withdrawal is permitted either on demand, by the issue of a cheque or by the use of an Automated Teller Machine, without the penalty or loss of any interest.

institute. To establish an entity or set of rules. To organise an educational body or a group for the investigation or research of a particular aim, objective or fact.

Institute of Bankers. *See* CHARTERED INSTITUTE OF BANKERS.

Institute of Bankers in Ireland. The Institute of Bankers in Ireland is the professional body for bankers in Ireland. Its mission is to promote, organise and co-ordinate educational activity within the banking profession and to develop and enhance recognised standards of professionalism among bank personnel. Its principal objectives are: 1. To ensure that appropriate educational qualifications are available to all members and that the means and opportunities are provided to enable members to attain these qualifications. 2. To identify members' needs for continuing education and development and to ensure that the means of satisfying these needs are provided. 3. To communicate the role of the profession to its members, other professional organisations and the public at large.

Institute of Bankers in Scotland. *See* CHARTERED INSTITUTE OF BANKERS IN SCOTLAND.

institution. An established law, practice or custom. An established body or committee and recognised for its work and acts.

institutional. Typical of institution. Regimented. Enforced by authority. Lack of imagination.

institutional broker. A broker who buys and sells securities for financial institutions, e.g. banks, pension funds, investment trusts, unit trusts, etc.

institutional investors. Banks, pension funds, investment trusts, unit trusts and insurance companies.

instrument. Any written document which has been drawn up in a formal manner which shows, for example, the rights, duties and obligations of parties named, e.g. a will, bill of exchange, deed, etc.

insufficient funds. A term sometimes used instead of 'refer to drawer', when a bank refuses to pay a cheque when the balance of the account is inadequate.

insurable interest. A condition of an insurance contract, whereby the person who wishes to enter into such a contract must be able to sustain a financial loss in that which is being insured. For example, a person may insure his/her own life, the life of his/her spouse, a company may insure a director, etc.

insurance. A contract in writing between an insurance company and the insured, whereby the insurance company will pay the insured a stated sum of money on the happening of a stated event. It is a contract of *uberrimae fidei*, which necessitates that the party wishing to have insurance will disclose all relevant facts, even though the insurance company will where necessary request the response to questions, other facts must be declared. Insurance will cover such areas as life, property, third party liability, accident, sickness, etc. Frequently the word insurance and 'assurance' are used in the same way. Any life insurance contract is a policy of assurance, since payment will be made either on death or reaching a stated age, so that the person is assured of receiving a financial payment. *See also* CREDIT INSURANCE; FIRE INSURANCE; GROUP INSURANCE; LIFE INSURANCE; MARINE INSURANCE.

insurance agent. A person or company that arranges an insurance contract between the insured and the insurance company. The agent will either be an employee of the insurance company or work for the company in a self-employed capacity.

insurance broker. An independent person or entity that seeks to obtain the best quotation on behalf of his/her client. The Insurance Brokers (Registration) Act 1977, makes it necessary for any person so registered to maintain proper books of account and maintain proper bank accounts for broking transactions and office expenditure. There is no right of set off between these accounts, nor is there likely to be any advances or overdrafts given for broking transactions. Where any advance is given by a bank, it is not the responsibility of such a bank to enquire whether the regulations have been complied with.

insurance certificate. A document issued to the insured certifying that insurance has been effected and that a policy has been issued. It is not transferable by indorsement and is therefore not usually acceptable under a documentary credit which stipulates for the insurance of goods. Such a certificate is not valid in a court of law without a policy, an is primarily used when goods are insured under the terms of a floating policy. It is widely used to save time and labour and is often prepared by the insured individual personally.

insurance policy. A document which is legal evidence of the agreement to insure, which may be issued at the time when the contract is made, or at a later date.

insurance premium. The payment of an agreed sum, whether in one amount of by instalments, to an insurance company by the person insured in return for the company's undertaking to indemnify the insured upon the happening of a stipulated contingency. *See also* POLICY UNDERWRITER.

intangible assets. Patents, trademarks or goodwill, which have a real value, sometimes a considerable one.

Integrated Circuit Card. *See* CHIP CARD.

inter. Between, among.

Inter alia. Among other things.

inter-bank market 'bid' rate (LIBID). The rate of interest which first-class banks are prepared to pay for deposits for a specified period. Such 'bids' may be limited in amount.

inter-bank market 'offered' rate (IBOR). The rate of interest at which funds are offered on loan for a specified period in the inter-bank market to first class banks. Offers are subject to availability within dealing limits, and may be limited in amount. The London inter-bank offered rate (LIBOR) is a possible alternative to a bank's base rate from which the bank relates its interest charges on lending. LIBOR is always a true reflection of the cost of funds to the bank, and it is logical to use it as a true base rate, particularly in the case of medium-term lending where the inter-bank market is the only assured source of term funds.

inter-bank sterling market. A market which consists of all banks, in order to allow banks to borrow and lend funds to each other in a quick, efficient and informal way, thereby allowing each bank to use its surplus funds to obtain interest, while those banks that are short of funds, have the opportunity of balancing their books. It can also be used to on-lend funds to customers. There is no market place. All transactions are carried out by telephone, usually via brokers. While security is neither required nor given, each bank will as a matter of practice have its own limits regarding how much it will lend to any other bank. Loans may be as short as overnight and up to one year.

inter-company loans market. A market that commenced in 1969, when the Bank of England imposed severe qualitative and quantitative controls on the banking system. It is a market where large sums of money are borrowed and lent between the large industrial and commercial organisations.

interest. 1. A payment of money by a borrower to the lender for the use of funds over a period of time. 2. The ownership of an asset, property or shareholding in a company. 3. The duty of a member of a local authority or a member of parliament to disclose his/her direct or indirect interest in a matter under discussion and would therefore not take part in a voting. 3. Law of Property Act 1925 sets out five interests. (*a*) An easement, a right or privilege in land for an interest equivalent to an estate in fee simple absolute in possession or a term absolute in possession. (*b*) A rentcharge in possession (*q.v.*) issuing out of a charge on land being either perpetual or for a term of years absolute. (*c*) A charge by way of legal mortgage (*see* LEGAL MORTGAGE. (*d*) Land tax (*q.v.*), tithe rental charge (*q.v.*) and other similar charges on land not created by an instrument. (*e*) Rights of entry exercisable over or in respect of a legal term of years absolute, or annexed, for any purpose to a legal rentcharge. (*f*) All other interests in land which are as equitable interests. *See also* COMPOUND INTEREST; CONTINGENT INTEREST; GROSS INTEREST; SIMPLE INTEREST.

interest clause bill. A bill more commonly met in eastern or Australian trading, which is drawn for a fixed amount plus interest at a stated rate per annum from the date of the bill or from the time of negotiation until the proceeds of the bill are received.

interest gearing. *See* GEARING.

interest in suspense. Interest calculated and passed to a suspense account because the borrowing customer is insolvent.

interest on account. It is current practice for banks and building societies to pay interest on most current accounts and at the same time have various types of deposit account also attracting interest at various rates. *See* INTEREST ON DEPOSIT ACCOUNTS.

interest on deposit accounts. Banks and building societies will offer a variety of deposit accounts which will attract different types of interest depending on (*a*) the amount deposited, (*b*) the term of that deposit. While it used to be the practice not to issue cheque books for such types of accounts, it is now quite common for cheque books to be issued, although there is from time to time some limitation, e.g. cheques to £100 or larger.

interest on overdraft. *See* CHARGES.

interest rate spread. Often referred to as the interest rate differential. It is the difference between the short-term interest rates prevailing in two money centres at any moment of time.

interest warrant. A cheque issued by the Bank of England on behalf of the government, or a cheque issued by a company, in favour of a specified payee, to pay the interest due on a particular loan.

interim accounts. Financial information circulated by a company within a period of the financial year, e.g. quarterly or half yearly, showing in broad detail the turnover, profits and an abridged balance sheet. This information is usually unaudited, but will contain a brief report from the directors on the progress of the company.

interim budget. The presentation of another budget during a financial year. It is now common government practice to present on occasion two interim budgets during any fiscal year.

interim dividend. A dividend usually payable when the interim accounts have been presented, leaving the remainder to be paid at the end of the year when the company's financial position is fully known.

interim payment. A payment made of account, damages or other debt for which a party may be liable, pending the final judgment in law in favour of the other party.

interlocking directorate. This occurs where several persons are directors of various companies all with the same trading policy, complementing each other, yet to the outside world it seems that they are in competition.

interlocutory injunction. *See* INJUNCTION.

intermediary. One who acts as go-between or a mediator; a middleman an agent, a broker.

intermediation. The depositing of funds with a financial institution, e.g. a bank, which then invests these funds with other institutions; government bond to obtain a higher return.

internal control. The establishment of a procedure within an organisation to ensure an efficient and common practice and the safeguard of assets.

internal debt. That part of a country's National Debt owed by a state to its own nationals.

internal loan. A public loan made within a country where the principal and interest are payable only in the same country.

international. Pertaining to, subsisting or carried on between, or mutually affecting, different nations.

International Bank for Reconstruction and Development (IBRD). In more popular terms this is known as the World Bank. The headquarters of this bank is situated in Washington DC, USA. It was established under the Bretton Woods Agreement of 1944 at the same time as the International Monetary Fund. The purpose of the bank is to provide financial assistance for those countries – particularly the lesser developed countries – experiencing financial difficulties and in the need of funds for reconstruction and development as implied by the name. The capital of the bank is provided by those countries that are members of the IMF, and further funds as required are borrowed from the world's capital markets. Interest charged on any loans are therefore related to international market conditions. Any loans provided to government agencies, companies and corporations are normally guaranteed by the government of that country.

International Chamber of Commerce. An international organisation established in 1920 for the purpose of the exchange of ideas, establishment of procedures in international trade. Its post-war publications include amongst others, 'INCOTERMS', 'Uniform Rules for Collection' and 'Uniform Customs for Documentary Credits'.

International Commodities Clearing House (ICCH). This organisation not only acts as a clearing house for the members of the London non-metal commodity markets, but acts as a guarantor for deals which take place in other international centres such as Hong Kong, Kuala Lumpur, Paris, etc. Its source of income is derived from registration fees on contracts, interest on deposits, and funds to cover contracts by the commodity brokers. Ownership is by the larger London Clearing Banks. *See also* INTERNATIONAL MONEY MARKET; LONDON INTERNATIONAL FINANCIAL FUTURES EXCHANGE.

international credit clubs. Organisations whose members are banks which are able to provide medium to long-term credit facilities for exporters across international borders.

International Date Line. The line on either side of which the date differs, running meridianally across the world from the poles and theoretically at 180° from Greenwich. When travelling westwards it is necessary to put one's watch back: this has the effect of lengthening the day or night for the westbound traveller. When travelling eastwards it is necessary to advance one's watch: this has the effect of shortening the day or night, for the eastbound traveller.

International Development Association (IDA). This association is administered by the International Bank for Reconstruction and Development (IBRD) and was established in 1960. The membership is open to all members of IBRD and its aims are the same as IBRD, but its purpose is to assist the poorest countries by longer term loans, i.e. up to 50 years with either no interest payable or at a very low rate of interest. As its lending is below market rates, it relies on subscriptions from members, special contributions and any funds that IBRD transfers.

International Finance Corporation (IFC) This organisation was set up in 1956 primarily to supplement the international loans provided by the IMF and World Bank specifically for non-governmental bodies in lesser developed countries.

International Law. An accepted system of laws or jurisprudence regulating intercourse between nations.

International Monetary Fund (IMF). The fund was set up in 1946 as one result of the international monetary conference held two years earlier at Bretton Woods, USA. The intentions were to develop some method of economising in the use of gold and currency reserves, to establish free convertibility between the currencies of the participating nations, and to set up a scheme for giving temporary assistance to member countries in short or medium-term balance of payment difficulties. The IMF is therefore, in effect, a bank which smoothes out the fluctuations of the world trade cycle. The member countries have contributed gold and currencies to the fund based on the relative importance of the member's economy and its share of world trade. The quota determines: (a) members subscriptions to the Fund; (b) within given limits the voting rights of members; (*c*) their borrowing rights on the Fund; and (*d*) their share of allocations to Special Drawing Rights (SDRs). When a country finds itself in difficulties it can apply to the Fund for a loan to finance its deficit. At that time it must show that it is taking appropriate action to correct its deficit and restore and maintain the external value of its currency. However, with the move to flotaing exchange rates in the 1970s, it was expected that such moves would reduce the role of the IMF in international financing. In fact this led to the huge payment imbalances of the less developed countries and very large demands on the resources of the Fund. The expansion in lending and the support of the IMF to these countries indicated to the financial community some form of approval of the borrowing countries' economic policies, so that private sources of finance were then readily available, and foreign creditors agreed to negotiate either new loans or rescheduling old ones. Although the IMF has faced many difficulties in its relationship with LDCs., it has the expertise and experience to make some contribution to assist those countries to formulate correct economic policies, providing adequate funding is available from its members. While the role of the IMF is to support LDCs, it must also attempt to reduce the large payment deficits so that the provision of finance must in the long term be based on private capital and internal political and economic adjustments. Finally, its prime concern is the assistance it can render to members in the adjustment of their economies and the proper performance of the drawing of funds within the arrangements made.

International Money Market (IMM). *See* CHICAGO MERCANTILE EXCHANGE.

international money order. A method of remitting a small amount of money from one country to another via the banking system.

International Primary Markets Association. The self-regulating body for banks involved in the Euromarket.

international securities. Securities which can be bought or sold on an international market, i.e. in several different countries, at more or less the same prices.

International Securities Regulatory Organisation (ISRO). A self regulating organisation that has been set up for the purpose of ensuring an orderly market in international investment business.

interplead. A situation where a third party holds property or funds claimed by two persons will call on them to appear before a court to decide who is the lawful owner.

interpleader. The person who takes out a summons on rival claimants, authorising them to appear in a court to decide who has the valid claim.

inter se. Amongst themselves.

intervention rate. The high rate or the low rate of exchange when it is required that the central bank should buy or sell its currency in order to return it, as far as it is possible, to its parity. With the UK joining the European Monetary System, the pound sterling may move 6 per cent either side of parity with the ecu, at that extreme the Bank of England should take some action.

interview. A formal meeting arranged between two persons to discuss a matter of mutual interest. This may be a manager meeting with a customer to discuss such matters as the conduct of the account, a request for an advance, etc. On these occasions, it is necessary for the manager to obtain all the information he has on the customer, so that a good and proper response is given and the customer knows that he/she has been fairly treated. A minute on the interview must always be recorded and kept. Managers at various levels will have regular interviews with staff concerning such matters as promotion, interests, discipline, etc.

inter vivos. Among the living.

intestate. Not having either made a will or having made a will that is not valid. In such instances, an administrator is appointed to total up the estate of the deceased.

in the money. *See* TRADED OPTIONS.

intimation. On the occasion of the asisgnment of a debt, it is the notice given to the debtor by the assignor. Such notice is unnecessary on the transfer of a negotiable instrument or securities.

in toto. Wholly.

in transitu. In the course of being transported from one place to another. *See also* STOPPAGE *IN TRANSITU.*

intra vires. Within the powers (usually of a company).

intrinsic value. Genuine or real value. When used of coin, it means that the metal in the coin is worth the face value of the coin.

introduction. 1. A method of bringing a company, through the medium of the Stock Exchange, into the market. 2. Formally making persons acquainted with one another. 3. The contracts made by an agent or employee on behalf of his/her principal or employer.

in trust. Indicating that property is held by a trustee. In banking, documents are often held in trust by a customer, who having signed a trust receipt, holds the documents of title on behalf of the bank and has agreed that having sold the goods will deliver the proceeds to the bank. *See* TRUST LETTER RECEIPT.

inventory. 1. A quantity of goods or raw materials kept in a store or warehouse for use as required. Often referred to as stock. 2. A detailed list of items or goods in a particular place, e.g. a list of items, furniture in a house or flat for letting, probate or insurance purposes.

inventory financing. Advances given for the purchase of stock of either consumer or capital goods. The security for the lender is often in the goods themselves and often the goods may be warehoused in the lender's name and only transferred to the borrower against the issue of a warehouse warrant and the completion of a trust receipt. Factoring companies will also advance funds when goods have been sold to customers and they have received copies of invoices. *See* FACTORING.

investment. The use of money to create more money either in the form of interest, dividend or profit. Investments can refer to the placing of funds into the capital of a business with the desire to obtain better than average dividends or an increase in the value of the capital invested. Alternatively, a person can purchase goods and with some physical effort sell the goods at a higher price and so reap a profit as a result of his/her business acumen. This should not be confused with speculation or savings.

investment appraisal. The perusal of an investment portfolio with the purpose to ascertain the strengths and weaknesses in any particular investment. It would then be necessary to consider the future benefits that are likely to occur, costs that are likely to be involved and the sale of any weak investments, before the price drops significantly. Any available funds may be used to purchase stocks/shares based on risk, spread and other factors.

investment bank. A bank whose function it is to act as an intermediary between the companies that wish to issue securities and the investing public. It may also provide capital for borrowing companies wishing to obtain long-term capital. Further, they may be involved in controlling private portfolios, advise on mergers, takeovers, broking, etc.

investment club. A group of persons (up to twenty) who have formed an association with the object of making investments in stocks and shares with money provided from regular contributions by each of the members. Besides this, it also has a social purpose, so that the members meet regularly and discuss investment strategies.

investment company. 1. The business of a company that consists of investing funds mainly in securities, with the aim of spreading risk and giving members of the ompany the benefit of the results of the management of its funds. 2. None of the company's holdings in other companies (apart from other investment companies) represents more than 15 per cent of the company's total assets. 3. Distribution of the company's capital profits is prohibited by its memorandum or articles of association. 4. The company does not retain more than 15 per cent of its income from securities. (Companies Act 1985 s. 266). The letter headings, forms, etc, must state that the company is an investment company (Companies Act 1985 s. 351(1)).

investment certificate. A certificate showing the amount invested in a particular savings scheme.

investment exchange. Company Securities (Insider Dealing) Act 1985 – 'An organisation maintaining a system whereby an offer to deal in securities made by a subscriber to the organisation is communicated, without his identity being revealed, to other subscribers of the organisation, and whereby any acceptance of that offer by any of those other subscribers is recorded and confirmed'.

investment grant. A grant given by central or local government to encourage the establishment of a new industry in areas of high unemployment.

investment income. Usually referred to as unearned income.

investment portfolio. *See* PORTFOLIO.

investment trust. A company registered under the Companies Act for the prime purpose of obtaining funds from the public and investing these funds in a wide range of securities. The holders of shares in these companies may if necessary, sell their holdings to other members of the public. This type of company allows the small investor to spread the investment risk which is under the control of professional investment managers. An investment trust is exempt from capital gains tax. They are also permitted to purchase thier own shares. *See* UNIT TRUSTS.

investor. A person who invests funds in government stock, Stock Exchange securities, etc.

investor protection. Protection for the investor has in the last decade expanded considerably. The spread does not lie in any one piece of legislation, but in a variety of areas: 1. Under the Banking Act 1987, depositors are protected up to 75 per cent of their deposits up to £20 000; 2. The Building Societies Protection Scheme gives depositors protection of up to 90 per cent of their deposits; 3. The Financial Service Act has established the Securities Investment Board, which through the various Self Regulating Organisations (SROs) offers protection to small investors by ensuring that only those authorised may advertise for investment business and prevents 'cold calling' on prospective clients. The SROs lay down stringent rules of conduct on its members and monitors their activities; 4. The Companies Act gives shareholders a measure of protection by the amount of disclosure that must be made in the report and accounts of public companies; 5. Insider dealing is also covered by the Companies Act – *See* INSIDER DEALING; 6. brokers, solicitors and others must keep the funds of their clients separate from their own funds.

investors in industry (3is). This unique company was formed in 1945 by the Bank of England and the major clearing banks, to help meet British industry's long-term capital requirements. It is the UK's largest venture capital company. At 31 March 1990, it had a portfolio of more than £2.3 billion and investments in over 4000 businesses. There is no lower or upper limit to their investments which can range from tens of thousands to investments in management buy-outs of between £50m or more. With a flexible approach, 3is will invest in either equity or loan capital often on a long-term basis. Funds are used to revitalise, expand businesses and encourage new businesses.

invisible exports. The various services performed in one country for persons in another, for which payment has to be made, interest, profits and dividends on investments abroad, air transport receipts, profits on plays abroad and royalties, all cause a flow of currency into a country. In the case of Great Britain, whose banking, insurance and shipping facilities regularly earn large sums of foreign money, it is often the case that her invisible exports go far to offset or even reverse a deficit on the balance of visible imports and exports. After the proceeds of investment abroad and the services performed by the City, the money earned by tourism is the next most important factor.

invoice. A list of goods dispatched, with particulars of quantity and price, sent to a consignee. *See also* CONSULAR INVOICE.

invoice discounting. The sale by a business of its book debts to a factoring company, who will pay the business the face value of the total of the invoices, less a discount which will take into consideration: the fee, interest rates appertaining at the time, risk of non-payment, etc. The seller of the invoices will do so in order to improve his cash flow. The factoring company, will not necessarily offer any other service, such as guarantee of bad debts, sales ledger accounting, etc.

invoice factoring. *See* INVOICE DISCOUNTING.

IOU. A written acknowledgment of a debt of a specified sum bearing these letters, addressed to the creditor, dated, and signed by the borrower. It is not evidence that money has been lent and it is not a negotiable instrument.

IPMA. *See* INTERNATIONAL PRIMARY MARKETS.

Irish Bank Federation. Nassau House, Nassau Street, Dublin 2, Eire. The Federation was formed in 1973 with the object 1. of providing facilities for the discussion of matters of common interest to Irish licensed banks, of protecting those interests, and, where appropriate, of making representations on their behalf; 2. of advising and assisting the authorities on all matters of material concern to Irish banking; 3. of representing Irish banking in matters relating to the European Economic Community. Membership is restricted to banks which are licensed under the Central Bank Act 1971.

irredeemable debenture. A debenture with no date for repayment, intended to be a permanent debt.

irredeemable stocks. Government stocks which have no date of redemption.

irrevocable credit. Article 10, Uniform Customs and Practice for Documentary Credits – ICC Publication No. 400. (*a*) An irrevocable credit constitutes a definite undertaking of the issuing bank, providing that the stipulated documents are presented and that the terms and conditions of the credit have been complied with; (*i*) if the credit provides for sight payment – to pay, or that payment will be made, (*ii*) if the credit provides for deferred payment – to pay, or that payment will be made, on the date(s) determinable in accordance with the stipulations on the credit, (*iii*) if the credit provides for acceptance – to accept drafts drawn by the beneficiary if the credit stipulates that they are to be drawn on the issuing bank, or to be responsible

for their acceptance and payment at maturity if the credit stipulates that they are to be drawn on the applicant for the credit or any other drawee stipulated in the credit, (*iv*) if the credit provides for negotiation – to pay, without recourse to the drawers and/or bona-fide holders, draft(s) drawn by the beneficiary, at sight or at a tenor, on the applicant for the credit or on any other drawee stipulated in the credit other than the issuing bank itself, or to provide for the negotiation by another bank and to pay, as above, if such negotiation is not effected.

irrevocable power of attorney. *See* POWER OF ATTORNEY.

ISDA. INTERNATIONAL SWAP DEALERS ASSOCIATION.

ish. In Scots Law, the expiry date of a lease.

Islamic banking. By the strict rules of the Koran, which lays down laws regarding the handling of money, a person is not permitted to earn interest (*riba*), on funds deposited with banks. Nor indeed are Islamic banks permitted to earn interest. In order to attract deposits and keep within the guidelines of the Koran, bankers will, instead of giving interest to their customers, allow them to participate in the profits/losses made on the loans of the enterprise. This is strictly not in accordance with UK banking practice, so that depositors' funds do not seem to be in accordance with the principle of true deposits as defined by the Banking Act 1987. In order to make a profit and yet not charge any interest, a system of '*mudaraba*' is utilised. This sytem involves the use of a depositor's funds for the purchase of commodities as requested by 'a borrower'. The borrower will at a later date purchase those goods from the bank at a price greater than that paid for by the bank. That premium, which represents the bank's profit, is closely related to the prevailing interest rates. The raw materials in the meantime are in the hands of the borrowing customer, who has transformed the raw materials to finished goods and sold them at a profit, so that repayment to the bank may be made within the terms agreed. During the time when the bank has the goods in its name and before settlement, there is a financial risk involved – the customer may fail to pay – the lending bank will therefore require as some collateral for the loan, a letter of credit issued by another bank, in its favour. This method of finance, project finance, is acceptable.

ISRO. *See* INTERNATIONAL SECURITIES REGULATORY ORGANISATION.

issue. 1. Shares, stocks, bonds, etc., sold by the government or entity at any given time. 2. Descendants – children and grandchildren. 3. The despatch or circulation of documents, notes, etc. 4. A matter for discussion at a committee meeting. *See* NEW ISSUE; PUBLIC ISSUE; RIGHTS ISSUE.

issued capital. That part of the authorised capital which is issued to shareholders and paid for by them, not necessarily fully paid up.

issue of a bill. The delivery by the drawer of a bill of exchange to the payee, and subsequently the bill can be transferred or negotiated to an indorsee or holder. It is only the drawer who can 'issue' a negotiable instrument.

issue price. The price stated on a prospectus or offer of sale at which the public may offer to buy the shares/stock. Occasionally, stock/shares are issued for tender, then there is a reserve price, but the actual issue price

is not decided until all applications have been received. Normally, the issue price is different from the nominal value.

issuing bank. A bank which has been given the authority by the applicant of a documentary credit to issue such a credit in favour of a named beneficiary. It is that bank's responsbility to examine the documents and ensure that they comply with the terms and conditions of the credit before payment is finally made.

issuing house. A financial institution that specialises in obtaining capital for clients. They are also involved in 'placing shares', 'offers for sale' and the sale of stocks and shares to the public by the issue of a prospectus. They will also be involved in seeking a quotation from the Stock Exchange for their clients. Many issuing houses are considered as merchant banks, while in the USA they are described as investment banks.

item. Any debit, credit or other documents used in banks for its accountancy, for transmission to the clearing house, or abroad, is in general terms described as an item. Amounts listed on sheets are often described as items. The only thing that does not normally carry this description is cash, either in coin or note form.

J

job. 1. A piece of work performed either by a machine or a person. 2. Regular employment of a person. 3. The performance of little pieces of work for numerous individuals. 4. The purchase and sale of securities.

job analysis. Reducing a particular working procedure into various skills and procedures in order to economise in time and energy involved, so increase efficiency and profitability.

jobber. A middleman. A dealer in the professional inter-bank money markets. Since the 'Big Bang' there are no jobbers in the Stock Exchange. They are now market makers.

job card. A card made out for recording the issue of raw materials, the labour hours used and the price of that labour and any other overheads used in arriving at the total cost of the job or process.

job costing. A process for evaluating the costs involved in an undertaking to make or perform a particular job for a particular customer.

job evaluation. The assessment of the requirements of a particular job, such as skills, experience, responsibility, qualifications, etc. This is necessary for the grading of staff and awarding them the appropriate salary/wage.

job rotation. Allowing employees to move from one job to another, to allow them not only to experience the work involved in that job, but to prepare them for promotion at the same time giving the office manager some flexibility, so that the movement of staff may be made smoothly and efficiently during staff shortages due to holidays, sickness, etc. It also helps to reduce monotony and boredom of one particular job.

job sharing. A situation whereby usually two persons share the same job. It may be that one person will do the job on mornings only, or alternate weeks or whatever the arrangement is agreed between the employer and employees. It is customary for an agreement to be made that should one employee be absent from his/her job then the other person, will for a short time undertaken the full-time job.

joint account. An account opened by a banker for two or more persons. The mandate must be signed by all parties which will contain instructions on the conduct of the account, e.g. 'All to sign', 'Any one to sign'. It is usual for that mandate to contain clauses for joint and several liability, the survivorship clause, etc.

joint and several liability. When dealing with the accounts of a partnership or a joint account, it is usual for the banker to have a clause in the mandate opening the account to include a joint and several clause. This allows the bank a right of action against each individual account holder until the debt has been fully paid.

joint and several liability of directors. 1. Company Directors Disqualification Act 1986 s. 15: 1. 'A person is personally responsible for all the relevant debts of a company if at any time *(a)* in contravention of a disqualification order or of section 11 of this Act he is involved in the management of the company, or *(b)* as a person who is involved in the management of the company, he acts or is willing to act on instructions given without the leave of the court by a person whom he knows at that time to be the subject of a disqualification order or to be an undischarged bankrupt. 2. Where a person is personally responsible under this section for the relevant debts of a company, he is jointly and severally liable in respect of those debts with the company and any other person who, whether under this section or otherwise, is so liable'. Insolvency Act 1986

s. 213: 'Where a director or directors of a company (which subsequently is involved in an insolvent winding up), continues to trade in a fraudulent manner, knowing that the company is insolvent and likely to go into liquidation, then the directors can be held personally liable to the creditors'. Under the Companies Act any breaches of warranty, liability for torts, operating with insufficient members, pre-incorporation contracts and if included in the memorandum of association may mean that each director whom has breached the regulations may be jointly and severally liable for the debts of the company. It is common practice with bankers when advancing funds to a company to request, perhaps as additional security, the joint and several guarantees of the directors, which ensures their participation in the company's activities and at the same time makes them personally responsible for the debts of the company.

joint and several promissory note. *See* PROMISSORY NOTE.

joint annuity. An annuity payable throughout the lifetime of two people (often husband and wife) and continuing until the death of the survivor.

Joint Credit Card Company. The company that promotes the credit card ACCESS. The company is jointly owned and promoted by Lloyds Bank, Midland Bank, National Westminster Bank and The Royal Bank of Scotland. *See* ACCESS.

joint heir. One who shares an inheritance with another.

joint liability. Joint holders are regarded by the law as together making up 'the owner', and before 1978 an action against joint debtors had to be brought against all of them together. Since that year, however, it has been possible to sue joint debtors one after another. *See* JOINT AND SEVERAL LIABILITY.

joint lives policy. A life assurance policy which is payable on the death of the first of joint policy owners.

joint obligation. An obligation undertaken by two or more persons who may be sued together or released from the obligation together.

joint promissory note. *See* PROMISSORY NOTE.

joint stock bank. A term no longer used as most banks, are usually public or private companies and not partnerships.

joint stock companies. Any company that has a quotation on a Stock Exchange, i.e. its shares are owned by members of the public.

joint tenancy. A tenure of land, property, etc., by more than one person. On the death of one joint tenant the property passes to the survivor to the exclusion of the personal representative of the deceased joint tenant.

joint venture. A partnership of a temporary nature usually for the purpose of carrying out one particular trading objective. On completion of the venture the partnership is dissolved.

journal. The ledger containing details of the daily transactions of a business; a diary, a daily newspaper, a periodical publication.

judge. An appointed person who has the power and authority to hear and settle disputes and decide the appropriate awards and/or penalties.

judge-made. The legal interpretation of statute or common law as interpreted by judges.

judgment. A legal and formal decision made by a judge in a court of law or tribunal which may or may not include his/her reasons for arriving at that decision.

judgment by default. A decision given in favour of the plaintiff when the defendant fails to appear.

judgment creditor. A creditor who has obtained judgment against a debtor for the payment of a debt. The creditor may enforce this in a number of ways, such as by a writ of *fieri facias*, by a garnishee order, by the issuance of a bankruptcy notice, by a charging order, etc.

judgment seat. A judge's bench, a tribunal, a court.

judgment summons. A legal summons for failure to settle a judgment debt.

junk bonds. A US term for tradable financial instruments of below the normal investment grade.

jurat. A person under oath, a person who performs some duty on oath; a municipal officer, especially of the Cinque Ports, corresponding to an alderman; a magistrate in the Channel

Islands; a memorandum at the end of an affidavit stating where, when and before whom the affidavit is sworn and bearing the signature and description of the person before whom it was sworn; in France, a municipal magistrate in certain towns, e.g. Bordeaux,

or a member of a company or corporation, sworn to see that nothing is done in contravention of its statutes.

jurisdiction. The power of a court to hear and decide the case. Within its authority, it has the power to legislate and exercise its authority.

K

kaffirs. A name given to South African gold mining shares.

keeping house. Under the bankruptcy Act 1914, the fact that a debtor kept to his or her house to delay or defeat creditors, was an act of bankruptcy. The liability to pay is now defined in the Insolvency Act 1986 s.268.

Kennedy Round. The name given to a GATT conference in 1967 in which the suggestion of President Kennedy was approved and accepted by members whereby the reduction of tariffs was achieved.

key industry. An industry which is of the utmost importance to the economy of a country and to other industries in that country.

key man insurance. Where a person, be he/she an employee, partner or director of a business entity, and is of particular value, that the loss to the organisation of that person may have severe repercussions on its operations, then that organisation will insure the life and/or injury of that person.

kick back. A reward to persons who place business with the company. Payment made secretly to a person for the introduction of business to the company making the payment.

kite. An accommodation bill; a representation of fictitious credit.

kite-flying. A method raising money by the utilisation of accommodation bills of exchange. The creation of artificial activity on a securities market to move the price upwards. Research into the reaction of the public to a particular proposal.

knock-for-knock. An agreement between insurance companies to pay only those insured with them and not bring an action to insurers of other companies.

krugerrand. A coin minted in South Africa in 1967 containing one ounce of pure gold. As it grew in popularity, so half, quarter and one-tenth ounce gold coins were minted.

L

labour. A factor of production, the other factors being capital and land. A human effort, whether it is physical or mental, manual or clerical. Many consider that all forms of labour except management, should be defined as labour.

labour intensive. A business enterprise that relies on a large pool of labour in order to carry out its operations or where labour as a factor of production is more important than capital, then that enterprise is described as labour intensive.

laches. Indolent or negligent. An unreasonable delay in pursuing a claim will defeat a party from obtaining his/her rights in a court of law.

Lady Day. A quarter day – 25 March.

lag. *See* LEADS AND LAGS.

laissez-faire. A French expression, free to do. The doctrine of non-interference by government in business and economic affairs. While this doctrine was true in the UK in the nineteenth century, it is now a fact in the twentieth century, governments play a large part in influencing business and economic affairs.

land. Law of Property Act 1925 s. 205(1) states: 'Land' includes land of any tenure, and mines and mineral, whether or not held apart from the surface, buildings or parts of buildings (whether the division is horizontal, vertical, or made in any other way) and other corporeal hereditaments; also a manor, an advowson, and a rent and other incorporeal hereditaments, and an easement, right, privilege, or benefit in, over or derived from land. Land is the oldest security available to bankers. It is always there and cannot be moved. Providing a good title is held, there is little risk. With proper maintenance, the value of land, with few exceptions, will generally increase.

land agent. A person employed by an estate owner to collect rents, let farms, etc.

land certificate. A document showing the particulars of a piece of land. It is issued by the Land Registry to the person who is registered as the owner. This certificate is divided into three sections. 1. The property register entry, showing the index number and title number given to the land. A short description of the property. A land registry map reference and whether the property is leasehold or freehold. 2. The proprietorship register entry, showing the name and address and description of the owner. The date of registration. Type of leasehold or freehold title and the consideration paid. 3. The charges register entry, showing any charges affecting the land, such as mortgages, restrictive covenants. It is the evidence of title to the land and any transfer will require the production of the certificate and subsequent endorsement.

land charges. The rights, interests and charges which affect unregistered land. These must be registered with the Land Charges Department by the holder of the charge. This is necessary so that any other person who obtains an interest in the land is given due notice by reason of the registration. *See* LAND CHARGES REGISTER.

land charges register. A register kept at the Land Charges Department of the Land Registry. The register will show six classes of charge which are: Class A, rent, annuities, or sums of money to be paid by a charge on the land created by some provision of statute. Class B, statutory land charges which arise automatically. Class C, consists of puisne mortgages, limited land-owners charges, general equitable charges, and estate contracts. Class D, charges for capital transfer tax, restrictive covenants, equitable easements. Class E, annuities created before 1 January 1926 and not registered as annuities. Class F, those charges affecting land due to the Matrimonial Homes Act 1967 and the Matrimonial Proceedings and Property Act 1970 (*Williams and Glyn's Bank* v. *Boland* (1980)).

Land Improvements Company. This company is now a subsidiary of Land Improvements Group, which is an investment company. The Land Improvements Company has been established for more than 100 years and its object is to make loans of a minimum of £50 000 with no maximum. Such loans are made to farmers for the purchase of land, the improvement of farms, purchase of machinery and equipment, livestock. Horticultural projects will not normally be approved unless supported by a reasonable amount of ordinary agricultural land. Loans are limited to a maximum of two thirds of the value of the security offered.

landing account. A document issued by a warehouse, giving details of goods and charges incurred.

landlord. One who has tenants holding land under him or her, the lord of the manor; the master of an inn or of a lodging house.

Land Register. The records at the Land Registry dealing with the registration of land. The Land Register is in three parts: 1. the Property Register; 2. the Proprietorship Register; 3. the Charges Register. *See also* LAND CERTIFICATE. The Land Register can be inspected only by permission of the registered proprietor: the customer's written authority must therefore be taken in appropriate cases. The registered land certificate is a copy of those entries in the Land Register which affect the land in question, with the addition of a copy of a Land Registry General Ordnance Map, with the property marked thereon, for purposes of identification. *See also* SASINE.

land registration. A system of registration of title of land based on the Land Registration Act and Rules. This system was set up in 1925 to simplify the procedure for transferring land. The title is entered in a central registry and a land certificate is issued to the title holder. The title is guaranteed by the state.

lapse. The termination of a legal possession due to negligence. The failure of a gift under a will due to the beneficiary pre-deceasing the testator. A slip of memory. A deviation from what is right.

lapse of offer. An offer is considered to have lapsed where no acceptance has been made within a reasonable time or the offer has lapsed if no acceptance has been made within a specified time. An offer would lapse on the death of either the offeror or the offeree.

lapsed policy. A policy of insurance is considered to have lapsed, i.e. become worthless due to the non-payment of the premiums.

LASH. *See* LIGHTER ABOARD SHIP VESSEL.

last in first out. Commonly known as LIFO. It is an accounting term used for the purpose of valuing stock. The pricing is based on the fact that any issue of stock is withdrawn from the latest delivery. With stocks that move out of the organisation rapidly, this method of stock valuation is more in line with current market values. Although it may appear that only stock from the 'top of the pile' is issued, in fact, the *physical* issue of the stock pays little attention to the *accountancy* method of valuation.

lateral combination. An integration of companies engaged in like stages of industrial production, whether in the same industry or in another.

laundered money. *See* MONEY LAUNDERING.

LAUTRO. The Life Assurance and Unit trust Regulatory Organisation. This is a self regulating organisation (SRO), established within the framework of the Financial Services Act 1986.

law. The written and unwritten rules imposed by a formal enactment or derived from custom which are recognised by the community at large as binding. They are enforced on individuals and if broken, appropriate sanctions are imposed. *See* CASE LAW; MARITIME LAW; STATUTE LAW; UNWRITTEN LAW.

law merchant. The law based on the customs and usages of merchants to settle their disputes, which was adopted as a body of regulations for the conduct of good commercial practice.

Law Society. The governing body of solicitors, established in 1925 with the objects of 'promoting professional improvement and facilitating the acquisition of knowledge'. Currently it is responsible for the admission of persons to the Society's Roll after passing the appropriate examinations.

lay days. Days allowed for the loading and unloading of a ship's cargo, during which the charterer is not liable to pay for demurrage.

lay-off. In popular terms this means that a person will not be required to work due to a recession, slowdown in production, poor performance or there is no work available. The reduction of a liability or commitment by selling the whole or part of it to another organisation.

leader. A company that holds a large percentage of the market product. A share that is doing better than any other in its sector of the market.

lead manager. The principal house in a syndicate handling a new issue, which co-ordinates and directs the efforts of the syndicate.

leads and lags. The expression generally used in the settlement of international trade meaning that on occasions some debtors will make payment early, while others tend to delay payment. Creditors will tend to act the same, but under different circumstances. A lead will refer to the settlement of a debt by an importer. Should sterling cheapen on the international exchanges, then an importer will settle his debt quickly. Should sterling strengthen, then an importer will tend to lag, i.e. delay payment. Similarly, should sterling weaken against other exchanges, and an exporter expects payment in a foreign currency, then he will tend to give longer credit, i.e. lag and lead if the opposite applies.

lease. The granting of ownership of land or an asset, for a payment or rent for a specified period. The owner of the property, granting the lease is the lessor and the user is the lessee.

leaseback. The sale of a property or asset to a leasing company and immediately the vendor becomes the lessee of the same property.

leasehold estate. The right of the lessee to have the use and possession of the estate or asset, for the term of years as state in the lease agreement.

leasing. A method of using an asset without necessarily purchasing it. The lessee will hire the asset for the duration of its life which has been purchased by the leasing company and at the end of the life of the asset they have no option to purchase. This system is particularly useful for large and expensive assets, e.g. ships, aircraft, plant and equipment, etc. It has the advantages of not having a large capital outlay, nor any down payment, but there are tax advantages for the annual leasing charges. The leasing company having funds available will use them profitably in leasing the assets, at the same time will defray depreciation charges to profits.

ledger. A book-keeping term meaning a book that contains a number of accounts in which financial transactions are recorded in accordance with the doubt entry concept. In a large business there may be a number of ledgers each containing different classifications of accounts.

legacy. A bequest, personal property bequeathed by will. *See also* STATUTORY LEGACY.

legal. Of, pertaining to, or according to law; lawful, legitimate.

legal assignment. *See* ASSIGNMENT.

legal entity. A person, corporation, company or any other organisation having, in the eyes of the law, the capacity to contract or assume legal obligations. It has the capacity to enter into contracts, own property, sue and be sued.

legal estate. The right to own and possess property and if desired to sell it. With regard to land this is a fee simple absolute in possession or in terms of years absolute. The holder of a legal estate taken as security from a borrower. A trustee holding property for the benefit of the holder of the equitable estate.

legal fiction. The assumption that something is a fact, in order to avoid technical difficulties, and to secure substantial justice.

legal interest. An easement, right or privilege in either freehold or leasehold land. A legal right to some claim against the property of another person. A charge by a legal mortgage or rent. Rights of entry on to the land of another.

legalisation. An official stamp of approval put on a document.

legal mortgage. A mortgage created by the conveyance of an estate or property as security for a debt. The property is charged by way of deed or by the demise of a term of years absolute.

legal opinion. A statement written by a member of the legal profession setting out the details of the issue involved and expressing his/her opinion on the legal aspects.

legal profession. Barristers and solicitors.

legal relations. The intention to create a contract between the parties. The opening of an account with a bank, forms the basis of a legal relationship between banker and customer.

legal tender. The settlement of a debt between debtor and creditor by an means of payment recognised by law. While a vast number of debts are settled by cheque, credit transfer, direct debit, etc., there is no legal obligation for the creditor to accept any means of payment other than that which is recognised by law. The creditor can be compelled to accept an unlimited amount of Bank of England notes as they are legal tender. Coins have limited legal tender as follows: £1 and 50p pieces up to £10, other cupronickel coins up to £5, bronze coins up to 20p. Legally, the debtor must present the exact amount of the outstanding debt, change cannot legally be demanded.

legal transfer. Any transaction that needs legal validation for the transfer of the property. This will apply to such assets as property, stocks and shares, etc.

legatee. One to whom a legacy is bequeathed. *See also* RESIDUARY LEGATEE.

lender credit. American banks in the UK and finance houses working through the so-called 'money shops' (*q.v.*) have developed an aggressive selling technique in a determined effort to provide the ordinary man with the kind of specialist consumer banking service which they believe is still not available at any of the big clearing banks. Their speciality is the provision of personal loans untied to specific shop or salesroom purchases. It is this type of distanced lending, known as 'lender credit', which distinguishes them from the UK's traditional finance house concerns, most of which specialise in hire-purchase finance and other forms of 'vendor credit', where the loan is made at the point of sale.

lender. A person or entity that offers money to a borrower with the expectation that repayment will be made, with interest, either by instalments or by one amount, by a specified date. Where necessary a lender will protect himself by asking the borrower to provide some collateral.

lender of last resort. A characteristic function of a central bank. In the UK this function is carried out by the Bank of England. When there is a shortage of funds in the market, it will be the discount houses only that will approach the Bank of England to either discount 'eligible bills' or to borrow money. These funds would be made available at a penal rate if necessary. The discount houses act as intermediaries to banks and other financial institutions in London.

lending ceilings. A self-imposed restriction by a bank on its lending to other banks, this is to ensure that lending risks are spread, both domestically and internationally, and that regular reviews are undertaken of limits applied. When the Bank of England imposed both qualitative and quantitative lending restrictions on the banking sector, maximum amounts were imposed on each individual bank.

lending ratio. The ratio between deposits and advances.

lesion. A Scots law term for injury or damage to a person.

lessee. The person to whom a lease is granted.

lessor. The grantor of a lease.

letter. A written or printed communication; to print in special lettering; to stamp a title on a book cover. *See also* FACILITY LETTER.

letter of advice. A letter notifying dispatch of goods, drawing of a bill of exchange or draft, receipt of an item for credit of a customer's account, etc.

letter of allotment. *See* ALLOTMENT LETTER.

letter of application. Usually a form included in a prospectus which has advertised the shares available. The form/letter will require the applicant to state his/her name and address, the number of shares required and enclose a cheque or bankers' draft for the amount.

letter of comfort. A letter from a holding company to a banker who has been requested to lend funds to a subsidiary of the holding company. This letter will be written in a situation when the parent company is either unable or unwilling to provide any form of guarantee or security, but would be willing to provide financial support for the subsidiary, and not let it go into liquidation. Before deciding to lend, a bank must carefully examine the balance sheets of both the parent and subsidiary company and ascertain whether other letters of comfort have been written by the parent company. Should the subsidiary in fact go into liquidation, then the liquidator can have grounds for stating that this repayment constitutes fraudulent preference.

letter of concern. A letter written by a bank to a customer expressing its concern, that the account or accounts have not been conducted in accordance with normal banking practice, or that the customer has not kept to the lending agreement and feels that its advance could possibly be at risk. It may also express its dislike of the attitude of the customer towards the bank and its staff. It may, in the final analysis, request the customer to close his/her account within a reasonable time.

letter of credit. *See* DOCUMENTARY CREDIT.

letter of deposit. *See* MEMORANDUM OF DEPOSIT.

letter of hypothecation. A letter addressed to a bank signed by a customer giving the bank a pledge over the goods and/or documents or title to the goods. Generally the goods will be warehoused in the bank's name. The bank will also have the power to sell the goods if repayment is unsuccessful. Often called a letter of pledge.

letter of intent. Any letter that indicates that a certain action will be undertaken on certain conditions being complied with. For example, a bank will confirm that it would be willing to advance funds, subject to certain conditions, e.g. the deposit of security.

letter of introduction. A formal letter given to a customer by a bank, which is addressed to its correspondents, branches and other companies abroad, requesting that the bearer should be given assistance regarding the introduction of local firms, details of local marketing opportunities, etc.

letter of licence. A letter embodying an agreement by the creditors of a defaulting and insolvent debtor that they will for a certain time permit the debtor to continue business without taking legal steps against him or her.

letter of lien. *See* LIEN LETTER.

letter of regret. A letter sent to an unsuccessful applicant for an allotment of a new issue of shares.

letter of renunciation. A letter signed by an allottee of shares surrendering them in favour of another person. This letter is usually found on the reverse side of the allotment letter.

letter of rights. *See* RIGHTS LETTER.

letter of set-off. Where an account is overdrawn and another account in the same name and in the same right is in credit, then the customer should be requested to sign a letter agreeing that the credit balance should not fall below a stated amount and that the bank has a right to set off one balance against the other without notice.

letter of trust. *See* LETTER OF HYPOTHECATION.

letter of weakness. A statement issued by an accountant of a business client, whose accounts have been audited by the accountant, detailing the accounting procedures that are weak or lack security and recommending how matters may be improved.

letters of administration. An authority issued by the Family Division of the High Court, appointing a person to act as an administrator for the estate of an individual who has died intestate or in circumstances where the executor is unable, unfit or unwilling to act.

letters patent. A grant from the Crown, under the seal of the state, granting some property privilege or authority, or conferring the exclusive right to use a design or an invention.

letters requisitory, letters rogatory. A document requesting the court of another country to procure evidence on behalf of the country issuing the request.

leverage. An American term for gearing. *See* GEARING.

leverage buy-out. The takeover of a company either by the management of the company or by an outside body. The purchaser will use borrowed funds and give the assets of the company as security. Repayment will be made out of future trading profits. *See* MANAGEMENT BUY-OUT.

leverage fund. A fund that obtains funds from the financial markets and uses them, and its own capital, to provide funds to clients to purchase companies.

levy of execution. A seizure of the goods of a debtor by the authority of a court. A creditor may obtain a writ of *fieri facias* under which the assets of the debtor may be seized and sold to obtain money to pay the outstanding debt.

lex loci. The law of the place.

lex non scripta. The unwritten law, common law.

lex scripta. The written law.

liabilities. The debts of a person, an estate or a company; the total of the liabilities side of a balance sheet. *See also* CURRENT LIABILITIES; LONG TERM LIABILITIES.

liability. A debt. A claim against a person or entity which will be settled usually in monetary terms. In a business concern, the liabilities are shown in groups in the balance sheet.

liability swap. A swap based on a liability, e.g. a bank loan, a bond issue, etc. It is a method of restructuring an existing debt or to gain access to another market. The borrower can also lock in the gain on a foreign currency borrowing.

libel. The publication of a statement in permanent form, e.g. writing, film, etc., which will tend to ridicule a person or expose him/her to contempt. If it is a breach of the peace, then it can be actionable.

LIBOR. *See* LONDON INTER-BANK OFFERED RATE.

library. An organised collection of information which is available for study and information. A bank computer centre will have a library of disks containing information and balances of customer's accounts, which are amended as necessary. Many banks also maintain cheque book libraries, from which

cheque books are issued, as requested by customers.

licence. The authority granted by the appropriate authority to act in a specified way. A licence may be granted for the importation of certain drugs. The Bank of England will grant a licence to an institution to accept deposits. The Director-General of Fair Trading will grant licences with regard to consumer credit services, etc.

licensed dealer in securities. One who is permitted by a Self-Regulating Organisation (set up within the framework of the Financial Services Act 1986) to purchase and sell securities to clients.

licensed deposit taker. A term brought in by the Banking Act, 1979. It was used to denote those financial institutions that could accept deposits – as defined by the Act, but were not able, unless permission had been granted, to use the word 'bank' 'banker' or 'banking' in its name. Since the introduction of the Banking Act 1987, the distinction between a licensed deposit taker and a bank has disappeared.

licensee. One who has been granted by a constituted authority the right to perform some act which would otherwise have been restricted or unlawful, e.g. to produce a play, to marry, to publish a book, to carry on a business (especially that of a licensed victualler selling wines, spirits, beers, etc.); a person let into occupation of land. *See* TENANCY AT WILL.

lien. Where a debt is due by one person to another, the creditor has the right to hold and retain the debtor's property until the debt has been settled. The ownership of the property still rests with the debtor, but the creditor retains possession. In general there is no power of sale. *See* BANKER'S LIEN; GENERAL LIEN; MARITIME LIEN; PARTICULAR LIEN; POSSESSORY LIEN; WAREHOUSEKEEPER'S LIEN.

lien letter. *See* LETTER OF SET-OFF.

life. The period of existence of a person or animal. The average age a person is expected to live. The subject of a policy of assurance.

life annuity. An amount paid by regular monthly, quarterly or by annual instalments, from a stated age until death.

life assurance. A contract in writing whereby the insured person will pay the insurance company stated premiums, so that he/she will receive a certain sum of money with or without bonuses on reaching a certain age or at death, whichever is the sooner. *See* ENDOWMENT POLICY; TERM POLICY; UNIT-LINKED INSURANCE POLICY; WHOLE LIFE POLICY; 'WITH PROFITS POLICY'.

life-belt. Security for a debt.

Lifeboat Committee Support Group. A rescue operation organised by the Bank of England in 1974 when many of the so-called 'secondary' banks were faced with liquidation. The crisis of confidence was so bad that it was thought that it might spread to the clearing banks, accepting houses and discount houses. Accordingly the sum required to support the ailing banks – £1200 million – was duly advanced and is thought to have been found by the lifeboat banks in these proportions:

Barclays	£300m
National Westminster	£300m
Midland	£225m
Lloyds	£150m
Bank of England	£120m
William & Glyn's, Coutts and the Scottish banks	£105m
	£1200m

The lifeboat operation was originally expected to last for six months, but it has turned out that several years have been required. The bulk of the security was in the depressed property market, which was slow to recover. It was therefore necessary to divide the secondary banks into: those which had some chance of recovery, so meriting continued support; those which might be taken over; and the others which could be abandoned to liquidation. At the time of writing there are still a few companies in the lifeboat. The Lifeboat Committee is technically known as the 'Support Group'.

life certificate. *See* CERTIFICATE OF EXISTENCE.

life insurance. *See* LIFE ASSURANCE.

life interest. An interest in an estate or property which continues for the life-time of another or one's own life.

life policy. The legal contract between an insured person and an insurance company, which gives the terms and conditions of the assurance as well as giving the personal details of the

insured, including his/her date of birth, the premium to be paid, the amount to be paid on reaching a certain age or death whichever is the earlier.

life rent. A rent which one is legally entitled to receive during one's life-time.

life table. A table of statistics, used by assurance companies, which estimate the expectation of life of persons at different ages.

life tenant. One who has a life interest in an estate.

LIFFE. *See* LONDON INTERNATIONAL FINANCIAL FUTURES EXCHANGE.

LIFO. *See* LAST IN FIRST OUT.

lighter aboard ship vessel (LASH). The transporation of a number of barges by a vessel, which are then released to seek their own way into a harbour or the estuary of a river.

limit. The maximum, the highest permissible amount. The amount up to which a banker may allow his customer's account to overdraw. In the sterling inter-bank market, the maximum amount of deposits that any one bank will make with another bank. The maximum or minimum price a client will instruct his broker to buy/sell shares.

limitation. A time when an action must be brought. The extent of an estate. A time period for an event to commence and cease. The size of an interest given.

limitation of actions. A period of time after which no action can be taken. This is to ensure that litigants bring their action promptly. A simple contract must have a period of six years from the date of the accrual of action, while for a contract under seal, the period is twelve years. Any acknowledgement of a debt in writing or part payment will restart the statutory period. Should a banker merely debit an account with interest, this will not have any effect on the period.

limited by guarantee. The members of a company have their liability limited to the amount each has guaranteed to contribute in the event of it going into liquidation. Few companies are limited by guarantee and those that are, would normally be social, charitable or educational establishments. Since December 1980, no company limited with guarantee may be formed with a share capital. Those that are in existence may continue.

limited by shares. In the event of a company going into liquidation, the loss to the shareholders is limited to the amount of their shareholding.

limited company. A legal entity which has been formed by its members and has a separate existence from its members. Each member will make a contribution to the capital. The liability of the shareholder is limited by the shares registered in his/her name or by the guarantee given. Should the company become insolvent, then the winding up process will not bankrupt any of the members. The most important type of company is that which has been formed by registration which must have a minimum of two persons. All companies must either have the word 'Limited' or the abbreviation 'Ltd' after its name or if it is a public company the words 'Public Limited Company', or the abbreviation 'PLC' or the Welsh alternative.

limited discretion. An agreement between a client and a broker/investment company allowing the latter to deal in a certain manner without consulting the client.

limited garnishee order. *See* GARNISHEE ORDER.

limited liability. The principle of limiting the liability of a shareholder of a company for the debts of the company to the nominal value of his/her shares or the amount of the guarantee.

limited liability company. Another term for limited company.

limited owner's charge. *See* LAND CHARGES REGISTER.

limited partner. A partner whose activities are restricted by virtue of his liability to the firm is limited to the capital invested. Because of this, he/she may not participate in the management of the business, sign cheques, or bind the business in any contract. He/she may inspect the books of account and in general offer advice to the other partners.

limited partnership. A partnership as defined by the Partnership Act 1890, but consists of one or more of the partners having limited liability. Such partnerships are governed by the Limited Partnership Act 1907.

limit order. An instruction to a broker to buy/sell stocks or shares within the price restriction given. Normally a broker will buy and sell for his client 'at best'.

line of credit. An agreement between a bank and its customer, for that customer to have the availability of funds to draw against for agreed trade purposes. For example, in international trade where an overseas buyer wishes to purchase goods from a UK exporter a bank can make available either sterling or currency at a stated rate of interest. The line of credit could be for either general purposes, i.e. to cover a variety of contracts or a project line where the buyer is often a governmental agency for a particular project, but utilising supplies from various suppliers.

liner bill of lading. A bill of lading issued by a shipping line operating liners following a predetermined route which has reserved berths, as opposed to a tramp steamer which picks up cargoes wherever it can.

linked transaction. A term used in the Consumer Credit Act 1974 s. 19(1) to refer to a debtor's transaction which is linked with a transaction of a different nature, but with the same supplier. A linked transaction is not only applicable to the buyer–supplier relationship, but to the debtor–credit–supplier relationship as well.

liquid. Readily convertible in to cash.

liquid assets. Assets in the form of cash, or any asset that can easily be converted into cash. Some examples for a business would be stock and debtors and balances in a bank. For financial institutions, then such assets as Treasury Bills, Discounted Trade/Commercial Bills, certificates of deposit are liquid assets.

liquidated damages. A sum of money agreed as payable in the case of a breach of contract and written into it as a term.

liquidating dividend. When the assets of a business in liquidation are distributed, the liquidator will decide how much and when a dividend is payable to the creditors. On the complete winding-up of the business, no further dividends would be payable.

liquidation. A company goes into liquidation at the moment it passes a resolution for voluntary winding up, or when the court makes an order for the winding up under s.124(5) Insolvency Act 1986.

liquidator. A person who is an insolvency practitioner appointed by the court or by the creditors of a company, or by the members of a company to get in what is owed to the company, to take charge of the assets and turn them into money, to pay the company's debts, and then, if there is anything left, to distribute it amongst the members in proportion to their shareholdings. A banker asked to open an account for the liquidator in a compulsory liquidation should ask to see the court order appointing him or her, together with the evidence of the sanction of the Department of Trade for the banker to maintain a banking account at a bank other than the Bank of England. In the other two cases a liquidator may bank wherever he or she pleases. The banker should see, as evidence of the appointment, the creditors' resolution in the first case, or a certified copy of it, and the members' resolution in the second.

liquid capital. Cash balances and other assets easily converted into cash.

liquid deficiency. The excess of current liabilities over current assets.

liquidity. The ability to meet debts as and when they are due. The excess of current assets over current liabilities.

liquidity ratio. A measurement or ratio to indicate the availability of assets to meet liabilities. The reserve asset ratio maintained by banks is popularly called a liquidity ratio. The formula for this ratio consists of the liquid assets, e.g. Treasury Bills, Commercial Bills, Short-Term Government Stock, certificates of deposit, short-term funds with the money market, etc., as a ratio or percentage of current and deposit accounts. This ratio is strictly controlled by the Bank of England. While in the past, such ratios were well known, it is now customary for such information to be available only to the Bank of England and the specific bank. *See* CONTROL OF THE MONEY SUPPLY.

list. A catalogue or roll of names, numbers, items, etc. Frequently any item forming part of a list would be entered in either alphabetical order, chrono-logical order, order of urgency, price, numerical order, etc.

listed company. A company whose shares are quoted on the International Stock Exchange Official List. Such quotations merely state the buying and selling prices of the shares as quoted by the market makers.

listed investments. Those investments which have satisfied the International Stock Exchange strict requirements and have been granted a quotation in the *Official Daily List.*

listed stocks. Stocks and shares dealt with on the Stock Exchange.

listing. Quotation on a stock exchange.

list of members. The list of shareholders of a company as at a given date. This is a return that must be submitted to the Registrar of Companies annually.

list price. The price which is quoted either in a catalogue, tender documents or quotation document. Such prices may be subject to trade and cash discounts.

Lloyd's policy. A policy of marine insurance written by Lloyd's underwriters and sealed by the Corporation.

Lloyd's Register of Shipping. An organisation established to survey and classify ships of all nationalities. Regular surveys are conducted on all vessels of 100 tons and over, and an opinion is given as to the seaworthiness and reliability of the vessel. Certificates are granted according to standards of efficiency, the highest being A1. A publication of British and foreign ships is revised ad re-issued annually.

loading. A part of a premium paid for a policy of assurance which is intended to cover the management expenses. The charges of a bank account to reflect the additional cost in the maintenance of an account. The interest placed on the opening of a personal loan account, and which the customer then pays off the total capital and interested debit to the loan account is 'front-end loading' or 'up-front loading'.

loan. The borrowing of a sum of money usually at a stated rate of interest for a specific time, either from a bank, a business, an individual or the government. In banking, the amount borrowed by a customer is usually debited to a loan account and credited to the current account. The loan is then repaid by a regular transfer from current account to loan account over an agreed period. The interest charged may be quarterly or half-yearly and debited either to the loan account or the current account. *See also* BACK-TO-BACK LOAN; LAND IMPROVEMENTS COMPANY; PERSONAL LOAN; SHORT-TERM LOAN; SUBORDINATED LOAN; SYNDICATED LOAN.

loan account. The account which records the amount borrowed by the customer, the amounts repaid, and the interest charged. Statements are sent to the customer at regular intervals.

loan application form. A form drawn up by a bank for the use of a customer who wishes to make a formal request for a loan. It will incorporate the necessary information required by the bank and will if necessary conform with the requirements of the Consumer Credit Act 1974. It may, if necessary, show a record of all items given to the bank as security for the loan.

loanback. A system whereby any person who pays into a personal pension plan may borrow a sum of money which should then be repaid after retirement. The insurance company hives part of the policy-holder's pension entitlement, which the policy-holder has to repay on retirement. The loan is not given from the pension fund, nor is the pension fund used as security for the loan, so that the borrower is obliged to offer some other form of acceptable security against the loan. The policy-holder will pay the normal rate of interest, plus management charges all of which must be repaid on retirement. Should interest charges accumulate, then the debit may amount to a sum greater than that permitted to be withdrawn from the pension fund. This of course can lead to financial hardship.

loan capital. That part of the capital of a company which has been derived from outside loans and is so described in the balance sheet.

loans guarantee scheme. *See* SMALL FIRMS LOAN GUARANTEE SCHEME.

Loans Bureau of the Chartered Institute of Public Finance & Accountancy. *See under* LOCAL AUTHORITY BONDS.

loan rate. The rate of interest that will be charged on the loan. It is usual to state the percentage above the bank's own base rate that will be charged and the minimum rate. For example '3 per cent above base rate, minimum 10 per cent'.

loan stock. Another name for a debenture. Usually it is redeemable at some future specified date. It may be unsecured, or secured by a fixed charge over the assets of the company. Interest may be paid either half-yearly or yearly. A trust deed is set up to protect the interests of the investors and trustees are appointed to look after their investment.

loans to directors. Section 330–339 of the Companies Act 1985 lays down stringent rules controlling the loans made by companies to their directors. While s. 330 states in general terms that it is illegal for a company or its holdings company to lend money to a director or enter into a guarantee or provide any security in connection with a loan to a director or shadow director, the Act continues to give some exceptions to this section. For example, in s. 332, a loan to a director of up to a total of a maximum of £1000 (a quasi loan) is permissible, if the sum is to be repaid within two months. Taking the matter further, s. 334 states: 'Without prejudice to any other provisions of ss. 332 to 338, paragraph (a) of s. 330(2) does not prohibit a company from making a loan to a director of the company or of its holding company if the aggregate of the relevant amounts does not exceed £2500'. Further, s. 335, permits a company to enter into minor transactions if the relevant amounts do not exceed £5000. In this case it is stated in s. 335(2a) that the transaction entered into by the company must (*a*) be in the ordinary course of business and (*b*) the value of transaction is not greater, and the terms on which it is entered into are no more favourable, than that or those which it is reasonable to expect the company to have offered to, or in respect of, a person of the same financial standing but unconnected with the company. For a director who has to incur expenses in order to perform his or her proper duties, providing the matter has had the approval of a general meeting and the liability is discharged within six months a loan of up to £10 000 may be granted. Section 338(6) does not prevent a company from making a loan to one of its directors for the purchase of a house which will be the director's main residence, or improving the main residence, or substitution of a loan made by an other person, providing such loans are ordinarily made by the company to its employees on terms no less favourable that those on which the transaction in question is made and the aggregate of the relevant amounts does not exceed £50 000. Finally a prohibition to s. 330 is contained in s. 338 (1) and (2) which permits a 'money lending company' to make loans, quasi loans and give guarantees, providing the loans so granted are no greater or more favourable than those offered to or in respect of a person of the same financial standing but unconnected with the company, on the condition that the loan is less than £50 000 unless the money lending company is a recognised bank.

lobby. The area of a branch of a bank, where it is usual for customers to transact their business with the bank. While many years ago, the staff of the bank were kept separate from the customers, it is now not unusual to see members of the bank staff sitting at desks in the lobby. This allows speedy access to customers who wish to make an enquiry, obtain investment/insurance advice and other personal services. It is also accessible for members of the public who wish to open an account with the least formality. While in the majority of branches, the cashiers are behind formal counters, in some cases where a customer needs to pay in a small amount, or withdraw a small amount this may be done in the banking area where there is a cashier for that purpose.

lobby banking. The name given to a banking system introduced in the late 1970s whereby a customer by using an ATM can make deposits and withdrawals, request cheque books, statements and balances.

local acceptance. See QUALIFIED ACCEPTANCE.

local authority. A body formed for the purpose of administrating local government under the Local Authorities Act 1972. This Act divided Great Britain into the Greater London Council (now repealed), county councils, London Borough Councils, district councils. Local Government (Scotland) Act 1973 gave the description 'a regional, islands or district council or any combination of those councils'. Finance Act 1974 s. 52(2): 'A local authority is defined as (a) any authority having power to make or determine a rate, (b) any authority having power to issue a precept, requisition or other demand for payment to be raised out of a rate'. Bank accounts of county councils must either be in the name of the county or in the name of the Treasurer and qualified by the description 'Treasurer of XYZ County Council'. Before opening the account of any local authority, a resolution must be obtained from the authority to open the account at the named branch. The signed mandate must include such formalities as signing instructions, endorsements, etc. Local authorities are authorised to lend or invest funds. They are also permitted to borrow funds, i.e. long-term borrowings would normally be secured by a mortgage on the rates while short-term borrowings are frequently unsecured. See LOCAL AUTHORITY BONDS, LOCAL AUTHORITY LOANS.

Local authority bonds, local authority loans. All local authorities will from time to time need to borrow funds. This may be done by going to the money markets, but it is not unusual for funds to be borrowed from the public by the issue of bonds – usually short term. The rates offered will vary according to the interest rates prevailing. In the immediate past, these bonds were for one year only and called 'yearlings'. The various bonds issued are normally advertised in the national press and available from the Chartered Institute of Public Finance.

local currency. In international trade this indicates the currency of the overseas country with whom the traders are dealing.

local searches. See LAND CHARGES REGISTER.

loco. In that place (the name of the place being next mentioned).

locum tenens. One who acts as a lawful substitute in an office, a deputy.

locus classicus. The authoritative passage in a judgement, the *ratio decidendi*, the principal authority.

Lombard Street. A street whose name is synonymous with the London money markets. Most of the head offices of banks and discount houses are situated in or around Lombard Street. The name originates from the Middle Ages, when Italian merchants from Lombardy, whose trade was money exchange and banking, settled in the area.

London Bankers' Clearing House. Now London and Scottish Bankers' Clearing House (LSBCH). *See* CLEARING HOUSE.

London Chamber of Commerce. An association, established in 1881, representing the various interests of commerce. This includes home and overseas trade, insurance and banking. This association collects information on all matters of interest to its members and makes representations to government on matters that affect its members. It is also an examining body in a variety of commercial subjects for UK and overseas students.

London Commodities Exchange. A market situated in Mincing Lane, dealing in a variety of commodities including tea, coffee, cocoa, spices and rubber.

London Discount Market. *See* BILL BROKER; DISCOUNT MARKET.

London Foreign Exchange Market. A market which has no fixed address, therefore conducted between the parties by the use of fax, telephone, telex, cable and other technological means. The purpose of the market is for the purchase and sale of sterling and foreign currency. The participants of the market are the various brokers that act as intermediaries, the banks that have been authorised by the Bank of England to deal in foreign currencies and the Bank of England. Contracts are made verbally and confirmed in writing.

London Gazette. The official twice-weekly publication, available from Her Majesty's Stationery Office (HMSO), that deals with public notices and legal notices and such insertions concerning bankruptcies, liquidations that are of importance to bankers. The acceptance of advertisements is subject to strict control and is as follows: 1. Advertisements purporting to be issued in pursuance of Statutes or Orders of Court will not be inserted unless signed or attested by a Solicitor of the Supreme Court or by a member of any body of accountants established in the United Kingdom and for the time being recognised by the Board of Trade for the purposes of Section 389(1) of the Companies Act 1985, or by a member of the Chartered Secretaries and Administrators. 2. Notices of dissolution of a partnership, signed by all the partners named therein or their legal representatives will be accepted if signed and attested as above. A notice not signed by all the partners or their legal representatives must be accompanied by a Statutory Declaration made by a Solicitor of the Supreme Court. 3. Advertisements purporting to be issued in pursuance of Section 27, Trustee Act 1925, will not be inserted unless they are authorised by a duly authorised official of a London Clearing Bank or the Grant of Probate or Letters of administration relating to the estate to which the advertisement refers. 4. Advertisements relating to Bills before Parliament will not be inserted unless signed by a Parliamentary Agent or a Solicitor of the Supreme Court.

London Gold Market. The gold market consists of five members that meet daily at the premises of N. M. Rothschild for the purpose of 'fixing' the price of gold in US.

London Inter-Bank Offered Rate (LIBOR). *See* INTER-BANK STERLING MARKET.

London International Financial Futures Exchange (LIFFE). The London International Financial Futures Exchange (LIFFE) was established in September 1982 as a response to continuing volatility in interest rates and exchange rates for which financial futures can provide protection. The contracts offered on LIFFE enable investors to control their exposure risk with great precision by using futures and options. The Exchange provides facilities for dealing in contracts including UK, US, Japanese, German and Italian government bonds, UK, US and European short-term interest rates, UK and European stock indices and ECU bonds. The London Clearing Houses (LCH) clears and guarantees all transactions carried out on LIFFE, thus eliminating all credit risk to users of the market. LIFFE has nearly 200 members representing many sectors of the international financial community. To become a member of the exchange one must purchase a share in LIFFE (Holdings) plc or lease a trading permit from a shareholder. Only LIFFE members are allowed to trade on the exchange floor. LIFFE's trading hours narrow the gap between the opening and close of trading in the major financial centres of North America and the Far East. Closer to home, LIFFE's trading hours encompass those of London and the European financial markets, where it remains the major international futures and options market within this time-zone. This position has been strengthened by merger between LIFFE and the London Traded Options Market (LTOM) to form a new exchange offering equity options to supplement LIFFE's existing range or products.

London Money Market. The term 'money market' is a general term for the whole cross-section of institutions which supply capital or demand funds for business, government or domestic uses. There is not an actual market place, rather the market exists in hundreds of dealing rooms linking together dealers, brokers and customers who are all either bidding for, or offering, large amounts of money. The market performs four main functions as follows: (i) Reallocation of funds between banks and other financial institutions on a daily basis. (ii) Reallocation of funds between industrial and commercial companies, banks and other financial institutions on a medium-term basis. (iii) Financing of short-term government debt. (iv) Operational link between official monetary policy and the rates of interest subsequently charged to institutional commercial and personal borrowers. Just as there is no single market place, there is in fact no single market but a collection of markets for several distinct and different instruments. We talk about 'the money market' because these instruments are closely linked by their pricing mechanisms and arbitrage opportunities. The five principal activities are dealings in: (a) Bills of Exchange, (b) Certificates of Deposit, (c) Treasury Bills, (d) Interbank Market, (e) Commercial Paper.

London Option Clearing House (LOCH). Was a subsidiary of the International Stock Exchange, where the buyers and sellers of traded options each had a contract with LOCH and not with each other, so that a person was able to trade his/her rights in the market without consent of the other party. Now merged with London International Financial Futures Exchange (LIFFE).

London Stock Exchange. *See* STOCK EXCHANGE.

London Traded Option Market (LTOM). This is a market which was established in 1978 as part of the International Stock Exchange. The traded option is an instrument which, due to its flexibility, controls an investment risk.

long bill. A bill having a usance of three months or more.

long end of the market. A term used in the gilt-edged market to indicate the movement of prices of stocks that have more than fifteen years to maturity.

long exchange. On the foreign exchanges, bills with a currency of sixty or ninety days or more.

long hedge. A situation where an investor has purchased a financial future to allow him/her to offset an adverse change in either interest rates or exchange rates within a given period.

long hundred. One hundred and twenty.

long rate. A term used to indicate the price in one country at which a long bill, drawn payable in another country, can be bought.

longs. Government stocks with a life of more than fifteen years to redemption date.

long tap. Tap *(q.v.)* having say, fifteen years or more to maturity.

long tenancy. A tenancy granted for a certain period of time which is over 21 years.

long-term debt. A debt or debts which are repayable later than twelve months time.

long-term liabilities. Liabilities which are not to be repaid for some years, e.g. mortgages, debentures, a company's loan capital. *See also* JOINT ACCOUNT; JOINT AND SEVERAL LIABILITY.

loro accounts. Third-party accounts in domestic or foreign currency.

loss leader. It is the practice of supermarkets, large stores and departmental stores to be deliberately offer some goods at either a very low price or a price below cost. In this way, customers are attracted to purchase these items, so that once the customer is in the store he/she will purchase other goods, so that overall, the store will make a profit.

lost bill/cheque. A payee or holder of a bill of exchange or cheque must in his/her own interest notify the drawer without delay, so that the drawee bank or entity will refuse to pay should the instrument fall into the hands of a thief. Should the drawer be absent, then notification to the drawee or the drawee bank should be made. No duplicate payment should be made without some form of idemnification as there is a possibility that the instrument may come into the hands of a third party who may be able to claim to be a holder in due course.

lost deed. Where a deed has been lost by the owner, an attested copy may be accepted by the purchaser of land. However, if such a copy is not available then a letter of declaration may be offered.

lost share certificate. In the instance where a share certificate has been lost by the shareholder, then an application may be made to the company registrar for the issue of a duplicate. However, before issue, a form must be completed on which there is an indemnity to be completed and signed by the shareholder's banker.

lot. A distinct portion, collection, or parcel of things offered for sale, especially at auction; a parcel of land; choice or decision by chance drawings; as in the redemption of some stocks, debentures or bearer bonds over a period of years.

lot money. The auctioneer's fee on each lot of goods sold by him or her at a public auction.

low-geared. *See* GEARING.

Ltd. The abbreviation for limited.

lump sum. A total sum, as in single payment of insurance, instead of instalments spread over several years; a sum of money paid on retirement as an alternative to instalments of pension or in reduction of such instalments.

M

MBO. See MANAGEMENT BUY-OUT.

MO, M1, M2, £M3, M3c, M4, M5. These represent the money aggregates as specified by the Bank of England. See MONEY SUPPLY.

macro-economics. The branch of economics that considers the relationships between the large-scale movements of unemployment, gross national products, savings and investments, etc. This should be contrasted to micro-economics which relates to smaller units.

made bill. A bill drawn, negotiated and indorsed in this country, but payable abroad.

magnetic card. A plastic card which contains data that can be used for recording and storing the information.

magnetic ink character recognition (MICR). With the expansion of information technology, more vouchers are being fed through computers, so that many more forms bear information that comprises magnetic characters being imprinted, usually at the foot of the form. In banking, cheques and credits are the most common form to have MICR characters. These characters will show the national sorting code number of the bank/branch, the customer's account number, cheque or credit number. When the item is presented to the collecting/presenting bank, the amount field is then completed. The computer or computers will then process the instrument and debit the cheque to the correct account or credit the paying-in voucher to the correct account.

mail transfer. This is often abbreviated to MT. It is the transfer of funds by a remitter in one country to a beneficiary in another, using banks as intermediaries. At the request of the remitter, the remitting bank will authorise the receiving bank either to 1. advise and pay; 2. pay against identification; or 3. advise and credit, the person specified in the instruction at a stated address. Funds can be in either local currency, the remitter's currency or a third currency. Settlement of the remittance is either by a credit to the account of the receiving bank in the books of the remitting bank (vostro). Authorising the receiving bank to debit the account of the remitting bank in its books (nostro) or requesting a bank in another country to debit its (remitting bank) account and credit the receiving bank (loro). To identify an M.T. the remitting letter should be properly signed and have a reference number. In countries that are contributors to the SWIFT system, then it is likely that M.Ts will be sent by this method. See SOCIETY FOR WORLD-WIDE INTERBANK FINANCIAL TELECOMMUNICATION.

maintenance. Means of support; keeping equipment in working order; helping a party in a law suit illegally.

maintenance fee. A fee charged to maintain certain types of accounts, items held on safe custody, etc.

make a market. The provision of the opportunities to investors to buy and sell particular investments or securities. The financial institution is willing and able to act either as a broker or adviser or both.

maker of promissory note. The drawer of a promissory note is designated the 'maker'. By writing up such a note, that person engages that he/she will pay it according to its tenor and is by law precluded from denying to a holder in due course that the payee exists and his/her capacity to endorse.

making-up day. A Stock Exchange phrase meaning the day on which accounts are balanced and settlement due. Also called Contango Day. On the introduction of TAURUS, this will disappear.

making-up price. On the Stock Exchange, the price at which stocks and shares are closed off for the settlement.

mala fide. In bad faith.

managed account. An account, usually an investment account that is managed by a bank's investment department on behalf of a customer.

managed bonds. An insurance linked investment spread over fixed interest securities, equities and property shares, the management having the power to vary the proportions of holdings from time to time as they see fit.

managed cost. A cost that is controllable.

managed currency. The currency of a country that is influenced by the intervention of the government in order to influence the rate of exchange.

managed funds. A fund that has a variety of assets. This is usually associated with insurance companies, unit trusts, unit linked savings plans. Frequently the management company will specify the area or areas in which funds are invested and for the small saver provide a safe low risk form of investment.

management. The administration, supervisory function of a person who will make decisions for the proper conduct of the branch, department or entity under his/her control, subject to the policy and directives of the owners of the business.

management accounting. That area of accounting which will assist management to formulate policies and plan and control the activities of the entity. A series of guidelines have been issued by the Institute of Cost and Management Accountants.

management buy-out. An agreement between the management of a business and the owners, whereby the managers will raise funds from their own resources, from other employees and from financial institutions willing to finance the operation. The managers and employees then become owners of the business. See LEVERAGE BUY-OUT.

management shares. The shares set aside for the directors and managers of a company as a reward for the increased profitability and/or to give them a stake in the company to ensure their loyalty and enthusiasm in the business.

management trust. A financial institution, e.g. unit trust, investment trust, etc. that has been given the authority and discretion to invest the funds at their disposal in accordance with their objectives.

manager. A person appointed by the owners or directors of a business to undertake the responsibility of running a department, branch of that business. A person appointed by the Court to manage the affairs of another, e.g. an administrator, receiver, etc.

managers' discretionary limits (MDLs). In all banks, a lending limit is imposed on all branch and lending managers. This limit will depend on the seniority of the manager and whether lending is with or without security. Normally the lending limit imposed when security is available is higher than one where there is no security taken. Any lending above a branch manager's discretionary limit will be referred to a higher authority. Loan officers within branches of banks have a lending limit imposed on them by the branch manager and any excess lending or any problems, should be referred.

managing director. A person who is a director of a company appointed to take charge of the day-to-day activities of the company.

managing trustee. Within the organisation of a trust, it is the responsibility of the trustee to buy and sell assets at the best prices for the benefit of the beneficiaries. The contrast between a managing trustee and a custodian trustee should be noted. See CUSTODIAN TRUSTEE.

mandamus. An order of the Crown requiring a person, corporation or inferior court to perform a particular duty.

mandate. A directive from an officer of a court. An order from a higher command. A contract of bailment whereby a mandatory undertakes to perform a gratuitous duty in respect of the property in his/her trust. An agreement from the electorate that the person chosen to serve their needs will do so as stipulated. An authority to a bank by a customer to allow the bank to pay cheques bearing a stated signature and conduct the banking business as directed.

mandatory injunction. *See* INJUNCTION.

manifest. A detailed list of a ship's cargo for the scrutiny of Customs officers.

manufacturing account. This account shows the direct cost of the production of goods, starting with the cost of the raw materials used and their transport into the factory, and then listing the three items of expense – fuel, power and labour – which are essential in the manufacture. Where there is a considerable amount of work which has passed from the raw materials stage but has not, by the date of the account, reached the status of finished stock, a further entry, work-in-progress, will be seen. A trading concern which buys goods for re-sale does not, of course, manufacture them, and will not, therefore, keep a manufacturing account.

manuscript signature. A hand-written signature as opposed to one that is printed or put on by a rubber stamp.

Mareva injunction. A legal procedure whereby the courts come to the aid of a plaintiff who fears that the defendant may dispose of the assets or abscond abroad before the case comes to trial, so that if the plaintiff is successful, there will be no assets to meet the claim (*Mareva Compania Naviera SA* v. *International Bulk-Carriers* SA, 1975). The Mareva injunction imposes an obligation and expense on banks to search the defendant's accounts at its various branches. In order to ease this situation, it is the plaintiff who must make a positive identification of the accounts held at any branch which he believes is relevant to the injunction and advise the bank precisely what is required. Any search made is at the cost of the plaintiff.

margin. In banking terms this is the difference between the value of the security offered against a loan the outstanding value of the loan. In commercial terms, it is the difference between the production and other costs of a product and the selling price, could also be known as the profit. In the foreign exchange market this would refer to the difference between the spot rate and the forward rate, which would be known as the premium or discount. A deposit of funds to a broker as a protection against loss.

marginal. Only just worth doing.

marginal cost. The extra cost of increasing output by one more unit.

marginal relief. Tax relief for a taxpayer who exceeds only slightly a figure which would entitle him to a greater relief of duty.

marginal risk. In the foreign exchange market it refers to the difference that is likely to occur should a customer fail to complete a transaction and the bank must 'close out'. It could happen that the rate of exchange has moved against the bank. A difference in the total of purchases and sales in various currencies and there can be a risk if there is a fluctuation in the exchange rates.

marine insurance. That part of the insurance market that relates to the insurance of vessels and cargo usually undertaken by Lloyd's underwriters and marine insurance companies. It covers losses due to perils on the sea for either a specified voyage or for a specified time. Cargo is covered for General Average or With Particular Average or Free From Particular Average. *See also* FLOATING POLICY; MIXED POLICY; NAMED POLICY; OPEN POLICY; TIME POLICY; VALUED POLICY; VOYAGE POLICY.

marine insurance broker. An agent between a shipper wishing to obtain cover on a ship or cargo and the Lloyd's underwriter.

maritime law. The law that is administered by the Court of the Admiralty and relates to sea and ships. In the UK such a court deals with collisions, prize jurisdiction and problems and interpretation of international maritime law.

maritime lien. The specific right for binding a vessel or its cargo, whether the vessel is at sea or not, due to a claim for payment.

maritime perils. Perils arising from sea, fire, water, piracy, the jettison of goods and any other perils as specified in the insurance policy.

mark. A visible sign, a character made by one who cannot write, a cross. A person signing cheques in this way, or signing a receipt, should put a cross in the presence of two witnesses to the act of marking, one of whom should add the name of the marksman and the fact that it is his or her mark. *See also* TRADE MARK.

mark down. To reduce prices or a valuation of securities held.

marked abstract. In order to obtain a good clean chain of title, it is often necessary to obtain other documents such as a probate certificate, marriage certificate, death certificate, etc. While these documents will not remain with the deeds, an abstract will be marked in the margin to show the date they were examined and found correct. Subsequent solicitors, checking the title will rely on the marking made by the previous solicitor.

marked cheque. Where a cheque or draft destined to be cleared through the Town Clearing System, but for some reason or other the collecting bank has failed to present the instrument at the proper time, that bank may make a special presentation to the paying bank requesting that it should be marked for payment, then it will be presented in the next day's Town Clearing, and the collecting bank can be assured payment will be made. It should be noted that a special presentation on a bank in the Town Clearing System cannot be made in the usual way.

marked transfer. See CERTIFIED TRANSFER.

market. A public place where goods are bought and sold. Often known as a market place. A number of persons who wish to buy and sell any commodity or service, but do not necessarily have a physical to buy and sell, e.g. the London Foreign Exchange Market.

marketability. The ease and rapidity with which a security can be sold in the market. That is, converted into cash. This concept is important to bankers when they take an asset – land, stocks and shares, etc. – as security for a loan.

marketable loan. A loan that can be transferred from person to person with ease. Many such loans are in the form of either a bond, certificate, note, etc. The instrument may be transferred by delivery or endorsement and delivery, or from time to time by change or ownership recorded in the books lending institution.

marketable securities. Securities dealt with on the Stock Exchange, or otherwise readily turned into cash. See also CERTIFICATE OF DEPOSIT; PARALLEL MARKET.

market analysis. The research undertaken to predict the movement of prices and recommend the appropriate action.

market capitalisation. The total value of a company by ascertaining the current market price of its shares in the market, then multiplying this amount by the number of shares issued. Although this will give an academic valuation of the company, it should be remembered that the value of shares on the market can fluctuate considerably and that the number of shares purchased and sold in any given period is usually small in comparison with the total number held by shareholders. The valuation of the company by a predator may be quite different from the valuation.

marketing. The ability to assess, by whatever means, the needs of the consumer, then using the available resources, design, produce, advertise, and deliver the goods at the right time and at the right place and price to the customer.

marketing boards. These were set up by statute in the early 1930s in order to purchase agricultural products from farmers and sell and distribute these products at controlled prices. The best known of these boards is the Milk Marketing Board.

market maker. A bank or securities house undertaking to make a secondary market for Eurobonds either by taking any bonds offered on to its own books or by finding takers for them among or through other banks active in the secondary market. Since the 'Big Bang' and the elimination of jobbers, member companies of the Stock Exchange undertake to make a market in certain ranges of shares i.e. to buy and sell shares on a continuous basis.

market overt. A public market where goods are on open offer. By custom, shops in the City of London form a market overt for articles which are sold in the normal business of such shops; elsewhere the term applies to markets established by grant or prescription. Stolen goods which find their way on to market overt become the property of the buyer in such a market, save only if the original thief is prosecuted to conviction, in which case the title reverts to the original owner. But the sale in 'market overt' must take place between sunrise and sunset for the buyer to obtain a good title. 'Market overt' does not apply to Scotland or Wales.

market price. The value placed on an article by the owner who wishes to sell it.

market report. An account describing the conditions of a market and listing the prices; a communication from a broker to banks and others who have money to invest, whether on their own behalf or on behalf of customers; a description of the previous day's trading on the Stock Exchange in the financial pages of a newspaper; a summary by a marketing manager of the results of market research carried out.

market research. The research undertaken to ascertain the size and potential of the market, ascertain the needs of a consumer so that the firm will be able to produce the goods/services and market its output.

marking. A Stock Exchange term to describe the prices recorded for business done in any security during the day.

marking names. Where an investor holds an US type of certificate, it will be seen on the reverse of the document that the investment is registered in the name of a company, but indicates from that point, the certificate has the attributes of a bearer document, i.e. transfer by delivery, so at that point it can be compared with a bearer document. However, the issuing company will send its dividends to the registered holder, so that any person holding the certificate, must claim the dividend due from the registered holder. A list of companies recognised by the International Stock Exchange as good for the receipt and payment of dividends has been made. The names quoted are considered as 'good marking names'. Those not on the list are merely known as 'other names'.

mark to market. The value of a swap in the books of a financial institution which is the 'agreed value' in its books. Where the mark to market takes into consideration the value of the swap if the institution wishes to sell or transfer the instrument.

mark-up. A term showing the amount or percentage added to the manufacturing cost or purchase price in order to obtain the selling price.

marriage settlement. A deed executed for the consideration that a marriage will take place for the settlement of property to either the husband or wife.

marry up. To join together. To link up. To connect a debit entry with a corresponding credit entry. To connect a query with a response obtained some time later.

marshal. To dispose in order, to arrange.

marshalling. The gathering together of data and arranging them in order.

marshalling of assets. Equitable principle whereby the executor of a will, will collect the assets together, for distribution to the beneficiaries in accordance with the will of the deceased. Where there are insufficient assets to satisfy the creditors and all the beneficiaries, some beneficiaries may lose their rights. The order in which they lose their rights is set out in the Administration of Estates Act 1925 s. 34(3) and Part 2 of the First Schedule of that Act.

marshalling of securities. An equitable principle regarding the position of creditors among themselves *vis-à-vis* the debtor. For example, where A mortgages properties X and Y to B, and later grants a second mortgage on X to C, C may demand that the claim of B shall be satisfied as far as possible from property X.

master card. An American credit card which is linked with ACCESS cards.

matching. The recognition that the purchase and sale of foreign currency must agree, that is that the buyer/seller who deliberately goes into a long or short position in any currency. Ensuring that the purchase/sale in any market agrees. The recognition that receipts and expenditure in a business is earned and expended in the particular financial period. A Bank of England term relating to 'matching' of a bank's assets and liabilities in terms of time.

material alteration. By Bills of Exchange Act 1882. s. 64(1): 'Where a bill or acceptance is materially altered without the assent of all parties on the bill, the bill is avoided except as against a party who has himself made, authorised, or assented to the alteration, and subsequent indorsers'. S. 64(2) 'The following alterations are material, namely, any alteration of the date, the sum payable, the time of payment, the place of payment, and where a bill has been accepted generally, the addition of a place of payment without the acceptor's assent. However if the alteration is not apparent, then the holder in due course may enforce payment according to its original tenor'.

mate's receipt. A receipt for goods received on board by a ship's mate. A mate's receipt is not a document of title and is purely temporary. It is later exchanged for a bill of lading.

matrimonial home. The place where a husband and his wife live. Under the Matrimonial Homes Act 1967, the spouse has a right of occupation to a house which the other is entitled to occupy by virtue of any contract or enactment. The wife has a precedence over any purchasers, creditors or mortgagees if her right has been registered as Class F land charge, at the Land Charges Department. In the reverse situation, a husband has a similar right of registration.

matrix. The place where anything is generated or developed; the centre of an organisational structure.

matrix organisation. The spread of the labour and skills of an organisation, so that such skills are fully utilised all the time, and that where there is a need to research a particular project, members of staff are chosen to be part of that project team. While project managers calculate the amount of time that each member needs to spend on the project, and when, the staff will remain at their posts and only be released to the project, when required. Additionally, an organisation in which managers will report to different superiors for different operations.

maturity. The date when a financial obligation, e.g. a bill of exchange, bond, stock is due for payment. In banking a bill of exchange or promissory note becomes legally payable on the last day of payment. However, should the last day of payment fall on either a Saturday or Sunday, or on any holy day, e.g. Good Friday, Christmas Day or on any holiday, e.g. Bank Holiday, Easter Monday, Boxing Day or any day appointed by Royal Proclamation to be a holiday, or any day under the Banking and Financial Dealings Act s. 2, to be a non-business day. Such bills are payable on the succeeding business day. The date that any instalment loan must be repaid.

maturity factoring. See FACTORING.

maturity ladder. A procedure whereby banks will arrange their reserve assets and the advances to customers in such an order that they can readily ascertain the ability to turn such assets into cash. In this way, the bank can readily establish the extent of any mismatch within a given time span. It will therefore give the bank time to adjust their position for any mismatch in their liquidity.

maturity transformation. The utilisation of short- term deposits to finance medium and long-term loans. While it has been the custom to 'borrow short – lend short', in practice many advances amount to nothing more than medium/long-term loans. Banks will lend large sums of money backed by funds borrowed from the money markets. However, it is only the larger banks and building societies that have a good desposit base, a high standing in the market that can utilise short-term funds for long-term loans.

Maundy Money. Money distributed annually by the Queen's Almoner to poor people on Maundy Thursday, the day before Good Friday. These silver coins of 1p, 2p, 3p and 4p become collectors' pieces.

maximum load line. See PLIMSOLL MARK; DEAD WEIGHT.

MBA. Abbreviation for Master of Business Administration. Within the educational qualifications of the Chartered Institute of Bankers, there is now the 'Lombard Scheme', which gives Associates the opportunity to gain a Master's degree in business administration.

mean price. See MIDDLE PRICE.

media. Popularly this refers to the television, radio, the press and any means of communication to the public at large. This term can also refer to the source of inputs and outputs to a computer. For example, a cheque is a medium whereby the computer will amend the balance of the drawer's account. Other forms of media are magnetic tape, punched cards, etc.

median. An average which indicates the middle item in a series of numbers arranged in order of values.

mediation. A method of settling industrial disputes between parties. A mediator, which is acceptable to all sides is brought in to assist in reaching a compromise agreement.

medium sized company. This is defined by the Companies Act 1985 as one which: (a) has a turnover between M£1.4 and M£5.75; (b) a balance sheet total between M£0.7 and M£2.8; (c) employees range from 50 to 250. A medium sized company is permitted to submit to the Registrar of Companies an abbreviated form of accounts.

medium of exchange. See MONEY.

mediums. Government stocks with a life of between five and fifteen years to redemption date.

medium-term credit. Loans which are now popular with banks for granting credit to businesses for capital purposes and expansion in working capital. Loans of this nature may be of five years duration and possibly longer.

medium-term notes. These notes were first issued in the USA in 1972. The market in the UK is still fairly young. These notes are similar to other bonds, but differ in the way they are offered to investors. A medium-term note (MTN) programme enables the issuer to deliver debts through dealers which can vary in amounts and maturities (two years plus). The issuers decide the rate of borrowing and the dealer receives a commission for finding investors.

meeting of creditors. The Insolvency Act 1986, has given creditors a certain amount of authority to ensure that the winding up of a company or the estate of a bankrupt is being dealt with in an efficient manner and in their interests. For the winding up of a company the administrator appointed by the court under an administration order must within 3 months give 14 days notice for a meeting of creditors to advise them of the purpose of the administration order and approve or disapprove of part or all of the administrator's pro-

posals. Any modification to the original proposal must be approved by the administrator. (ss. 23 and 24). Where a meeting has been summoned, the meeting if it thinks fit, may establish a creditors' committee to act on behalf of the creditors as prescribed by the act (s. 26). Where a company is being wound up by a creditors' voluntary winding up, then a meeting of creditors must be called within 14 days of the company resolution for its voluntary winding up. The notice of the creditors meeting must contain (a) the name and address of the person qualified to act as the insolvency practitioner and; (b) the place where on the two days prior to the meeting the list of company creditors is available for inspection (s. 98). Should the winding up of a company take longer than one year, then by s. 105, the liquidator shall at the end of the first year summon a general meeting of the company and a meeting of creditors. At this meeting the liquidator will account for his or her acts and conduct in the winding up process. This will be done for each successive year during the winding up period. Should the winding up of a company be done by the court, then a meeting of the creditors is called by a liquidator nominated by the creditors. In the case of an insolvent debtor where an interim order has been made by the court, the liquidator will summon a meeting of the creditors to decide whether to approve the voluntary arrangements made (ss. 257/8). Section 294: where in the case of any bankruptcy (a) the official receiver has not yet summoned, or has decided not to summon, a general meeting of the bankrupt's creditors for the purpose of appointing the trustee; and (b) a certificate for the summary administration of the estate is not, for the time being in force; any creditor of the bankrupt may request the official receiver to summon such a meeting for that purpose. Section 301: subject to certain rules a creditor's committee may be formed to exercise certain functions unless the trustee in bankruptcy is the official receiver, in which case, the functions of the committee will be exercised by the Secretary of State.

meetings, company. *See* ANNUAL GENERAL MEETING; EXTRAORDINARY GENERAL MEETING; STATUTORY MEETING.

member. An organ of the body. A person or an entity that belongs to a particular organisation, group or society.

member bank. A bank that is either a subsidiary of another bank, or part of a group of banks formed into a union to pursue a common interest. A bank that is member of one or all of the clearing companies. In the USA it refers to those banks that are affiliated to the Federal Reserve System.

member of a company. A person who has applied and received an allotment of shares in a company, or a person who has purchased shares in a company.

members' voluntary winding-up. *See* VOLUNTARY LIQUIDATION.

memorandum. A note or reminder, a brief record; a summary, outline or draft of an agreement.

memorandum of association. Frequently known as the memorandum. It is a document that must be drawn up by the founder members of a company, presented to the Registrar of Companies, for his approval and for registering that company. The document will contain such facts as: 1. The name of the company with PLC (Public Limited Company), or the Welsh equivalent, or Ltd (Limited), if the company is a private limited company. 2. The address of the company's registered office. 3. The objects of the company. 4. A statement that the liability of the members is limited. 5. The capital structure of the company and the number of shares and nominal value of these shares. In the case of a company limited by guarantee, a statement to the effect that each member undertakes to the assets of the company, in the eventuality of its winding up. For banks the objects clause states the purpose of the company and what it is capable of doing. Any activity not stated in the memorandum is *ultra vires* (beyond its powers). However, by the Companies Act 1989, s. 108 which has amended s. 35 of the 1985 Act does not limit the company to contract. Any transaction with third parties (bankers), providing that the third party has entered into a contract in good faith shall be deemed free of any limitations under the company's constitution. The interpretation of s. 9 European Communities Act 1972 has also varied the provisions of the *ultra vires* principle.

memorandum of deposit. This is the form which is normally signed by a customer who wishes to receive an advance and is willing to offer some security for the advance. The document is evidence that whatever security has been offered and taken, is evidence of the intention of the parties. It allows tha bank to take an equitable charge, but if it wishes to perfect its security, convert to a legal charge. It also permits the bank, if necessary to sell the security. A customer may also be requested to undertake to maintain a specific margin of cover.

memorandum of interview. After an interview with a customer, it is customary for the manager or bank official to record the details discussed, so that it is (*a*) kept as a record and (*b*) for immediate information, circulated to the relevant persons in the office. Such a memorandum of interview should be filed either in paper form or on the computer file. It is also used for the regular interviews with staff, so that a comprehensive record of the person's career is maintained.

memorandum of satisfaction. A notice addressed to and filed with the Registrar of Companies, to the effect that a mortgage or charge has been wholly (or partly) satisfied. The notice is originated by the creditor.

memory card. *See* CHIP CARD.

mental incapacity. The incapacity of a person will include such conditions as psychopathic disorder, disability of the mind, dependency on drugs or alcohol, mental impairment, or such a development of the mind as to impair intelligence or abnormal or aggressive conduct. For the banker, any such conditions, makes it difficult to decide whether the customer is able to conduct his/her own affairs. Should a customer be admitted compulsorily to a mental ward of a hospital, or when the customer is placed under the guardianship of the local authority social services, then it can be assumed that the customer has no mental capacity to conduct affairs. All mandates at this stage must be cancelled. Should a customer enter a hospital as a voluntary patient in order to obtain treatment, then this fact does not necessarily justify the cancellation of the banker/customer relationship.

mercantile. Pertaining to commerce, relating to buying and selling.

mercantile agent. A person or business that has the authority to sell and buy goods, consign goods, raise money on the security of the goods, as an agent for another person or trading organisation.

merchandise. Commodities bought and sold in home or foreign markets.

merchandise advances. *See* PRODUCE ADVANCES/LOANS.

merchandise marks. Marks on the outside of cases, packets, bales, etc., containing goods, especially those being imported or exported. The marks are used for identification purposes and are specified on the bill of lading and insurance policy.

merchant banks. The current description for these banks is Acceptance Houses, since they are all members of the Accepting Houses Association (*see* ACCEPTANCE HOUSE). Their main functions are dealing with the acceptance and discounting of bills of exchange, finance of international trade. They are also involved in dealing with mergers, take-overs, share and stock placings, new issues, investment management, etc. Their origins stemmed from trading as merchants, with specialised knowledge in certain commodities or certain areas in the world, so with London being a major centre of international trade, overseas merchants kept funds with them in London and drew and accepted bills of exchange on their account with these merchants. Eventually, as banking became more important to them than acting as merchants, they were given the popular name of 'merchant banks'. There is no apt definition of these banks, nor is there any one activity that dominates. They all have their own specialist activities, e.g. gold markets, underwriting, etc.

merger. An amalgamation of two or more businesses to improve the total capital base, have a greater influence in a market. The shareholders in each company will receive shares in the new company in an agreed proportion of the shares in the old company.

methods of payment. The banks offer their customers a variety of methods for settling their debts, which not only include cheques, credit transfers, direct debits, standing orders but the ability to transfer funds by home banking, i.e. using some means of identification (PIN). Other means of debt settlement, now being expanded is by the use of debit cards for payment of goods at retail outlets. In international trade, the use of bankers' drafts, mail transfers, telegraph transfers, SWIFT, bills of exchange, promissory note.

metric system. A decimal system of weights and measurements based on the French metre, at present in use in most countries of the world. There are seven base units: length (metre); mass (kilogram); time (second); electric current (ampere); temperature (kelvin); luminous itensity (candele); amount or substance (mole). The system is being gradually introduced into the UK at the present time.

Michaelmas Day. A quarter day – 29 September.

MICR. *See* MAGNETIC INK CHARACTER RECOGNITION.

microcomputer. *See* COMPUTER.

micro-economics. The branch of economics dealing with unit productions, e.g. single firms, their raw materials, costs and output; or the wages or salary of one man, or the fashioning and sale of one product, etc.

middleman An intermediary between the producer/manufacturer and the consumer or between the wholesaler and the consumer. They will very often take the risk of ordering and storing goods, before they have a contract to sell. Buy in bulk and sell in small or single units. Accept distribution costs and make their profit between the buying and selling prices.

middle price. In any market or exchange there will be two rates – the buying rate and the selling rate. When rates are published in newspapers or through TV channels, rather than stating both rates, the half-way rate only is quoted, so that the reader, whether a buyer or seller can make his/her own valuation. The margin between the buying and selling prices will differ up to about 5 per cent.

Midsummer Day. A quarter day – 24 June.

milker. One variety of thief specialising in travel cheques. He takes a book of travel cheques from a wallet, handbag, or hotel room, and tears out half-a-dozen cheques from the middle of the book before replacing it. The victim will probably not find out for a little while that any are missing, so the loss will not be reported quickly.

milling. In order to stop the clipping or the sweating of coins a ridge was introduced to coins that had an intrinsic value. Currently there is no temptation to shave pieces off any coin, since no coin has any value in itself. The milled-edged coin was introduced in the latter part of the seventeenth century, and it has been the custom, until fairly recently to retain milled-edge coinage for cupro-nickel coins.

mini-bond. Mini-bonds are single-premium policies which make use of share-exchange techniques, developed for the taxpayer who has a very high income and therefore pays a top rate of tax. The value of the bond is reflected by the value of the underlying assets. An individual taking out a single-premium mini-bond policy does not have to pay the premium in cash. Instead he or she can hand over investments in listed shares and will be credited with their value, less a small management charge taken by the assurance company. This counts as a disposal for capital gains tax (*q.v.*) purposes. The advantage which makes mini-bonds attractive comes from the fact that life assurance companies pay tax on the income from their investments at a maximum rate of 37.5 per cent – considerably lower than the higher rates and investment income surcharge levied on the individual. Thus the assurance company can pass on the benefit to the client. The usual procedure is to time the policy so that it matures after the policy holder has retired, because then the policy-holder's income will be comparatively low and thus liability to higher rate tax and the investment income surcharge will be correspondingly lighter.

minicomputer. *See* COMPUTER.

minimum lending rate. In October 1972 the bank rate was discontinued and a minimum lending rate was introduced by the Bank of England. This rate was calculated by taking the average rate of discount at the Friday bill tender, then adding one half of a per cent, and rounding this figure up to the nearest quarter per cent. The authorities had the right to vary this rate without reference to the Treasury Bill Rate. The minimum lending rate was suspended in August 1981. Nowadays the authorities can discount bills in accordance with an unpublished interest rate band.

ministerial trust. A trust where the will of trust deed gives the trustee(s) no particular discretion to vary the investments in the trust, or in the running of it, but calls merely for the exercise of normal prudence and business judgment in carrying out the express terms of the trust; as opposed to a discretionary trust (*q.v.*).

minor. A person under the age of eighteen. While there is no objection in opening a bank account for a young person – some banks encourage these persons to develop the banking habit at an early age – providing such an account is kept in credit. Money lent except for necessaries cannot be recovered. However, under the Minors' Contract Act 1987, a minor on reaching the age of eighteen years, may now ratify a contract or loan which he/she made while still a minor. A bank may at its discretion may lend, if it knows the person is of an honourable character and in receipt of a regular income, or knows that the minor's parent or guardian would if necessary put matters right. The law was amended by the Minors' Contract Act 1987, as it now recognises that a guarantee is enforceable against the guarantor, even though the original debt was unenforceable against the minor.

A minor may act as a witness, act as an agent, sign and draw cheques on the account of a principal. A minor is bound to pay a reasonable price for necessaries and contracts of employment are not voidable.

minor interests index. A record kept at the Land Registry for the purpose of registering a class of interest which is not in land, but an equitable interest which is additional to (*a*) those which can be registered in the Land Registry and (*b*) overriding interests – namely minor interests. These interests may in some cases be binding on a purchaser, if registered, or are equitable interests created under a trust for sale, which will be over-reached on a sale. Minor interests are protected by notices, restrictions, cautions or inhibitions, e.g. (*a*) land held upon trust for sale could have a restriction to make sure that sale funds are paid to two trustees or to a trust corporation, (*b*) a pending action affecting the land would be the subject to a caution, (*c*) a receiving order, of an inhibition. Any of these, except a notice will appear in the charges section of the Land Certificate.

minority interests. A subsidiary company which is owned by another company, but has a small number of shareholders which is in no way related to the holding company or other subsidiary companies. Such interests are shown separately in the balance sheet, while in the profit and loss account, the interest due to the minority shareholders is also shown separately.

minority shareholder. A shareholder of a company whose interests are not the same as the holding company or the major shareholder. A shareholder who has at an annual general meeting, or an extraordinary general meeting voted against the resolution/s accepted by the majority of shareholders.

mint. The place where money is coined under governmental supervision; to make by stamping, as of coins; fresh, unused, new. *See also* ROYAL MINT.

mintage. A charge made by a mint for turning bullion into coins; the process of minting coins.

mint par of exchange. A par of exchange between the coins of two countries both using the same metal, e.g. silver. The weight and fineness of one, compared with that of the other, will give the mint par of exchange by reference to the amount of pure metal in each coin.

mint price. The value of the quantity of coins into which a bar of metal can be made.

mint ratio. Where a bimetallic currency is in circulation, the ratio between the values of the two metals.

minute book. A book for recording the business carried through at company meetings.

minutes. The official record of business transacted at a meeting. Minutes of all company meetings are to be entered in books kept for that purpose. They are signed by the chairman of the meeting. They list the date and place of the meeting, name those present, and record all resolutions proposed. They are read over as the first item of business at the next meeting to check their accuracy.

Miras. *See* MORTGAGE INTEREST RELIEF AT SOURCE.

mirror account file. An exact duplicate of an account held in the books of another company/bank. An account held abroad (Nostro), will have a variety of debits and credits passed through it. In the books of the account holder, there will be an account also recording these entries to ensure speedy reconciliation and management information.

misappropriation. The conversion of funds by an employee or other person for improper or dishonest purposes, e.g. the use of employer's funds to pay the individual's own expenses.

mismatching. Using assets in one currency to finance advances in another currency (leading to a risk of loss flowing from adverse movements of exchange rates), or using short-term deposits to finance longer-term lending. *See* MATURITY TRANSFORMATION.

misrepresentation. Give a false account, incorrect presentation. Under the Misrepresentation Act 1967 any misrepresentation whether done innocently, negligently or fraudulently, will invalidate a contract.

mis-sort. In banking terms this means that an item has been sorted into the wrong compartment/file, so that there could either be a difference in the book-keeping or an error of commission/principle. Should a cheque or credit be mis-sorted for any reason, then that item would be forwarded to the bank/branch concerned after notifying the remitter of the occurrence.

mixed economy. An economic system planned and directed partly by the State, and partly by private enterprise.

mixed policy. A marine policy combining voyage and time insurance, in that a ship is insured from one certain place to another over a certain period of time.

MLR. *See* MINIMUM LENDING RATE.

MMC. *See* MONOPOLIES AND MERGERS COMMISSION.

mobile bank. A motorised caravan fitted out as a small bank, which can tour outlying districts on one or more days per week, or go to fairs or agricultural shows.

mode. A statistical formula to show an item that occurs most frequently.

modifying agreement. A regulated agreement which varies or supplements an earlier agreement. A modifying agreement revokes the earlier agreement, but its provisions reproduce the combined effect of the two agreements.

monetarism. An economic theory that inflation is caused by an excessive supply of money. Where there is too much money it will cause the price of goods to rise, i.e. the value of money will fall.

monetary. Concerning money or the coinage.

monetary asset. Cash in hand or balances in the bank or a claim to money which is immediately available.

monetary authorities. A term to describe the Bank of England, the Treasury or any governmental department that is responsible for the regulation of the monetary policies.

monetary base. This refers to a bank's reserve assets, cash held by a bank and the balances held at the Bank of England. By relating the reserve assets to eligible liabilities, the Bank of England can control the ability of a bank to lend and thereby control the money supply and interest rates.

monetary economy. An economic system in which exchange is effected by means of money, as opposed to barter.

monetary policy. The rules and regulations imposed by the monetary authorities in order to control the money supply, control inflation and achieve the economic policy that is required for the good of the country generally. This may be achieved by a variety of ways such as, change of interest rates, directives, open market operations, amendment of the reserve asset ratios, special deposits, etc.

monetary reform. The introduction of a new currency after a period of hyper-inflation, or the introduction of a new decimal currency unit.

monetary system. The provisions laid down by government for the monetary arrangements of the country. It covers such matters as the monetary unit and its divisions, whether such units have unlimited or limited legal tender, the production of banknotes, the minting of coinage. Externally it deals with the provisions of foreign exchange and exchange controls, if any.

monetary union. An agreement between countries to maintain a fixed exchange rate between their currencies.

monetary unit. The standard unit of a country's currency.

monetary working capital adjustment. *See* INFLATION ACCOUNTING.

money. This is regarded as any commodity that can be used as (*a*) a medium of exchange, (*b*) a store of value, (*c*) a unit of account, (*d*) a standard for deferred payments. While the pound sterling is the legal tender of the UK and therefore notes and coins are acceptable for the settlement of debts, other forms of debt settlement are being used more frequently, e.g. cheques, interbank transfers – direct debits, standing orders – credit cards, etc.

money at call and short notice. A description of a bank liquid asset which covers day-to-day advances to members of the money markets. Such short-term loans are from overnight up to fourteen days.

money broker. A firm in the City of London whose function it is – in the money markets – to marry borrower to lender, or buyer to seller. For this function they will be paid a commission.

money laundering. Banks and other financial institutions may be unwittingly used as intermediaries for the transfer or deposit of funds derived from criminal activity. Criminals and their associates use the financial system to make payments and transfers of funds from one account to another; to hide the source and beneficial ownership of money; and to provide storage for banknotes through a safe deposit facility. These activities are commonly referred to as money laundering. In January 1989 the Basle Statement of Principles on Money Laundering was circulated to all institutions authorised under the Banking Act. The Statement of Principles does not restrict itself to drug related money laundering, but extends to all aspects of laundering through the banking system, i.e. the deposit, transfer and/or concealment of money derived from illicit activities whether robbery, terrorism, fraud or drugs. It seeks to deny to those involved in money laundering by the application of the following principles: (*a*) Know your customer – banks should make reasonable efforts to determine the customer's true identity, and have effective procedures for verifying the bona fides of new customers. (*b*) Compliance with laws – bank management should ensure that business is conducted in conformity with high ethical standards, laws and regulations being adhered to and ensuring; that a service is not provided where there is good reason to suppose that transactions are associated with laundering activites. (*c*) Co-operation with law enforcement agencies – within any constraints imposed by rules relating to customer confidentiality, banks should co-operate fully with national law enforcement agencies including, where there are reasonable grounds for suspecting money laundering, taking appropriate measures which are consistent with the law. The statutory exemptions to which the above refers are as follows: Drugs Trafficking Offences Act 1986 s. 24, Prevention of Terrorism Act (Temporary Provisions) Act 1989 s. 11. Criminal Justice Act 1988 s. 98. *See* BASLE STATEMENT.

moneylender. A person whose business it is to lend money. The business must be licensed by the Director-General of Fair Trading.

money lent and lodged. A comparison between the total advances made by a bank, whether by way of overdrafts, loans, discounts, etc., and the total of money deposited with it, whether by way of current, deposit, or savings accounts, or by borrowing from the inter-bank market. This comparison gives the bank's lending ratio.

money market. The market consists of the Bank of England, the money brokers, Discount Houses and all the banks. In this market which has no physical site, wholesale funds are borrowed and lent for short periods. *See* LONDON MONEY MARKET.

money of account. A denomination (e.g. the guinea) not actually coined, but used for convenience in keeping accounts.

money shops. These are best described as financial retail outlets, financed by major banks. They are not a cohesive group but fall into two sections according to their objectives and background. Some have a number of retail outlets and conduct their business directly with their customers, while others do not have more than one or two outlets and conduct their business by post. Generally, they do not have commercial customers, but attract individuals. Their popularity stems from the fact that they tend to have longer opening hours and have a less formal attitude to their customers and bright and comfortable offices designed to attract individuals. The main services tend to be the acceptance of deposits and lending services at various rates of interest. Due to the type of borrower that is attracted to them, they are vulnerable to bad debts, so loan rates tend to be higher than the major banks. They do not offer the wide range of services available in a major bank.

money supply. Money supply and monetary policy commences with the simple assumption that there is a connection between the rate of growth in the money supply and the rate at which prices rise – inflation. The government in its 1981 Green Paper stated that while the money supply and prices may diverge in the short term, they do not in the longer term. It therefore set itself the responsibility of controlling inflation by controlling the money supply. The relationship between the money supply and inflation has never been straightforward and the various monetary targets and measurements of the money supply have from time to time been called into question. Over recent decades, the monetary targets have been revised upwards several times, so that as recently as March 1987 targets have been set and in May 1987 a new set of money aggregates were introduced, they are $M0$ = Notes and coin in circulation with the public, in bank tills and in banks' current accounts at the Bank of England; $M1$ = Notes and coin in circulation with the public, plus private sector sterling sight bank deposits, both interest and non interest bearing (includes current account, call money and overnight money held in the UK banking sector); $M3$ = M1 plus private sector sterling time bank deposits and private sector holdings of sterling bank certificates of deposit; $M4$ = M3 plus private sector holdings of building society shares, deposits and sterling certificates of deposits *less* building societies holdings of bank deposits and bank certificates of deposits, notes and coin; $M5$ = M4 plus private sector (excluding building societies) holdings of money market instruments (Bank bills, Treasury Bills, Bank deposits) certificates of tax deposit and national savings instruments (excluding national saving certificates, SAYE and other long term deposits). $M2$ = Non interest bearing component of M1 plus private sector interest bearing retail sterling bank deposits, plus private sector holdings of retail building society shares and deposits and National Savings Bank ordinary accounts. $M3c$ = M3 plus private sector holdings of foreign currency bank deposits. Money consists of a small proportion of notes and coin, the rest being deposits of which some perform all the functions of money, while others only some. This makes it difficult to give an accurate definition of money. Further, some definitions of money refer to 'Narrow Money' – money for immediate spending, e.g. M0, M2, and 'Broad Money' – money for transaction purposes and as a store of value e.g. M3, M5. The definitions of money supply are, therefore, to some degree arbitrary and with possible future developments to change can be invalidated.

money transmission services. The ser-

vice operated by banks for their customers for the clearing of cheques, bills of exchange, giro credits, bankers orders, direct debits, etc. With the establishment of the Association of Payment Clearing Services in December 1985, for the purposes of transmission of funds and clearing of items presented to banks, three clearing companies were set up *viz;* 1. Cheque and Credit Clearing Co. Ltd – high volume paper clearing; 2. Chaps and Town Clearing Co. Ltd – high value same day clearing; 3. Bankers Automated Clearing Services Ltd – electronic clearing of direct debits, standing orders, etc.; 4. In due course a system to cover EFTPOS (Electronic Funds Transfer Point of Sale) will be set up. *See* ASSOCIATION OF PAYMENT CLEARING SERVICES.

monopoly. An exclusive right secured to one person, group or company to make, supply or sell a certain commodity. A monopoly supplier is therefore one with no competitors, who is able to charge whatever price he or she likes unless restrained by legislation. The Fair Trading Act 1973 s. 6(1) defined a 'monopolist' as one having a quarter or more of the market; such a company may be examined by the Monopolies and Mergers Commission.

Monopolies and Mergers Commission. This commission was set up under the Monopoly and Mergers Act 1965, to investigate those take-overs and mergers which are likely to operate against the public interest. Under the Fair Trading Act 1973, it will, where necessary, refer any merger to the Department of Trade and Industry to take any action required.

monthly investment plan. A service operated by all major banks and other financial institutions to assist personal customers to save on a regular basis. Often banks will offer attractive interest rates on their deposit accounts, while other institutions such as unit trusts will offer facilities to invest a minimum of £25 each month to build up an investment in a trust of the customer's choosing.

Moody's Investor Services. A debt rating agency.

mopping up. When there is a surplus of money in the discount market the Discount Houses, who never refuse money offered to them by the banks, will lower the price for money by quoting a very low rate of interest for such funds. The banks will not wish to avail themselves of this and money which should have been lent out overnight or at call will be very much more difficult to place. In these circumstances the Bank of England will come to the rescue by selling Treasury Bills to the banks, or houses, thus 'mopping-up' the spare funds. *Also called* operating in reverse.

moratorium. An act authorising the suspension of payments or reparations by a bank or debtor state for a certain period of time; the period of suspension of payments; the agreement by creditors with an insolvent debtor that they will not enforce payment for a certain time.

mortgage. The conveyance of a legal or equitable interest in real or personal property as security for a debt or for the discharge of an obligation. In relation to Scotland, the terms includes any heritable security. *See also* ENDOWMENT MORTGAGE; EQUITABLE MORTGAGE; FIRST MORTGAGE; LEGAL MORTGAGE; POWERS OF MORTGAGEE; PUISNE MORTGAGE; SECOND MORTGAGE; SUB-MORTGAGE.

mortgage annuity scheme. This scheme can be attractive to elderly persons who are in need of income and can use their property to take out a mortgage. The sum raised can then be invested to buy an annuity. Usually no capital is repaid – only interest – in the lifetime of the person/s, so that on the death of the survivor, the property is then sold to repay any outstanding debt.

mortgage bond. A bond backed by mortgage of real property. Mortgage bonds carry a specified maturity and interest rate. In Italy and Germany this is the main method of housing finance. Special mortgage banks arrange the issue, and then lend the money so raised to house buyers.

mortgage debenture. A debenture accompanied by a charge on the assets of the borrowing company.

mortgage deed. The document containing the conditions of a loan secured by the property.

mortgagee. The person to whom property is mortgaged by a borrower.

Mortgage Interest Relief at Source. Commonly known as MIRAS. This is a method whereby the taxpayer who pays mortgage interest is given immediate relief from income tax. The mortgagor deducts income tax at the basic rate from the interest component of the repayments.

mortgage market. In the US, a government-sponsored secondary market in mortgages, that is, long-term loans for house purchases. No corresponding market of this nature exists in the UK.

mortgage of company assets. *See* REGISTRATION OF CHARGES.

mortgage of equitable interest. Where a person is likely to be a beneficiary of property under a will, then that person has an equitable interest against which he/she may borrow. Such a person may be a joint tenant, a beneficiary under a trust for sale, or a remainder-man. While the property in the trust will one day be sold, there will be an income from this property which will be paid by the trustees to the life tenant. From the lending bank's point of view, there is no legal estate to be obtained, so that the bank cannot take a legal charge over the property. The deeds of the property are held by the trustees, nor can the mortgage be registered with the Land Charges Department, as it is not a mortgage on land, but on the proceeds of sale of the land. However, if the land is registered land, a mortgage of the equitable interest can be protected by registration on the Minor Interest Index. All the bank can do is to take a legal assignment by way of a mortgage of an equitable interest. A mortgage will be drawn up by the bank's solicitor, and notice of the charge will be given to the trustees. Their acknowledgment must be obtained and they must confirm that no notice of any prior charge has been received. If the borrower's interest is contingent only, the security must be supported by a life policy to repay the loan if the borrower should die before his/her interest becomes vested in him.

mortgage of a ship. For a lending banker, the taking of a ship as security has many disadvantages. It is difficult to value, it is difficult to sell and importantly, it has a high rate of depreciation. Any mortgage taken on a vessel must be in the form as prescribed in the Merchant Shipping Act 1894. British ships are registered in their home ports in the UK. A ship is divided into 64 shares and each share can be owned by one or more persons. The mortgage of a ship must be registered in the register of the ship's port of registry and the entry is recorded for purposes of priority on the hour and day of registration. The bank's own mortgage form will also be completed as it contains the various clauses giving the bank protection. As with any other property, a prior search of the register is made to ensure that there are no prior entries, adequate insurance cover must be available to cover the various marine and war risks. Should the vessel be owned by a limited company then the charge should also be registered at Companies House. While it has been stated that the capital of the vessel is divided into 64 parts, it is desirable from the lending banker's point of view to have a majority holding of these shares in order to control its operation.

mortgage offer. A formal letter from a bank or building society stating the details, terms and conditions on which the loan is offered to the borrower.

mortgage protection policy. A policy of assurance taken out by a borrower to cover the outstanding loan. Each year the premium paid is reduced slightly in line with the reduction of the loan. In the event of the borrower's death, repayment of the loan is made by the insurance company. Should the borrower survive the period of mortgage loan, no return or repayment of money will be made.

mortgage term. The period for which land is vested in the mortgagee by the mortgagor.

mortgagor. The person who mortgages personal property in favour of the lender.

mortmain. This phrase was used in instances where land could not be alienated. This law which related to mortmain was abolished by the Charities Act 1960 s. 3.

motion. A formal proposal either made orally or in writing at a meeting for the purpose of discussion, rejection or adoption. An application to a judge or Court for a ruling or action in favour of the applicant.

movables. A term embracing all property other than land.

mudaraba. A method of lending funds without breaking the rules of the Koran by obtaining interest on funds lent to borrowers. See ISLAMIC BANKING.

multilateral. Having several participants.

multilateral trade. A state of complete freedom of trade between countries unhampered by tariffs, quotas, or any other restrictions.

multinational company. A company or corporation that has manufacturing or trading interests in two or more countries. It may take the form of a holding company based in one country with subsidiary companies in other countries.

multiple agreement. In the Consumer Credit Act 1974, an agreement whose terms are such as 1. to place a part of it within one category of agreement mentioned in the Act, and another part of it within a different category of agreement so mentioned, or within a category of agreement not so mentioned; or 2. to place it, or part of it, within two or more categories of agreement so mentioned.

multiple exchange rates. In countries that have exchange control regulations in operation, it can be the policy of the government to impose two or three different exchange rates according to the purpose for which these funds are intended, e.g. commercial rate, tourist rate, etc. A discount or premium will be imposed depending on the use of funds.

municipal. Pertaining to a corporation or city, or to local self-government in general.

municipal corporation. See LOCAL AUTHORITY.

muniment. A title-deed, charter or record kept as evidence or defence of a title.

mutatis mutandis. After making the necessary changes.

mutilated banknotes. It is the policy of the Bank of England to call in and accept banknotes which are either soiled and/or mutilated and a refund will be made if a sufficient part of the note is available. It is usual for members of the public to obtain this service by presenting these notes to any of the major banks or the Post Office.

mutilated cheque or bill. Should a bill or cheque be torn or mutilated in any way the drawee or drawee bank in the case of a cheque would be entitled to receive some explanation for the mutilation. This tear may be ignored if it is only slight and in no way interferes with the tenor of the instrument, but where the cheque/bill has been torn right through, then the payee or indorser should endorse the instrument with the words 'torn in error' and signed, or 'mutilation confirmed' and signed or perhaps some form of indemnification inserted for any loss due to the mutilation.

mutual funds. A US financial institution, similar to the UK unit trust as the investor will place his funds with the institution for investment in various securities. An annual fee is made by the corporation for this service.

mutual wills. Wills made by two or more persons, each giving mutual benefits to each other and agreeing that there will be no changes in either wills without the consent of the other party.

mutual savings banks. In the US, thrift institutions which have no stockholders but are owned by the depositors.

N

naked debenture. An acknowledgement of indebtedness, not accompanied by any security.

naked trustee. A person acting as a trustee has no beneficial interest in the property and whose sole function is to act in the interests of the beneficiaries of full age and transfer as necessary, such property to its owners.

name. A person who is a sleeping partner for Lloyd's underwriters. He/she takes no active part in the day-to-day business, but is liable for the debts to which their name has been put. Such persons must have a financial standing of at least £75 000.

name day. A Stock Exchange term indicating the day on which the names of the buyers are transmitted to the sellers. It is also called the Ticket Day.

named policy. A policy of marine insurance in which the name of the vessel carrying the insured goods has been specified.

narration. An accountancy term meaning the explanation or reason why a particular entry has been made to an account.

narrow market. When there is only a small supply of any particular security available on the Stock Exchange.

NASDAQ. National Association of Securities Dealers and Automated Quotations.

NASDIM. National Association of Dealers and Investment Managers.

National Association of Investment Clubs. This association was established to assist small groups of persons (not more than 20) who meet regularly for the purpose of combining their contributions in a mutual investment fund and to invest such funds in stocks/shares as decided by the group. The association will assist in drawing up a constitution and in general, offer guide-lines in running an investment fund.

national capital. The financial value of the total real capital of a country at any particular time.

national debt. The borrowings of governments. The government borrows funds by the issue of gilt-edged stock which, in general terms, can be regarded as long term, while the government's short-term borrowing is by the issue of Treasury bills. The national debt is managed by the Bank of England.

National Economic Development Council. Commonly known as 'Neddy'. The council consists of government ministers, members of the TUC and the CBI to discuss major economic issues in order to improve the economic performance of Great Britain. The main functions of the Council are: 1. To advise the Treasury. 2. To search for ways to stabilise industrial incomes. 3. To research into the reasons for Great Britain's disappointing economic growth in recent years. 4. To educate the public in the importance of applying developed new ideas to industry. For these functions, small committees – often known as Little Neddies – have been set up to deal with individual industrial sectors.

National Enterprise Board (NEB). This board was set up under the Industry Act 1975 for the purpose of acquiring on behalf of the state, an interest in companies in the private sector.

National Girobank. *See* GIROBANK.

national income. The value in a country's money of the total production of goods and services in that country for one year.

National Institute for Economic and Social Research (NIESR). A non-profit making research centre set up in 1938, which works closely with the Treasury in making quarterly projections of the economic trends in the country, using a computer-based model of the British economy.

nationalisation. The acquisition and management of industrial and distributing organisations by the State.

National Research Development Corporation (NRDC). Established in 1948 and financed by the Government. The corporation exists to provide 'innovation capital' to assist the development of British inventions. An application for assistance, if approved, will be furnished with funds to patent the idea, set up a working model, and eventually market the product. The corporation, which is part of the Department of Trade and Industry, is repaid by a levy on the sales of the successful project. *See also* VENTURE CAPITAL.

National Savings Bank. The original name for this bank was the Post Office Savings Bank, which was established in 1861, but changed its name in 1969. This bank offers basic banking services, i.e. deposit and withdrawal, to any person that wishes to have the convenience of being able to deposit and withdraw funds from the Post Office network of nearly 20 000 retail outlets. Although some clubs, charities and companies may have existing accounts they are no longer eligible to open such accounts, but those that are still open may continue to function. For those who wish to open an Ordinary Account, then the minimum deposit is £5, for which a deposit book is given and the maximum that can be held on this account is £10 000. Instant withdrawal of up to £250 may be made at any Post Office, the entry is recorded in the pass-book and returned over the counter with the funds. Any larger amount will mean verification of the transaction at the Head Office and payment made a few days later. One special feature of this account is that no interest is charged on the first £70 (£140.00) if the account is in joint names, but interest earned must be declared to the Inland Revenue. While the National Savings Bank acknowledge that the interest offered is not high, the rate at the time of writing is 2.5 per cent on balances up to £500 and 5 per cent on balances over this figure. Interest is paid at the end of the calendar year. The Investment Account is the only other type of account available from the National Savings

Bank. For the non-taxpayer this account offers a good rate of interest payable gross – at the moment 12.75 per cent – but interest earned must be declared to the Inland Revenue. The account may be opened with a minimum deposit of £5 and the maximum is £25 000, but existing holdings of more than £25 000 are permitted but no further deposits may be added. As with the Ordinary Account, societies, clubs, charities and companies are no longer eligible to open accounts, but may continue to make deposits in an existing account. One month's notice is required for withdrawals.

National Savings Capital Bonds. These are bonds which have a life of five years and like any other national savings investment offer a safe deposit for funds earning, at the moment, an average 11.5 per cent interest per annum compound and therefore attractive to non-taxpayers. The current issue is series 'C' which may be purchased in amounts of £100 up to £100 000. Any early encashment will be penalised by a lower rate of interest. No interest will be paid if the bonds are encashed in the first year.

National Savings Certificates. These certificates are available at all Post Offices and some banks. They are designed for persons who require absolute security, a guaranteed rate of return for a period of five years, and to be totally free of income tax and capital gains tax. The present issue (36th) has a minimum investment of £25 and a maximum of £5000 plus any holdings from other issues of savings certificates. Should any certificates be held over the five years, they will still attract interest but at the 'extension rate'. The capital and interest is payable at maturity. For any person wishing to encash the certificates before the fifth anniversary, then the interest rates will be at a lower, but sliding rate. For persons wishing to have not only safety and a hedge against inflation, then index-linked certificates are available. The present issue offers a basic rate of interest of 4.5 per cent to which is added an index-linked percentage, providing the certificates are held for the five-year period. The index-linked interest is calculated by reference to the Retail

Prices Index (RPI) which is published monthly. Each unit costs £25 and a maximum of 400 (£10 000 may be held). For those investors that hold the certificates over the five-year period, index linking will continue, but an additional bonus is payable as well. This type of investment is attractive to the high rate of taxpayer.

National Savings Children's Bonus Bonds. The first issue of these bonds was announced in the budget of March 1991 and became available from July 1991. It is particularly attractive for parents, grandparents, friends and others who wish to give bonds as gifts. They can be purchased for any child up to 16 years of age and will keep on growing until the person is 21 years of age. All interest and returns are exempt from Income and Capital Gains Tax. The main features of this form of savings are: 1. Bonds are purchased in units of £25 up to a maximum of £1000. 2. The present rate of interest is averaged at 11.84 per cent. 3. If the bonds are held longer than the first five years, a bonus is payable each five years until the person reaches 21 years of age. Should the bonds be encashed before maturity, then a lower rate of interest is paid.

National Savings Guaranteed Growth Bond. Introduced in the Budget of March 1992 to become available in the summer of 1992. The bond will offer a fixed rate of interest guaranteed for one year. Interest will be added annually after basic tax has been deducted. The minimum holding is to be £1,000 and the maximum £250,000.

National Savings Income Bonds. Unlike National Savings Capital Bonds, these bonds offer all holders a regular monthly income. The interest is paid gross, so they are ideal for non-taxpayers who have a lump sum to put away for some time and are looking for a regular income with nothing taken off for tax. The minimum investment is £2000 which may be increased in multiples of £1000 to a maximum of £50,000. Holdings of bonds above this figure may still be held but no further purchases may be added. Societies, clubs and companies are no longer eligible to buy these bonds, except to increase their current holding. The rate of interest, currently 11.75 per cent, is variable at six weeks notice and is available in all Post Offices and in the national press. After the bond has been held six weeks, interest is paid monthly on the 5th of each month, and may be credited to the holder's account either at a bank or building society. To obtain repayment in multiples of £1000, three months notice must be given.

National Savings Premium Bonds. These bonds give investors a regular chance to win tax-free prizes. While the investment is perfectly safe, holders receive no interest, but have the opportunity of winning prizes ranging from £50–£250 000. Prize-winners are notified direct. To pay these prizes, a sum equivalent to interest of 6.5 per cent is paid into a prize fund to pay out weekly and monthly prizes chosen by Electronic Random Number Indicator Equipment (ERNIE). Minimum purchases may be made as follows: under 16 years of age, £10. Over 16 years of age £100. Further purchases may be made in multiples of £10 with a maximum of £10 000. Bonds become eligible for the prize draw three months after purchase. Withdrawals need eight working days notice.

National Savings Save As You Earn. This form of savings is only available to employees who are entitled to buy shares in their company under a share option scheme approved by the Inland Revenue.

National Savings Stock Office. A wide range of Government Stock (Gilts) may be purchased through National Savings. Application forms and envelopes are available at Post Offices. The special feature of this service is that *(a)* interest is paid gross, *(b)* it is cheaper than purchasing/selling through a stockbroker, *(c)* a maximum of £10 000 may be purchased in any one day, but there is no limit to the amount of gilts that could be held.

National Savings Yearly Plan. This is a method of regular monthly savings for a one year period, when at the end of the year a savings certificate is issued. Providing this certificate is held a further four years, the capital and interest is repaid free of Income or Capital Gains Tax. The amount invested may be paid away by standing order from a building society account or bank account. The minimum fixed monthly payment is £20 and a maximum of £200 each month. Savers who wish to stop payment, may simply cancel the standing order, but withdrawals in the first year do not receive any interest.

'natural deposit'. When financing a particular asset, it is usual for a bank to obtain funding via the interbank sterling market. Natural deposits are funds which are derived from an industrial or commercial company as opposed to the former.

natural rights. The rights of a person as imposed by the law of nature. These rights are usually incorporated in the laws of a country.

near (or quasi-) money. A term used to describe any assets that are quickly and easily convertible to cash. This term is frequently applied to such intruments as bills of exchange, cheques, processing notes, credit cards, etc. or any such instrument, but does not include banknotes, coins or deposits in banks payable on demand.

necessaries. Goods that are required by a person in accordance with his/her standard of life. A minor may bind himself/herself in a contract for such food, drink, apparel and other necessaries (employment, study) (*Nash* v. *Inman*, 1908). A man is not generally liable for the debts of his wife, except if they are necessaries for domestic purposes.

negative. A statement that implies a denial or refusal or lack of a definite commitment.

negative cash flow. A situation in which a business spends more money than it receives during any financial period.

negative certificate of origin. A certificate or invoice, often referred to as a legalised invoice and must be approved by the importing country's consulate or embassy in the seller's country before the goods are allowed to be imported. This document is frequently required by countries of the Middle East.

negative dealing. Eurocurrency market operations not always viewed with approval by the authorities, e.g. US dollars are borrowed for one year fixed, swapped into sterling on a three-month swap (fully covered), and the sterling proceeds lent out for three months, at the end of which period (depending on rate movements) a further three-month swap can take place as before, or the dollars can be lent out for nine months.

negative income tax. Payments from the State to people with incomes below subsistence level.

negative interest. A charge made by a bank for retaining funds on a deposit account. This rarely occurs, but does so when a hard currency country, e.g. Switzerland, wishes to discourage foreign residents from placing deposits.

negative pledge. A pledge given by a borrower, usually a company, when funds are lent without any collateral being taken, it is signed to the effect that should the company borrow from other sources, no security would be given to that other lender without the consent of the first lender.

negligence. A lack of reasonable care, a breach of common law duty. It is a tort in its own right. A plaintiff must show: 1. That the defendant owned a duty of care to him. 2. There was a breach of that duty. 3. The plaintiff suffered some loss or damage. In banking, negligence is likely to be seen in a banker/customer relationship, e.g. the non-payment of a cheque drawn by a customer that will harm his/her reputation. The collection of a cheque and the credit to the wrong customer's account. The lack of making a reasonable enquiry when such an enquiry should have been made. Under the Unfair Contract Terms Act 1977, it means the breach of any obligation arising from the express or implied terms of a contract, to take reasonable care or exercise reasonable skill in the performance of a contract, or the breach of any common-law duty to take reasonable care or exercise reasonable skill or the breach of the common duty of care imposed by the Occupiers' Liability Act 1957. *See also* CONTRIBUTORY NEGLIGENCE OF PLAINTIFF.

negotiable instrument. Any instrument that has the following characteristics is deemed to be a negotiable instrument: (*a*) title passes on mere delivery or indorsement and delivery, (*b*) the holder may sue in his own name, (c) no notice of assignment need be given, (d) the holder takes the instrument in good faith, has given value, and has no notice of defects in the title of the transferor. Negotiable instruments are: banknotes, bearer bonds, bills of exchange, promissory notes, cheques, Treasury Bills, Certificates of Deposit, bearer share certificates, debentures payable to bearer. Any bill of exchange that is overdue, discharged by payment or has a restrictive endorsement will no longer be negotiable. Cheques which are crossed 'not negotiable' or crossed 'A/C Payee' or 'Not Transferable', would lose their attribute of negotiability.

negotiation. A conference with a purpose of arriving at an agreement. Bring in a desired result. A method of finance in international trade whereby the banker will discount an exporter's clean bill of exchange or documentary bill of exchange and therefore credit his account with the face value of the bill less interest and other charges. Should the bill be dishonoured on presentation, then the bank has the right of recourse. This method of finance differs from discounting, inasmuch it is usual for bills to be discounted when (a) they have been accepted, (b) drawn in sterling, (c) the bill is payable in the UK. Under the Bills of Exchange Act 1882 s. 31(1) negotiation is defined as 'the transfer of a bill from one person to another in such a manner as to constitute the transferee as the holder of the bill'. There can be no negotiation without delivery and therefore it gives the transferee the right to sue in his own name. If a bill is stolen, then neither delivery nor negotiation has taken place. By s. 34(4) 'Except where an indorsement bears the date after the maturity of the bill, every negotiation is prima facie deemed to have been effected before the bill was overdue'.

negotiation credit. An issuing bank under a documentary letter of credit will from time to time instruct or nominate an advising bank to negotiate a credit, or make it freely negotiable in the exporter's country. Should a bank negotiate a credit, then it will examine the draft and documents presented under the credit and if they comply with the terms and conditions of the credit, the negotiating bank will advance the amount subject to recourse. That bank will then seek reimbursement from the issuing bank. If the negotiating bank has been asked to add its confirmation then payment to the beneficiary is then without recourse.

negotiation fee. A fee charged by a bank for arranging a loan.

negotiator. For the purposes of the Consumer Credit Act 1974, the person by whom negotiations are conducted with the debtor or hirer.

net, nett. Left after all deductions.

net asset value (NAV). The total value of all the assets, less all short-term and long-term liabilities. The net figure is then divided by the number of shares issued to give the result which will show the net worth of the entity. It should be noted that these figures are available from the balance sheet and would not necessarily be the same date as the valuation.

net book value (NBV). The original cost of an asset less its aggregate depreciation. It may also be known as 'current value', 'depreciated value' or 'written down value'.

net cash. The request by a supplier that no credit will be permitted with the transaction and the purchaser must therefore pay either on receipt of the goods, or send payment with the order.

net cash flow. Retained profits for the year, plus depreciation as charged (i.e. gross cash flow less dividends paid).

net dividend. The dividend paid by a company, after deduction of the tax credit.

net income. Usually refers to a person's total income after deduction of income tax and other compulsory deductions, e.g. national insurance charge, pension, etc. For a business this will refer to the profit generated less all expenses.

net investment. The total investment made by a company in its financial year, less any depreciation of the asset/s.

net loss. A situation where the income is exceeded by the expenses.

net price. Cash price without discount.

net profit. The gross profit of a business entity, less all its expenses including taxation and interest paid on the long-term loans. Schedule 4 Companies Act 1985, states this item must be shown as 'profit for the financial year'.

net rate of tax. The amount that a person will need to pay, depending on his earned and unearned income less allowances. The rate of tax will be calculated by reference to a given band of tax, e.g. 20 per cent or 40 per cent, or whatever is the rate laid down by government.

Net Relevant Earnings (NRE). Net profit from all employment often deducting business charges and capital allowances – or if employed could be salaries plus bonuses and overtime.

net rental. The rent of a property after payment of all sums for repairs, taxes and expenses.

net saving. Total savings less adjustments for depreciation and stock appreciation.

nett. Left after all deductions.

netting. An arrangement whereby it is not necessary to re-exchange currencies when a swap arrangement is terminated. For example, if company X and Y each in different countries sell each others' currencies against their own local currency and during the period of the swap agreement, one currency has moved up and the other down, then the agreement could provide for a 'netting' whereby neither party will gain or lose by the transaction.

net weight. The weight of goods without their packaging.

network. A communications system for speedy transmission of information throughout an organisation. A computer system where there are a number of terminals at some distance away from each other and connected by a telecommunications system.

net worth. The total value of all the assets (not including fictitious assets), less all current and long-term liabilities. This should equal the value of the invested capital plus reserves. Often known as the owner's equity.

net yield. A yield which is assessed after deduction of tax.

new issue. When a company needs to raise funds either for expansion purposes or to reduce its borrowings, it may make a new issue of shares to the public. This will be arranged by an issuing house which will make itself responsible for the issue. New issues may also be for new companies or for companies that have been 'privatised'. A new issue may be made by an 'Offer for sale'. In this instance the issue house will purchase the total amount of shares available and then will find purchasers to take up the shares. A new issue may also be undertaken by a 'placement' whereby the issuing house will place blocks of shares with financial institutions. An issue to the public will be by the issue of a prospectus, usually placed in major national newspapers and members of the public may apply for a stated amount. *See also* RIGHTS ISSUE.

next friend. One who acts on behalf of another who is unable, from infirmity or legal incapacity, to act for themselves.

next-of-kin. Nearest blood relative.

NIFS. *See* NOTE ISSUING FACILITIES.

night safe. A safe whose door is on the outside wall of a bank which will allow customers to place their valuables and cash into the bank when the bank is closed. To use this facility a customer must obtain a key to the safe and a wallet, which is capable of being locked. When a deposit in the safe is made, the customer will open the safe and insert his wallet which will drop down a chute and land in the bank's strongroom. In the morning, the wallet can either be opened by a member of the bank staff and the proceeds credited to the account of the customer or alternatively, the customer may go to the bank and retrieve the full wallet and pay in the proceeds personally.

Nikkei Average. The Tokyo Stock Exchange Index which indicates the overall movement of transactions each day.

nisi prius **(unless before).** A name given to trials by jury in civil cases, the words *nisi prius* being the first in the old Latin form of the writ commanding the parties to appear at Westminster 'unless before' this the case had been dealt with on circuit.

NMS. *See* NORMAL MARKET SIZE.

node. A substation, housing a computer, on a packet switching network.

Each node will determine the route for the next step which the message will take.

nominal. Existing only in name, formal, ostensible.

nominal account. An account which records an expense or gain of a business, e.g. wages, rent, commission received, etc. Often referred to as impersonal accounts. These balances would normally be transferred to the profit and loss account at the end of the financial year.

nominal capital. An alternative name for Authorised Capital (*q.v.*).

nominal consideration. In order to ensure the validity of a contract, some consideration must be given and received. Any consideration which is less than the real consideration value is but nominal and therefore adequate for the purposes of the contract.

nominal partner. A person who is ostensibly a partner of a firm, although he takes no active part in its management, but allows his name to be used to show that he has some financial interest.

nominal price. The amount given to the value of a share, which may have quite a different value to the price for which it could be purchased or sold.

nominal value. *See* NOMINAL PRICE.

nominal wages. The value of wages in monetary terms, but this does not include wages paid in other forms, which represents the true value of the wage.

nominee. A person nominated to a post of office. A person on whose life an annuity or lease depends. A person or company who holds shares on behalf of another. Under the TAURUS method of share transfer, the nominee may be known as the commercial account controller, who will hold the share records of his clients. Banks or their subsidiaries give nominee services for those customers who for some reason wish that the control of a portfolio is in the hands of experts, while they receive the income from such investments. It should be emphasised that any person having a 5 per cent shareholding in a company must declare this fact, even if the shares are held by a nominee. With regards to s. 390 Insolvency Act 1986 – the person nominated to act as an insolvency practitioner – as a trustee or otherwise. S. 52: An insolvency practitioner who

has consented to supervise the winding-up or administration of a company.

nominee company. A company formed by a bank or financial institution for the purpose of holding stocks and shares transferred to it by a customer. Frequently such a service is used by the bank itself for the purpose of transferring a portfolio into the name of the nominee company, as such a holding is being retained as security for a loan.

non-. A prefix in the formation of compound terms signifying absence or omission.

non-assented bonds. Bonds for which a plan of financial re-organisation has not been approved by the bondholder.

non assumpsit. A general legal plea by which a defendant refutes entirely the allegations of his or her opponent.

non-business day. A day which is not counted as one on which normal business is transacted. For the purposes of the Bills of Exchange Act 1882, non-business days are 1. Saturday, Sunday, Good Friday, Christmas Day; 2. a bank holiday under the Banking and Financial Dealings Act 1971; 3. a day appointed by Royal Proclamation as a public fast or thanksgiving day; 4. a day declared by an order under s. 2 of the Banking and Financial Dealings Act 1971 to be a non-business day. Any other day is a business day. Where, by the Bills of Exchange Act 1882, the time limited for doing any act or thing is less than three days, in recknoning time non-business days are excluded. Where a bill is due and payable on a non-business day it is payable on the succeeding business day. *See also* MATURITY.

non-claim. A failure or omission to make a claim within the prescribed limits of time.

non-commercial agreement. A consumer credit agreement or a consumer hire agreement not made by the creditor or owner in the course of business.

non compos mentis. Not of sound mind.

non-contributory pension. A pension awarded on the grounds of age and not on contributions paid during a working life; an old-age pension.

non-essential. In international trade, this is a description for goods which are not of prime importance to the economy of the country.

non est factum. A plea which denies that the deed was made by the defendant. It is put forward to avoid liability on the grounds that (*a*) either the signature was not his/hers, (*b*) in cases where the signature was in fact genuine, but was given by mistake as it was obtained by misrepresentation. A person must take care and have responsibility for what he/she is signing, so that the plea 'it was not made by me' (*non est factum*) will only be successful in exceptional cases. However, banks must be aware that a possible successful plea exists, so they must be careful when taking a guarantee.

non-feasance. Failure to perform an act that is legally incumbent upon one.

non-intervention. Not intervening or interfering in the affairs or policies of another, especially in international affairs.

non-joinder. Failure to join with another as party in a suit.

non-marketable securities. These are securities that are not dealt with on the Stock Exchange. Most are part of the National Debt and are in the form of National Savings Certificates, Premium Bonds, National Savings Income Bonds, National Savings Capital Bonds, etc. Other securities are Certificates of Deposit, annuities, etc.

non-participating policy. A policy of assurance that does not attract profits. A fixed amount is payable at maturity.

non-payment of a bill/cheque. Dishonour of a bill by the acceptor or the non-payment of a cheque by the drawee bankers. Whereas the dishonour of a bill may be noted or protested by the holder, a cheque need not go through this procedure as evidence of presentation by the collecting banker's crossing and the reason for non-payment by the drawee bank are written on the face of the cheque.

non-profit making. An organisation, e.g. a charity, club, etc., which has been established to provide a service or donate funds to a good cause. While the object of the organisation is not to make a profit, it must generate sufficient funds to meet its day-to-day expenses. *See* NON-TRADING PARTNERSHIPS.

non-provable debts. Where a person is in the proceeds of being made bankrupt, then certain creditors cannot claim on his/her assets, e.g. debts of an illegal contract, debts arising after the commitment of an act of bankruptcy, maintenance payments to the debtor's wife.

non-recourse finance. This is finance given by a bank to a borrower, and which the borrower has no liability to repay. Repayment will come from other sources, e.g. the purchaser of the borrowers services or goods. Non-recourse finance is available by various methods: (*a*) an exporter may obtain non recourse finance by making available to a lending banker an ECGD guarantee; (*b*) export finance departments of the major bankers will offer similar facilities to those of ECGD, to customers that conform to the conditions that they lay down; (*c*) factoring – the sale of book debts, with the agreement of the factor, cover for the client's bad debts is given, so that invoices presented to the factor that are presented in accordance with the agreement between the parties will be paid without recourse; (*d*) with the confirmation of a documentary credit, the confirming bank will pay the beneficiary, providing the terms and conditions of the credit have been complied with, payment will be without recourse; (*e*) by the forfaiting of a bill of exchange or similar instrument, a bank may agree to forfaiting, that is, should the instrument be dishonoured for any reason, then there will be no recourse to the drawer. With time and the expansion of financial services, there is no reason why other methods of non-recourse finance are made available to borrowers.

non-residents. Anybody whether it is a person, firm or company who is ordinarily resident outside the UK (including the Channel Islands, Gibraltar and the Isle of Man) so that any interest earned on an account would be exempt from UK Income Tax. Any unearned income from investments would also be exempt from tax. While the UK has no exchange control regulations, the distinction for the transfer of funds outside the UK does not apply. To have the status of non-resident, the person must not stay in the country more than an average of three months each year.

non sequitur. 'It does not follow': an illogical inference, an irrelevant conclusion.

non-suit. The renunciation by the plaintiff of a suit before a verdict is given. The withdrawal by a judge of a case.

non-trading partnerships. This consists of professional persons, e.g. doctors, dentists, solicitors, who are concerned in providing a service. Usually by the rules of the professional association limited liability is not permitted. It is possible to have more than twenty persons in the partnership as is evidenced by the large accounting partnerships. For banking purposes, the usual mandate is obtained and therefore any partner can be liable for the debts of the partnership.

non-transferable. A crossing placed on a cheque to ensure that the cheque is paid to the named payee only. An alternative would be to make the cheque out to the payee and then to add the word 'only'. To make the drawer's intention quite clear, the words 'order' or 'bearer' should be struck out and the alteration initialled by the drawer.

non-user. Neglect to use a right, by which it may become void.

non-voting shares. A share in a company which does not permit its holder to vote. The purpose of such an issue of shares is to allow a smaller group of shareholders of another set of shares to have voting rights and therefore control over the company. This usually occurs when a family wishes to expand the capital base of its company, yet still retain its influence over its operations. This type of share is not popular with investors and very gradually they are being converted to ordinary shares.

no par value. Shares issued with no stated nominal value, but valued according to the current stock exchange assessment.

normal market size (NMS). Early in January 1991, the words 'alpha', 'beta', 'gamma' and 'delta' were dropped by the Stock Exchange as words describing types of shares. Instead, it has introduced a twelve-level system which identifies how easy or difficult it is to buy/sell any particular share. In other words it reflects the liquidity of the shares without affecting the market price. For example, the purchase of £100 000 worth of shares in a major international company would not necessarily cause any reaction in the market, while a purchase of a similar amount in a very much smaller company would have a sharp reaction. The NMS of any share is calculated quarterly by adding the turnover of the previous four quarters, dividing the total by 10 000 and dividing this again by the market price at the end of the quarter. The final figure is then placed into one of the twelve bands ranging in size from 500–200 000 shares.

nostro account. Accounts maintained by home banks with banks abroad. *See also* VOSTRO ACCOUNT.

notarial act of honour. If, after a bill of exchange has been protested, a third party intervenes to pay the bill for the honour of the party on whom it is drawn, such a payment must be attested by a notary public and is known as a notarial act of honour.

notary public. A person, usually a solicitor, authorised to record statements, to certify deeds, to take affidavits, etc., on oath, especially for use in legal proceedings abroad. When a dishonoured bill is 'noted' it is presented again by a notary public and 'noted' for non-acceptance or non-payment. If necessary, the noting can be extended into a protest. It is very common in the US for documents to be notarised or authenticised by a public officer who is known as a notary public. The notary is called to acknowledge, attest and certify deeds as well as official forms, usually under his or her official seal, for a small charge. Notaries public are licensed by the state in which they operate after passing an examination.

note. A memorandum. A written reminder to oneself or another person. A brief record of facts of a speech, interview, etc. Often the abbreviated meaning of a banknote or some other form of payment.

note issuing facilities. Popularly known as NIFS. A bank or financial institution pledges to lend money to a borrower if his note issue falls flat.

note of hand. A promissory note, a written promise to pay a certain sum by a stipulated time.

note reserve. The difference between the amount of banknotes in circulation and the highest permitted legal limit.

notice. A formal advice in writing giving either information or data. A written indication to a person that his/her contract of employment will cease at some future date. A warning. A notice to the Land Registrar to protect a minor interest, such as a deed of arrangement affecting land. A notice under the Consumer Credit Act 1974 must be in writing. *See* DEFAULT NOTICE; NOTICE OF DISPENSATION.

notice deposit. A term deposit account whereby notice of withdrawal must be given otherwise some penalty is incurred, e.g. loss of interest or some charge being made.

notice in lieu of *distringas*. *See DISTRINGAS.*

notice loan. Where the borrower or the lender wishes to repay a loan before the agreed date then a period of notice to the other party.

notice of assignment. *See* ASSIGNMENT OF LIFE POLICY.

notice of cancellation. For the purposes of the Consumer Credit Act 1974, a notice served within a specified period by the debtor or hirer under a cancellable agreement on 1. the creditor or owner; or 2. the person specified in the notice; or 3. a person who is the agent of the creditor or owner. If the notice, however expressed, indicates the intention of the debtor or hirer to withdraw from the agreement, it shall operate to cancel the agreement and any linked transaction, and to withdraw any offer by the debtor or hirer, or his or her relative, to enter into a linked transaction.

notice of deposit. Where a banker has received a land certificate from a borrowing customer which is to serve as an equitable charge, the banker will complete a Land Registry form which is notice to the Land Registry that the land certificate has been lodged with the bank as security. The registrar enters the details in the charges register, thereby giving notice to any future purchaser or mortgagee. Should the owner wish to sell the land or use the land in any way other than by legal mortgage, then the registrar will notify the bank.

notice of dishonour. Section 47, Bills of Exchange Act 1882; 'where a bill has been dishonoured by non-acceptance or by non-payment, notice of dishonour must be given to the drawer and each indorser, and any drawer or indorser to whom such notice is not given is discharged provided that: (1) Where a bill is dishonoured by non-acceptance and notice of dishonour is not given, the rights of a holder in due course subsequent to the omission shall not be prejudiced by the omission. (2) Where a bill is dishonoured by non-acceptance and due notice is given, it shall not be necessary to give notice of a subsequent dishonour by non-payment unless the bill shall in the meantime have been accepted. Notice of dishonour may where necessary take the form of returning the bill to the drawer or indorser. The dishonour of a cheque by the drawee bank will usually mean that notice of dishonour will be notified to the drawer and the cheque returned to the collecting bank with the reason for non-payment specified on the face of the cheque.'

notice of dispensation. For the purposes of the Consumer Credit Act 1974, it is an authority signed by a joint account holder, to waive his/her rights to receive a separate bank statement.

notice of a second charge. Where a lending banker who is holding a first charge on a security receives notice of a second charge, must stop, or rule off the customer's overdrawn account in order to prevent the *Rule in Clayton's case* operating against him. He must also retain this information in his records as he holds the deeds in trust for the second mortgagee. In the case of registered land, notification will come from the Registrar, if the second mortgage has been registered and from mortgagee himself. If the bank has an equitable charge and a notice of deposit has been given, then the second mortgagee will be unable to register his mortgage until the bank's interest is re-registered as a legal charge. For a company, a second registration must be made at Companies House and a notice is then inserted in *Stubbs Weekly Gazette.* Should a bank take a second charge, it must give notice to the first lender. *See also* SECOND MORTGAGE.

notice to suspend payments. Where a debtor notifies his creditors that he is unable to pay his debts a petition for bankruptcy may be made by (*a*) one of the creditors or jointly by more than one of them (*b*) by the individual himself, (*c*) by a supervisor under a voluntary arrangement, (*d*) or by the courts under a criminal bankruptcy order (s. 264 Insolvency Act 1986). Following such a notice, a bankruptcy order, or voluntary arrangement, may be directed, but much will depend on the information regarding the debtor's assets and liabilities presented to the court.

noting a bill. *See* NOTARY PUBLIC.

notional amount. A term used by the International Swap Dealers Association to indicate the amount calculated in any period in a rate swap.

notional income. An income which is assumed from an investment, e.g. land, but in fact the owner receives no financial income at all.

not negotiable. A statement inserted on a crossed cheque, indicating that the negotiability, but not the transferability, is destroyed. Bills of Exchange Act 1882 s. 81: 'Where a person takes a crossed cheque which bears on it the words "not negotiable", he shall not have and shall not be capable of giving a better title to the cheque than that which the person from whom he took it had'. In simple language, while a 'not negotiable' cheque can be transferred from one person to another, the receiver of a cheque with this general crossing should take care that his title is only as good as the transferor's.

novation. A contract between two persons which has been replaced by a new contract between the same persons.

null and void. A contract that will have no legal effect and in consequence will be inoperative.

nursery finance. The provision of funds for a new or favoured company that requires an injection of equity or long-term borrowing on favourable terms. The bank or other financial institution will maintain a watching brief, even have its own representative on the board of directors and if necessary provide additional capital, encouragement, etc., until such time as the company is fully able to compete in the market.

O

obiter dictum. A passing remark of a judge. A persuasive opinion. A statement made on a point of law, not necessarily relevant to the case and not binding. It is the judge's own opinion on some point of law.

objects clause. The clause in the memorandum of association of a company which lists the business objectives which the company will pursue. *See* MEMORANDUM OF ASSOCIATION.

obligation. A duty either legal or moral to perform, or not to perform, a given function. A debt, represented by a bond, on which an interest is payable.

obligor. A person that has an obligation to fulfil a function, e.g. to repay a debt with interest, by a due date.

obsolete. A word to describe an asset that no longer has any function or use in a business. It has lost its value, because it is no longer up to date and efficient. While the asset may still function, it is often necessary to either sell or scrap the item and replace it.

obtaining credit by undischarged bankrupt. Under the Insolvency Act 1986 s. 360, a bankrupt is guilty of an offence if alone or jointly with another person the bankrupt obtains credit without notifying the person that he or she is an undischarged bankrupt.

odd lot. The purchase/sale of a smaller number of shares than usual. Often this is done by an investor to round up or down his holding in a particular company. Obviously such a purchase or sale will attract a higher commission.

off-balance sheet finance. Sources of funds which do not appear in a balance sheet and consequently are not owned by the entity. As no capital outlay had been made, there is no reduction in the working capital. An example of this would be a financial lease.

offer. 1. A proposal to make or do something that forms part of a legally binding contract. From the conduct of the individual an offer may be implied or expressed. 2. A price at which a person wishes to sell. In securities this is often known as the asking price. Goods displayed in a window with a price label, or a prospectus advising the issue of shares at a stated price, is not an offer but an invitation to make an offer. *See* OPEN OFFER.

offered price. The price at which a security is offered for sale by a market maker or the price quoted by a Unit Trust Company. *See* BID PRICE.

offer for sale. A method of selling shares in a new issue. The total of shares available that have been taken up by an Issuing House who then sells then to any person or institution that wishes to make an investment.

Office of Fair Trading (OFT). A government agency set up in 1973 to protect both consumers and traders against unfair practices. Its function is to notify the public of its rights and responsibilities, promote fair compensation, recommended changes in law governing trade practices, credit facilities and consumer protection. It will pursue traders whom it suspects of having broken the law. It is controlled by the director-general of fair trading.

official. A person that holds an office for the time being. The holder of an office, with a responsibility to make and take decisions. The person may be elected or appointed.

official list. The daily publication by the International Stock Exchange of all bargains made for all securities quoted on the exchange. It will also include such data as rights issues, dividend payments, etc.

official quotation. The buying and selling prices as stated in the Official List.

official rate. In countries that still have some form of exchange control, it is likely that there is two or more rates of exchange, e.g. commercial rate which is the official rate and the travellers rate which is an inducement to travellers to visit the country.

official receiver. Under the Insolvency Act 1986, the Official Receiver must be a qualified insolvency practitioner who will be appointed by the court so that the bankrupt may submit his statement of affairs within 21 days (s. 288). It is the duty of the Official Receiver to investigate the affairs of the bankrupt and report to the court. At all times the Official Receiver is the trustee of the estate of the bankrupt, but the bankrupt may apply to the Secretary of State for the appointment of a person to act as trustee instead of the official receiver.

official search. The search by the registrar at the request of a bank, solicitor, etc., to find any encumbrance on a piece of land that a prospective purchaser is intending to buy. The certificate issued is evidence that he or she is free from any liability that has not been disclosed by the search.

off market deals. Dealings other than through the recognised Stock Exchange.

off market purchase. A purchase of any goods not made in the recognised market for those goods. In the UK an off-market purchase by a company of its own shares is so defined if either 1. the shares are purchased other than on a recognised stock exchange; or 2. the shares were purchased on a recognised stock exchange but were not subject to marketing arrangement on that stock exchange (Companies Act 1985).

offshore funds. Funds which have been invested in the various tax haven countries, e.g. Channel Islands, Isle of Man, Bahamas, etc. which are not subject to UK tax, nor to the UK Depositors Protection Scheme. It is a useful investment vehicle for non-UK residents, but it does not necessarily have any advantage to a UK resident as any income remitted into this country would be subject to income tax deductions. The various offshore fund prices are quoted in the major national financial papers.

OFT. *See* OFFICE OF FAIR TRADING.

old-age pension. The weekly allowance paid by a government to persons who have attained a certain age and fulfil certain conditions, usually known as the *retirement pension.*

Old Lady. The popular name given to the Bank of England. Often called *The Old Lady of Threadneedle Street.*

oligopoly. A situation where the production of a commodity is in the hands of a relatively few companies and consequently controls the market price.

ombudsman. A Commissioner appointed by the government to investigate any complaints against the body concerned, e.g. Local Government, Insurance, Banking. *See also* BANKING OMBUDSMAN.

omnibus resolution. *See* RESOLUTION TO BORROW.

omnium. On the Stock Exchange, the value of the aggregate stocks in a funded loan.

on account. A payment made in partial settlement of an amount outstanding. Often when a loan of a bank customer has not been reduced in accordance with the loan agreement, a reminder from the bank will often induce a payment on account, to assure the bank of the good faith of the borrower.

on-board bill of lading. A bill of lading that will have a clause which states 'received on board the above mentioned vessel . . . '. This phrase indicates that the goods described on the document are in fact in one of the holds of the vessel, or if the vessel is a container ship, it is quite likely on deck. Unlike a 'received for shipment' bill of lading, the goods will be taken to the port of destination as stated.

on consignment. Goods sent to an agent who will sell them at the best terms obtainable.

oncost. A production overhead cost and therefore a charge to be included in the cost of production or manufacture.

on demand guarantee. This type of guarantee can be found in a Performance Bond, whereby the buyer, in whose favour the guarantee is made out, may on demand and without any proof, demand payment of the amount stated.

one-man business. *See* SOLE TRADER.

one-man company. A company – usually with two shareholders only – where one person has the majority shareholding and the other person or persons have a nominal holding simply to comply with the Companies Act.

one-off. The manufacture of one item or the production of one process to satisfy the requirements of a particular buyer. The making of such an item, or the giving of such a service is not likely to be repeated.

onerous. Burdensome, oppressive.

onerous covenants. Promises and obligations concerning land which will be expensive for the estate owner to fulfil, as where a leashold in its last stages requires the repair of the property before it is handed back to the free-holder. A trustee in bankruptcy may, with the leave of the court, refuse to accept the land possessed by the bankrupt if, because of onerous covenants, it is likely to prove a liability rather than an asset.

on-line. In banking this refers to an office or department that is directly linked with a computer or computer centre. Practically every banking service has a computer link. Additionally, the expansion of home/office banking, provides customers with on-line facilities to obtain up-to-date balances, transfer sums of money to and from different accounts and transfer funds to different persons.

OPEC funds. See PETRODOLLARS.

open. Without restrictions; to establish or set going.

open account. A method of trading in international trade, whereby the seller not only sends the goods direct to the buyer, but will send the invoice, document of movement and any other commercial documents direct to the buyer, who will then pay the amount due in accordance with the agreement. The seller loses all control over the goods and must therefore have complete trust not only in the buyer to pay in accordance with the contract, but also in the buyer's country so that he is confident that there is political and economic stability and no control will suddenly be imposed to stop the remittance of funds from that country.

open cheque. A cheque which does not have a crossing and therefore is payable on demand at the counters of the bank and branch on whom it is drawn. Section 60, The Bills of Exchange Act 1882, gives a bank protec-tion against paying the wrong person, providing it has made payment (a) in good faith (b) in the ordinary course of business.

open contract. A contract for the sale of property, which does not contain all the terms but merely identifies the property, names the buyer and seller.

open ended. A situation whereby a bank willing to lend funds against some security and the form the security will take has not yet been decided. A lending situation where money has been loaned and agreed that when necessary a further advance/s may be made. A trust that gives the trustee the authority to vary the various investments.

opening a crossing. To open a crossing on a cheque, usually by writing 'pay cash', has the effect of making the cheque an open one. While the Bills of Exchange Act has never recognised this action, it is the practice of banks to permit this. However, practice among the banks has grown to permit only the drawer to open a crossing against his initial or signature for the alteration and that payment made must be to the drawer or his known agent.

opening an account. To open an account establishes a relationship between a banker and his customer. In order to open an account, some small amount of money is deposited, a mandate form is completed, including a specimen of the signature of the customer/s and references are normally taken. Once the referees have given a satisfactory reply, a cheque book is issued. For joint accounts, the procedure is the same but the mandate will include a joint and several liability clauses and a survivorship clause. For a company, memorandum and articles of association are deposited with the bank and sight of a certificate of incorporation, or a certificate to commence trading must be made. A resolution passed by the directors of the company must be signed appointing the bankers, plus of course specimen signatures of those that will have the authority to sign on the account.

opening balance. A balance in an account at the beginning of a trading period indicating whether there is an asset or liability.

opening stock. The value of stock either at cost or realisable value at the commencement of the trading period.

open market. A market where prices are decided solely by supply and demand.

open market operations. A method of controlling the monetary movements of the country. It is the Bank of England that will make the day-to-day decisions on the amount of money available, so that if there is a need to reduce the amount of money in circulation, the Bank of England will sell bills of exchange, treasury bills or stocks to the market, thereby calling funds in from the banks which will have the effect of reducing liquidity. To increase liquidity the bank will buy short-term instruments.

open offer. An offer to a shareholder by a company to take up any amount which is already held. See also RIGHTS ISSUE.

open order. An order to a stockbroker which has not been executed. Such orders may instruct the broker to buy/sell securities at a stated price, but this particular price has not yet been reached in the market.

open outcry. The dealings that take place in the pit or ring of an exchange by means of dealers calling to one another. The dealers are identified by the type of jacket they wear and in addition to shouting, hand signals are also made. If two traders agree, a note is made and a contract is recorded.

open policy. A type of marine policy covering goods, the value of which is not stated, but has to be proved in the event of a loss occurring.

open position. A situation in a money market, whereby any purchase or sale, whether spot or forward, has not been covered by the institution.

operating in reverse. See MOPPING UP.

operating lease. See FINANCE LEASE.

operation. The act or process of operating; working, action, mode of working; activity, performance of function; effect.

operational. In production, working, effective.

operational research. The study of the procedures within an organisation, to ascertain the various methods of work and the costs involved, in order to arrive at the most efficient and cost effective method.

operative clause. The words in a deed of conveyance which actually have the effect of transferring the property from one party to another.

opportunity cost. The value of an alternative procedure that could have been brought into operation and compared with the current methods of work that had been costed.

opposed bid. Where a company makes a bid to take over another company, the directors of the latter company may, for any number of reasons object to the bid and recommend to their shareholders that they should reject the offer and oppose the bid.

optimum. The most favourable view of the system. Often used in relation to finance, economics, production, etc.

option. The right to choose, to buy or to sell. The Traded Options Market of the Stock Exchange will allow a person to obtain the right to buy or sell a specified number of shares within a given period (3, 6 months) at an agreed or striking price. An option to buy (call option) an option to sell (put option). For this right to buy/sell, the buyer/seller will pay the other party called the writer a fee or premium, which will be forfeited if the option is not excercised before the date of the maturity. In the foreign exchange market currency can be purchased or sold between two given dates. The option in this case is not whether the transaction will be carried out, but when. See SHARE OPTION SCHEME; TRADED OPTIONS.

option forward rate. In the foreign exchange market, it is a legally binding contract, between parties, whereby a fixed amount of currency is bought/sold at an agreed rate, but the delivery of the currency will be between two dates at the option of the buyer or the seller. Where the contract is between a banker and his customer, then it is customary for the option to be at the customer's discretion.

option mortgage scheme. A scheme whereby a borrower could opt for a lower mortgage rate and forgo tax relief. This scheme was abolished early 1983 on the introduction of MIRAS. See MORTGAGE INTEREST RELIEF AT SOURCE.

option pit. The area where the dealers for the commodity fix their deals in open outcry.

option premium. The amount paid by the buyer/seller to the writer for the right to buy/sell the named security at an agreed price before a specified period.

option spread. The margin between the buying and selling prices.

option writer. The financial institution that sells put options and buys call options. For giving the buyer/seller the right to obtain a put or call option, the writer will charge a premium-option premium for this service.

oracle. See VIEWDATA.

order. An instruction. An order from a court, which is a directive that must be obeyed. The word 'order' as stated on a negotiable instrument is a request from the drawer that payment should be made in accordance with the tenor of the instrument. An instruction to a broker to buy/sell a commodity or security in accordance with the verbal or written instructions given, or buy/sell at best. In commerce, this refers to an offer to buy goods as either specified in a catalogue, or by agreement.

order bill. A bill payable to a specified person or to his or her order.

order cheque. A cheque payable to a named person or to his or her order.

order for foreclosure. See FORECLOSURE ORDER.

order in council. An order issued by a British Sovereign with the advice of the Privy Council.

order of payment of debts in bankruptcy. When a bankrupt's trustee has converted the estate into cash, as far as possible, by the sale of the bankrupt's assets, he or she has the task of paying the creditors whose proofs the trustee has passed for payment. The trustee is obliged to pay creditors in a certain order of priority, set out in Sch. 6, Insolvency Act, 1986. Where the bankrupt has sufficient funds, then the order of payment of debts from the estate of the bankrupt will be as follows: (a) the fees and expenses of the insolvent practitioner; (b) secured creditors, but any deficiency in the value of their security will mean that they will prove for the balance as unsecured creditors; (c) preferential creditors; (d) other creditors.

ordinary income. The income derived from the normal trading activities of a business or a sole trader. This should be shown quite separately from exceptional or extraordinary income.

ordinary partner. See PARTNER.

ordinary resolution. One which may be passed by a simple majority.

ordinary shares. Since this is considered as the risk capital it is known as 'equities'. These are the basic shares of any company. The ordinary shareholders will receive a dividend after all expenses of the business have been paid. Should there be any preference shareholders, then they rank first for dividends then the ordinary shareholders will receive theirs. In years of good profits, then they should receive good dividends, but in poor years, the dividend could be passed. The ordinary shareholders have voting rights in proportion to the number of shares held.

organisational chart. A chart that shows the relationships between persons or department of any organisation.

organisational development. A strategic plan to implement planned procedures that will develop and change the organisation, so that it will have greater efficiency, be more competitive and be more profitable.

Organisation for Economic Co-operation and Development (OECD). This organisation was established in 1960 for the purpose of (a) achieving higher economic growth and employment, (b) a rising standard of living in member countries, (c) contribute to the development of the world economy, (d) expansion in world trade on a non-discriminatory basis.

Organisation of Petroleum Exporting Countries (OPEC). See PETRODOLLARS.

original bill. A bill drawn and discounted before it has attracted any indorsement.

ostensible authority. An implied authority of an agent in a particular trade or business.

other names. See MARKING NAMES.

out clearing. See CLEARING.

outgoing partner. A partner who, for any reason is leaving the firm. Up to the date of retirement, he/she is responsible for its debts, but from the date of departure, he/she is no longer liable, providing due notice has been given to creditors in writing and by advertisement in the *London Gazette* and local papers. For bankers, the partnership account should be stopped or ruled off to retain the outgoing partner's liability and a new account for the new partnership should be opened.

out-of-date cheque. *See* ANTEDATED CHEQUE.

out of the money. *See* TRADED OPTIONS.

output. Production, the amount of goods produced in a given time, the produce of a factory, mine, etc.

output media. Reports, print-outs, documents, punched cards, tape, are examples of output media. In fact they are any methods (or media) of transferring data from the memory of the computer to some external source.

outright transaction. A transaction in the forward foreign exchange market that is not linked to a spot transaction.

outside broker. A broker not belonging to the Stock Exchange.

outstanding. A bill or an account that has not yet been paid.

over and short account. An account in a branch where any differences in the tills of cashiers are placed and recorded. By this procedure, any claims and refunds can be linked and any continuous shortages or surpluses can be isolated.

overcapitalised. Said of a company whose assets are worth less than its issued capital, if when its earning capacity is insufficient to pay interest on the capital.

overdraft. A form of borrowing from a bank which entails a debit balance on current account, i.e. withdrawals exceed receipts. Such a borrowing should be an agreement between banker and customer and a debit balance limit should be agreed. As items are paid in, reducing the balance and withdrawals increase the overdraft, so the cost of borrowing will be cheaper than a loan as the interest rate charged in on a daily closing balance. From a customer's point of view, this is possibly the cheapest form of borrowing, while from a banker's point of view it is more difficult to monitor the account, nor has the bank any control on the use of the funds.

overdue bill. A term bill of exchange which has matured and has not yet been presented for payment. A bill payable on demand is deemed to be overdue within the meaning of the Bills of Exchange Act, and for the purpose, when it appears on the face of it to have been in circulation for an unreasonable length of time. What is an unreasonable length of time for this purpose is a question of fact, s. 36(3) Bills of Exchange Act. For practical purposes an unreasonable length of time would be 10–15 days. One of the conditions of a holder in due course is that he/she became a holder of the bill before it was overdue – s. 29 Bills of Exchange Act 1882, so that any person taking a sight bill/cheque which has been in circulation for an unreasonable length of time or has taken a term bill that has matured cannot claim to be a holder in due course.

overdue cheque. While the provisions of an overdue bill applies equally to an overdue cheque it should be noted that bankers who collect cheques for themselves, i.e. to pay off or reduce an overdraft or loan, must take care that the cheque is not overdue otherwise they will lose the attributes of being a holder in due course. An overdue cheque should be distinguished from a stale cheque which is considered to be at least six months old.

overfunding. The deliberate action of the central bank, in the course of its duty to control the money supply, to create a shortage of funds, by deliberately selling gilts so as to reduce bank lending.

overhead cost/expenses. The indirect costs of a business, which will include labour and material costs.

overheating. This refers to an economic situation where factors are becoming out of control, so that there is an increase in bank borrowing, prices and wages are beginning to increase, and imports exceed exports widening any balance of payment deficit.

overlines. Overlines are credits made available to borrowers of correspondent banks whose legal limit has been or is about to be reached. US banks are constrained by law from lending more than a specific proportion of the value of their capital and reserves to a single customer and, because of the proliferation of regional and local banks, many of which are very small compared with their European counterparts. the legal lending limit can be very quickly reached. In this situation, the bank with the limit constraint will look for a larger correspondent bank to take over a portion of the commitment; this is referred to as an overline.

overnight loans. Loans given by bankers to discount houses using bills of exchange as security. Such loans are repayable the next business day. This loan is usually to rectify a long position taken by the discount house.

overriding interest. This phrase was highlighted in the case of *Williams & Glyn's Bank* v *Boland* (1981). Overriding interests in registered land should be recorded on the Land Certificate, while for unregistered land a search of the Land Charges Register (class D (iii)) or Local Land Charges Register should be made. Other interests such as easements, rights of way, light, drainage, may not necessarily be recorded so that a prospective purchaser of land should visit the property and note of any such rights exist.

overseas trading company. A UK trading company which does all its business in overseas markets and little or no trading in the domestic market.

oversubscribed. A term used to indicate that there has been more offers to purchase shares than the number of shares available. Either some applicants will get no shares in the issue and/or will be cut back and only receive a proportion of the number of shares requested. It is quite likely that on the first day of dealing, the price of the shares will be at a premium.

over the counter. The description of shares that have not got a full listing on the Stock Exchange, but are available on a secondary market.

overtrading. The rapid expansion of production and sales without having the necessary financial resources to back the operations. The signs of overtrading will be quickly noticed in a bank account, are the increase in the bank overdraft and/or there is a hardening of the overdraft position. It can also be noticed when cheques payable to creditors are for round amounts. This is done to delay full payment, yet pay something in order to keep the suppliers quiet. It will also be noticed that there is likely to be a difficulty in paying regular expenses including salaries and wages.

owner's equity. That part of a business that belongs to the owner/s. In simplistic terms, it is the total assets less the liabilities i.e. the creditors and lenders to the business.

ownership. The exclusive rights to chattels and property. The owner has the legal right to do whatever he/she wants to do – subject to legal constraints. Possession need not necessarily include ownership.

owner's risk. Where goods are transported from one place to another, particularly by rail or road, it is not infrequent to have the document of movement claused 'owner's risk'. This means that the responsibility of the carrier would be due to either the negligence or dishonesty of an employee.

P

p.a. The abbreviation for per annum, or personal assistant or personal account.

packing note/list. A document drawn up by a seller showing the details of the goods, method of packing, the nett and gross weight of each individual item and the total weight of the consignment.

paid cheque. A cheque that has been honoured by a bank. A cheque if it is an open one may be presented to the banker on whom it is drawn, either by the payee or indorser for payment over the counter. If it is a crossed cheque, by the presenting banker, either specially or through the clearing system. Once paid, the amount on the cheque is debited to the drawer's account. The cancelled cheque is retained by the drawee bank unless there is a special arrangement for the customer to have his/her cancelled cheques returned to him/her with the bank statement. With the possible extension of truncation, it is quite likely that the cheque on presentation by the payee for credit to his account, the collecting bank will not remit the cheque through the clearing system, but will retain it and merely transmit, via its computer terminals, the details of the cheque.

paid-up capital. The nominal amount of capital that has been bought by the shareholders. This may be the same as the authorised capital, it could be less, but never greater than the authorised capital.

paid-up policy. A life assurance policy in respect of which no further premiums are payable.

paid-up shares. *See* FULLY-PAID SHARES; PARTLY-PAID SHARES.

panel. A group of persons gathered together to discuss a situation or topic, to make a decision, give a judgment or a recommendation.

paper. A newspaper, a document, bills of exchange, promissory notes, a set of examination questions.

paper bid. When a predator company wishes to make a take-over bid for another company, it could offer its own shares in exchange for the shares of the company it wants to take over.

paper currency. The legal tender of a country in the form of banknotes.

paper money. Banknotes, bills of exchange, promissory notes, cheques, or any other instrument in paper form, which are acceptable in settlement of debts.

P & L. The abbreviation for profit and loss.

paper profit or loss. The comparison of the present price of an asset or investment and the original cost. The difference between these two amounts would indicate a profit or loss if the asset or investment was realised.

par. Equal to the nominal or face value. Government stocks are redeemable at par, but during the lifetime of that stock, the price could be above or below par. In the foreign exchange market, par is the current spot rate and any forward rate would be at a premium, i.e. a margin above par, or at a discount, i.e. a margin below par.

parallel. Precisely corresponding, similar; a thing exactly like another, a counterpart, a comparison.

parallel market. Operating alongside the short-term money market in which the discount houses are the centre of activity, there are the other short-term markets consisting of the inter-bank sterling market, certificate of deposit markets, local authority market, Eurocurrency market. All these markets are used by all banks and major financial institutions for borrowing and lending overnight funds, short and long-term funds which are used to lend to their own customers, or to balance overnight or short-term liquidity positions.

parallel rate of exchange. In countries where there are two rates of exchange, it is the unofficial rate.

paraph. The flourish beneath a signature, originally intended as a precaution against forgery; to initial or sign.

parcel. Goods wrapped in a package or in a bundle. A number of similar items in a group, or in an auction forming a lot. A plot of land, a term used in the conveyance of land to aid the description of the property conveyed. The collecting together of bills of exchange or other negotiable instruments of the same tenor, so that on maturity they may be presented in time, or where there is a need for discounting, they may be delivered as a parcel to the transferee.

parcener. A joint heir. See CO-PARCENERS.

parent company. The company that owns and controls subsidiaries by having the majority shares in those companies. Where the parent company is merely a shell and does not operate in its own right, then the description of holding company is used. See HOLDING COMPANY.

pari. Par.

pari passu. At the same rate or pace, with equal step, in the same degree or proportion, likewise, enjoying the same rights.

parity. Equal. In commercial terms the value of one commodity with another, or a currency having the same value or pegged to the currency of another country.

parking. The funds received from the sale of investments, are placed in a high interest account while considering what other investments ought to be made and when.

parol. A simple contract given by word of mouth.

par rate of exchange. The value of coins which are related to their gold content.

partial. Affecting a part only, incomplete, not total, biased in favour of one party, unfair, having a preference for.

partial acceptance. Under the Bills of Exchange Act 1882 s. 19(2) the acceptance of part of the face value of the bill is considered as a qualified acceptance only and therefore the holder may consider it as dishonoured and notification must be given to all previous parties and the drawer.

partial intestacy. A situation where a testator has given instructions for the disposal of some but not all of his/her assets.

partial loss. The damage or loss, short of a total write-off of an insured item, e.g. a ship or its cargo, which has been insured.

partial payment. An amount paid to a creditor which is in partial settlement of the outstanding debt. Partial payment of a bill of exchange should not be considered as settlement of the bill but can be protested for dishonour.

participating loan. A loan to an entity where there is more than one lender – a syndicated loan. The bank arranging this loan – lead bank or manager – obtains agreement from other banks or financial institutions to participate in the loan up to an agreed amount. The lead manager, acting for the lenders negotiates with the borrower the terms of such a loan.

participating policy. See 'WITH PROFITS' POLICY.

participating preference shares. A type of preference share that not only gives the shareholder his/her right to a dividend before the distribution or before other shareholders, but is entitled to an additional dividend should the ordinary shareholder receive a dividend above a certain amount.

particular. Distinguishing one thing from another. Having a different characteristic. More precise or exact than usual. Attention to detail. Noteworthy or remarkable.

particular average. Originates from the Italian *avaria particolare*, meaning partial losses. See GENERAL AVERAGE; WITH PARTICULAR AVERAGE; FREE OF PARTICULAR AVERAGE.

particular lien. The right of a dealer, warehousekeeper, etc., to retain goods in possession until the debt in respect of those particular goods is paid.

partly-paid shares. Shares on which there is a percentage of uncalled capital. They are comparatively rare, and are not popular with shareholders because of the liability to further calls. However, the offer of partly-paid shares in recent privatisations has, with the exception of British Petroleum, proved successful. Although the value of the shares may increase as the calls are paid, and in the long-term the shareholder should suffer no loss, nevertheless in the short-term the investor has to find the money at a time which may be inconvenient.

partner. A person who is in a profession or business with other persons. *See* DECEASED PARTNER; DORMANT PARTNER; INCOMING PARTNER; LIMITED PARTNER; NOMINAL PARTNER; ORDINARY PARTNER; OUTGOING PARTNER; QUASI-PARTNER; SALARIED PARTNER; SURVIVING PARTNER.

partner by estoppel. *See* QUASI-PARTNER.

partnership. Defined in the Partnership Act 1890 as 'The relationship that subsists between two or more persons carrying on business with a view to profit'. It is possible to form a partnership without any written agreement, but it is often useful to have either 'Article of Partnership' or a 'Deed of Partnership' drawn up so that there can be no misunderstanding. A partnership can consist of up to twenty persons, but a professional partnership, such as solicitors, accountants, etc. may have an unlimited number.

partnership agreement. This can take the form of either articles or deed of partnership. The agreement will cover such matters as capital invested, division of profits, objects of the partnership, responsibilities of each partner, retirement, bankruptcy of any partner, etc.

part payment. A payment for less than the amount owing. Where an acceptor of a term bill of exchange or the drawee of a sight bill of exchange offers only part of the amount due on the bill, then it must be considered as dishonoured. The drawer and previous parties must be notified of this fact, so as to retain their liability and if necessary a protest must be made. It is correct to receive the amount offered, but the bill must be retained by the holder and the amount received recorded on the back of the bill. In England, a cheque must be either fully paid or returned unpaid, but in Scotland where a customer is in credit, but does not have sufficient funds to meet the cheque, then those funds are attached as an assignment of funds.

par value. Nominal value.

passbook. A book issued, usually by a building society and the National Savings Bank, to record the financial transactions between the customer and the society. This was a method used by banks, but was discontinued when handwritten statements were introduced.

passing the dividend. Where trading has been poor, or profits have been low, or perhaps no profit at all, the final dividend may not be paid.

passport. A document issued by the Foreign Office of a country to its own citizens and intended to ensure their safe passage through a foreign country. In practical terms it is often used as a means of identification and for the purposes of encashment of cheques, travel cheques while abroad, opening accounts for non-residents and payment of funds in favour of non-customers of the bank.

pawn. Under the Consumer Credit Act 1974 s. 189, it is the delivery of a chattel by the owner – the pawnor – to the pawnee (the pawnbroker) as security for a loan. The chattel remains the property of the pawnee, and on repayment of the loan, the pawnor may reclaim the chattel. Should the debt not be repaid by a specified date, the pawnee may sell the item.

pawnbroker. A person or company that has received a licence to engage in the business of lending money against the security of goods or items deposited by the borrower. The goods are pledged up to six months, and if repayment of the loan is not made then the pawnbroker may sell the goods to obtain reimbursement of his loan.

pawnee. One who accepts goods as security for a loan. For the purposes of the Consumer Credit Act 1974, the term includes any person to whom the rights and duties of the original pawnee have passed by assignment or operation of law.

pawner, pawnor. One who pledges goods. For the purposes of the Consumer Credit Act 1974, the term includes any person to whom the rights and duties of the original pawner have passed by assignment or operation of law.

pawn receipt. A term used in Consumer Credit Act 1974 to describe a receipt in a prescribed form given by a person who takes any article in pawn, under a regulated agreement, to the person from whom he receives it at the time of receipt. A person who takes any article in pawn from an individual who he or she knows to be (or who appears to be and is) a *minor*, commits an offence. The above has no application to a pledge of documents of title or a non-commercial agreement (s. 114 of the Act). *See also* NON-COMMERCIAL AGREEMENT; REGULATED AGREEMENT.

pay. The transfer of money to another person. The settlement of a debt, wages or salaries given to employees. An award of compensation.

pay as you earn (PAYE). A method of tax deduction from the weekly wage or monthly salary of an employee. The amount deducted will depend on the code number issued to the employee and the employer by the Inland Revenue. This code number is calculated subject to personal allowances acceptable to the Inland Revenue. The employer has a copy of the tax tables which he refers to before the salary or wage is given, so that deductions are made and the transfer of the gross tax collected is then sent to the Collector of Taxes at regular intervals.

pay day. The last day of the settlement on the Stock Exchange. Also called account day or settling day. *See* PAYMENT.

payee. The person or persons named or to whose order a cheque or other negotiable instrument is payable. The payee may transfer the rights in the instrument by indorsement and delivery. Where the payee is fictitious, then the bill is payable to bearer. *See* FICTITIOUS PAYEE; IMPERSONAL PAYEE.

paying banker. A paying banker is obliged to act in accordance with the mandate given to him by his customer, and may only pay cheques, charge direct debits, debit standing orders in accordance with the authority held. The banker is open to risks as follows: he may pay in contravention of the mandate held, or where a stop has been placed, or where there has been a material alteration on the instrument. Perhaps the greatest risks are in paying cheques, so that in theory the clerk responsible for payment must before cancellation of the signature ensure that the signature corresponds with the record of the signature held, since there is no defence against payment of a cheque with a forged signature unless there is a plea of estoppel. The other points that must be checked are as follows: 1. Cheque drawn on the bank and branch (*Burnett* v. *Westminster Bank*). 2. Date in order – not postdated or stale. 3. Words and figures do not differ. 4. Funds are available or an agreement to overdraw. 5. Payee's name stated. 6. No material alteration or multilation. 7. No legal bars, i.e. no imposition by the court, customer not bankrupt, no notification of the death of the customer, no notice of mental incapacity. 8. No countermand of payment. 9. From time to time, cheques are issued with a large 'R' printed on the front of the cheque, when this happens, the payee must indorse the cheque in the space provided. The banker does get statutory protection when paying an open cheque across his counter, but any cheque form payable to 'Cash' or 'Wages' or similar words, is by definition not a cheque, but a demand by the drawer for payment from his own funds, and therefore the bank must not pay except to the account holder or his/her known agent. *See* PAYMENT OF CHEQUES.

paying-in slip. Also known as a credit slip. In broad detail there are three types. The first is in book form which is encoded with the customer's details, the second are blank forms available at the bank counter for completion by any customer who has not got a paying-in book. Lastly, personal cheque books contain paying-in slips which have been collated between blank cheque forms. When a customer wishes to pay in cheques and/or cash he/she will write the details and amount of the cheques on the reverse of the paying-in slip and carry the total forward to the face of the slip. That, plus any notes and coin that are being paid in will equal the total amount that will be credited to the customer's account. Except for the paying-in slips available at the counters, they are all personalised showing the branch sorting code number and the account number. The amount field is completed when the total cheques and cash are agreed. Before the customer leaves the counter, the paying-in slip is withdrawn from the book and the counterfoil stamped and initialled by the cashier, counter paying-in slips also have a counterfoil which is receipted and given to the customer.

Paymaster General. The officer appointed to make payments on behalf of the various Departments of the British Government.

payment. The settlement of an outstanding account or bill. For the purposes of the Consumer Credit Act 1974 payment includes tender. Payment of a bill of exchange completes the discharge of the bill which may be by the drawee or acceptor. Payment for the purchase of government stocks via the Stock Exchange is on a 'cash' basis, while the settlement of the debt for the purchase of shares will take place on settlement day.

payment by mistake. Where a bank has paid in funds to a customer's account in error the possibility of obtaining the return of those funds depends on: 1. Whether the customer has been advised of the funds. If not, then the bank can reverse the entry and no problem arises. 2. Had there been a series of incorrect payments by mistake to the customer's account and this has taken place over some period of time, then the situation can be serious for the bank. It would be up to the bank to prove that the customer knew or should have known that the entries passed were a mistake, but if the character of the customer is such that he/she was perhaps elderly, had no understanding of business figures and readily accepted the balance shown on the statement, then it is quite likely the bank cannot reclaim these funds. 3. Where the bank had overpaid a person at the counter, then that amount could be irrecoverable. 4. Payment of a stopped cheque. In this instance, the bank has been negligent and has paid by mistake and cannot debit the customer's account. 5. Under a documentary credit, where the paying bank has issued a draft to the beneficiary, then the applicant refuses to reimburse the bank owing to the fact that there was a discrepancy in the documents and therefore did not strictly comply with the terms and conditions of the credit, the bank has paid by mistake.

payment date. The date on which a declared dividend will be paid. The date a debt will be settled.

payment for honour *supra* protest. *See* NOTARIAL ACT OF HONOUR.

payment in due course. Defined by the Bills of Exchange Act 1882 s. 59(1) as payment at or after maturity, to the holder, in good faith, and without notice of any defect in the holder's title. If all these conditions have been complied with the payer has fulfilled his/her obligation and has obtained a valid discharge.

payment of cheques. Cheques are normally paid by the paying banker who has protection by ss. 60 and 80 of the Bills of Exchange Act 1882. Before final payment is made and the customer's account is debited, the banker must ascertain that the cheque is complete and regular on the face of it, i.e. it is correctly dated; there is a payee; words and figures agree; the signature is in accordance with the mandate; there are no unauthorised alterations; the cheque is not mutilated and any endorsements are correct; there are funds on the account or proper arrangements have been made and there has been no countermand of payment; there is no legal bar; lastly, the cheque is not crossed by two clearing banks.

payment of wages. It is an offence for employees to be paid other than in legal tender. However, by the Payment of Wages Act 1960 it is now possible with the agreement of the employee for wages to be paid direct into a bank account.

payment on account. The partial payment of a debt due, a deposit. The intention is that when the work has been completed, the balance will be paid.

pecuniary advantage. The opportunity to obtain a larger remuneration or employment. When obtaining a loan or overdraft on improved terms. To obtain money by pecuniary advantage by deception is a breach of the Theft Act 1968.

peg. To stabilise. To fix. It is the intervening with the price of a commodity or shares so that a steady market is maintained. The retaining of a rate of exchange, so that government is able to control prices.

penalty. A punishment for an offence, a sum to be forfeited for breach of a rule or contract.

penalty clause. A clause found in a commercial or financial contract providing for a penalty to be paid should any of the terms of the contract be breached.

pence rates. Rates of exchange quoted in pence per foreign unit.

pending action. An action or proceedings to be heard in court relating to land or interest in land. Any pending action in the case of unregistered land must be registered on the Pending Actions Register at the Land Charges Department or in the case of registered land by the registration of a caution on the Land Register. The intention is to warn possible purchasers than an action is pending and the title is not perfect. An action pending to the validity of a will may lead to the appointment of an administrator.

penny. A coin of the realm, which until the thirteenth century was the only coin of the realm although there were half pennies and quarter pennies (farthings). Copper coins were introduced in 1797 and replaced by bronze coins in 1860. There were 240 pence to one pound sterling. It was indicated by the letter 'd', which was taken from the Latin *denarius*, but for the current penny introduced with decimalisation in 1971, it is indicated by the letter 'p' and is worth one hundredth of a pound sterling. There are now no half pence or quarter pence in circulation.

penny bank. A savings bank of the late nineteenth century, so called because it would accept a sum as small as one penny on deposit.

penny stocks. Shares that are quoted at very low prices, usually 50p or less each. Many are regarded as speculative.

pension. A monthly or annual payment to a person on retirement from full-time employment. The amount paid is calculated with reference to the final salary, times the number of years service, divided by either eighty or sixty, whichever is the regulation of the organisation. Many pensions are linked to the cost-of-living index, so that a pensioner is likely to receive an annual increase. Under the national insurance scheme, men and women who have made regular contributions will receive a pension at 60 years of age for women and 65 years of age for men. *See also* CONTRIBUTORY PENSION; NON-CONTRIBUTORY PENSIONS; OLD-AGE PENSION.

pension funds. These are funds that have accumulated by the regular contributions of employees and the employer. Some pension funds are controlled by the company's own managers or investment subsidiary, while others prefer that the funds should be managed by an insurance company. These funds are then invested in a wide range of stocks and shares, some will invest part of their funds in works of art and antiques. Their aim is to obtain the best possible returns for their investment.

PEP. *See* PERSONAL EQUITY PLAN.

peppercorn rent. A nominal rent.

per annum. By the year, yearly.

p.e. ratio. The abbreviation for price/earnings ratio.

per capita. Individually, each, per head.

per cent. per centum. By the hundred.

per contra. On the other side (of the account), to balance it, on the other hand.

per diem. By the day, daily.

performance. The discharge of an act in accordance with the contract. Settlement of a debt.

performance bond. A type of guarantee which is an undertaking that should the seller fail to carry out the terms of the contract, then the buyer may claim a certain amount of money. These bonds are usually issued in connection with work overseas. The overseas buyer who awards a contract to a builder or constructor will request a performance bond, so that he is reassured that should the job not be finished owing to liquidation or other reasons, he will obtain recompense. The bank, on the authority of its customer, will issue a performance bond usually in favour of a bank in the importers country. That bank will convey its own performance bond to the importer. The validity period of the bond will vary according to the terms of the contract and the value is likely to be between 5 and 10 per cent of the contract price, but from time to time a higher percentage is demanded. Frequently a number of performance bonds have to be issued in accordance with the different stages of the contract. Some performance bonds are unconditional, that is the buyer, without giving any reason, may call for payment under the bond, and the UK bank will be obliged to pay. Other bonds are conditional, so that some evidence must be provided to show that there has been a breach of the terms of the contract. A bank will always take either a counter indemnity or cash cover before a performance bond is issued.

perestroika. The introduction by Mr Gorbachev, when President of the USSR the principal of reforms into the economy of the country, whereby industrial efficiency will be improved, businesses will be denationalised and eventually the rouble will be an international convertible currency.

performance fund. An investment or unit trust where the investment policy is intended to yield higher than the average.

period of account. The period for which the final accounts and balance sheet have been prepared. The period for which the entries in an account relate. The date between one accounting period and another.

period of grace. The time allowed after the balancing of an account during which time a debt must be settled. Days of grace for the payment of bills of exchange are no longer permitted.

peripheral. All calculations performed by computer central processing units (*q.v.*) ultimately come down to an ability to 'sense' the presence of an electrical impulse. All data on which we require a computer to work must therefore be presented to it in the form of electrical impulses. The function of peripheral equipment is: 1. to translate words and figures into 'computer-recognisable' impulses, e.g. terminals (*see under* ELECTRONIC DATA PROCESSING); 2. to store data for presentation to CPUs when needed, e.g. magnetic tape and disk units; 3. to present results of computer operations in humanly understandable form, e.g. visual display units (*q.v.*).

per mensem. By the month, monthly.

permissive waste. Allowing the buildings on an estate to fall into a state of decay, thus a wrong of omission.

perpetual. Unending, eternal, persistent, continual, constant.

perpetual annual rent charge. *See* FEE FARM RENT.

perpetual annuity. An annuity payable for ever.

perpetual debenture. A debenture with no date for repayment, intended to be a permanent debt.

pepetual injunction. *See* INJUNCTION.

perpetuity. The number of years purchase to be given for an annuity; a perpetual annuity. *In Perpetuity.* For ever.

per procurationem (per pro). By the agency of, by proxy. A form of words used by an agent when signing for a principal, i.e. *'per pro* John Jones, S. Smith', where Jones is the principal and Smith the agent. *'Per Pro'* is also shortened still further to *'p.p.'.*

per se. By itself, or itself.

personal. Peculiar to a person as a private individual; directed against a person; of possessions, belonging to a person.

personal account. The account of a person, persons or any legal entity held in the account of a business.

personal bar. The Scots law equivalent of the doctrine of estoppel (*q.v.*)

personal cheque. A cheque usually issued by a building society for those customers who maintain an account for which a cheque book is not issued. When funds are required for payment to another person, the building society will issue a cheque in favour of a named payee.

personal equity plan (PEP). A method of savings brought in by the 1986 budget which allows the ordinary person to invest up to £500 per month or £6000 a year in equities either through a bank, building society, insurance company or any other financial institution that offers this service. Profits and income will be exempt from tax if the holding is retained for a given length of time.

personal estate. Any property other than freehold land is personal estate.

personal identification number (PIN). This number is issued by a bank, credit card company or building society to a customer, so that a sum of money may be withdrawn from an ATM, transferred to the account of a retailer when using an EFTPOS card, or in the case of home banking, transferring funds from one account to another.

personalisation of cheques and credits. At the foot of each cheque and each credit, the following details are printed: (*a*) the cheque or credit number, (*b*) the branch/bank sorting code, (*c*) the customer's account number. There is also a space for the amount. Due to this personalisation, customers are advised to ensure that the credit and cheque is only used for the account for which they are intended as when these items are passed through the work in the bank, the sorting takes place by computer, so that the characters are read and the appropriate account is debited/credited and then the item is sorted, again by computer, and despatched to the branch.

personal liability. A person is jointly and severally liable for the debts of a company if he or she, as a director or shadow director, contravenes s. 216 Insolvency Act 1986. A person who is a party to a joint account or a partner in a trading concern, is also normally jointly and severally liable for the debts owed.

personal loan. A loan to an individual as opposed to a business loan. Whereas it was the general practice to put the interest 'up front', this is no longer done. A loan account is opened in the name of the customer, which is then debited with the agreed amount and the current account credited. Interest charges may be debited quarterly or half-yearly to either the current account or the loan account at the option of the customer. The period of the loan is usually from six months to about three years, in some cases it could be extended to five years. Any loan under £15 000 is subject to the Consumer Credit Act 1974. It is therefore unlike a hire purchase loan and the bank has no rights over the item purchased.

personal poinding (*Sc. Law*). *See* POINDING.

personal property. Movable property, goods, money, etc., leasehold estates.

personal representative. A person that administers the estate of another. This may be due to the fact that a person has died intestate and the court has appointed him as the administrator of the estate or where there is a will he is then appointed as the executor.

personal security. Security for an advance which consists of a guarantee by a third person.

personal tax. The income tax on earned and unearned income.

personalty. *See* PERSONAL PROPERTY.

petition. A written application, request or prayer to the courts, Parliament or the sovereign for a relief or remedy. For example, an application by a creditor for the bankruptcy of a debtor.

petition for bankruptcy. By s. 264, Insolvency Act 1986, a petition in bankruptcy may be presented to the court as follows: (*a*) by the individual himself; (*b*) by the supervisor or other person bound by the voluntary arrangement; (*c*) in the case of criminal bankruptcy, by an official with powers under the Powers of Criminal Courts Act 1973. A bankruptcy petition should not be presented to the court unless the debtor is (*a*) domiciled in England or Wales; (*b*) personally present in England or Wales on the day on which the petition is presented; (*c*) has, at any time in the period of three years, been ordinarily *resident* or has had a place of *residence* in England or Wales or has carried on *business* in England or Wales (s. 265).

petrodollars. These are funds that oil producing countries have paid into their accounts with Western banks, usually for a short term. As oil is invoiced and paid in US dollars the term 'petrodollars' indicates the source of these funds. They were important sources of finance during the 1970s, since these funds were used by the banks to finance oil-importing countries. By the mid 1980s, their importance diminished as the surpluses shrunk. The flow of these funds in the 1990s while not having the same importance as in the 1970s still require some attention in the current economic situation.

petty cash. The amount spent on small or minor items in a business.

petty cash book. The book which records the minor expenses of a business and the funds which are from time to time received for such purposes.

pie chart. A circular diagram of a quantity divided up into sections showing how each section makes up the whole. Frequently used to show as a circle the profit of a business and the sectors in proportion to their contribution to the profit.

piecemeal distribution. A procedure whereby a business in the process of liquidation, sells its assets and settles the debts due, then distributes funds to the owners' of the business. Any funds due to them are on a pro rata basis.

piece rates. A rate of pay based on a person's work on a unit of production or manufacture.

piggy bank. Originally this referred to a china model pig with a slot for money, so that a person could save his farthings, halfpennies and pennies, for whatever purpose. Currently this describes any savings box, in whatever shape, that children are encouraged to use to teach them thrift. Can also refer to an account that is used for small disbursements.

pin. *See* PERSONAL IDENTIFICATION NUMBER.

pin money. An allowance to a person, e.g. son or daughter for the purchase of personal items. A wage or salary of a person, who does not need this money for household expenses, but for expenditure on luxury or inessential items.

pip. A digit after the whole number and decimal point in an amount which specifies the rate of exchange.

pipe. A system for the exchange of share information between the various European Stock Exchanges. It will give information on quoted companies, prices and volumes of trade. It is intended to be the forerunner of a single European market in the shares of large European companies.

pit. The area on the 'floor' of LIFFE where dealers deal by open outcry.

P & L a/c. The abbreviation for profit and loss account.

placing. A method of issuing a new issue of stocks/shares. Either the whole issue is placed with one institution or large blocks are placed with a small number of institutions. Some or all of these shares/stocks will find its way to the market.

placing broker. An insurance broker who places various percentages of a risk he or she is employed by a client to cover with various syndicates at Lloyd's.

placing power. The ability of a bank to sell new Euro bond issues to investors.

plaint. The cause for which a written complaint is made.

plaintiff. The one who sues in a court of law.

plant. The group name for assets which comprise fixtures and fittings, equipment, etc.

plastic card. The general or common name given to all the various credit, cash, cheque, store cards being used.

playing the market. A phrase used to describe a person who during times when the Stock Exchange indices are going up, moves into a stockholding and quickly moves out again when a profit is shown.

plc. The abbreviation for public limited company.

plead. To put forward an answer to a plaintiff's accusation. An address to the court.

pleader. One who pleads, especially a lawyer who makes a plea in a court of justice, an advocate.

pleading. The art of conducting a case, as an advocate. *See also* SPECIAL PLEADING.

pleadings. Written statements of plaintiff and defendant in support of their claims.

pledge. A security of goods which are transferred to the possession of or in the name of the creditor or lender. Once the borrower has repaid the debt, then the goods so pledged will be returned to the debtor. Consumer Credit Act 1974 gives the pawnee rights over an item taken into pawn. *See* NEGATIVE PLEDGE.

pledgee. A person to whom goods are pledged.

plimsoll mark. A line required to be placed on every British ship, marking the level to which the authorised weight of cargo sinks her.

plus value. Appreciation in price.

poinding. *(Sc. Law) personal poinding* is the seizure of personal property of a debtor in settlement of the debt. As a preminary there must first be an order of the court, called a *decree* (*q.v.*)

leading to a formal requisition, served personally on the debtor if he or she can be found, or by *edict* (*q.v.*) if he cannot, by a sheriff officer. This requisition, or schedule of charge, will specify the days of charge – usually seven days – within which payment must be made. If payment has not been made at the end of this time, the creditor may then proceed to poind. It is the sheriff officer who actually seizes the property (all corporeal movables belonging to the debtor and in possession), which is then valued, listed, and offered for sale. *Real poinding,* or *poinding of the ground,* is a diligence (*q.v.*) which can be called into service where a debt, or the interest on it, in respect of an obligation incurred on the *security of land,* is in arrears. The person entitled can poind the movables on the ground, i.e. he or she can, after obtaining a decree, seize any movable chattels or movable fixtures on the property. In the case of tenants the right extends only to the amount of rent due but unpaid.

point. In investment terms, a digit representing 1 per cent is often referred to as a point. When an index is quoted in a number then a movement up or down is referred to as 2 points up or 2 points down as the case may be. In the foreign exchange market or a commodity market a change of 1 per cent less is referred to as points.

Point of Sale Terminals. *See* ELECTRONIC FUNDS TRANSFER AT POINT OF SALE (EFTPOS).

poison pill. A move by a company that is likely to be taken over so that the attractiveness of the shares are reduced and a takeover less likely.

polarisation. Under the Financial Services Act, banks must choose between selling their own life assurance and financial products or, acting as an independent intermediary and selling the products of other companies. At the time of writing, Barclays, Lloyds, Midland Bank and National Westminster Bank sell their own products.

policy. The legally binding contract between the insurance company and the insured. *See also* COMPREHENSIVE POLICY; ECGD POLICY; ENDOWMENT POLICY; FAMILY PROTECTION POLICY; FLOATING POLICY; GENERAL POLICY; INDUSTRIAL POLICY; LIFE POLICY; LLOYD'S POLICY; MIXED POLICY; NAMED POLICY; NON-PARTICIPATING POLICY; OPEN POLICY; PAID-UP POLICY; SHORT-TERM POLICY; SINGLE PREMIUM POLICY; SURVIVORSHIP POLICY; TIME POLICY; TONTINE POLICY; UNIT-LINKED POLICY; VALUED POLICY; VOYAGE POLICY; WHOLE LIFE POLICY; 'WITH PROFITS' POLICY.

policy holder. The person who has a policy in his or her possession or under his or her control, usually the insured.

policy underwriter. One who writes his or her name under a policy of marine insurance, thus undertaking to indemnify the insured against the risks specified in the policy; a member of an underwriting syndicate at Lloyd's.

portfolio. A case, collection or file containing investment certificates held by an individual, company, financial institution. The bundle or file of bills of exchange or other negotiable instruments held by a bank, discount or other financial institution.

portfolio management service. A service offered by any financial institution or its subsidiary, whereby it will retain, in its own name, the securities of a customer, deal with the dividend received, by either crediting the amount received in an account held in-house, or credit the customer's usual bank or building society account. Deal with bonus and rights issues. Review the portfolio at regular intervals and buy or sell an investment in accordance with the customer's authority. Regular statements are sent to the customer showing the income received and a list of investments held.

portion. A part, a share, an allotment, a dowry, the part of an estate descending to an heir.

position. A situation or state. In banking a position may be taken in foreign exchange to hold an excess or deficit in any particular foreign currency. A bank may take a position in its lending policy. In the interim bank results of 1991, due to the massive provision for bad debts, which resulted in major reductions in profits, a more cautious attitude was taken in regard to lending to small businesses. In the commercial sense, it is the financial condition of a business. An investor, will take up a position in a particular group of securities or market.

position building. The gradual purchase of shares in a particular security, so as to avoid a sudden rise in price.

possession. The physical ownership, occupation or control of property, goods, wealth, etc. It must be contrasted with ownership. In cases of the deposit of equitable security, while a bank may have possession of that security, the borrower will retain ownership.

possessory lien. The right to retain or detain the property of another until the outstanding debt is settled. There is no right of sale, except where it has been authorised by statute.

possessory title. The title to land by a person unable to establish his right in the usual way. It can be acquired by possession of property for a period of twelve years or more, during which time no rent has been paid, nor has any other person acknowledged any right to that land. With registered land, the title is granted when the examination shows no more than the applicant was in possession of the land. A purchaser must always investigate the title of the land, prior to registration. The registrar has the power to convert a possessory freehold into an absolute freehold title after fifteen years and a possessory leasehold title into a good leasehold title after ten years.

post. An official position. A job description. An entry into an account or ledger. To despatch by mail.

postal giro. A method of transmission of funds through the postal system, rather than through the banking system. This method is particularly prevalent in European countries. See GIROBANK.

postal order. A means of payment provided by the Post Office. This order may be purchased for small fixed amounts, but in order to increase its value, postage stamps may be added. A poundage or commission is paid when the instrument is purchased. There is no formality in obtaining a postal order from any Post Office and it is useful for those persons who do not have a cheque book. Strictly, they are not negotiable instruments, but in practice, they can be transferred. Postal orders may be paid into a bank account or encashed at a Post Office.

postdate. To insert on an instrument, e.g. a cheque, a date later than the date of drawing or issue. The intention of postdating a cheque may be a deliberate act of the drawer, but if this happens with any degree of regularity, then it is obvious that there is some form of financial embarrassment for the customer. From the bank's point of view, it is bound to accept the customer's mandate and not pay the cheque until the due date, so should a postdated cheque be presented for payment, then it must be dishonoured with the reply 'Cheque postdated, please represent'. Should a bank inadvertently pay such a cheque, then it runs the risk of (a) the cheque being stopped before the due date, (b) due to lack of funds dishonouring a cheque whose date is correct, thereby damaging the customer's credit, (c) a legal bar may be operative, e.g. death, mental incapacity, notice of bankruptcy or liquidation, attachment of funds by a garnishee order. The cheque is not invalid by reason of it being postdated – Bills of Exchange Act 1882 s. 13(2).

posting. The act of recording an entry in a ledger account.

Post Office Register. See DIRECTOR OF SAVINGS.

pound. The British money of account consisting of one hundred pence, a sovereign, written £.

poundage. Commission, allowance or charge of so much in the pound.

pound cost averaging. Where stock or shares are bought in instalments over a period at varying prices, an harmonic mean will be established (as with unit-trust linked life assurance policies). The lower this average price, the higher the ultimate profit is likely to be when the securities are sold.

pound sterling. The British standard pound of one hundred pence as a gold coin or a paper note.

power. A value. A force. An authority given to a person or an office to perform certain functions, e.g. enter into a legal contract, purchase, sell property, engage and dismiss staff.

power of attorney. An instrument authorising one person to act on behalf of another. Such an instrument is created by a written or typed document signed by the donor or maker, sealed and delivered to the agent. Powers of attorney are now regulated by the Powers of Attorney Act 1971 and the Enduring Powers of Attorney Act 1985. The powers granted by the principal or donor can be either (a) for a specific transaction, (b) for a series of transactions or (c) in respect of all his/her transactions. When a power of attorney is lodged with a bank, the banker should carefully inspect the document to see whether it contains general powers or specific powers. The bank should also note the effect this will have on the banker/customer relationship, e.g. can the agent overdraw the account? Can the agent charge securities registered in the principal's name? These factors should be expressly provided for. Where the power of attorney is for a specific transaction, e.g. for the purchase of land, then on the completion of the transaction, the powers of attorney are revoked. When a power of attorney is presented to a bank it is common practice for the bank to request the customer to complete his/her own mandate form, so that the bank has clear instructions that will be enforceable. Where powers of attorney are to be effected under the Enduring Powers of Attorney Act 1985, the bank must ensure that such powers are registered with the Court of Protection.

power of attorney clause. An equitable mortgage is created by the desposit of the title deeds or the land certificate to the property, usually with a signed memorandum of deposit. Where a memorandum of deposit is taken under seal, then it will incorporate a clause which gives the bank irrevocable powers of attorney, appointing the bank or its nominee as attorney to sell or grant leases on the property and give the bank a legal mortgage. Alternatively, it will incorporate a declaration of trust, whereby the customer declares that he/she holds the property in trust for the bank and at the discretion of the bank he/she may be removed as trustee and a fresh trustee appointed. This enables the bank to carry out the sale of the property without resort to the courts and are not affected by either the death or bankruptcy of the mortgagor.

power of sale. In any lending situation where security has been taken by a bank, the bank should, if necessary, be able to sell that security. Where a legal charge has been taken, then the bank as the legal owner can do so without seeking permission of the customer. However, where an equity charge has been taken, then the ownership is still with the borrower, so that the memorandum of deposit must have a clause which insists that the customer will realise the named security for the benefit of the bank. In practice, the customer, at last resort, may not give this authority, so that the bank will have to seek the authority of the courts. As an alternative to this, the bank may request the signing of an undated authority to transfer that security to the bank or its nominee. Any repayment can then be done without notice to the customer.

power of a mortgagee. A legal mortgagee may on the default of the mortgagor, have the following options: 1. Sue for the debt on the personal covenant of the morgagor. 2. Appoint a reciever, who under the Law of Property Act 1925 s. 109, may apply any rents to any outstanding amounts to prior mortgages, payment of community charge and other outgoings, payment of receiver's own charges, insurance and repairs and reduction of amount due to the bank. 3. Foreclose. The property is vested in the name of the mortgagee. 4. Enter into possession – the same effect as appointing a receiver – rarely used. 5. Sell the property. This right is available under s. 101, Law of Property Act 1925. With an equitable charge, a mortgagee has only the right to sue on the covenant to repay or to resort to the court.

powers of an administrator or administrative receiver. Under s. 14 Insolvency Act 1986, the powers given to the administrator allow him to do whatever is necessary to manage the affairs, business and property of the company. He must act in accordance with the directions of the court or apply to the court for such directions as he/she consider necessary for the appointment. Under Schedule 1 the powers include: 1. Take possession of land. 2. Dispose of property either privately or by public auction. 3. Borrow such money and create charges over the company property to secure such borrowings. 4. Appoint solicitors, accountants and other professional advisers and agents and to bring and defend any actions or legal proceedings on behalf of the company. 5. Maintain the insurances of the company property. 6. Use the company seal and to execute any deed, receipt, bill of exchange, promissory note, document on behalf of the company. 7. Carry on the business of the company, form subsidiaries and transfer property to a subsidiary. 8. Grant or surrender leases or to take tenancies. 9. Call up any uncalled capital of the company. 10. Appoint directors and remove directors. 11. Call meetings of members and creditors and exercise any powers under the Memorandum and Articles of Association. For all purposes the administrator is an agent of the company.

powers of liquidator in a winding up. In accordance with the Insolvency Act 1986, Sch. 4, the powers exercisable with sanction are as follows: 1. To pay any class of creditors in full. 2. To make any compromise or arrangement with creditors or persons claiming to be creditors, or having or alleging themselves to have any claim (present or future, certain or contingent, ascertained or sounding only in damages) against the company, or whereby the company may be rendered liable. 3. To compromise on such terms as may be agreed (*a*) calls and liabilities to calls, debts and liabilities capable of resulting in debts, and all claims subsisting or supposed to subsist between the company and a contributory or alleged contributory or other debtor or person apprehending liability to the company and (*b*) all questions in any way relating to or affecting the assets or the winding up of the company, and take any security for the discharge of any such call, debt liability or claim and give a complete discharge in respect of it. The following power is exercisable without sanction in voluntary winding up, with sanction in winding up by the court. 4. Power to bring or defend any action or other legal proceeding in the name and on behalf of the company.

5. Power to carry on the business of the company so far as may be necessary for its beneficial winding up. The following powers are exercisable without sanction in any winding up. 6. To sell any of the company's property by public auction or private contract with the power to transfer the whole of it to any person or to sell the same in panels. 7. To act and execute, in the name and on behalf of the company, all deeds, receipts and other documents and for that purpose to use, when necessary the company's seal. 8. To prove, rank and claim in the bankruptcy, insolvency or sequestration of any contributory for any balance against his estate, and to receive dividends in bankruptcy, insolvency or sequestration in respect of that balance, as a separate debt due from the bankrupt or insolvent, and rateably with the other separate creditors. 9. To draw, accept, make and indorse any bill of exchange or promissory note in the name and on behalf of the company, with the same effect with respect to the company's liability as if the bill or not had been drawn, accepted, made or indorsed by or on behalf of the company in the course of its business. 10. To raise on the security of the assets of the company any money requisite. 11. To take out in official name letters of administration to any deceased contributory, and to do in his official name any other act necessary for obtaining payment of any money due from a contributory or his estate which cannot conveniently be done in the name of the company. In all such cases the money due is deemed, for the purpose of enabling the liquidator to take out the letters of administration or recover the money, to be due to the liquidator himself. 12. To appoint an agent to do any business which the liquidator is unable to do himself. 13. To do all such other things as may be necessary for winding up the company's affairs and distributing its assets.

powers of the liquidator in bankruptcy. By Sch. 5 of the Insolvency Act 1986 the powers exercisable with sanction are as follows: 1. carry on any business of the bankrupt if it is beneficial for the winding-up; 2. bring, institute, or defend any action relating to the property of the bankrupt's estate; 3. accept payment for the sale of the property of the bankrupt's estate, subject to certain stipulations; 4. mortgage or pledge any property to raise money to pay debts; 5. make payments or incur liabilities for the benefit of creditors; 6. refer to arbitration, any claims by third parties on the property of the bankrupt; 7. make such arrangements as are thought expedient with respect to claims out of the bankrupt's estate.

powers of trustee in bankruptcy. For insolvency purposes, the trustee may with the permission of the creditors' committee and the court exercise the following powers: 1. Carry on any business of the bankrupt as far as may be necessary for winding it up beneficially without contravening any requirement imposed by or under any enactment. 2. Bring, institute, or defend any action or legal proceedings relating to the property in the bankrupt's estate. 3. Accept as the consideration for the sale of any property comprised in the bankrupt's estate a sum of money payable at a future time subject to such stipulations as to security or otherwise as the creditors' committee or the court thinks it. 4. To mortgage or pledge any part of the property comprised in the bankrupt's estate for the purpose of raising money for the payment of his debts. 5. Where any right, option or other power forms part of the bankrupt's estate, to make payments or incur liabilities with a view to obtaining, for the benefit of the creditors, any property which is the subject of the right, option or power. 6. Refer to arbitration or compromise on such terms as may be agreed on, any debts, claims or liabilities subsisting or supposed to subsist between the bankrupt and any person who may have incurred any liability to the bankrupt. 7. Make any such compromise or other arrangement as may be thought expedient with creditors, or persons claiming to be creditors, in respect of bankruptcy debts. 8. Make such compromise or other arrangement as may be thought to be expedient with respect to any claim arising out of or incidental to the bankrupt's estate made or capable of being made on the trustee by any person or by the trustee in

person (Insolvency Act 1986 Sch. 5 Part 1). Without permission the power that can be exercised as shown in the Insolvency Act 1986 Sch. 5 Pt 11 are as follows: 9. Sell any part of the property for the time being comprised in the bankrupt's estate, including the goodwill and book debts of any business. 10. Give receipts for any money received by him, being receipts which effectually discharge the person paying the money from all responsibility in respect of its application. 11. Prove, rank, claim and draw a dividend in respect of such debts owing to the bankrupt as are comprised in his estate. 12. Exercise in relation to any property comprised in the bankrupt's estate any powers the capacity to exercise which is vested in him under Parts VIII to XI of this Act. 13. Deal with any property comprised in the estate to which the bankrupt is beneficially entitled as tenant in tail in the same manner as the bankrupt might have dealt with it.

practical insolvency. See INSOLVENCY.

preamble. The introduction to a statute or bill. It gives the broad outline of the intention of the bill, e.g. Company Directors Disqualification Act 1986: 'An Act to consolidate enactments relating to the disqualification of persons from being directors of companies, and from being otherwise concerned with a company's affairs'.

pre-authorised payment. The US equivalent to direct debits and standing orders.

precatory trust. A trust which arises from a construction of words of supplication or entreaty, which are interpreted to show that the donor intended to impose a trust.

precept. A written order. A command. An order, warrant, writ demanding the payment of a debt.

pre-emption. The right to purchase before others, e.g. the purchase of shares in a company by its members before members of the public do so, or to buy back property from the original purchaser.

pre-emptive bid. A high offer for shares of a company by a predator, so as to make it difficult for another to attempt a take over. The high bid at an auction to dissuade others from bidding.

pre-emptive right. The right of shareholders to bid for shares before it is offered to others.

preference. The act of favouring one person or thing before another or others. *See also* FRAUDULENT PREFERENCE.

preference creditor. A creditor of an insolvent person or company whose debt has priority over other classes of creditors.

preferential creditors. In the winding-up of a company or the bankruptcy of an individual, the person, company or institution that is entitled to receive settlement of debts before other creditors (Insolvency Act 1986 Sch. 6).

preferential debts. In the event of bankruptcy or winding-up, it is those persons who are entitled to receive settlement of debts before the distribution of the assets to others. By Sch. 6, Insolvency Act, 1986, the preferential debtors are: 1. Inland Revenue: 2. Customs and Excise; 3. Social Security Contributions; 4. Contributions to occupational pension schemes; 5. Remuneration to employees.

preferential wages account. *See* WAGES/SALARIES ACCOUNT.

pre-finance bill. A bill drawn under a pre-finance credit. *See* DOCUMENTARY CREDIT.

preliminary expenses. Often known as formation expenses. Expenses which are incurred in the formation of a company.

premium. A recompense, a prize, a bounty; a fee paid to learn a profession or trade; the amount exceeding the par value of shares or stock; the periodical instalment paid for insurance. *at a premium.* Above par, in great demand. *to put a premium on.* To act as an incentive to.

premium bond. *See* NATIONAL SAVINGS PREMIUM BONDS.

premium bonus. A term applied to any system whereby a worker is paid according to his or her output in a given time, but receives an additional payment if this output exceeds a certain standard.

prepay. To pay in advance.

prerogative. A privilege or right vested in a person or office, e.g. the sovereign to an advantage or option.

prerogative orders. Instructions, directives issued by courts to protect the rights of individuals from the abuses or excesses of power by public authorities, government departments, etc. *See* CERTIORARI, MANDAMUS; PROHIBITION.

present. Here or at hand; writings or documents; the offer of a bill for acceptance or payment.

presenting bank. When dealing with clean or documentary collections, it is the collecting bank which requests the presenting bank to present the financial document, with or without commercial documents attached, to receive acceptance/payment of the instrument or documents.

presentment. The act or state of presenting, representation, delineation, the laying of a formal statement before a court or an authority; notice taken by a grand jury of an offence from their own knowledge or observation.

presentment for acceptance. Bills of Exchange Act 1882 s. 39 states that a 'bill of exchange is presented for acceptance (i) to fix its maturity date, if it is payable after sight (ii) if it expressly stipulates that it shall be presented for acceptance (iii) where a bill is payable elsewhere other than the residence or place of business of the drawee, it must be presented for acceptance before it can be presented for payment.' To comply with the law a bill must be presented for acceptance (a) on behalf of the holder (b) to the drawee or some person (bank) authorised to accept or refuse acceptance on his/her behalf (c) at a reasonable hour on a business day (d) before the bill is overdue.

Where the bill is a documentary bill, i.e. with commercial documents attached, the bill should be accepted before the commercial documents are released to the drawee. They should as part of normal practice not be left with the drawee, unless the principal has authorised such a procedure. Where a clean bill of exchange is presented for acceptance, then subject to the standing of the drawee this may be left on the premises for not more than 24 hours awaiting acceptance or refusal.

Acceptance must be unconditional, i.e. must not be for a lesser amount or extension of the time.

presentment for payment. Bills of Exchange Act 1882 s. 57: 'A bill is duly presented for payment which is presented in accordance with the following rules: 1. Where the bill is not payable on demand, presentment must be made on the day it falls due. 2. Where the bill is payable on demand, presentment must be made within a reasonable time after its issue in order to render the drawer liable and within a reasonable time after its indorsement, in order to render the indorser liable.' S. 45(3) 'Presentment must be made by the holder or by some person authorised to receive payment on his behalf at a reasonable hour on a business day, at the proper place either to the person designated by the bill as payer, or to some person authorised to pay or refuse payment on his behalf if with the exercise of reasonable diligence such person can be found'. With a cheque, presentment of a cheque must also be made within a reasonable time. For promissory notes, presentment for payment must be made at the place specified in order to make the drawer/maker liable.

In dealing with documentary collections, where the instructions state that documents must only be delivered against payment of the bill of exchange (D/P collection), such presentation must be made without delay – London practice – within 24 hours or the next business day and the commercial documents will only be delivered against good payment.

present value. The value today, of a future payment. The amount which will be paid at present by a bank discounting a bill payable at a future date. The present value of a sum of money that is likely to be received at some future date, e.g. the present value of £100 to be received in ten years time at a discount rate of 10 per cent p.a. compound. For investment purposes, a calculation is made on how much should be invested today, in order to obtain a sum of money at some future time.

pre-shipment credit. Funds that are available to an exporter to finance either the purchase or manufacture of goods until final payment has been received from the importer. Such finance is available by the use of a 'Red Clause' Documentary Credit. Funds are also available from banks under their own export finance arrangements, whether it is for capital (one-off) projects or consumer goods with or without ECGD cover.

prestel. A television link originated by British Telecom (BT) in 1979 which is available to the public on their television sets and can give up-dated information on a large variety of topics including financial and stock exchange movements.

presumption. An assumption made until the contrary is proven. A conclusion that a certain fact exists because other facts exist which can lead to or be proven to have a conclusion.

presumption of fact. An inference as to a fact from facts already known.

presumption of law. The assumption that there is truth in fact until it is proven otherwise.

presumption of value. The assumption that value has at some time been given. 'Every party whose signature appears on a bill is prima facie deemed to have become a party thereto for value' (s. 30(1) Bills of Exchange Act 1882).

presumptive evidence. Evidence derived from circumstances which necessarily or usually attend a fact.

price. The amount at which a thing is valued, bought or sold; value, cost.

price consumption curve. A curve on a diagram showing how the demand for the consumption for a commodity is relative to its price changes.

price control. A governmental policy to maximise the price of a commodity or commodities, to protect the consumer against high prices. This is done for political reasons on occasions when the government wishes to keep down wages/inflation.

price discrimination. The charging of different prices to different groups of customers for the same or similar service. It is currently alleged that there is a discrimination against small businesses and that interest and other charges are forcing them into bankruptcy or liquidation. While each bank is an independent body, there are suggestions that a bank must advertise a tariff for its charges and that interest and loans should not be on a 'what the customer can bear' basis.

price earnings ratio. The relationship that exists at any one time between the market price of a share and its current profit after the deduction of tax. Its purpose is to show the number of years it will take an investor to recoup his/her investment if profits were distributed. It also reflects the market's own expectations of the future profitability of the company. This is frequently referred to as the P/E ratio.

price fixing. *See* PRICE CONTROL.

price range. The highest and the lowest range of prices in any commodity. In newspapers stocks and shares, show the highest and lowest in the year. Foreign exchange rates show the highest and lowest rates of the day.

price spread. The price range in any given period.

price support. The support given by a government or an authority, for example, the government may support farm prices, while the Bank of England will from time to time support any large run on sterling.

pricing. *See* DIFFERENTIAL PRICING.

prima facie. On the first view, on the first impression, at first sight.

prima facie check of documents. A brief examination of documents to see that all the documents that are listed in the covering letter are on hand. 1. Article 2, Uniform Rules for Collections state: 'Banks must verify that the documents received appear to be as listed in the collection order and must immediately advise the party from whom the collection order was received of any documents missing. Banks have no further obligation to examine the documents'. 2. On receipt of deeds it is customary to examine the contents to see that a good root title is held, i.e. for at least fifteen years. 3. Check the holding deed is in the correct name, i.e. the person wishing to borrow against the security.

primary dealer. A broker or financial institution that deals in government stock or treasury bills.

primary market. That market that involves the discount houses and deals with the issue and sale of government stock and treasury bills. The sale of a new issue of shares through the Stock Exchange.

primary period. *See* FINANCE LEASE.

prime. Original, foremost, first in degree or importance.

prime bank bill. *See* FINE BANK BILL.

prime costs. The costs that directly affect the cost of manufacture or production. This includes direct wages, direct material and direct expenses.

prime entry. The details taken from an invoice or some other document and recorded in a book or ledger of original entry.

prime paper. *See* ELIGIBLE BILL.

prime rate. An American term, but it is used in the UK where it is the equivalent of the UK minimum lending rate. It refers to the best possible lending rate which is available to the most-creditworthy customers of banks. A prime company will be able to borrow at the prime rate plus about 1 or 2 per cent.

principal. A capital sum invested. The person for whom an agent will work. The leading or head person. The head of a department or college.

principal amount. The sum of money invested, or the amount due on a debt. This will not include any interest paid or payable.

principal's mandate. The deed or contract setting out the functions and duties of an agent. Each function and duty must be clearly specified. Should the agent exceed his/her powers, then the principal will not be bound.

prior charges. The charges that will rank ahead of the current lender. Before a bank will lend funds against any security, it will be in the bank's own interest to investigate to see whether any prior charges have been registered. In the case of a policy of assurance being deposited as security, the bank must check with the insurance company that there are no prior charges. Any security on land, whether equitable or legal, should be checked to ascertain that the Land Registry has not recorded any prior charges.

priority of debts. *See* PREFERENTIAL DEBTS.

priority notice. The establishment of priority will depend on whether the land is registered or unregistered, so that in the case of the first legal or equitable mortgage by individuals: 1. For unregistered land, and the deeds are held, no registration is necessary, if at the time of the mortgage, the land charges register showed no encumbrances against the owner, but a search is essential. 2. For registered land, registration at the District Land

Registry is necessary and priority is subject to entries on the register and overriding interests. For subsequent buyers of unregistered land, and the deeds are not held, registration as puisne Class C(i) legal charge or Class C(iii) equitable charge is necessary. For registered land, registration is necessary at the District Land Registry Office. For mortgages by limited companies, then in addition to registration as mentioned above, registration is also necessary at the Companies Registrar, as required by the Companies Act 1985 s. 395–8.

private. Not public, belonging to or concerning an individual, secret, not publicly known; not holding public office, confidential.

private act, private bill. An Act of Parliament concerned with private persons and not affecting public policy or to have a general application.

private bank. Strictly speaking, very few private banks exist today. Before the introduction of limited liability and company law, all businesses including banks were by necessity small partnerships. The first bank with limited liability was the Bank of England which was given Royal Charter in 1694. With the advent of joint stock companies and joint stock banking, private banks either merged or were taken over by the more powerful banks with limited liability. At present the major banks are those with branches throughout the UK. Private banks, can be defined as either small limited companies, incorporated in the UK with one or perhaps only a few branches, or being a subsidiary of a major clearing bank, e.g. Adam and Co plc, Brown Shipley & Co Ltd. While Hoare & Co remains a partnership, Coutts & Co is a subsidiary of National Westminster Bank plc. In theory, there is no reason why in the future a private bank could not be opened, providing the organisation can satisfy the criteria laid down by the Banking Act 1987 and is accepted as a bank by the Bank of England.

private company. A company whose shares are not generally available to the public at large. Capital is raised from a small number of persons although there is no limit to the number of persons that can have shares in that company, but the minimum number of persons is two. It is an offence for a private company to invite the public to subscribe for capital. The shares are transferable, but there is no organised market to buy or sell shares in private companies. All private companies will have the letters 'Ltd' after their name.

private company shares. From the viewpoint of the lending banker, the shares of a private company given as banking security must be treated with caution. First, the acceptance of these shares as a legal charge, may deprive a director of his/her directorship because a condition of his/her appointment is that he/she must have a stated number of shares in his/her name. Secondly, as there is no market for these shares, it is difficult to have a valuation and if necessary sell the shares to recoup any loan. Thirdly, if a bank is offered shares in a private company it will not necessarily be able to register its name as a registered holder because the company may not be able to accept a limited company as a shareholder.

private enterprise. The opposite to state-run enterprises, or nationalised industries. Private persons either individually or collectively establish businesses or whatever legal nature, run them for reasons of profit. Of course, such businesses are subject to the laws of the land and taxes are deducted from profits.

private placing. *See* NEW ISSUE; PLACING.

private practice. The setting up of a service by a professional person or persons. Such a service, e.g. accountancy, legal, medical, must normally be run by qualified individuals and within the framework laid down by their professional association that has awarded them 'a licence to practice'. There are, however, many persons that have a private practice, where there are no qualifications and consequently no restrictions placed on their activities. e.g. book-keeping service.

private sector liquidity (PSL). *See* MONEY SUPPLY.

private treaty. A legally binding contract

between two persons for the purchase/sale of land or property.

private trust. A trust that is established by beneficiaries as opposed to a charitable or public trust.

privatisation. It has been the policy of the Conservative Government to sell, i.e. return to the private sector, public companies, which have been owned by the State. Among the companies which have been sold to the public or 'privatised' are: British Gas, British Petroleum, British Telecom, TSB England and Wales. The sale of other companies whose capital is totally or partially owned by government, is likely to continue during the life of the present Government.

privity of contract. Those persons that have offered and accepted the conditions of a contract and are willing to be legally bound by its conditions. By its nature a contract cannot bind persons that have no obligations to it, nor have any rights to it. In banking there is a privity of contract between banker and customer. Any other person, not a customer has no legal relationship with the bank. The service of responding to status enquiries, imposes a duty of care on a banker giving an answer, i.e. he must answer truthfully based on the knowledge of the customer, but the banker need not seek information from outside sources, but there is no contract. It is customary for a disclaimer clause to be inserted in the reply letter.

privity of estate. The relationship between two parties who respectively hold the same estates as those created by a lease, e.g. lessor and lessee, lessor and assignee from the lessee, lessee and assignee of the reversion of the freehold estate. *See also* PRIVITY OF CONTRACT.

pro. For, before, in front of, on behalf of.

probate. The process by which a last will and testament is legally authenticated after the testator's death; an official copy of a will.

probate action. An action in the courts for the granting of probate of a will or

a letter of administration. The revocation of the grant of probate or requesting the courts to pronounce the will as invalid.

probation. A test for the character of an individual. The court may instruct an offender to be put on probation, i.e. remain under the supervision of a probation officer and comply with the conditions of the probation. A period between the employment agreement and the final acceptance of that person as an employee. The period before complete acceptance of a person to full membership of a club or association.

procedure. The method of conducting business in an office, bank, court or other place, so that the procedure is watertight and that it will not react to the detriment of the person, department or business, nor have any legal consequences arising from any default.

proceeds. A sum of money after deduction of expenses realised from a sale. The amount remitted by a bank to another bank or beneficiary on settlement of a collection, negotiation or documentary credit.

process costing. Where goods are being produced on a continuous basis, it is the costs involved for the production of all the goods in a given period.

procuration fee. The money paid for an agent who negotiates a loan.

procuration signature. *See* PER PROCURATIONEM.

procurator. One who acts for another, especially in legal affairs, an agent.

produce advances/loans. A loan made to a customer to pay for the goods purchased using the goods as security. It is customary to give such loans to customers who know their trade well and knowing (*a*) that there is or likely to be a demand for the goods, (*b*) there is a contract in existence with an ultimate buyer/s for whom the bank has already received a favourable reply to a status enquiry and (*c*) a report on the foreign exporter is favourable, so that it is unlikely that goods of an inferior quality will be shipped. It is good banking practice to obtain a margin between the loan and the c.i.f. value of the goods. As security the goods are pledged to the bank and deposited in a warehouse in the name of the bank. When the customer wishes to sell part or all of the consignment, he/she will sign a trust receipt, indicating that the customer is an agent of the bank and that all proceeds will be remitted to the bank. In exchange the bank will give the customer a signed letter addressed to the Warehouse Keeper, requesting the release of some or all of the goods to the person named in the letter. All warehouse, insurance and other charges are debited to the customer's account. This type of loan is generally short term, liquid, and profitable.

produce broker. A person buying and selling on a produce exchange.

product. A unit, item, or service produced or provided by an entity.

product cost. The labour, materials and other costs used in the course of production and added together. To obtain the cost per unit, the total costs are divided by the number of units produced.

production. The transformation of raw materials to finished goods, by assembly, chemical process or other method. This will include direct and indirect costs and other costs involved until delivery to the ultimate buyer.

pro et con. For and against.

profit and loss account. A final account drawn up at regular intervals when all the nominal accounts are closed and the balances transferred to this account. The excess of income over expenditure will show a profit and where the expenditure is greater than the income there will be a loss or deficit. Within this account any prepayments, accrual and depreciation of assets must be taken into account before the final balance is produced. Any exceptional or extraordinary items must also be considered. Profits will be distributed as decided by the owner, partners or directors of a company.

profit and loss appropriation account. This account is drawn up after the production of the profit and loss account

and will first show the transfer of a calculated amount to a taxation account, the net balance, plus any amount carried down from the previous year, will be distributed (a) to a reserve account, (b) for payment of preference and ordinary dividends, (c) any small balance remaining will be retained for the future period.

profit margin. The calculation of the profit as a ratio to (a) the net sales, (b) capital.

profit sharing. This usually refers to a bonus to the employees of a business that is given either in the form of cash or shares, based on a percentage of the profits.

pro-forma. As a matter of form.

pro-forma invoice. 1. An invoice which has been drawn up by the seller and sent to the buyer to confirm the details of the sales contract. 2. It is used as a polite reminder that a debt is due for payment. 3. For despatch to an agent when goods are sent on a consignment basis. 4. By an exporter to an importer to indicate the various charges, e.g. freight, insurance, packing, etc., before despatch of the goods.

program. The procedure for feeding instructions into a computer.

progress payments. An agreed sum of money paid to a contractor for the completion of a given stage of the contract. Such a payment is made against evidence that completion has been made by a given date and that it is in accordance with standards laid down in the contract.

progressive tax. A principle of taxation which involves the payment of a greater percentage of tax as income increases.

prohibition. An order from the courts to prevent a person or entity from acting in a certain manner. An authority from government to prevent a certain course of action, e.g. the importation of dangerous drugs without a licence.

prohibitory injunction. *See* INJUNCTION.

project finance. The finance either by a bank or financial institution or a group of financial institutions/banks to provide funds for the construction of a named project. Such projects tend to be 'one-off', so that special lending criteria must be applied particularly if it is to be constructed overseas. The lenders would want some form of guarantee, that payment, if necessary, by instalments will be made at the proper time against the proper documentation. Interest rates will usually be based against LIBOR. For overseas contracts, it is customary to involve ECGD, or another credit insurance company.

project team. A group of persons from various disciplines formed to examine a new scheme, enterprise, etc. Their function is to consider all available resources and make recommendations to achieve the best and most profitable result.

promise. An assurance by one person to another that they will undertake to do something or desist from doing something. While there is no legal obligation to fulfil a promise, it could form part of a contract which therefore must be fulfilled.

promissory note. Defined in the Bills of Exchange Act 1882 s. 83(1) as 'An unconditional promise in writing made by one person to another signed by the maker, engaging to pay, on demand or at a fixed or determinable future time, a sum certain in money, to, or to the order of, a specified person or to bearer'. There is no acceptor, only the maker and the other parties are the payee, indorser, bearer and holder. The maker has prime liability while the other parties have secondary liability. Should the promissory note be made by two persons, then they are jointly and severally liable on the note according to its tenor.

promoter. An entrepreneur who has the initiative to arrange a new venture or business. One who supports the promotion of a venture. A person or company that is involved in the formation of a new company.

promotion. Advancement, preferment, a higher rank; the advancement of a business interest by advertisement or exhortation.

promotion money. The initial fund available to the founder directors or shareholders of a company for the formation of that company.

proof. The establishment that a certain fact exists or does not exist. Verbal or written evidence presented and accepted.

proof of death. A requirement by a bank or other institutions, e.g. pension fund, building society, insurance company on receiving a communication that a customer has died. It is necessary to have sight of the death certificate or probate or letters of administration.

property. Something that can be owned, land, goods, money, and chose in action. The owner is entitled to any profits that can be obtained from property and he/she has the right to transfer it to another. Property can be inherited from a deceased owner.

property register. *See* LAND CERTIFICATE.

proposal. An offer by a person to an insurance company to have life assurance cover or obtain some other form of insurance. The offer, which takes the form of the completion of a questionnaire or proposal form, may be accepted or rejected at the option of the insurance company.

proprietary. Belonging or pertaining to an owner; made and sold by a firm or individual having the *exclusive rights* of manufacture and sale.

proprietary company. A parent company owning a quantity of land suitable for mining, etc., which it lets out to other interested companies on a joint proprietorship basis, all profits to be equally divided.

proprietor. The owner of a business in other words, the sole trader. The owner of land.

proprietorship register. *See* LAND CERTIFICATE.

proprietor's stake. The funds invested by the owner or owners in a business. As a going concern the amount invested will include not only the invested capital but any retained profits and reserves.

pro rata. In proportion.

prospectus. A note, invitation, circular or other advertisement or an invitation to the public to subscribe to shares in the company in accordance with the Companies Act 1985, and the regulations of the Stock Exchange.

pro tanto. For so much, to that extent.

protected goods. Consumer Credit Act 1974 s. 90. Goods which are subject to a regulated hire purchase or credit sale agreement to which the debtor has paid at least one third of the total price of the goods. They cannot be recovered except by court order or the voluntary surrender by the debtor.

protected shorthold. *See* SHORTHOLD LETTING.

protection. In the Eurobond market it is an undertaking by a lead manager that during a selling period, it will ensure a favoured bank will receive a stated amount of a new issue in full.

protection of depositors. *See* DEPOSIT INSURANCE.

protective trust. A condition in a trust document stating that the beneficiary is entitled to the income from the trust until some event occurs. From that moment, he/she will no longer be entitled to receive any further funds, e.g. on bankruptcy. Should this event occur then the income would be held for his children or next-of-kin.

protest certificate. A document bearing a seal, given by a notary attesting that the bill of exchange has been dishonoured either for acceptance or payment. Such a document is attached to the bill of exchange and is accepted as proof in a court of law that presentation of the bill has been made and dishonoured. A formal claim or statement in an insolvency. *See* FORMAL PROTEST; HOUSEHOLDER'S PROTEST.

proving a debt. Under the Insolvency Act 1986, the proving of a debt has been simplified. No longer is it necessary to swear an affidavit in front of a practising solicitor, but the Trustee if he so wishes can call for a sworn proof of debt. To prove for a debt a form from the Trustee must be completed and returned to him/her, so that any dividends from the estate may be received. A creditor including a bank may attend and vote at the meeting of creditors. Where a bank holds security it has the following options. (*a*) The security may be surrendered to the trustee, and the bank can prove as an unsecured creditor for the whole debt. (*b*) The bank may assess the value of the security in the proof of debt and claim as an unsecured creditor for the outstanding balance. (*c*) The bank may realise its security, and if there is a shortfall, prove for the balance. (*d*) The bank may realise its security, and if the advance is repaid, then it will lodge no proof, but will pay any surplus to the trustee in bankruptcy.

provision. A measure taken beforehand; an amount retained to provide for depreciation; a sum retained to offset against a bad or doubtful debt; a sum of money set on one side to meet a known payment which has to be made, e.g. payment of pensions to retired staff.

provisional certificate. Evidence of ownership of a new or scrip issue of shares, before the definite certificate is ready.

provisional liquidator. An insolvency practitioner appointed to act as a temporary liquidator for a company that has been ordered by a court to be wound up. At a later date a liquidator is appointed by the creditors and in practice it is usual for the provisional liquidator to be appointed as liquidator.

provision for bad and doubtful debts. A sum set aside from profits of a business to meet the possibility that some current debts, payable in the future, will not be settled. The calculation of the amount of the provision may be a list of debit balances that may be considered as doubtful and/or a percentage of outstanding debts at the end of a financial period.

provisions. The articles of an instrument or statute.

proviso. A condition, clause or stipulation in a contract. In a contract it is a condition that may render the contract inoperative if an event took place, e.g. bankruptcy of a person would be a breach of covenant and would make the lease contract inoperative.

proximate damage. The immediate cause not the remote cause must be considered. It is the damage which arises out of a breach of contract or extraordinary damage which was agreed could be a possibility. An award of compensation may be given.

proxy. A person appointed to represent another at a meeting. A document authorising one person to vote instead of another.

prudential ratios. *See* CAPITAL ADEQUACY.

public. Pertaining to the people as a whole, open to general use; the community or its members.

public act, public bill. One involving the interests of the community.

public company. The formation of a company by registration with the Registrar of Companies and has received a

Certificate to Commence Trading. Its Memorandum of Association states that it is a public company and is therefore permitted to invite the general public to subscribe for shares to participate in loan capital. Every public company must have a minimum of £50 000 authorised capital and will have the words 'Public Limited Company' or the abbreviation 'PLC' after its name, or the Welsh equivalent.

public corporation. Any company or industry that is owned and controlled by the state. This will include local authorities and nationalised industries.

public examination. Insolvency Act 1986 s. 133(1): 'Where a company is being wound up by the court, the official receiver or in Scotland, the liquidator, may at any time before dissolution of the company apply to the court for the public examination of any person who (*a*) is or has been an officer of the company or (*b*) has acted as liquidator or administrator of the company or as receiver or manager, or in Scotland, receiver of its property, (*c*) not being a person falling within (*a*) or (*b*) is or has been concerned, or has taken part, in the promotion, formation or management of the company. Under s. 290 of the Act "Where a bankruptcy order has been made, the official receiver may at any time before discharge of the bankrupt apply to the court for the public examination of the bankrupt...." ' The following may take part in the public examination of the bankrupt and may question him concerning his affairs, dealings and property and the causes of his failure, namely (*a*) the official receiver or the Official Petitioner, (*b*) the trustee of the bankrupt's estate, if his appointment has taken effect, (*c*) any person who has been appointed as special manager of the bankrupt's estate or business, (*d*) any creditor of the bankrupt who has tendered proof in the bankruptcy'.

public funds. Debts owing by the government; government stock and public securities; the National Debt.

public issue. An issue of shares publicly offered to investors.

public law. International Law.

public relations. The relations of an organisation or authority with the general public.

public sector. In the UK, the term includes the Civil Service, Local Authorities, and nationalised industries.

public sector borrowing requirement (PSBR). First introduced in 1970 for the amount required by central government to finance the difference between the immediate future receipts and the expenditure. This is done by the issue of short-term loans, i.e. Treasury Bills, gilt-edged securities.

public trust. *See* CHARITABLE TRUST.

public trustee. A public official appointed by the State to act as an executor or trustee to any person wishing to use his services. In practice little use is made of this office except when the estate is so small that it is inappropriate for such services to be performed by banks, solicitors, accountants, etc.

public utilities. Another phrase meaning the basic public services, whether they are nationalised industries or in the private sector, available to the public. This includes, gas, electricity, water, telephones, etc.

Public Works Loan Board (PWLB). A government body whose purpose is to make loans to local authorities, particularly during times when it is difficult to obtain funds from other sources. The funds are obtained from the National Loans Fund and repayments of capital and interest are repayable to the National Loans Fund.

puisne mortgage. A legal mortgage not protected by deposit of the title deeds. It should be registered at the Land Charges Department as a land charge, Class C (i). *See also* LAND CHARGES REGISTER.

punitive damages. *See* EXEMPLARY DAMAGES.

purchase. To obtain the goods and/or services from a supplier in exchange for cash paid on receipt of the goods/services or at some future time by cash or other benefit.

purchaser. A person or entity that acquires goods or land in exchange for money or other benefit. The term includes any lessee, mortgagee, or other person who for a consideration obtains an interest in land or property.

purchasing power. The theory that endeavours to explain the rates of exchange in relationship to the purchasing power of the home currency for goods and services.

pursuer.   Scots law term for *Plaintiff.*

put option.   *See* OPTION.

put and call option.   *See* OPTION.

put of more option.   *See* OPTION.

pyramiding.   The control of a number of subsidiary companies which together have a large amount of capital, yet are controlled by a holding company or a major shareholder with a controlling interest whose capital is relatively small in comparison.

pyramid selling.   A scheme whereby an agent or distributor, for payments, delivers goods or obtains the services of others who in their turn, offer. the same benefits to others. Under the Fair Trading Act 1973, the promoter is required to buy back any unsold goods. Before a person joins, there is a cooling-off period.

Q

qualified. Having the necessary qualifications. Competent by law, by examination, by test or attaining some standard of competency. Limited or modified.

qualified acceptance. S. 19(2) Bills of Exchange Act 1882: 'A qualified acceptance in express terms varies the effect of the bill as drawn. (*a*) Conditional, that is to say, which makes payment by the acceptor dependent on the fulfilment of a condition therein stated. (*b*) Partial, that is to say, an acceptance to pay part only of the amount for which the bill is drawn. (*c*) Local, that is to say, an acceptance to pay only at a particular specified place. (*d*) Qualified as to time. (*e*) The acceptance of some, one or more the drawees but not all'.

qualified audit report. A report by an auditor which brings to the attention some important aspect of his examination of the vouchers, papers, accounts etc., which prevents him/her from giving his/her opinion that the statements give a true and fair view.

qualified indorsement. An indorsement where an indorser has added after his signature an express stipulation. 1. negativing or limiting his or her own liability to the holder (e.g. *'Sans recours'*); 2. waiving as regards himself or herself some or all of the holder's duties.

qualified opinion. *See* AUDIT REPORT.

qualified title. A rare situation whereby the registrar is unable to grant an absolute title, possessory title to the applicant.

qualifying policies. For tax purposes, life policies are divided into two classes (*a*) qualifying policies, (*b*) non-qualifying policies. So far as the insurance company is concerned it has little or no effect on the basic insurance contract. It is only relevant for the individual policy holder's tax position. The advantages of having a qualifying pol-

icy, i.e. a policy taken out prior to 14 March 1984, as as follows: 1. The person is eligible for tax relief on premiums. 2. While the policy is in force, all income and gains attributable to the policy and the tax thereon are the responsibility of the life company. 3. Gains made under the policy are not liable for basic rate tax when realised by the policyholder. 4. The proceeds are usually entirely free of tax, provided premiums are kept for at least ten years (or three-quarters of the term of an endowment policy).

qualifying share. The shares needed by a person to qualify as a director of a company.

qualitative directives. Directives from the Bank of England to the lending banks and financial institutions as to classes of customers who may be allowed to borrow.

quality certificate. A certificate that goods are of a required standard, issued by a third party after an inspection.

quality control. Checks made at various intervals during the production process to ensure that at each stage of manufacture, the standard of quality is maintained. Within banks, internal audits and visits from various officials ensure that the quality of service given to customers is of the standard expected by the bank.

quantitative directives. Directives from the Bank of England to the lending banks and financial institutions as to the total amount of money which they may lend.

quantity rebate. A discount or reduction of price on the purchase of a large number of quantity of a product.

quantity theory of money. This theory relates prices to money by relating the volume of production with the velocity of the circulation of money. The formula is expressed as $MV=PT$, where M represents the quantity of money, V is the velocity of its circulation. P is the general price level and T is the sum total of all transactions that take place for money. This then shows that the changes in general price levels can be influenced not only by changes in the quantity of money, but also in the changes in the velocity of circulation of money. Additionally any changes in production and in the change in money or its velocity will also offset a change in the total transactions.

quantum merit. The amount earned. Where a breach of contract has occurred, the injured party may sue for work done or services performed, as an alternative for a claim for damages. Where no agreement regarding payment has been made, it is expected that payment will be based on a reasonable payment by one person or another.

quarter days. *In England:* Lady Day, March 25th; Midsummer Day, June 24th; Michaelmas, September 29th; Christmas Day, December 25th.

In Scotland: Candelmas, February 2nd; Whitsunday, May 15th; Lammas, August 1st; Martinmas, November 11th.

Quarterly Bulletin. A publication of the Bank of England available in March, June, September and December of each year, which gives economic commentaries, financial reviews, information about credit control, savings, foreign exchange markets, policy decisions, and various tables of statistics.

quasi-. Apparent, seeming, not real.

quasi-loan. A transaction under which one party (the creditor) agrees to pay, or pays otherwise than in pursuance of an agreement, a sum for another (the borrower) or agrees to reimburse or reimburses otherwise than in pursuance of an agreement, expenditure incurred by another party (the borrower) (a) on terms that the borrower will reimburse the creditor (b) in circumstances giving rise to a liability on the borrower to reimburse the creditor' (Companies Act 1985 s. 331(3)). Simply put, it is where X Ltd, agrees to pay some financial obligation of Y, its director, on condition that Y will a some short-term future date reimburse X.

quasi-money. *See* NEAR MONEY.

quasi-negotiable instrument. An instrument which contains some but not all the attributes of negotiability. A prime example of this is a bill of lading which can be transferred by delivery and indorsement and gives the transferee the title to the goods specified in the bill, but the transferee cannot get any better title than the transferor, even though he may have taken it in good faith and given value.

quasi-partner. A partner by implication. Should a person act in such a way as to make people think that he is a partner, then he is stopped from denying that he/she is in fact a partner can be held liable for debts of the partnership. Should partners for all practical purposes imply that a member of their staff is a partner, when he is not, then by implication, that person can be made a partner.

quasi-rent. A term used for the rent of any property other than land, e.g. as in the case of the leasing of a capital asset to a manufacturing company by a finance company.

quayage. A charge for the use of a berth alongside a quay.

Queen. *See* SOVEREIGN.

queuing time. A timetable operated by the Bank of England so that the raising of funds (more than £3m) by new issues can be in an orderly manner. Abolished in 1989. A preparation and readiness of materials to go on to a production line or process, so that the machines are as idle as little as possible.

quick assets. Assets which can be converted into cash quickly and easily. *See* LIQUID ASSETS.

quid pro quo. A term used when giving one thing in exchange for another. Consideration.

quiet possession. There is implied in any contract, that the purchaser shall be able to enjoy his purchase without any encumbrances, except by the true owner.

quittance. Discharge from a debt or obligation, acquittance, receipt, requital, repayment.

quorum. The least number of persons that will validate a meeting in order to transact official business. Such a number will appear in the constitution of a club, or for a limited company in the articles of association.

quota. A stated amount which must not be exceeded. In international trade, quotas may be introduced by a government to restrict imports of certain commodities, this may be to conserve foreign currency, protect an infant industry or any other economic factor.

quotation. A price for a service to be performed or for work that is likely to be done. When a quotation has been agreed, it forms the basis of a contract. In the Stock Exchange or other exchange a quotation for a stock is given in two prices to the enquirer, so that he/she knows both the buying and selling price. Under the Consumer Credit Act 1974, any person or company that has a consumer credit business, must notify any prospective customer of the terms on which he/she is prepared to do business.

quotations committee. The committee appointed by the Stock Exchange to decide the conditions on which an official price quotation can be granted to a company, and to consider such applications and to decide upon them.

quote. *See* QUOTA.

quoted company. *See* LISTED COMPANY.

quotes. Prices, being selling and buying rates of exchange, or bid and offered rates of interest given by brokers or dealers, to customers or other enquiring parties in the market.

R

R & D. *See* RESEARCH AND DEVELOPMENT.

rack rent. A rent which is the highest level obtainable at a particular time.

raider. A private or company investor whose intention it is to take over a targeted company by the purchase of its shares.

random remittances. Whereas in previous years, the branches of the clearing banks sorted cheques payable at other banks/branches (out clearing), into bank order before despatch to the clearing department, it is now customary not to do the sorting at branch level, but merely to despatch all the cheques, unsorted, to the clearing department, leaving the branch staff more time to deal with customers and other services, while the clearing department makes a more effective use of its computer sorters.

railway consignment note. *See* CONSIGNMENT NOTE.

rally. To recover, a recovery, as in the price of a commodity, or of stocks and shares on the market.

random walk theory. A theory that prescribes to the view that the movement of the prices of stocks and shares in the past have little or no value for predicting the prices in the future. It is information that comes to the market piecemeal and in random fashion that really influences the markets.

rate. Degree, standard, proportion, value, price; to estimate, to assess, to calculate, to appraise. *See also* CHEQUE RATE; INTERVENTION RATE; LONG RATE; SHORT RATE.

rateable value. Prior to the introduction of the community charge (poll tax), all private and business properties were assessed by local authorities as to the rental the property could obtain. On this assessment, a rating figure was fixed, and the rate of so many pence in the pound was payable by the owner either every six months, or by equal instalments over a period of ten months each year.

rate of exchange. *See* PARITY.

rate of inflation. *See* INFLATION.

rate of interest. A payment for the use of money by a borrower for a period of time, but will vary according to the rate at the time of borrowing and the risk involved. Banks and other financial institutions advertise a base rate to which all other borrowing and lending rates are related. In general, banks will borrow from customers and give them a very low rate of interest on current account – if any interest is payable – while on deposit account, a higher rate of interest can be obtained. On the principle that the larger the amount and the greater the agreed length of time of the agreed deposit, the greater is the interest rate. The interest may be given quarterly, half-yearly or yearly and may be subject to a deduction of tax at source. Interest on loans and overdrafts is payable at a percentage above the base rate. The highest rate of interest charged to a borrower, is on unauthorised borrowing, that is frequently practised by the private customer.

rate of return. For investment theory this will refer to the gain in the purchase of stocks and shares and the profit made on selling. It is also the annual return on a portfolio, usually expressed as a percentage of the total holding. In business, this will refer to the profitability of the business as a percentage of the capital invested.

rate of stock turnover. In order to show the number of times stock will be bought and sold in a trading period, a formula of average stock divided by the cost of sales is calculated. This may be shown either as a ratio or in periods of time, e.g. days, weeks, months.

rate of turnover. The number of times the value of an average stock figure is sold in a given trading period.

ratification. Confirmation or approval. Where an agent has exceeded his/her authority in a contract, it may be ratified by the principal. In banking where discretionary limits are laid down for each area or responsibility, it is often necessary for a branch manager to make an on-the-spot decision and at a later date obtain ratification from regional or head office.

rating. The grading of a risk or comparing one institution or one measure with another. One of the major rating companies in the UK is Standard & Poor's, which also deals with global ratings, using such grades as AAA, AA+, AA–, etc. Ratings are also used for insurance purposes on which to base premiums.

ratio. Relationship between one value and another.

ratio decidendi. The main legal principle which forms the core of a case.

rationalisation. A term used to describe the reorganisation of a business, so that it becomes more efficient and profitable. Frequently this may mean the reduction in the number of employees, the sale of parts of the business that are either unprofitable or not relevant to the core purpose of the enterprise. Currently it is concerned with the slimming down of an organisation and the more efficient use of labour and capital.

ratios. *See* BALANCE SHEET RATIOS; PRUDENTIAL RATIOS.

raw materials. The basic products to be used in production. Not yet part of the work in progress or finished goods.

RCH. Recognised Clearing House.

R.D. Can be extended to RDPR. *See* REFER TO DRAWER.

ready money. Cash; money paid, or ready to be paid, for a purchase, etc.

real. True, genuine; consisting of fixed and permanent things, e.g. lands or houses, as opposed to personal things.

real account. An account that records the entries of fixed assets which have been bought and sold. The balances on the real accounts are not transferred to the profit and loss accounts, but are shown in the balance sheet.

real cost. Generally known as opportunity cost. The value of any factor of production that could be used for other purposes.

real estate. Immovable property covering freehold land and buildings and proprietary rights in or over lands, e.g. mineral rights.

real income. Money income in terms of the goods and services which it will buy.

real investment. The purchase of a capital asset, e.g. machinery, instead of an investment in stocks or shares.

realisable value. On looking upon a business as a 'Gone Concern', any assets would be valued at an amount that would probably be received if they were sold. The basis of this valuation could give a more precise value of the resources employed than the current book value.

realisation account. An account maintained when a business is being wound up or sold, or on the dissolution of a partnership.

realised profit. An investment which has appreciated since it was bought is showing a paper profit until such time as it is actually sold, when the paper profit becomes a realised profit.

real property. Property that can be recovered by an action and the owner dispossessed. It is land and buildings as opposed to personal possessions and choses in action.

real time. The operations of a computer, during which time information is processed and updated. This should not be confused with the time taken to plan and process such information before feeding it into the computer.

real wages. *See* REAL INCOME.

reasonable. A word frequently used in banking, finance, law etc., e.g. reasonable time, reasonable man, reasonable doubt. Having the ability to make a sound but moderate judgment of a situation. Being fair and tolerable.

rebate. A deduction from a price or debt for some particular reason. A term bill of exchange could be subject to a rebate if the acceptor is willing to pay before maturity. The settlement of a debt before its due date at an amount less than the outstanding balance.

recap or recapitulation. The word recapitulation is often abbreviated as recap. Often used in banking to show the grouping of totals from batch sheets or proofing machines and to transfer amounts to a clearing department, cost centre, or control centre.

receipt. An acknowledgement in writing that a person or entity has received something. Stamp duty on receipts was abolished in 1971. Cheque Act 1957 where cheques have been paid into a bank for the credit to the payee's account without indorsement it is sufficient evidence of receipt. Some cheques – those which have the letter 'R' printed on the face – will require the signature of the payee before payment is finally made. Cheques of this nature are usually drawn by insurance companies and pension funds as evidence that the person entitled to the funds has in fact received them.

receipts and payments account. Usually drawn up by a small social or non-business organisation to show a summary of all the financial transactions that have taken place in the financial period. As it shows cash records only, it will therefore not show any prepayments or accruals, so for a more sophisticated organisation, a receipts and payments account has very little use.

receivables financing. See FACTORING.

received for shipment bill of lading. A bill of lading indicating that the goods have been received by the shipping company, but has not yet been loaded on any vessel. For banks that are likely to have the goods as security, this is not a good document, because it opens up the questions, where are the goods – on the quay-side, in a warehouse? Are they subject to the elements, deterioration, pilfering? Have they been insured? When the carrying vessel is available such a bill of lading will be replaced by an 'on board' bill of lading.

receiver. An officer appointed by the court to collect debts or rents from property which is in dispute in a suit in that court. Under the Insolvency Act 1986 s. 29, it is an officer appointed by the court as either a receiver, manager or adminsitrative receiver to a company. While under s. 287, the official receiver may act either as a receiver or special manager of the estate of a bankrupt.

receiver for debenture holders. A person appointed by a court or a debenture holder, under the terms of a fixed or floating charge, to crystallise the assets of the business from the day of his/her appointment and apply them towards repaying the debts due to the debenture holder/s. His appointment is the signed, sealed and delivered instrument of his appointment and his/her powers arise through the terms of the debenture deed or the Companies Act. To open an account for a receiver the bank will require evidence of his appointment and the account will be opened 'A.B receiver of DEF Ltd'.

receiver of rents. One of the remedies open to a mortgagee, upon default by the mortgagor, is to appoint a receiver to collect the rents and manage the estate; this is particularly appropriate for property which is let, e.g. a block of flats. On appointment, the receiver takes possession of the property and therefore collects rents and profits, applying them in reduction of the mortgagor's debt. The receiver is regarded as agent of the mortgagor, who is therefore responsible for his or her defaults. See also OFFICIAL RECEIVER.

receiving order. An order made by the court (a) to deprive the bankrupt of disposing of his/her estate, (b) to appoint an insolvency practitioner to be responsible for the property, (c) distribute the proceeds of the assets to the creditors in order of priority.

recession. The reduction of business activity in a country. This will mean that businesses will reduce stocks, reduce the numbers of persons employed. Confidence in the economy will be impaired, investment will not be encouraged, unemployment will increase and there will be a greater number of businesses going into liquidation.

reciprocal business. An arrangement in international trade where one country will make concessions to another country for similar or equal concessions. In banking, each bank with international business will utilise the services of banks abroad, providing the bank abroad provides services of equal value. This can also apply to utilising the services of a bank abroad for a service which is chargeable, but the charge both ways is of equal value, e.g. the transmission of travellers cheques back to the country of domicile for collection and credit to the remitter's account. In all banks records are kept of the amount of work directed to and from banks abroad. Where banks maintain their own branches or subsidiaries abroad, there will be a tendency to give them the major and most profitable business.

recognised bank. Any financial institution that has been given authority by the Bank of England to act as a deposit taker as defined by the Banking Act 1987.

recognised investment exchange. A body declared by the Secretary of State as being recognised as an Investment Exchange for the purposes of the Financial Services Act 1986 s. 207(1).

recognised marking names. *See* MARKING NAMES.

reconciliation statement. An analysis of the difference between two sets of figures. Since there are always cheques drawn, credited to the Cash Book, but not always presented within a reasonable time, a difference between the balances shown in the Cash Book and a bank statement will vary. Consequently a statement of reconciliation is drawn up taking into account any debits and credits originating from the bank, plus any credits still in the course of collection and cheques drawn but not yet presented.

reconstruction of a company. The reorganisation of a company (*a*) to obtain new capital, (*b*) to redistribute the various classes of capital, (*c*) to amalgamate or merge with another company. (*d*) Where a company plans to merge with another, then the approval of the majority of shareholders must be obtained.

reconvention. A counter-action in a suit brought by the defendant against the plaintiff.

reconveyance. The transfer of the title to land to the original owner. A receipt on the mortgage deed is now sufficient evidence to extinguish a mortgage.

record. To make a note in writing, in a file, portfolio, computer with information of a similar nature.

recorded delivery. A service provided by the Post Office for a fee, whereby the sender completes the name and address of the addressee on a form, part of which is stuck on the front of the envelope. The receipt given to the sender is proof of despatch, and on delivery the addressee will sign for the letter or package so that a record has been made of both despatch and delivery.

recourse. A right of a person to obtain repayment of debt that he/she financed. The discounting of a bill of exchange, is with recourse to the drawer or payee or previous holder. The negotiation of a bill under a letter of credit, an advance against a collection, etc. are all done with recourse. Any cheque presented for collection and credited to a customer's account is done so on the understanding that should the cheque be unpaid for any reason, the bank has the right to debit the account.

recourse factoring. The payment by a factor to a client of any outstanding funds, but with the right of recourse, should a buyer not pay for any reason whatsoever. *See* FACTORING.

recovery. A part of the economic cycle when business grows more confident, consumers are willing to spend more and the economy expands.

recovery stock. A stock which has its price at the lowest quotation, but investors consider that with an efficient management in place, and an up-turn in trade, the profitability of the company will improve. The purchase of shares in such companies can be speculative.

rectification. Setting right an act or a situation. The amendment to a contract which both parties agree need correction.

red clause. A clause in a documentary credit, which originally was written or typed in red, hence the name, which contains an instruction from the issuing bank to the advising bank to make an advance payment, to the beneficiary, prior to the shipment of the goods. Repayment of this advance will be made by deduction of the amount and interest when the documents have been presented and payment made under the credit. The advance may be conditional on signing an undertaking that the money will be used to collect the goods together, and that all receipts for the goods must be presented before the advance is given or, unconditionally, when the beneficiary is given the funds against a receipt.

redeemable. A debt or money which can be repaid. The discharge of a mortgage. The repayment of a loan to a pawnbroker and the retrieval of the goods or chattels deposited as security. Redeemable bonds or stock. Preference shares, debentures and government stocks which are repayable at some future date or between two given dates. *See* REDEEMABLE DEBENTURE; REDEEMABLE PREFERENCE SHARES.

redeemable debenture. A debenture that is repayable at a certain date or repayable when notice has been given. It is possible for debentures to be repaid in whole or in part. When a new debenture is issued to take the place of or repay the redeemed debenture, then the purchasers of the new debenture have all the priorities of the holders of the old debenture. Old debentures must be cancelled and retained.

redeemable preference shares. Redemption of preference shares must be made out of profits or from the proceeds of a new issue. They must be paid at par and any premium that is payable on redemption must come from profits.

redemption dates. The dates between which redeemable stock is repayable.

redemption period. For the purposes of the Consumer Credit Act 1974, a pawn is redeemable at any time within six months after it was taken. Subject to this, the period within which a pawn is redeemable shall be the same as the period fixed by the parties for the duration of the credit secured by the pledge, or such longer period as they may agree.

redemption yield. A return calculated on the total profit obtainable on a fixed interest stock redeemable at a predetermined price. It is composed of 1. the flat yield, and 2. the present value of the future capital profit which will be obtained on redemption. Where redemption is to be at a point in a range of years, it is usual to base the calculation on the latest possible redemption date. Although redemption yield is worked out by reference to a term of years, it is expressed in annual terms for comparison purposes.

red herring. A preliminary prospectus distributed to potential investors giving some but not all the details of the new issue.

re-discount. The act of a person who has discounted a bill of exchange in subsequently selling to another person; for example, a bank discounts a bill for a customer and then has it rediscounted by the central bank.

reducing balance method of depreciation. A method of depreciation where a given percentage is calculated on the closing balance of the asset at the end of the financial period and charged to the profit and loss account.

reduction of share capital. Share capital of a company can only be reduced by special resolution of the members and then subject to the confirmation of the courts who must be satisfied that the creditors have consented or have been secured. Among the reasons for wishing to reduce the capital may be to extinguish or reduce an unpaid liability or adjust the nominal value of the capital as the share value has fallen below this figure, or return share capital which is in excess of the company's needs. On the amendment of the articles of association, a copy must be filed with the company registrar and the bank should be notified of this as well so the records can be amended.

redundancy. The dismissal of an employee as the job he was doing ceased to exist, or there is a scaling down in numbers of employees. Where this occurs, the employee is entitled to be compensated for his/her loss of a job, fringe benefits and other earnings. Such compensation will depend on the length of service and earnings. Compensation is met partly by the employer and partly by the state.

re-entry. The reclaim of the property or land by the lessor due to the failure of the lessee to observe the covenants of the lease. The return of the land to the original owner. It is unlawful to force a re-entry with the order of the courts.

re-exchange. This refers to the loss resulting from the dishonour of a bill in a country different from that in which it was drawn or indorsed. The holder may recoup himself by drawing a sight bill on either the drawer or one of the indorsers. That is called a re-draft bill.

The indorser who pays a re-draft bill may in a like manner draw upon the antecedent party. The holder is entitled to draw a bill to cover not only the value of the dishonoured bill, but include protest expenses, interest and other expenses. To ascertain the total sum due, it would be necessary to find the cost to purchase a sight bill at the existing rate of exchange drawn at the time and place of dishonour.

re-export. A commodity re-exported; to export after having been imported. Re-export trade is carried on by a country which has a good location for redistributing goods to other countries and good air and shipping facilities to carry the goods. Also known as *entrepôt trade.*

referee. A person to whom a dispute is referred. A person who is referred to for an opinion. A person whose name and address is given by a person who wishes to open a bank account. A person who is willing to give a reference to an employer for one who wishes to seek employment.

referee in case of need. *See* CASE IN NEED.

referential settlement. *See* SETTLED LAND.

refer to drawer. When dishonouring a cheque due to lack of funds, a bank will use this phrase as the reason for non-payment. It does so, in order to protect the confidential relationship between banker and customer, so that should the payee or holder wish to know the real reason for non-payment, then he/she should refer the cheque to the drawer. Popularly, 'refer to drawer' is understood to mean that the drawer has no funds, and the abbreviation R/D is not only known by bankers but other members of the public that have some experience in banking and financial matters. Occasionally the dishonour of a cheque might be 'RDPR', or 'Refer to Drawer, Please Represent'. This is a request to the collecting bank and/or payee to represent the cheque when funds may be available and payment may be made. It is no promise that payment will be met when the second presentation is made.

re-finance bill. A bill drawn under a re-finane credit (*q.v*).

re-finance credit. Where the exporter requires immediate settlement under a letter of credit, but the importer needs time (say three months) to pay, then an arrangement can be made between the issuing bank and the issuer (importer) so that when the exporter has presented his sight draft and documents in accordance with the terms and conditions of the credit, and the issuing bank has been advised that payment/negotiation has been made by the bank in the exporter's country, the issuing bank will then, in reimbursement, accept the importer's bill of exchange at thirty days, discount the bill and reimburse the paying/negotiating bank abroad. By maturity, the importer would have sold the goods, received payment, then have sufficient funds to meet the bill of exchange at maturity.

reflation. A deliberate government policy to improve the economy. Various methods are available, such as the easing of credit restrictions, injection of money, encourage investments by one means or another, encourage banks to lend more money, reduce taxation. At present, the government's policy is to reflate the economy by very gradually reducing interest rates, so that reflation will be brought about in a controlled manner.

refunding. A replacement of a debt by another debt. As interest rates fall, so it is in the interests of a business to repay a loan and obtain a fresh loan which would be at a lower rate of interest.

regeneration. The improvement or to renew life. In city areas which have become slums or left derelict, it is a government policy to encourage house building, setting up shops, and encourage the return of businesses, so that city centres return to an improved and vibrant way of life.

regional trade. Trade between countries with common borders or situated in the same region, as the result of an agreement between them to pursue a common trade policy, e.g. the European Common Market.

register. A formally written record. An official list of facts, names, addresses, etc., which it is intended to be maintained and up-dated as necessary. Such information may be kept in a file, book, computer, etc. Statutory registers, e.g. register of companies, register of shareholders, Land Charges Register, etc.

registered capital. *See* SHARE CAPITAL.

registered charge. When taking a legal charge over registered land, the banker must obtain the land certificate from the customer, obtain his/her signature on the legal charge form, make a search on the register. The banker then sends the land certificate with copies of the mortgage form to the registrar, with a fee. The registrar will retain the land certificate, make an entry in the register and issue a charge certificate to the bank as evidence of his/her interest. The original mortgage form is inserted inside it.

registered company. A company formed in England and Wales, or in Scotland, by registration in accordance with the Companies Act 1985, with the Registrar of Companies. Such a company may be a limited private company, a limited public company, or an unlimited company.

registered land certificate. *See* LAND CERTIFICATE.

registered office. An address which is the head office of a registered company and that has been notified to the Registrar of Companies. At this address such registers as required by law are held, e.g. register of shareholders, directors, debentures, etc. All communications to the company must be served to this address.

registered post. A postal delivery service for the carriage of valuable goods and documents. Such letters and parcels are insured against loss and damage while in transit.

register of charges. A register held at Companies House of all charges made by limited companies that need registration under the Companies Act 1985 (s. 396). Inspection may be made by any person on payment of the appropriate fee. Additionally, at the registered office of a company, a register of all charges is maintained. This register is also available for inspection by any member of the company or members of the public.

register of companies. A list of companies that have been given a Certificate of Incorporation or a Certificate to Commence Trading by the Registrar of Companies. This register is open for in-

spection by any member of the public. *See* REGISTRAR OF COMPANIES.

register of debenture holders. A register held at the registered office of a company listing the names and addresses of debenture holders. Inspection of this register is available to shareholders and members of the public.

register of directors and secretaries. At the registered office of every limited company there is a register of directors and secretaries. The name, address, nationality, occupation and any other directorships held of each director. If the director is a corporation, then the corporate name and registered office must be shown. For each secretary, the register must show the full name and address. If the secretary is a limited company, its name and registered office must be shown.

register of members. Every registered limited company must keep at its registered office a register of all its members, showing the names and addresses of the members and if the company has share capital, then the number of shares held by each member, the date of being registered as a member and when a member has sold his/her shares, the date on which the shares were transferred. The register is open for inspection by any shareholder free of charge and also by members of the public for whom a small charge will be made.

register of transfers. *See* TALISMAN.

registrar. An official whose duty it is to keep a register or record of transactions.

Registrar-General. A public officer who superintends the registration of births, deaths and marriages.

registrar of companies. An official appointed by the Secretary of State to be responsible for receiving, approving and registering the applications for the incorporation of new registered companies.

registration Act of registering, entry or record, e.g. of births, etc.; a form of insurance on postal packages; the insertion of a company's name on the Register of Companies.

registration fee. *See* REGISTERED POST

registration of charges. To obtain a first legal charge on unregistered land the procedure to be adopted is as follows:

1. Obtain the title deeds, (a) check the good root title, (b) check the first legal charge is not subject to prior interests. 2. Carry out searches at (a) Land Charges Register, (b) Local Land Charges Register 3. Check value of property. 4. Execute bank's charge form 5. Check insurance. For registered land, the following is the procedure to be adopted: 1. Complete the searches at (a) Local Land Charges Register, (b) companies registry (if necessary), (c) District Land Registry. 2. Send to the District Land Registry, the land certificate, bank mortgage form duly executed, a signed certificate indicating the extent the bank is relying on the security, complete registration form (A4) plus fee, official search form for stamping. A charge certificate will be received from the Land Registry with the original land certificate stitched to the inside. As to companies, the Companies Act 1985 (s. 396) gives a list of charges that must be registered with the registrar of companies within 21 days.

registration of share transfers. See REGISTER OF TRANSFERS.

regressive tax. A tax falling more heavily upon people with low incomes than on those with high incomes; thus as the income falls the proportion of tax increases.

regulated agreement. Under the Consumer Credit Act 1984, a consumer credit agreement other than an exempt agreement.

regulator. The name given to the power of the Chancellor of the Exchequer to vary the rates of indirect taxation to meet the economic and monetary needs of the time.

reimbursement credit. This type of credit is used in merchanting, when an applicant in one country, e.g. India, requests his bank to open a credit in favour of a beneficiary in another country, e.g. Germany, but settlement will be in Sterling. The opening bank will undertake to reimburse the negotiating/paying bank in London. On presentation of documents the negotiating/paying bank will contact the London correspondent of the opening bank and request reimbursement by credit to its account with that bank in London or by payment to its account

with another bank in London. If the issuing bank is the paying banker, they will authorise the London correspondent to debit its account and transfer funds to the account of the account of the German bank.

reinsurance. An insurance will be prepared to cover an insurance risk up to a certain amount, above that figure the excess risk is re-insured with another company, so that the risk will be spread.

re-issue. To issue again, to republish, to make again available; a reprint.

re-issue of a bill of exchange. Bills of Exchange Act 1882 (s. 37): 'Where a bill is negotiated back to the drawer, or to a prior indorser or to the acceptor, such party may, subject to the provisions of this Act, re-issue and further negotiate the bill, but he is not entitled to enforce payment of the bill against any intervening party to whom he was previously liable.'

re-issue of debenture. See REDEEMABLE DEBENTURE.

related company By s. 92, Sch. 4, of the Companies Act 1985, a related company is any company that holds a long term qualifying interest for the purpose of securing a contribution to that company's own activities, by the exercise of any control or influence arising from that interest.

relation back. The power to go back to an early time or early action. This is especially important in bankruptcy and liquidation, whereby the trustee in certain circumstances can ignore certain transactions and claim/reclaim property from a third party.

release. To set free from restraint or confinement, to loosen, to exempt from an obligation; to remit a claim; exemption, a discharge of a right.

remainder. In instances where a trustee holds property and assets for the benefit of a life tenant until his/her death, then such property/assets passes to a remainderman, e.g. trustees hold property in trust for a widow (life tenant), but on her death, the estate passes to the children absolutely.

remainderman. See REMAINDER.

remedies of mortgages. See POWER OF A MORTGAGEE.

remedy. The right in law to obtain redress or compensation for a wrong.

remise. Putting back, remittance, delivery, rebate; a surrender, a release, as of a claim; to resign property by deed.

remission. The act of remitting an accused person or a case to another court.

remittance. *See* TRANSMISSION OF FUNDS.

remittance advice. The covering letter specifying the items sent for collection and instructions regarding advice of payment or non-payment of any item.

remittance letter. A letter sent by a bank to its correspondent or branch, which encloses cheques and other negotiable instruments for collection and payment. The remitting bank will request the collecting bank to credit its account under reserve, or after payment. The collecting bank will sort the cheques and other instruments into particular order and make a presentation either, through a clearing system or direct. The remitting letter should instruct the collecting banker on how to deal with any items which have been dishonoured.

remitting bank. Under a documentary collection it is the bank to which the principal has entrusted the operation of the collection. The bank that has remitted to its correspondent or branch clean collections, e.g. cheques, travellers cheques, etc. for payment and credit to its account.

remoteness of damage. As a general rule, where there is a loss that is too remote to be recovered, then compensation will not be awarded. It is necessary for a person to establish liability for direct consequences of the accident or breach of contract.

remote parties. The parties to a bill of exchange who are not in immediate relationship with each other.

remuneration. The consideration given for a service. This can be in the form of either a fee, wage, or salary.

remuneration certificate. A certificate from the Law Society to a client of a solicitor confirming that the charges for non-contentious works are fair and reasonable.

remuneration of directors. The remuneration of directors must be stated in the articles of association and any change must be sanctioned by a general meeting. This amount must be shown in the balance sheet of a company.

remuneration of trustees. This is not usually permitted, except where authorised by the Trust Instrument, or the court, or by statute. Where a bank acts as trustees, then it would be usual to have this fact recorded in the trust instrument.

renewal. To revive or regenerate, to restore or replace, to continue after some interval. To replace a new note for an old one. To continue a loan beyond the final payment.

renewal bill. The replacement of a bill of exchange with another not necessarily with the same term. A method of extending finance.

rent. A period payment made by the tenant or occupier of land to the owner for use of that land. An amount paid by a person for the use of plant, machines, computers etc., to the owner.

rental. A rent-roll, the annual amount of rent payable.

rental contract. *See* FINANCE LEASE.

rentcharge. Rentcharges Act 1977 s. 1. 'Any annual or other periodic sum charged on or issuing out of land except rent reserved by a lease or tenancy or any sum payable by way of interest'. The creation of rentcharges is now prohibited under 2(1) of the Act, and under s. 1(4) rentcharges are extinguished at the expiry of sixty years either from the date of the Act or the date on which the rentcharge became payable whichever was the first.

rent rebates. A sum of money deducted from the rent payable by tenants of homes let to them by the local authorities as calculated by the rent rebate scheme under the Housing Finance Act 1972 and Housing Benefits Act 1982.

rent-roll. A schedule of rents, a list of those who pay rents.

rent service. A regular payment made by a tenant to the landlord for the right to live on land.

renunciation. A statement or action of surrender of interest, disclaiming responsibility or liability. On the allocation of shares in a new issue, the recipient may renounce the allocation either in part or in full in favour of another. This is done by completing the form on the reverse side of the letter of acceptance and returning the form, duly completed to the named bank involved with the new issue. The renouncement by a holder of a bill of exchange renounces his rights against the acceptor, then the bill is discharged. To be effective, the bill must be delivered to the acceptor, but if it is not then the renunciation must be in writing addressed to the acceptor.

replacement cost. The cost at which a identical asset may be bought. To replace an asset a sum of money, either identified as a depreciation of an asset and/or the retention of funds so that at the end of the useful life of asset, it may be scrapped and a new one purchased utilising the funds set aside for the purpose. As there is annual inflation, it is quite likely that the cost of replacement will be greater than the original cost, so that additional funds must be made available.

report on title. It is of major importance that a banker, when accepting deeds as security for an advance, sends them to a solicitor in order to check on the title and request that he/she advises the bank on any points that might affect the bank's rights. It must be the bank's aim to receive a good title so that if necessary, the bank should be able to sell the security to recover its loan.

repossession. A word that has come to prominence in 1991, due to the recession in the years 1990–1, particularly in the housing market where those house owners who have not been able to keep up their mortgage repayments to banks and/or building societies, due to redundancy, inability to find work, etc. Their homes have been repossessed by the lender who has then either sold the property in the open market or by auction. It often happens, that due to a very depressed market, the property is sold at a price that does not cover the outstanding debt, so that the borrower no longer has his/her home and still has an outstanding debt.

With tens of thousands of families losing their homes and put into temporary accommodation or in bed and breakfast hotels by the local authorities, or going to live with relatives, the government has had to take quick and drastic action to alleviate the distress caused.

represent. To present a cheque, promissory note or bill of exchange the second or third time after its original dishonour. To take the place of someone else, to correspond to.

representation. The making of some form of protest, a statement during the course of negotiating a contract. Taking the place of another Acting as an executor or representative for a deceased person. For the purposes of the Consumer Credit Act 1974 s. 189(1): 'Any condition or warranty and any other statement or undertaking whether oral or in writing'. *See also* CHAIN OF REPRESENTATION.

representative. A person deputising for another. A person who is typical of a group of persons. A person who has been elected to an assembly or council to represent his/her constituency, group, etc.

repudiation. The breach of one or more conditions of a contract. The refusal to be bound by a contract.

repurchase agreements (repos). An agreement between a buyer and a seller of securities, whereby the seller agrees to buy back that security at a specified time and at an agreed price. Also known as buybacks. It gives a financial institution (a bank) immediate funds for a short-term loan to a customer and then funds are available for repurchase when the customer repays the loan. It is a very flexible way of obtaining funds from the market and reverse repurchase agreements are also available. *See also* INTER-BANK STERLING MARKET.

reputed ownership. The apparent ownership by a person or firm of property giving the impression to third parties of ownership as well as possession of the property, when in fact this is not the case. Where a person has been declared bankrupt, his/her property passes to the insolvent practitioner, who has the ownership of such property and may act in such a manner as to be the owner.

requisition. A written order for materials or supplies, a formal demand; to seize.

requisitions on title. The demand by a purchaser of land or his/her solicitor to ask questions to the vendor or his/her solicitor on the chain of title or other relevant points.

requisitor. An official empowered by a court to investigate facts.

re-registration of companies. The Companies Act 1985 ss. 43–55, defines the terms whereby (*a*) a private company can become public; (*b*) a limited company can become unlimited; (*c*) an unlimited company can become limited; (*d*) a public company can become private.

resale price maintenance. An imposition of the maintenance of minimum prices imposed by a manufacturer or group of manufacturers on retail outlets. Such agreements are illegal unless it can be proven to be in the public interest. The manufacturer, however, has the right to cut off supplies to a retailer if he/she so wishes.

rescheduling of debts. This refers to the spreading of debts over a longer period. This happens in the international field, particularly for sovereign debts, but during the recession in the UK agreements to reschedule debts between lender and borrower were seen as a method to stave-off liquidation or bankruptcy.

rescind. To annul, e.g. a law or decision; to cancel, to revoke, to repeal, to reverse, to abrogate.

rescission. The act of annulling or abrogating. An *equitable remedy* for the relief of a party to a contract where *mistake* has been a vital factor.

rescissory action. An action whereby deeds, etc., are declared void.

research & development. This is covered at length in SSAP 13 which seeks to standardise the treatment of research and development. It also lays down rules to be observed when any such expenditure is carried forward to a later period. There are three categories of research and development, they are: 1. Pure research – original investigation undertaken to gain new technical knowledge. It is not directed to any specific practical application. 2. Applied research – as above but directed to a practical application. 3. Development – the use of technical knowledge to produce new or improved products before the commencement of commercial operations. Basically all fixed assets should be written off or depreciated over their useful lives. Items of revenue expenditure should be written off but where the expenditure is of a continuing nature and the benefits are difficult to quantify, then amounts may be carried forward.

reservation. A clause or proviso in a conveyance or lease by which some right or easement is retained by the vendor or lessee.

reserve. A fund set aside to meet some specific contingency. The lowest price the seller will accept in an auction. The short-term assets of a bank.

reserve assets. These are the short-term or current assets of a bank, which can very quickly be converted into cash. During the period of Competition and Credit Control, all banks were required to keep at least 12½ per cent of their eligible liabilities in the form of reserve assets. With the change in policy by the Bank of England, this was abandoned in August 1981, but reserve assets are still held in accordance with Bank of England directive. *See* CAPITAL ADEQUACY; CONTROL OF THE MONEY SUPPLY.

reserve currency. A currency which has international strength and other countries are prepared to use this as a unit of account and settlement of debts. A currency of one country, held by another as part of its monetary reserves, e.g. US$, Deutschmarks, Sterling.

reserved power. A reservation made in deeds, settlements, etc. The most common example is perhaps the clause in a lease whereby the lessor reserves the right to re-enter upon the property if the rent is not punctually paid.

reserve fund. A reserve or provision containing funds to meet some future expense.

reserve liability. A liability for members of a company who hold partly paid shares and may be called upon to pay either in one lump sum or by instalments the oustanding amounts. Unless this is a new issue, the amount members are required to pay, shall not be called unless a special resolution has been passed when the company is expected to be wound up.

reserve price. A price below which no offer will be accepted.

reserves. Profits and surpluses that have been made after payment of tax and the distribution of dividends and are retained in the business. In a limited liability company, such reserves must be shown clearly and separately in the accounts. Share premium is considered as a reserve, but must be shown in a separate account. The balances of gold, foreign currencies and other balances with international financial institutions, e.g. International Monetary Fund, held by the Bank of England.

resettlement. *See* SETTLED LAND.

re-shipment. The re-export of imported goods.

residence. The place where a person has his home. A residence is where a person lives. For a compnay it is its registered office. For tax purposes, providing a person, not necessarily a British citizen, is resident in the UK, then he/she is liable to pay UK tax.

resident. A person whether a UK citizen or not who has voluntarily settled in the UK and made it his/her home then that person is a resident of the country, irrespective of nationality. For tax purposes, a resident is a person who has lived in the UK for 183 days in any calendar year.

residual value. Often referred to as scrap value. The value of an asset at the end of its useful life.

residual devisee. The person who takes the real property after other gifts under the will have been distributed.

residuary estate. The property not bequeathed under the will.

residuary legatee. The person to whom the residue of personal estate is bequeathed after all other claims are discharged.

residue. After the payment of funeral expenses, personal debts and other debts and bequests, it is the balance remaining of the estate.

res ipsa loquitur. The thing speaks for itself, e.g. where in an accident the negligence of the defendant is so obvious that proof is hardly required.

resolution. The decision of a court or the vote of an assembly; motion, declaration; a proposition put before a meeting of company shareholders for discussion, passed by a majority. *See also* EXTRAORDINARY RESOLUTION; ORDINARY RESOLUTION; SPECIAL RESOLUTION.

resolution to borrow. Whenever a limited company wishes to borrow, a resolution must be approved by the directors or by the members at a general or extraordinary general meeting. This resolution, which is signed by the secretary as a true copy of the entry in the Minute Book, is passed to the bank with details of the purpose for which the funds are going to be used. Frequently, the secretary/directors will obtain their banker's own resolution form for completion and return to the bank. The amount and purpose of the borrowing should be checked with the Memorandum of Association to see whether such borrowings are *intra vires* the company and with the Articles of Association to check that the borrowing is *intra vires* the directors. Rather than complete a resolution form each time an advance is required, the form will contain a clause which reads 'such funds as the company may require from time to time and the bank be willing to lend'. Whether any collateral or security is put up, will depend on the bank's willingness to lend with or without security.

resolution to wind up. A company may be wound up voluntarily if when the period fixed for the duration of the company by the articles expires, or the event occurs which the articles provides that the company is to be dissolved, and the company in general meeting has passed a resolution requiring it to be wound up voluntarily (*a*) if the company resolves by special resolution that it may be wound up voluntarily or (*b*) if the company resolves by extraordinary resolution to the effect that it cannot by reason of its liabilities continue its business and that it is advisable to wind up. Where a company has passed a resolution for volntary winding up, it shall, within 14 days after passing the resolution, give notice of the resolution by advertisement in the *London Gazette* (Insolvency Act 1986 s. 84 and 85).

respondent. One who answers in certain proceedings, especially, in a chancery or divorce suit, the defendant.

respondentia. A loan raised by the master of a ship upon its cargo, for which he is personally responsible; the instrument of hypothecation by which such a loan is raised. The money is repayable only if the ship safely reaches its port of destination, and the loan is for the purpose of paying for repairs to the ship urgently needed if it is to continue its voyage.

restraint of trade. All contracts restraining trade are illegal unless approved by the courts and found to be reasonable or against the public interest. It can be found for example in an employer–employee relationship where as a condition of employment the employee agrees not to set up in competition with his employer for some time in the future. This could be enforced if it is necessary to protect any knowledge gained in the service of the employer, but it is not intended to reduce or eliminate normal competitive business. It may also occur when the seller of a business agrees not to set up in competition with the buyer of the business.

restricted circulation. A standing procedure that certain categories of circulars, notes, memoranda, etc. may only be advised to various staff levels. For example, some notes will only be circulated to directors, others to directors and senior management. By this means, matters of business policy and sensitive information will only reach persons who need to be aware of particular policies and events, rather than all employees.

restricted-use credit agreement. Consumer Credit Agreement 1974 s. 11: (*a*) to finance a transaction between the debtor and the creditor, whether the transaction forms part of the agreement or not; or (*b*) to finance a transaction between the debtor and a person (the supplier) other than the creditor; or (*c*) to refinance any existing indebtedness of the debtor's, whether to the creditor or to another person.

restriction. The imposition of a limitation upon an action. A restraint (in trade). A notification to the Land Registrar for the protection of a minor interest. A control in the free transmission of funds from one country to another.

restrictive covenant. A covenant by which the use of the covenantor's land is restricted for the benefit of the covenantee's land which ajoins it.

restrictive indorsement. A bill of exchange will cease to be negotiable if it contains a restrictive indorsement

(Bills of Exchange Act 1882 s. 36(1)). While the Act does not define an indorsement, but is merely the writing of a payee or indorsee of his/her name of the reverse side of a cheque/bill. An example of a restrictive indorsement is where the bill is indorsed 'Pay X only', or 'Pay X only for the account of Y', or 'Pay X or order for collection'.

Section 35(2) 'A restrictive indorsement gives the indorsee the right to receive payment of the bill and to sue any party thereto that his indorser could have sued, but gives him no power to transfer his rights as indorsee unless it expressly authorises him to do so'.

restrictive trade practices. In general terms any restriction on trade is illegal under the Restrictive Trade Practices Act 1956, 1968, 1976 and 1977, unless it is considered to be in the national interest. Any such practices must be registered with the Director-General of Fair Trading so that these agreements can be investigated.

resulting trust. A trust which arises out of circumstances due to the conduct of the donor or his/her representatives; for example, if funds are left in trust for a marriage settlement and it is later found that the marriage is void. A settlement on children on reaching majority, but the children die before reaching that age.

retail banking. Regarded as banking in the high street. The provision of the basic services of a bank to the individual as opposed to 'wholesale', 'international', 'merchant' or 'investment' banking. This type of banking is made possible by having branches of banks in shopping complexes, college campuses, industrial estates as well as in the high streets of cities and towns.

retail cost. The price of an article in the shop where it is sold.

retail price index. *See* GENERAL INDEX OF RETAIL PRICES.

retail trade. The final stage of the commerce in the selling of goods and services to the ultimate consumer, i.e. from shops, market stalls, mail-order organisations, etc.

retaining fee. A preliminary fee paid to a barrister or other professional engaging his or her services.

retention funds. The withholding of final payment on a manufacturing or construction contract for a period of time, e.g. six months, to ensure that the complete job is in accordance with the contract and up to the specification and quality. Any costs for repairs and alterations necessary will be deducted from the amount withheld.

retire. To withdraw from circulation, e.g. a bill of exchange, a note, etc. Scrapping or selling a fixed asset. To give up a full-time occupation and receive either a private pension, a company pension or state pension. At the moment the compulsory age for retirement in most jobs and professions is 60 years for women and 65 years for men. In banks the normal retirement age is 60 years of age, although many members of staff are offered the benefits of retirement from 50 years of age and upwards.

retirement of a bill. The payment of a bill of exchange before its date of maturity, by the acceptor, drawer or any indorser, to the transferee. In effect the bill is withdrawn from circulation and considered paid and all rights are extinguished.

retiring partner. *See* OUTGOING PARTNER.

retirement of trustees. A trustee can only retire either by statutory power under the Trustee Act, or by power of the Court, or by agreement of all the beneficiaries.

return. A refund of money. A return of goods to the supplier. A report made by one person to another giving either information, a formal statement of affairs, or an opinion on a future course of events. The election of a person to an office. The receipt of funds as a result of an investment.

return day. The day on which a defendant is instructed to appear in court.

returned cheque/item. A cheque or other item that has not been paid by the paying banker. In accordance with the instructions of the Committee of London and Scottish Clearing Banks, any item dishonoured and returned, must state the reason for its dishonour.

revaluation. A change in the value of an asset, commodity or a currency. Where an asset in the books of a company has been revalued it is customary to credit a reserve account with the difference between the original balance and the increased new balance.

revenue Income derived from any source, especially the annual income of a state or institution; proceeds, receipts, profits. *See also* INLAND REVENUE.

revenue account. An account showing the income of a company and the expenditure chargeable against it.

revenue expenditure. The payment of expenses which are charged to the profit and loss account.

revenue reserve. A sum which has been built up out of favourable profit and loss balances in previous years.

reverse. To turn the other way round, to give a contrary decision; to repeal, to revoke.

reverse arbitrage. Borrowing from the market to clear off a bank overdraft when rates permit this.

reverse auction. A situation in which the Bank of England takes bids from the market for the purchase of designated gilts stock. This way it saves paying large premiums to investors. The first reverse auction took place on Friday, 13 January 1989. For the £500 million it required to purchase, it received offers of £1.6 billion.

reverse income tax. *See* NEGATIVE INCOME TAX.

reverse takeover. A takeover of a larger company by a smaller one.

reverse yield gap. A situation that exists when the yield on equities is less than the yield on gilts. This occurs when there is an awareness of the effects of inflation which increases the price of equities and there is a reduced demand for gilts and fixed rate interest securities.

reversion. Where the owner of land has granted a lease for a number of years to a tenant, the land will then revert to the owner at the end of that period.

reversionary bonus. A bonus added to the value of a 'with-profits' life policy on a periodic valuation of the profits made by the assurance company in the preceeding period.

reversionary interest. *See* REMAINDER.

revival of a will. The restoration of a will to have its original effect. This may be done by adding a codicil to the current will or to execute a fresh will in order to restore the effect of the original will.

revocable credit or revocable documentary credit. Articles 7 and 9, Uniform

Customs and Practice for Documentary Credits. 'Where a letter of credit does not stipulate whether it is revocable or irrevocable, then it is considered to be revocable.' 'A revocable credit may be amended or cancelled by the issuing bank at any moment without prior notice to the beneficiary. However, where a bank has received documents for payment, acceptance or negotiation prior to notice the issuing bank is bound to reimburse that bank if the documents conform to the terms and conditions of the credit.'

revocation of a will. The cancellation or annulment of a will by a testator. This may be done by the drawing up of a fresh will. By the destruction of the old will. By a subsequent marriage, which will have the effect of revoking the existing will unless such a will was drawn up in contemplation of marriage.

revoke. To annul, to repeal, to reverse a decision.

revolving credit. A facility given to a borrower for the automatic renewal of the initial amount of credit available. When the credit has been utilised and the borrower has repaid some or all of the amount, he/she has the right to borrow up to the amount of the facility again. Under a documentary letter of credit a letter of credit may be utilised up to the amount of the credit again and again until the date of expiry of the credit.

riba. An Arabic word meaning interest of funds deposited. This is strictly not permitted by the Koran. *See* ISLAMIC BANKING.

rider. An addition to a manuscript or other document; an additional clause, as to a bill; a supplement tacked on to the original motion or verdict.

RIE. Recognised Investment Exchange.

rigged market. A manipulation of the price of a security to induce either buyers or sellers.

right. A just claim, a legal title.

right *in personam*. A right which can be enforced only against a limited number of persons.

right *in rem*. A right enforceable against the whole world.

right of action. A right to commence an action in court.

right of survivorship. The right of the survivor to the whole property. On opening a bank account for two or more persons, a survivorship clause is in the mandate, so that the account may be continued in the name of the survivor/s.

right of way. A right, established by custom, to use a path over or through private property; such a path.

rights issue. A rights issue occurs when a company wishes to raise additional funds from its shareholders in order to make an acquisition, pay off short or long-term liabilities, or expand. The company offers its shareholders new shares in proportion to the number already held at a price lower than that quoted in the market. The shareholder has the right, but not the obligation, to apply for the new shares and since they are attractively priced it is an incentive to take up the offer, in this way the shareholder increases his stake in the company without incurring any dealing costs. For the ordinary investor, the dilution of his/her stake is of minor importance. On the announcement of a rights issue, the market will adjust the price of the share.

rights letter. The formal letter advising a shareholder of the details of the new issue and his/her right to take up the allocation of shares. Should the shareholder for some reason not wish to take up the new allocation, the rights can be sold in the market and any profit made will be given to him/her.

rights of holder of bill. The holder may sue on the bill in his or her own name. Where the holder is a *holder in due course* the bill is held free from any defect of title of prior parties and payment may be enforced against all parties liable on the bill.

rights of unpaid seller. Where the ownership of goods has been transferred from the seller to the buyer, but the seller has not yet been paid, he has; 1. a lien on the goods until the price has been paid; 2. where the goods are in transit, and he hears the buyer is insolvent, he has the right to stop the goods being transferred to the buyer; 3. he has the right of resale.

ring. A group of persons or traders that control prices of a commodity so that it shall not fall below a given level. The place where dealers in financial paper or commodities do their trading.

risk. The chance of losing or gaining value in either money or a commodity. Any future uncertainty is subject to risk of loss of funds or property, so that there are markets and institutions that would, for a premium insure against any future loss, e.g. foreign exchange, life assurance, property insurance, interest rate, risk of liquidity, political and economic, etc.

risk-asset ratio. The Bank of England's system for controlling the banks and deposit-taking institutions under its supervision has obliged it to make certain definitions. *Risk-asset* ratio is defined as the free capital plus a figure for premises relative to all assets; substantially, the bank's loan portfolio; and its investments. *See also* CONTROL OF THE MONEY SUPPLY.

risk capital. This is the ordinary share capital of a company, often referred to as the 'equity' capital. Dividends are paid on ordinary capital, but the amount will depend on the profits made. From the banking point of view this will refer to advances made to customers which has hardened and the customer is finding it difficult not only to pay the interest due but to reduce the capital.

risk management. The management of the risks involved in financial futures and options arising from the volatility of interest rates, exchange rates, equity prices, etc.

roller coaster. A phrase used to describe large rises and falls in the movement of share prices in a single day, week or account period.

roll forward. The move from one option situation to another. The closing down of one position either before or simultaneously establishing another. If the new position means a higher exercise price it is called a roll up and forward, if a lower exercise price it is called a roll down and forward.

roll-over. The review of a loan at regular intervals by the lender, and providing the loan is within acceptable limits it may continue. In large syndicated loans, a roll over, especially for foreign currency borrowings, may be part of the agreement whereby the borrower may roll over the loan in the currency borrowed using LIBOR as the base lending rate, but where another currency is attractive, it can also be agreed that the loan can roll over into another currency.

Romalpa case. A stipulation in a contract that the ownership in the goods shall not pass to the buyer until payment has been made. This is an important case to bankers, who having given an advance to customers against a floating charge, need to know that creditors to the borrowing company have not inserted retention clauses in their contracts so that they have prior rights to the bank. *Aluminium Industrie Vaasen B.V.* v. *Romalpa Aluminium Ltd.*

root of title. *See* GOOD ROOT OF TITLE.

round lot. The minimum number of shares that are accepted for purchase or sale on a Stock Exchange. The actual number will depend whether the shares are active or inactive.

round tripping. *See* HARD ARBITRAGE.

royal assent. The authorisation by the sovereign of a bill that transforms it into an Act of Parliament. The preamble to the Act would start 'Be it enacted by the Queen's most Excellent Majesty, by and with the advice and consent of the Lords Spiritual and Temporal and Commons, in this present Parliament assembled, and by the authority of the same as follows: . . .'. It is highly unlikely that Royal Assent would not be given.

royal charter. A document originating from the sovereign creating a legal entity. A century or two ago, royal charter was granted to trading companies, these days it is now given to universities, charitable institutions, professional associations, e.g. Chartered Institute of Bankers.

Royal Mint. A government department under the Chancellor of the Exchequer which is responsible for the production and distribution of coins of the realm. It is also responsible for the manufacture of coins of other countries. In addition it makes medals, decorations and seals for governmental purposes. It is situated at Llantrisant, near Cardiff.

royalty. Payment to an owner of land for the right to work minerals, or to an inventor for the use of his or her invention; payment to an author dependent upon the sales of a book.

RUFS. Revolving underwriting facilities.

rule against accumulations. Where a person wishes that income is invested as it accrues and given to his/her descendants at some future date, by the Law of Property Act 1925 and Perpetuities and Accumulations Act 1964, any person with this intention must choose only one of the following periods: (*a*) the life of the settlor/s; (*b*) not more than 21 years from the date of the settlor; (*c*) the duration of minority of a person living or *en ventre sa mère* at the death of the settlor; (*d*) the minority only of any person/s who under the limitations of the settlement would if of full age become entitled to the income directed to be accumulated; (*e*) a term of 21 years from the date of settlement; (*f*) the duration of the minority of any person/s in being at the date of the settlement.

rule against perpetuities. In English law, the rule that is not permissible to suspend the vesting of interst in property (usually land, but not necessarily so) for longer than a life in being plus twenty-one years. From 1964, a settlor may instead specify a fixed period of time not exceeding eighty years. The rule came to be used to defeat the unbarrable entails by which families sought to keep their estates in perpetuity. Unbarrable entails were first defeated by the introduction of the devices of fines and recoveries. The objection to the remoteness of interests emerged later with the recognition of the trust. A *fine* was no more than a judicial proceeding used for conveying land. For this it was necessary to institute a fictitious suit which was compromised with the consent of the court, an agreement being entered into by the parties concerned as to the disposal of the land in question. A *recovery* was a judgment in a collusive suit brought by a plaintiff against the tenant in tail. The subsequent procedure was rather complicated, and of hisorical interest now as both fines and recoveries were abolished in 1833 and replaced by a simple disentailing assurance.

rule in Clayton's case. *See* CLAYTON'S CASE.

run. To flee, to flow; to continue in operation; to continue without falling due, as a promissory note or bill; to have legal force; to manage (a business); a frantic rush on the part of depositors to withdraw their money from a bank believed to be in difficulties.

running. Successive (Numbers); continuous (e.g. an order of account).

running account credit. Defined in the Consumer Credit Act 1974 s. 10: 'A facility under a personal credit agreement whereby the debtor is enabled to receive from time to time (whether in his own person or by another person) from the creditor or a third party cash, goods and services (or any of them) to an amount or value such that, taking into account payments made by or to the credit of the debtor, the credit limit is not exceeded at any time'.

running days. Consecutive days, including Saturdays and Sundays, as opposed to business days.

running margin. A man who borrows money to invest is at interest both pays and earns interest. The difference between the interest paid for the loan and the interest derived from the investment, is the running margin.

running yield. *See* FLAT YIELD.

run on a bank. Where customers of a bank have lost confidence in that bank or they have heard rumours about the loss of liquidity of the bank, they will, all in one day or a short period of time, try to withdraw their balances. Unless there is some support either from other financial institutions or the central bank, a bank could effectively have to close its doors.

S

safe custody. As one of the functions of a bank is to act as a bailor, it will, when necessary be prepared to accept envelopes, boxes, parcels and documents for depositing for safety in its strongrooms. All items – with the exception of documents – must be sealed before handing them into the bank for safe custody. The bank will if required issue a receipt for the item, which is usually recorded in the bank's books as 'contents unknown'. The bank is therefore not responsible for any loss or damage to any item in the box, envelope or parcel. Should the customer wish to safeguard himself, then he/she should be advised to take out insurance for the items deposited. The contract between banker and customer is one of bailment. The bank will make a quarterly or half-yearly charge for maintaining the item within the strong-room and will also charge each time the customer wishes to inspect the box and its contents. Any withdrawals must be made to the customer only against his/her signed receipt.

safe deposit. A safe deposit service is offered by some banks and private companies. In this instance, the customer has their own box which is rented from the company and the customer may personally put articles in the box. The customer keeps the key to the box, while the bank keeps a duplicate key in case of emergency.

salaried partner. A person who is regarded as a partner in a firm, but receives a regular salary.

salaries and wages accounts. *See* WAGES/SALARIES ACCOUNT.

salary. A payment made under a contract of employment, which is calculated on an annual basis, but is paid to the employee monthly. Any bonuses or profit sharing will be based on the annual salary.

sale. In business terms it is a contract for the supply of goods to a person, firm or company in return for payment as agreed within a stated time. Once the parties have agreed to the conditions of the sale, it is a legally binding contract and providing the goods are in accordance with the standard, the buyer must accept the goods and pay for them in due course. *See also* BARTER.

sale and lease back. A form of leasing arrangement whereby the company will sell its property or other asset to the leasing company and immediately lease it back and continue to use it as before. In this way the company raised immediate finance without losing the use of the asset. The ownership passes to the lessee, while the lessor will pay a leasing rental for the duration of the life of the asset.

sale by auction. *See* AUCTION.

sale of description. Where there is a contract for the sale of goods by description, there is an implied condition that the goods shall correspond with the description.

sale by sample. Where the sales contract has terms, one of which is that the sale is by sample it is implied that: 1. the bulk of the goods shall correspond with the sample in quality; 2. that the buyer shall have a reasonable opportunity of comparing the bulk with the sample; 3. that the goods shall be free from any defect, rendering them unsaleable, which would not be apparent on an examination of the sample.

sales ledger. That ledger that contains the accounts of the customers that purchase goods on credit and a record to the transactions.

same day funds. *See also* VALUE DATE.

sampling. A method of arriving at the quality of the merchandise by a random choice of some of the parts. This is important when dealing with such commodities as tea, grains, etc. A method of auditig the financial records of a large organisation is by a random choice of accounts/transactions so an opinion can be formed as to the standard of efficiency and accuracy in the organisation. Consumer organisations use a sampling method to obtain the attitude of the public towards various products, political parties, etc.

sanction. The permission given to pursue a certain course of action. In politics this could mean to cut off economic, financial or other relationships to a country that has committed some misconduct. In banking a sanction refers to the authority given by a bank to a customer which will allow him/her to overdraw the current account or have a loan.

sans recours. These words mean 'without recourse'. This may be added to the signature of an indorser. *See* WITHOUT RECOURSE.

sasine (*Sc. Law*). The act of putting a person into possession of land, by completing an appropriate conveyance and registering it in the General Register of Sasines.

savings. Money put aside for the purchase of some household commodity, the purchase of a car, or for some important occasion, e.g. a wedding or holiday. It differs from investment as savings are put in some form of risk-free deposit, e.g. a bank or building society, whereas as investment is perhaps a little riskier as the value of the shares or stock may increase or decrease.

savings bank. A term that used to cover a variety of banks whose function it was to encourage small savers. The major services were the deposit and withdrawal of cash, with interest paid on balances. With the changes that have taken place in the banking systems, such banks as TSB and the Yorkshire Bank can no longer be regarded as purely savings banks. The only bank which is covered by this term is the National Savings Bank, whose outlets are the Post Offices and sub-post offices in the country. *See* NATIONAL SAVINGS BANK.

savings bonds. *See* NATIONAL SAVINGS DEPOSIT BOND; INCOME BOND.

savings certificates. *See* NATIONAL SAVINGS CERTIFICATES.

savings-related share option scheme. A scheme offered by companies to directors and staff which provides them with the opportunity of purchasing shares in the company with money that has been set aside from salary, bonuses, etc. As the scheme provides some tax advantages it must have the approval of the Inland Revenue.

scalar principle. A management function to grade persons according to authority and areas of responsibility. Within a banking organisation, personnel are graded for clerical, supervisory and managerial duties. Within each group, there are also grades to which a person may be promoted. Using as an example a clerk who is a cashier, he/she will be directly responsible to the chief cashier, who may either be a senior clerk or a supervisor. In turn, that person would be responsible to the administration manager. Managers are of course answerable to an area, regional or local head office manager and so on. Each person will have a job specification, which states his/her duties, responsibilities for work procedures and subordinates, and targets that will have to be met during the course of the year.

scarcity value. This describes a situation where the supply of a commodity is small and difficult to increase with the consequence that it will always command a high price.

schedule. A timetable for a sequence of events. Additional information provided in a report, Act of Parliament, etc. A list of items attached to a document. *See* SCHEDULE OF INCOME TAX.

scheduled territories. Formerly a list of countries whose currencies were linked to the £ sterling – since 1972 consisting only of the UK, including the Channel Islands and the Isle of Man and Gibraltar.

schedule of income tax. For the purposes of payment of income tax on earnings, the Inland Revenue have six different categories of earned income which are: Schedule A. Income from land and buildings; Schedule B. Income from woodlands; Schedule C. Profits from UK and overseas gilts; Schedule D. Case 1. Income from a trade; Case 2. Income from a profession or vocation; Case 3. Income from interest, annuities, and other annual payments; Case 4. Income from other overseas investments not covered by Schedule C; Case 5. Income from foreign ownership of possessions; Case 6. All other miscellaneous income not by an schedule or case; Schedule E. Case 1. Income from employment by persons living and working in the UK; Case 2. Income from employment by persons working in the UK but not resident in the UK; Schedule F. Dividends from companies in the UK working and residing in the UK.

scheme of arrangement. An arrangement between a debtor and his/her creditors allowing the debts due to be paid as agreed by the creditors, rather than allow the debtor to go bankrupt.

scrap. Anything that no longer has any use or value and can either be sold or discarded.

scrap value. An asset which at the end of its working or useful life has some value. This approximate value is considered when calculating the annual depreciation of an asset. The value of an asset at the end of its working or useful life.

scrip. The certificate or document given to a person showing the number of shares or stock that he/she has agreed to purchase or in the case of oversubscription, has been allotted.

scrip issue. The issue of additional shares to members of a company issued in proportion to the number of shares already held. It is a transfer from reserves to issued capital. No money is given by the shareholders nor received by the company. After the issue, the shareholder holds an additional number of shares. There are more shares available in the market. The price of the shares in the market will fall in proportion to the number of shares issued.

scorched earth policy. When a company does not wish to be taken over, it may adopt the technique of not making itself attractive to the predator, by selling off an attractive and profitable part of the business. *See also* POISON PILL.

scripophily. The hobby of collecting share and stock certificates for either interest, their scarcity, or purely the appreciation of their artistic designs. Many certificates issued in the nineteenth and early twentieth century had extremely attractive designs not only on the certificate itself, but also on the coupons attached to the certificate. These were mainly the old oil companies, railway companies of South American countries, etc.

scrivener. One who draws up contracts or other documents; one who places money at interest on behalf of clients; a public writer, a notary.

scrutineer. One who examines votes cast at an election; one who computes the votes of members at a company meeting.

seal. A small impression by a person on a document to signify his/her acceptance of the conditions stated on that document. It used to be a drop of melted wax on the paper or parchment impressed either by the pattern on a ring or by a metal instrument which has impressed a personal or company motif. Currently it is a stamped wafer, or an adhesive wafer is attached to a document, which is signed by two witnesses to certify that the seal was fixed in their presence. A contract given under seal needs no consideration.

SEAQ. Stock Exchange Automated Quotations. A method of displaying share trading information anywhere in the UK. The system is capable of showing the buying and selling prices of shares within minutes of the deal.

searches. An investigation made by a person or persons before entering into a formal contract. Investigation into unregistered land titles carried out on behalf of a bank will be made on the Land Charges Register, while for registered land, the despatch of the Land Certificate to the Land Registry for up-to-date completion. Searches for charges made on companies will be made at Companies House. Searches, for example, may be made at credit reference agencies, libraries, etc. Legally, the power to search an individual or the premises of an individual or company is vested in government and can be given to the police, the Department of Trade, customs and excise authorities, Serious Fraud Office, etc.

seasonal. The occurrence of an event on due time or in accordance with the season or calendar. The increase in advances will occur when business persons need to pay funds due to the

Inland Revenue authorities, or value added tax. The need to borrow funds, prior to the Christmas shopping period in order to restock. The final accounts and balance sheets of the major banks are normally for the year ended 31 December.

seat. In commercial and financial terms this means a representation or membership of a clearing house, market or exchange, e.g. a seat in a clearing company 'BACS' 'CHAPS and Town Clearing', a seat in LIFFE, the Stock Exchange, etc.

secondary market. The primary market in stocks and shares is the original issue by the government or the company. The secondary market is the purchase and sale of these stocks and shares after the first issue, i.e. second hand stocks/shares.

secondary offering. The placing of parcels of shares held by individuals or by groups.

secondary risk. *See* PRIMARY RISKS.

second mortgage. A mortgage taken on a property on which there is already a first mortgage. This form of mortgage can be on either unregistered land or registered land. With unregistered land, the title deeds will be held by the the first mortgagee, so that the bank will have to send a questionnaire to the first mortgagor in order to cover such points as amount outstanding, insurance, consolidation, tacking, other mortgages – do they exist? The charge must be registerd with the Land Registry as a Class C (i) charge. For registered land, a questionnaire as above is sent to the first mortgagee and a copy of the Land Certificate is obtained from the Land Registry. Notice of the bank's interest must in all cases be given to the first mortgagee.

second of exchange. *See* BILLS IN SET.

secrecy. The witholding of information from persons not authorised to receive it. Confidentiality in all matters in the affairs of others. Perhaps one of the most important banker/customer relationships is that of the non-disclosure of the affairs of a customer to those not entitled to have such information. Banks in general will take every possible precaution to ensure that confidentiality is not breached, but case law has authorised the disclosure of a customer's affairs under the following circumstances: 1. Compulsion of law. 2. In the public duty. 3. In the interest of the bank. 4. When the customer has given his/her expressed or implied consent. Bank employees when joining the staff will sign a declaration of secrecy and many banks will insist that this declaration is renewed annually. In such matters as money laundering, or the deposit of proceeds of drugs, etc., banks are compelled by public duty to reveal the evidence of such matters. When a warrant or writ has been issued, then under the compulsion of law banks must show their records either to a visiting authority, or produce such evidence in a court of law.

secretary. Under the Companies Act 1985, every company must have a secretary. He or she is an official of the company, having specific statutory duties.

secret commission. An agent must not accept any money, goods, services or favours from a third party as an inducement to act in a way that is favourable to a third party that will give him/her any of the above considerations. An agent must not act in any way that is prejudicial to his principal or accept a bribe of any nature. Should this happen, then any inducement given becomes the property of the principal. Both the giver and receiver of a bribe may be guilty of an offence under the Prevention of Corruption Act 1916 and Representation of the People Act 1983.

secret reserve. *See* HIDDEN RESERVE.

secured creditor. A creditor – a bank or financial institution – that has a legal charge or an equitable charge on an asset belonging to the debtor. The creditor may also be secured against non-payment by holding third party security, e.g. a guarantee with or without some form of cover. Insolvency Act 1986 s. 248(a): 'secured creditor, in relation to a company, means a creditor of the company who holds in respect of his debt a security over property of the company, ...'. For the bankruptcy of an individual a secured creditor as s. 2619(1) states: 'A debt which is the debt, or one of the debts, in respect of which a creditor's petition is presented need not be unsecured if either (a) the petition contains a statement by the person having the right to enforce the security that he is willing, in the event of bankruptcy order being made, to give up his security for the benefit of all the bankrupt's creditors, or (b) the petition is expressed not to be made in respect of the secured part of the debt and contains a statement by that person of the estimated value at the date of the petition of the security for the secured part of the debt'. *See also* SECURITY.

secured debenture. A debenture providing a fixed charge on specified company assets.

securities. In a wider and less precise sense a word meaning investments generally, e.g. 'Stock Exchange securities'.

Securities and Futures Authorities (SFA). The Securities and Futures Authority is the organisation responsible for regulating firms acting as dealers or advisers in the securities and derivatives market. It was formed in April 1991 through the merging of the Securities Association with the Association of Futures Brokers and dealers which were themselves established by the Financial Services Act 1986. SFA's powers are delegated to it by the Securities and Investments Board who in turn is responsible through the operation of the Act. It is the primary requirement of the SFA that anyone carrying on investment business in the UK should be authorised by the appropriate self-regulating organisation. Consequently, SFA has the ongoing task of considering applications for membership and for changes to members' business profiles. There is also an examinations department which is responsible for setting the examination through which SFA's 'Registered Representative' status can be achieved. There are now eighty inspectors in the enforcement division, who monitor member firms' compliance with SFA rules through a combination of visits to firms and financial reporting statements which firms have to submit. The work of authorisation and enforcement is supported by a large computerised database and records system. In the event of disciplinary action being taken, the prosecutions group is involved. SFA maintains close relations with other SROs, the SIB, the Bank of England, the Treasury, Parliament and international authorities.

Securities Investment Board. Under the Financial Services Act 1986 it is responsible for enforcing codes of conduct in their appropriate area of investment.

Securities Management Trust Ltd. ('SMT Money'). A wholly-owned subsidiary company of the Bank of England. It is used by the Bank as a nominee company for the placement of funds at market rates in the security and money markets on behalf of, and at the request of, Bank of England customers.

securitisation. The borrowing and lending of funds between market operators, with the intermediation of banks, using such securities as commercial paper, euronotes, certificates of deposit, etc.

security. The protection of property, to make safe any article or asset or person. In banking this can refer to the protection of its cash and other valuables, belonging to the bank or its customers retained on its premises. The protection of customers' funds, by giving each customer a personal identification number (PIN) when transferring sums of money via a home banking service, or ATM. The confidentiality of the customer's affairs. The depositing of an document or asset with a Memorandum of Deposit to be retained either as a legal or equitable charge for an advance. This form of security may include, stocks and share certificates, debentures, insurance policies, guarantees, deeds, etc. For the purposes of the Consumer Credit Act 1974 s. 189(1) security in relation to an actual or prospective consumer credit agreement or hire purchase agreement, or any linked transaction, means a mortgage, charge, pledge, bond, debenture, indemnity, guarantee, bill or note or other right provided by the debtor or hirer (express or implied), to secure the carrying out of the obligations of the debtor or hirer under the agreement. An item of security for banking purposes, must have the following attributes: 1. It must have value.

2. Capable of being owned by the bank. 3. Marketable.

seigniorage. The power or right of a feudal lord or sovereign. The charge made for turning gold or silver ingots into coins. A mining royalty. The difference between the bullion value of gold, siler and copper and cupronickel coins and their face value.

seisin. Possession of land under a freehold; the act of taking possession; the thing possessed.

self-liquidity. An important concept of an advance most favoured by bankers, whereby the loan for raw materials, finished goods, exports, imports, etc., are repaid from the proceeds of sales.

self regulating organisation. For the purposes of s. 8(1), Financial Services Act 1986, a body which regulates the carrying on of an investment business of any kind by enforcing rules which are binding on persons carrying on business of that kind, either because they are members of that body or because they are subject to its control.

self-service. A retail outlet that permits a customer to help themselves to goods they require and to pay for them before leaving the shop. There is a slow move towards self-service in banks, whereby customers can now withdraw funds from an ATM situated either inside or outside the bank. Some banks have a facility for the deposit of funds outside banking hours and the larger banks have a restricted service whereby certain shares may be sold via a computer terminal situated in the banking hall and operated by the customer.

seller. A person who sells, or agrees to sell, goods or services.

seller's interest. Where the terms of trade are either FOB or C & F and the exporter is unhappy that when selling goods to some countries, he is unlikely to be paid against claims made on an overseas insurance company, he may obtain an insurance policy, without the knowledge of the importer, to protect himself against claims which have been dishonoured.

seller's market. A condition of markets in which goods are scarce, and there is a great demand for them, so that the seller can make his or her own terms.

seller's option. The right of a seller to

deliver the security at some time before maturity, e.g. foreign exchange forward option contract.

selling group. A group of dealers or syndicate formed for the purpose of selling bonds or a new issue of shares to the public at large or to selected investment institutions. The lead manager will draw up an agreement which sets out the conditions, commissions, etc.

selling group terms. The issue price minus the discount (usually 1¼–1½ per cent) allowed to the selling group allows a commission or 're-allowance' of (usually) ½ per cent, to authorised dealers.

selling off. When the prices of securities have declined and it is anticipated that there is likely to be a further drop in prices, then under pressure, dealers will sell off whatever they can to avoid any further losses.

selling out. Action taken by a seller on the Stock Exchange when the buyer fails to complete. This consists of an instruction to the Stock Exchange official broker to sell the securities in question, any loss arising being charged to the defaulting purchaser.

send direct. *See* SPECIAL CLEARANCE.

separate entity. A concept that a business is completely separate from its owner or owners and the financial transactions of one should not be confused with the other.

sequestration. Where a person fails to obey an injunction or an order of the Court, then a writ may be issued for the sequestrators to enter his/her premises and retain possession of the items until the order has been complied with.

series. All options, in the traded option market, of the same class, having the same exercise right and expiry date.

Serious Fraud Office. The Serious Fraud Office was set up under the Criminal Justice Act 1987, to investigate and prosecute the most serious or complex cases in England, Wales and Northern Ireland, following public concern about existing arrangements for dealing with such crime. It began its operations in April 1988. It aims to (*a*) increase the efficiency of the criminal justice system in investigating and prosecuting serious fraud, (*b*) to deter fraud and maintain confidence in the UK's financial systems. The present director of the SFO is Mrs Barbara Mills QC who took over the office in September 1990. It employs over 100 persons and includes lawyers, accountants, information technologists and others with relevant expertise, and works in close co-operation with the police and other investigative authorities. The SFO is accountable to the Attorney-General and to Parliament. In the 1990–91 annual report it was stated that the commonest type of fraud was on investors, representing 28 per cent of referrals, closely followed by fraud on creditors 23 per cent.

SERPS. State Earnings Related Pensions.

set off. A banker has the right to set off different accounts that are in the same right and in the same name of the customer. This is done by calculating the balances on those accounts that are in credit and the balances of those accounts in debit and arrive at a net credit or net debit balance. There is a statutory or common law right to set off balances on the occurrence of certain events: bankruptcy (Insolency Act 1986 s. 323), winding up of a company (Insolvency Act 1986 s. 323), winding up of a partnership (Insolvent Partnerships Order 1986), mental incapacity or death of a customer, receipt of a garnishee order, notice that a customer has assigned his/her balance, receipt of a notice of a second mortgage. It is customary for a bank to obtain a letter or authority from a customer giving it right of set off.

settled land. Land which is subject to the terms of a settlement; land held under certain conditions by a tenant for life. A strict settlement was a device to preserve land in a family for as long as possible. This was done by the device of a conveyance of the land to trustees upon trust to hold it for the settlor for life, with remainder to the eldest son in tail and successive remainders, in the event of the death of this son without issue, to the younger sons in tail. On the attainment of majority by the son, a re-settlement was made, whereby the land was reconveyed to the trustees on trust to hold it

for the settlor for the remainder of his life, subject to an annual sum of money charged on the land in favour of the son, with remainder to the son for life and then to *his* eldest son in tail. A similar re-settlement was made every generation. The re-settlement, read together with the original settlement, was known as a *Compound Settlement.* A settlement taking effect by reference to another settlement was called a *Referential Settlement.* In this way land could be kept in the family, but it was so tied up that it could never be sold. In 1925, in pursuit of the principle of free alienation, it was provided by the Settled Land Act 1925 that after that year settlements must be made by two deeds. The trust instrument declares the trusts upon which the land is to be held. The vesting deed declares that the legal estate in the land is vested in the person who is, for the time being, entitled to the enjoyment of it as tenant for life. The latter is thus made the 'estate owner' and entitled to sell the land. A purchaser is only permitted to examine the vesting deed and deals with the estate owner therein named. He or she has to pay the money, however, to the trustees, who must hold the money in place of the land, invest it, and apply the income according to the trusts of the settlement.

settlement. Where a business or financial transaction has taken place and an invoice, statement or bill has been sent to the debtor, and payment of the amount outstanding has been given. In a court of law, an agreement between the parties has taken place. The creation of an interest in land.

settlement day. A specified day in the Stock Exchange calendar which occurs every two weeks. Occasionally there is a three week period, when the accounts for the previous accounting period are settled.

sever. To part or divide by violence, to sunder, to cut or break off; to make a separation, to act independently of others in a joint law suit. *See also* WORDS OF SEVERANCE.

several liability. *See* JOINT AND SEVERAL LIABILITY.

severalty. A freehold estate held solely by a tenant in his or her own right.

severance payment. An amount paid to an official or an employee as compensation for either termination of his or her employment contract, or having been dismissed.

shadow director. By the Companies Act 1985 s. 741, a shadow director means any person in accordance with whose directions or instructions the directors of the company are accustomed to act. This will not include advice given by a person acting in a professional capacity. The position of a bank manager, who advises, requests or directs the company to act in a certain way, is not clear, but it could be construed by his or her conduct that the bank manager could be in the position of a 'shadow director'.

share. The proportion of interest in the capital of a company which a shareholder has. *See also* DEFERRED SHARES; FULLY-PAID SHARES; GROWTH SHARE; INCENTIVE SHARES; NON-VOTING SHARES; ORDINARY SHARES; PARTLY-PAID SHARES; PREFERENCE SHARES; REDEEMABLE PREFERENCE SHARES; SUBSCRIPTION SHARES; UNQUOTED SHARES.

share capital. The amount of the contribution that can be made by investors or members of the company. The amount of capital that can be invested or authorised is shown in the Articles of Association. However, the directors may only wish to issue a percentage of the authorised capital, so that the number of shares actually issued is called the issued share capital, but if the issued capital is in instalments, then the capital that has been called in is called the paid-up or called capital. The balance would be known as the uncalled capital. Shares would usually have a nominal value, e.g. £1, 50p, etc. this is known as the nominal capial amount.

share certificate. A document issued by the company to its shareholders as evidence of the number of shares registered with the company in the name of the shareholder/s. *See also* TAURUS.

shareholder. One who has an interest in a joint property, particularly a member of a limited company.

share option scheme. An arrangement between the company and its directors, employees or any other person (an option holder) whereby the company agree to allocate shares to a person under a share option scheme agreed by the shareholders at an annual general meeting. The person – director or employee – has the right to purchase a stated number of shares at a price fixed when the arrangement was made.

share parking. A situation where someone buys shares on behalf of the real buyer in an attempt to hide the true ownership. Usually a deal has been agreed for the nominal buyer to sell the shares at a prearranged price and time.

share premium. The amount by which the issue price of a share exceeds the nominal value. This normally occurs when a fresh issue of shares is made some time after the first issue. Under the Companies Act 1985, the value of the share premium must be credited to a share premium account.

share pushing. The sale of shares by aggressive methods, when the salesmen make glowing and extravagant reports on the shares in order to sell them at a price well above their worth. Such statements are a criminal offence if it can be proven that such statements were made deliberately to mislead investors.

share register. Often called the register of members. It is a statutory obligation that a company keeps such a register at its registered office, showing the names and addresses of its members and the number of shares held, the date of purchase and the numbers allocated to the group of shares held – if relevant. The register must be available for inspection, by shareholders, free, but to any other person wishing to inspect the register, there is a charge.

shares of no par value. *See* NO PAR VALUE.

share or stock transfer form. *See* TAURUS.

share warrant. Certificates issued by a limited company certifying that the bearer is entitled to the shares specified therein.

sheriff. The Crown's representative and the chief officer in the county. He is responsible for the conduct of a parliamentary election and the execution of the laws. *See also* UNDER-SHERIFF.

shilling. The old name for a 5p piece.

ship. Any type of vessel other than a rowing-boat that can be navigated. It is used for the carriage of passengers and/or the carriage of freight. The name of the vessel must be shown and also its port of registration. British vessels for the purposes of ownership are divded into sixty-fourths and any person may own some or all shares or own part of a share. British vessels are usually registered with Lloyd's Register of Shipping.

ship bill of sale. The document used for the transfer of ownership of a ship or a share in a ship.

ship-broker. An agent for a shipping company who transacts business for a vessel lying in port; one who transacts marine insurance deals.

shipment. The process of shipping; that which is shipped; a cargo. *See also* GROUPAGE SHIPMENT.

ship mortgage. *See* MORTGAGE OF A SHIP.

shipped bill of lading. In the absence of an 'on board bill of lading' owing to the fact the goods are held in a warehouse or on the quayside because the carrying vessel cannot be loaded, a shipped bill of lading is issued evidencing receipt of the goods by the shipowners and showing that space has been reserved for the named goods of a specified vessel. Once the goods are actually on board, then an 'on board bill of lading' will be issued.

shipping agent. One who arranges the shipment of goods or passengers.

shipping bill. An invoice of goods shipped; customs documents used where drawback is claimed.

shipping note. A document prepared by exporters and used to accompany goods to the dock, setting out the details of the ship, dock and the goods themselves.

ship's husband. A person appointed by the owner or his agent who is responsible for the maintenance and repair of the vessel, ensure that it has adequate provision and stores before commencing a journey. For ensuring the seaworthiness of the vessel he may as an agent borrow funds. His/her name must be registered at the port of registration of the ship.

shopping list credit. This refers to a transferable documentary credit, often for a very large amount, where the UK

beneficiary is an agent of the applicant, or a major supplier of goods, but is unable to supply the variety of goods described in the credit. He would then, via the advising bank, be responsible for allocating and transferring portions of the credit to numerous suppliers of particular goods. Hence the description – shopping list credit. This large-scale purchase of UK goods may be the result of a UK government loan to an overseas government or central bank, or by a large company involved in a major project, or by a commercial attache of the applicant's country purchasing supplies from a variety of manufacturers. Sometimes known as 'a shopping bag credit'.

short. A measurement which is too little either in time or space. Does not reach from one end to another. A cash deficiency or in a commodity. Where a broker has greater sales than purchases, e.g. stocks and shares, foreign exchange, etc.

short bill. A bill of exchange which has only a few days to maturity.

short-dated paper. Bills of exchange drawn at not more than three months.

short end of the market. The market that deals with government stock that has less than five years to run. Often referred to as 'shorts'.

short exchange. On the foreign exchanges, bills payable within ten days.

short form bill of lading. A bill of lading which does not contain all the conditions of carriage.

short gilt. Government stock which has a five years' security or less.

short hedge. A term used in the London international financial futures exchange (*q.v.*) which indicates that an investor has *sold* a financial futures contract to enable him or her to offset an adverse change in interest or exchange rates within a specified future period. *See also* LONG HEDGE.

shorthold letting. This came into force with the Housing Act 1980 s. 52, whereby a tenancy agreement of between one and five years cannot be terminated by the landlord, except on cerain conditions, i.e. non-payment of rent, or breach of an obligation. At the end of the term the landlord has the right to regain possession of the dwelling.

short lease. A lease for not more than 21 years.

short position. The sale of shares by a market maker or an investor, who is not in possession or ownership of those shares and therefore needs to buy them to square his books. A situation where the sale of shares in any particular exceeds purchases.

short rate. The price in one country at which a short-dated draft drawn on another country can be bought.

shorts. Short-dated stocks, repayable inside five years.

short tap. Tap (*q.v.*) having, say, five years or less to maturity.

short-term liabilities. *See* CURRENT LIABILITIES.

short-term loan. A loan for up to three years; Government stocks issued for a similar period.

short-term money market. Part of the London Money Market that provides funds for those institutions that need to borrow funds from over-night to a period of up to one year. The participants in this market are the banks, discount houses, local authorities, etc. There is no one short-term market as the Discount Houses are prepared to deal in short-term funds and so is the interbank market, intercompany market, Euro-currency market, and so on. The rate of interest, particularly for the very short term is subject to negotiation and depending on the borrowing entity, it is usual that no security is offered or accepted.

short-term obligation. A current liability.

short-term policy. An insurance policy which covers risks for a short period only, as where a businessman is taking a trip abroad.

short-term rate of interest. The rate of interest for loans of up to three months.

short-ton. A unit of weight equal to 2 000 lb.

shutting the window. *See* WINDOW.

SIB. *See* SECURITIES INVESTMENT BOARD.

sight bill. A bill payable as soon as the drawee sees it.

sight clause. *See* EXCHANGE CLAUSE.

sight credit. A credit where the beneficiary is to obtain payment immediately, either against a sight draft accompanied by documents of title, or against the documents only.

sight deposits. Current accounts, money deposited overnight, and money at call.

signatory. The person who has placed his/her signature on a document and is liable for the terms of that document.

signature. The writing of a person's name on a document. If the person is unable to read or write, then a fingerprint will do, or 'x' will do, providing it is witnessed by a person who can read and write. The authentic signature of a customer is the authority to a bank to comply with the customer's mandate.

simple. Single, not complex, entire, mere.

simple arbitrage. *See* DIRECT ARBITRAGE.

simple contract. One evidenced in writing, or formed orally.

simple debenture. Debentures which are unsecured.

simple interest. Money paid on the principal borrowed, but not on the accrued interest as in compound interest.

Simplification of International Trade Procedures Board (SITPRO). This board was set up in 1970 with the object of rationalising international trade procedures and the standardisation of documents. It is funded by the British Overseas Trade Board, but the board membership consists of persons from shipping companies, freight forwarders, bankers, insurers, government officials, etc. It has produced a 'master' document which carries all the relevant information and with overlays and masks will produce any commercial document necessary for international trade. It is also interested in computerisation of documents and the marketing of its ideas to interested parties.

sine. Without.

sine die. Without a day being set, indefinitely.

sine qua non. An indispensable condition, an essential.

single costing. A system of quantifying cost where one commodity only is in question.

single entry. A method of book-keeping which does not conform to the double entry concept. Entries are only made into one account or book.

single premium policy. An insurance policy where one premium only, usually for a large sum, is payable at the time when the policy is taken out.

sinking fund. A sum of money set aside at the end of each financial period for the purpose of investing the money outside the business in order to pay off a debt due sometime in the future or replace an asset.

sixpence. The name of a coin no longer in circulation worth 2½p.

slander. The use of word or gesture used for the purposes of defamation. It may include attacking a person's title, false or malicious comment.

sleeping partner. See DORMANT PARTNER.

slump. A term used to describe a depression or recession. This would occur in a period of high unemployment, increased bankruptcies and company liquidations, a fall in consumer spending. Internationally it would have a knock-on effect, so that where a slump occurs in one major country, it would, by a process or balance-of-payment difficulties, restriction in trade, influence economic conditions in other countries.

small agreement. Under the Consumer Credit Act 1974, it is defined as an agreement for credit, not exceeding £30. This does not include a hire purchase or conditional sales agreement or a regulated consumer hire agreement for payments of less than £30.

small company. A small company is defined in the Companies Act 1985 as one that does not (*a*) have a turnover exceeding £1.4 million, (*b*) its balance sheet does not exceed £700 000, (*c*) its weekly average employees during the year does not exceed 50 persons. By conforming to these criteria for the current year and the preceding year, it may register modified accounts to the Registrar of Companies.

Small Estates Payout Procedure. See DEATH OF CUSTOMER.

small firms loan guarantee scheme. A government guaranteed loan scheme available to small businesses, i.e. firms with less than 200 employees, that need finance but because of lack of capital or inadequate security are unable to obtain finance from banks or other financial institutions. By providing a guarantee for each loan, any lending institution would then find the proposition more attractive. The borrowers can be sole traders, partnerships, co-operatives or limited companies who are already trading or intend to start trading in the near future. The trading activities that are acceptable include manufacturing, construction, wholesalers, retailers, service organisations. The groups that are not acceptable include banking and related services, estate agencies, insurance and related services, sporting and leisure organisations and travel and related services. The scheme provides loans between £15 001 and £100 000, but a smaller loans scheme is available for amounts from £1000 to £15000. The guarantee covers loans for periods from two years to seven years and the Department of Employment will guarantee up to 70 per cent of the outstanding balance. The loan may be drawn in one lump sum, or by four instalments over a period of two years, but this will not apply to the smaller loans amount. Repayment may be made by monthly or quarterly instalments and the bank's interest charges would be about 2.5 per cent above their base rate. Some security may be requested by a bank for that part of the loan that is not guaranteed by the Department of Employment. The Department will charge the borrower a commitment fee which is payable when the loan has been sanctioned. To ensure that the loan is properly monitored, the borrower will be required to provide the bank with regular funds flow statements, profit and loss accounts and any other financial returns that are considered necessary.

small investor. The individual or 'man in the street' who invests relatively small amounts of money in stocks and shares. The government with its policy of 'privatisation' has encouraged the ordinary person to obtain holdings of shares in companies. Generally speaking, the holding in any one company would average about £1500 to £2000. While the numbers of individual investors may be very large, the amount actually invested is comparatively small when compared with the major institutions.

Smithsonian agreement. In December 1971, a meeting of the Group of Ten (the world's leading central bankers) at Washington resulted in an agreed realignment of currency parities. The Smithsonian agreement widened the limits of permissible fluctuations of one currency against another. The US dollar was given the role of providing the 'middle rates' around which the system revolved. *See also* SNAKE IN THE TUNNEL.

snake in the tunnel. The exchange rate operated by the EC for those countries whose currencies that are linked to the ECU. The tunnel relates the maximum and minimum limits that a currency can have, while the snake represents the movement of the exchange rates above and below parity. Most countries have a margin of 2.25 per cent while the UK and Portugal have a margin of 6 per cent. *See also* EUROPEAN MONETARY SYSTEM; EUROPEAN CURRENCY UNIT.

social responsibility. While it is accepted that the major businesses in the country are motivated by profit, it is also recognised that because of their size and importance, they have a responsibility not only to their shareholders and employees, but to society at large. They are and must be conscious of possible pollution of the atmosphere and take steps to avoid such actions. They make donations to charitable organisations, make grants to social organisations and sponsor both local and national sporting activities. By these actions the large business will improve its public image.

society. A relationship that exists between persons to pursue some common activity, whether it is for social reasons, pleasure reasons. It may be a club or incorporated by law. The rules of the society will be its constitution which will permit it to have a bank account or accounts, but may or may not give it authority to borrow and use any assets as security. Should any unincorporated society wish to borrow funds then the constitution must be carefully studied and if necessary a joint and several guarantee must be taken from the officers or other members of the club which will make each person individually liable for the debt.

Society for Worldwide Interbank Financial Telecommunication (SWIFT). A co-operative society created under Belgian law and registered in Brussels. It is used by all major banks throughout the developed world and is linked with the domestic inter-banking networks in all participating countries. The aims of SWIFT are to enable members to transmit between themselves international payments, statements and other messages connected with international banking. The SWIFT system has enabled the money transmission services of banks – whether mail, cable or telex transfers – to be sent faster, more efficiently and safely. With the continuous improvement in computers and telecommunications, the system is continuously improving and expanding.

Society of Investment Analysts. A society formed by persons whose work is concerned with portfolio management and investment analysis. The members are usually employed in investment companies and fund management companies. An associate of the society obtains his/her diploma by examination or has received exemption from it.

soft arbitrage. Taking advantage of two different prices for the same commodity which is being traded in two different markets. An occasion when persons switch between borrowing from a bank and utilise those funds for money market investments.

soft currency. That currency of a country which is not necessarily acceptable in exchange for hard currencies as the rate of exchange and/or its convertibility is not good. For example, a trader would be reluctant to exchange Deutschemarks for the currency of Bolivia.

software. The program or the set of instructions for the computer which is readily available to the user or can be purchased by the user.

sola bill. A bill consisting of one document only, as contrasted with a bill in a set.

sole. Single, only, alone in its kind; unmarried.

sole proprietor. The owner of a one-man business.

sole trader. One who works in a wholesale or retail trade for himself or herself only.

solicitor. A person legally qualified to represent another in a court of law, a lawyer, a law agent; a legal practitioner authorised to advise clients and prepare cases for barristers, but not to appear as an advocate in the higher courts.

Solicitor-General. A law officer of the Crown, ranking in England below the Attorney-General and in Scotland below the Lord Advocate.

solicitors' accounts. Solicitors must maintain at least two bank accounts. The first is the office account which relates to income received, expenses of the practice, salaries and other expenses. The second is a client's account which must be operated in accordance with the rules laid down in the Solicitors' Accounts Rules 1975, the Solicitors' Trust Accounts Rules 1975. Any funds received by a solicitor on behalf of a client must be placed into a client's account which has been opened for this express purpose. From a banking point of view, the client's account must never be overdrawn. There is no right of set-off against the office account or any private account of the solicitor. Under normal circumstances when funds are transferred from the client's account to the office account, the bank is not put under any enquiry, but if any unusual circumstances occur, it may be necessary for the bank to make such enquiries for its own protection.

solicitor's undertaking. An undertaking signed by a solicitor that the documents, securities or deeds in his/her possession for inspection will be returned to the bank in the same state as they were received. An undertaking is also given where a customer has sold his house or property, the deeds, or certificate, are sent to the solicitor in exchange for his undertaking that on receipt of the proceeds of the sale, the funds will be remitted without delay to the bank. This is essential for a bridging advance, when the bank requires these funds in order to make available other funds for the purchase of the customer's new property. Should a bank not know the solicitor it is usual before having dealings with him/her, that a status enquiry is made which should be responded to in a favourable manner.

solicitor-trustee. A solicitor who is a sole trustee, or who is co-trustee only with a partner or employee.

solvency. The state of being able to pay all one's debts.

solvency ratio. *See* CAPITAL ADEQUACY.

SORP. *See* STATEMENT OF RECOMMENDED ACCOUNTING PRACTICE.

sorter/reader. A computer that can read the encoding on a document, e.g. a cheque, and sort these documents into a given order.

sorting. Arranging in numerical, date or alphabetical order or any logical arrangement of the data. This can refer to cheque sorting, filing of correspondence in customer files.

sorting code number. This is a number given to each office or branch of a bank or other financial institution that have been allocated a sorting code number. These code numbers are used for the purpose of clearing cheques, dividend and interest warrants, standing orders and direct debit mandates, giro credits. It is usual for each branch of a bank to have its own six-figure number. The first two numbers indicates the bank and the second and third group is the number of the branch. This number will appear in the top right-hand corner of a cheque and also in Magnetic Ink Character Recognition (MICR) characters at the foot of the cheque. All other documents will only have the code number at the bottom of the document in MICR symbols. A sorting code directory is issued annually.

sources and application of funds statement. A statement usually prepared when the final account and balance sheets of a company are produced. This statement would normally show how funds are received i.e. from profits, sale of assets, increased capital, etc. It will also show how these funds have been used, i.e. payment of dividends, purchase of fixed assets, repayment of loans, etc. The date on this statement is usually the same as that on the final accounts and balance sheet.

South Sea Bubble. The name given in the UK to an early example of widespread and reckless speculation. The South Sea Company was incorporated in 1710, and was given a monopoly of trade in the Pacific Ocean. The company was also engaged in various financial dealings at home: in particular the directors had worked out a scheme for taking over most of the National Debt from the government. Parliament was persuaded to agree to this, although there was strong opposition. The price of South Sea stock rose dramatically and people rushed to buy shares, recklessly investing all their life savings. When the share value reached ten times the nominal value people began to realise that the shares were not worth nearly as much as their quoted value, and confidence suddenly evaporated. There was a rush to sell and prices dropped catastrophically. Thousands of people were ruined.

sovereign. A gold coin that was worth £1. As the coin is made of gold so its value increased and it finally ceased to circulate in 1915. However, for collectors of coin, the sovereign is being minted from time to time and although its legal tender is £1 only, it is being bought and sold at a value nearer to the value of gold.

'sovereign lending'. Loans made by banks and banking syndicates to foreign governments. Banks have become very cautious in their 'sovereign lending' as in the past debts have had to be rescheduled or written off, and as a consequence large provisions have had to be made for bad debts.

sovereign risk. The risk that a foreign government will default on a loan. This may be due to economic difficulties, but could also be due to a change of government , or the restriction imposed by government in the release of funds to settle its international debts. *See* RESCHEDULING OF DEBTS.

special agent. One authorised to act only on a particular occasion or for a specific service, e.g. to bid at an auction on his or her principal's behalf.

special attorney. *See* POWER OF ATTORNEY.

special buyer. The Bank of England agent in the Discount Market.

special category company. For the purposes of the Companies Act 1985 s. 257, a special category company can be either a banking company, shipping company or an insurance company. A banking company is defined as a company recognised as a bank under the Banking Act 1987.

special clearance, special collection.

The accelerated clearance of a cheque for a customer, by posting the cheque direct to the branch on which it is drawn with a subsequent telephone call to ascertain its fate.

special crossing. *See* CROSSED CHEQUE.

special deposits. One of the techniques used by the Bank of England in the 1970s to control the lending abilities of banks and other financial institutions. The Bank of England requested all banks to deposit funds in a special account which could not be used for operational purposes and therefore could not be calculated as part of any reserve asset ratio. This method was eventually abandoned for open market operations and interest rates as a means of controlling credit.

special drawing rights. Often abbreviated as SDR. It is a type of international money – a unit of account of the International Monetary Fund. Its value is calculated against the US dollar, while contribution to IMF funds consists of a basket of currencies weighted according to the international trading importance of each contributing country. Drawing rights are available to all member countries and are used particularly as a type of bridging loan when a country has payment difficulties.

special indorsement. Bills of Exchange Act 1882 s. 34: 'a special indorsement specifies the person to whom, or to whose order the bill is payable'. A blank indorsement can be converted to a special indorsement by writing above the indorser's signature the person to whom the bill should be payable (e.g. Pay A. Baker or order Charles Deeks).

special manager. A qualified insolvency practitioner appointed by the court under s. 370, Insolvency Act 1986, to deal (a) with the bankrupt's estate; (b) the business of the undischarged bankrupt; (c) the property or business of a debtor in whose case the official receiver has been appointed interim receiver under s. 286.

special pleading. Unfair argument; bending the rules to suit one's case.

special resolution. A resolution at an annual general meeting or extraordinary general meeting which requires a majority of at least 75 per cent of those voting to vote in favour of the resolution. At least 21 days notice must be given of the meeting stating that the resolution was to be proposed at the meeting.

speciality contract. One executed under seal.

speciality debt. A debt which is acknowledged in a document under seal.

special verdict. A verdict stating the facts, but leaving the decision to be determined by the court.

specie. Gold and silver coins, and bullion.

specie points. In a situation where the currencies of two countries have a fixed relationship to the value of gold, and the rate of one of them moves above the mint par exchange rate, then together with the cost of insurance and transport, it becomes cheaper to import gold, if the rate falls below mint par value, less the cost of insurance and transport, then it becomes cheaper to export gold. These extreme points are the specie points.

specification. A commercial document which gives the details of work to be carried out, or a description of materials to be used by a builder, contractor. A document which specifies the range of goods, with the measurements, weights, etc. that are shown on the invoice.

specific performance. An equitable remedy ordered by the court, where a person is obliged to perform an obligation. It is granted where damages is not the most satisfactory solution.

specific reserve. A sum set aside out of profits to meet a future specific liability, e.g. to meet a tax liability. This amount is shown as part of the capital structure, but is not part of the issued capital.

speculation. A risk on the purchase of an asset that it will rise at some time in the near future and can be sold for a profit, or the sale of an asset on the assumption that its price will drop and it can be purchased at a lower price, hence make a profit. Such speculations will occur in the purchase/sale of foreign currency, purchase/sale of stocks and shares and on the options market. When these procedures are carried out by professionals they can

by various methods of hedging techniques limit the risk of loss. This is different risk than that taken by a gambler who risks his/her capital in a random manner.

spin-off. The restructuring of a holding company by divesting itself of a subsidiary either by a management buyout, or selling the entity to another company.

split capital trust. A method of dividing the equity capital of a trust company between income shares and capital shares. Holders of the income shares will receive dividends, if the trust is profitable, durings its life. Holders of capital shares will receive a proportion of the assets of the company on liquidation, after the holders of the income shares have been repaid their capital plus a specified increased valuation. If the company has traded profitably then the holders of the capital shares should receive an amount substantially greater than their original investment.

splitting. A method of making shares more marketable is by splitting the nominal value into smaller units. For example, if a share has a £1 value, it is possible with the order of the Court to double the amount of shares available by giving each share a nominal value of 50p. Each shareholder would have twice the number of shares, but at the same time the value of the shares would have halved on the Stock Exchange. Splitting can occur when a bonus issue or new issue takes place. The holder by completing the renunciation section on the reverse of the letter of acceptance, splits the issue between himself and another person.

sponsor. A person or company that makes himself or itself responsible for the carrying out of an event, by accepting the financial responsibility. Banks will sponsor sporting events, concerts, plays and other forms of entertainment. It assists in keeping the name of the bank in the eye of the public.

spot, spot price. Cash price for immediate delivery.

spot against forward. *See* SWAP.

spot check. An inspection carried out by the internal audit staff to check that procedural instructions have been complied with, stocks are in accordance with the records and accounts show a true and correct record. In banks there are inspectors that make spot checks on branches, to satisfy themselves that the branch is performing in accordance with instructions and that the record of cash held agrees with the books. Where a bank has a subsidiary which is responsible to a regulatory organisation under the Financial Services Act, then a compliance officer will from time to time ensure that there has been no breach of regulations and returns are made on time.

spot rate. The price paid for goods paid for and delivered immediately. In foreign exchange deals, customers pay or receive sterling on the day the deal is contracted. In the foreign exchange market settlement of any spot deal takes place in the overseas centre two working days later.

spread. The width or depth. In the foreign exchange market this will refer to the margin between the lowest selling price and the highest buying price of the day, or the closing prices for the day. In investment the policy for the small investor is to have as wide a portfolio as possible so as to minimise any possible risk or loss. The lending bank would always like to see a borrowing business have a wide range of debtors, so that the risk of bad debts is reduced. In Stock Exchange prices, the company is quoted in national newspapers showing the spread between the highest and lowest in the year, as well as the closing spread of prices for the day.

spreadsheet. A form or computer printout which shows the trading profit and loss accounts and balance sheet for a business at the end of a financial period. It not only shows the figures, but also various percentages and ratios, so that the figures can be analysed and comparisons made. Investment portfolios can also be spread between different types of investment, an analysis given and comparisons made.

square mile. The common name for the City of London or the financial centre of London.

squeeze. The tightening of interest rates and money becomes scarce or scarcer. Borrowing becomes expensive and in-

creased costs reflects in increased prices to consumers.

SRO. *See* SELF REGULATING ORGANISATION.

SSAPS. *See* STATEMENT OF ACCOUNTING PRACTICE.

stag. A speculator who will apply for a new issue of shares with the object of selling the shares at a profit as soon as dealing takes place on the Stock Exchange. It is now illegal to make more than one application for new shares. The name is also given to a person who purchases shares for the purpose of selling them as soon as a profit has been made. There is no intention of holding them as an investment.

stagflation. A word coined to express the co-existence over many years of high rates of unemployment and a high rate of inflation.

stale cheque. *See* ANTEDATED CHEQUE.

stamp duty. When certain contracts are to be performed, e.g. conveyancing, then an *ad valorem* stamp duty is imposed as a form of tax.

Standard & Poor's Corporation. Standard & Poor's Corporation, a subsidiary of McGraw-Hill Inc., is one of the world's leading rating agencies. S&P has offices in New York, San Francisco, London, Paris, Stockholm, Tokyo and Melbourne. It assigns debt ratings to a broad range of issuers located around the world. The ratings are based on an in depth financial analysis of each issuer and are assigned on different rating scales, depending on the maturity of the debt rated. Debt with a maturity of one year or greater is rated on a scale which has AAA as its highest rating, while debt of under one year is rated on a scale starting with A-1+. Once published, the ratings are in the public domain. They are disseminated via a variety of print and electronic products, which also contain analyses of individual issuers, industry sectors and market developments.

standard contract. Where the contract is of a type which is constantly occurring, a standard contract will emerge, which will have generally accepted terms which are normal and usual. Either or any of the parties to the contract may stipulate a variation to the standard form, but if they do not, they are bound by its terms.

standard costing. A costing technique in

which the total cost of the product is calculated which will include total of materials, labour and other items of expense. By using this method of costing management can assess the cost of the operation through the various stages. On completion of the product, a comparison is made between the actual cost and the standard cost. Any deviation will be investigated so that future production may be more efficient and the business more profitable.

standard liner waybill. This document is occasionally offered in place of a bill of lading. It is merely a receipt for the goods given to the shipping company. Unlike a bill of lading it is not transferable, nor is it a document of title. Frequently it merely staes that the goods have been received for shipment. Where goods have been received on board a vessel, then the waybill may state so. It can be compared with an air way bill.

standard security (*Sc. Law*). Since 1970 the 'standard security' is the only means whereby a security over heritable property can be created. It is a deed in a form laid down by the Conveyancing and Feudal Reform (Scotland) Act 1970, which had as one of its aims the simplification of the then existing land law, which in turn has led to a simplification for lenders taking security deeds. The deed is very short and simple, and refers to standard conditions which formerly had to be incorporated by the lender in the form of charge, but now are listed in Sch. 3 of the Act. It has thus been made possible for much repetitive matter to be eliminated.

standby letter of credit. A letter of credit, that is only used if certain events take place. It is a form of insurance that if payment is not made in the usual way to the seller/exporter, then a claim can be made under the standby letter or credit. For example, in many countries, banks are not permitted by law to issue guarantees, so that a customer may request a bank to issue a letter of credit in favour of a beneficiary, who may claim a stated sum either by presenting a simple claim – unconditional – or some form of documentation supporting the

claim – conditional. A standby letter of credit can also be used in open account trading. Should the buyer at any time default, then payment can be claimed under the credit, against the presentation of an invoice or some other documentary evidence. Where documentary collections are used on a regular basis, a buyer may as evidence of good faith, issue a credit in favour of the exporter, so that should a collection be unpaid or a bill of exchange be dishonoured, then payment may be made under the credit.

standing. Fixed, established, permanent.

standing credit. *See* CREDIT ADVICE.

standing order. An order by a customer to his banker to make a regular payment to a named payee to the debit of his account.

standing orders. The rules or constitution of any society or organisation, which lay down the procedure and conduct of meetings. Responsibilities of the officials and committees.

statement. A formal account, recital or narration; a declaration of fact or circumstance.

statement clerk. A statement clerk in a bank is frequently a junior clerk whose responsibility is either (*a*) to post the various debits and credits to the appropriate accounts, or, with computerised accountancy systems, he or she may have the responsibility (*b*) to verify the entries and vouchers before despatching a statement to a customer.

statement *in lieu* of prospectus. Where a company limited by shares does not issue a prospectus in order to obtain its capital it must send to the Registrar of Companies, a statement *in lieu* of the prospectus, signed by all the directors at least three days before the shares are allotted.

statement of account. A document sent to a customer or a client on which is entered the financial transactions between that customer/client and the business. It will also indicate the balance owed to or by the remitting entity. *See also* BANK STATEMENT.

statement of affairs. A statement presented to the Official Receiver by a debtor within three days of the receiving order if presented by the debtor himself or within seven days if presented by a creditor. This statement must show all the details of the assets, liabilities, plus the names and addresses of all creditors. In the case of a company, then this statement is prepared and presented to the administrator or liquidator so appointed.

Statement of Recommended Accounting Practice (SORP). The series of these statements issued jointly by the British Bankers' Association and the Irish Bankers' Federation are intended to supplement the Statements of Standard Accounting Practice (SSAPs). There is growing pressure, both domestically and internationally, for the accounts of banks to be more informative. The primary aim of the drawing up of SORP is to narrow the areas of difference and to enhance the value of the accounts to those that use them. While accounts of banks are prepared within the statutory framework laid down in the Companies Act, both in the United Kingdom and in the Republic of Ireland the legislation provides somewhat different rules for banks from those applying to the generality of companies. These rules will undergo substantial changes as a result of the implementation of the EC Bank Accounts Directive (86/635/EEC). The SORPs provide guidance on how the requirements of a SSAP can best be interpreted in the circumstances of a bank, but they cannot override those requirements. The international standard IAS 30 issued by the International Accounting Standards Committee on disclosures in the financial statements of banks and similar financial institutions is also relevant. The recommendations in the SORP are, of course, also subject to the overriding requirement that the account must present a true and fair view. Although they are intended to be authoritative and persuasive, it is recognised that it is not compulsory to disclose the fact or nature of any departure from recommended practice. For the moment the following statements or exposure drafts have been circulated: 1. Securities; 2. Off balance sheet instruments; 3. Advances; 4. Segmental reporting by banks. No doubt in time other publications will be issued.

Statement of Standard Accounting Practice (SSAP). A statement made by the accountancy bodies which proposes rules which should be followed when preparing final accounts. It is recommended that a 'true and fair view' of the business will not be presented unless the financial statements comply with the SSAP publications.

statistics. Numerical data which has been acquired by measurement, enquiry, observation and experiment then organised or arranged so that it may be interpreted to provide information.

status enquiry. A service given by banks to banks and authorised enquiry agents which has been initiated by a customer of one bank who wishes to know the financial status of a customer of another bank or branch. It is common practice that no bank will respond to a status enquiry from a non-bank or enquiry agency. In responding to status enquiries, banks must not break the code of confidentiality, therefore any response will, for example, not give specific descriptions or addresses of customers, nor will they seek information other than that held in their own records. Status enquiries tend to be in terms of 'Is Mr X good for £500 per month'? 'Is ABC Ltd good for £10 000'? etc. The reply will always carry a disclaimer clause and will be in general terms as follows: 'Good for your figures and purpose'. 'A properly constituted company, but the figures you quote are higher than we have seen, but they have always fulfilled the engagements they have undertaken'. When a customer opens an account, it is implied that the bank will respond to status enquiries, even though the customer may or may not be aware that this service exists. Status enquiries are made and given both domestically and internationally. *See also* CREDIT RATING.

Statute. An Act of Parliament.

statute-barred. A debt which cannot be recovered at law, because more than six years have elapsed since the cause of action arose. *See* LIMITATION OF ACTIONS.

Statute Book. The complete record of legal enactments.

Statute Law. The law which originates

in Acts passed by Parliament (also known as *Written Law*).

statutory books. The books that every limited company must keep in order to comply with the Companies Act. This includes a record of the minutes of meetings (Minutes Book). A register of shareholders. A register of directors. Records of all income and expenditure, assets and liabilities, purchases and sales.

statutory company. A company authorised by special Act of Parliament, e.g. a nationalised industry.

statutory declaration. A statement made to a solicitor, commissioner for oaths or in a court of law as to knowledge or fact that he/she possesses. Where it is proposed to wind up a company voluntarily, the directors must make a statutory declaration to the effect that they have made a full enquiry into the company's affairs and have formed the opinion that the company will be able to pay its debts in full together with interest, within such period not exceeding 12 months from commencement of the winding-up (Insolvency Act 1986 s. 89(1)). This declaration must be made within five weeks immediately preceding the date of the passing of the resolution for winding-up, or that date, but before the passing of the resolution and it must be delivered to the registrar of companies for registration before the expiry of fifteen days from the date on which the resolution was passed (s. 89(2)). Where a creditors' winding-up occurs, then a declaration in the prescribed form is given to the meeting of the creditors showing the assets, debts and liabilities, the names and addresses of all creditors and any securities held by any of them plus any other information required. In the Companies Act 1985 s. 156 dealing with the cases in which a private company may give financial assistance to any person so that he or she may acquire shares of the company, calls for a statutory declaration by the directors that describes the particulars of the assistance to be given and of the business of the company of which they are directors and to name the person to whom assistance is to be given, plus an assurance that the company will be able to pay its debts. The Companies

Act will also permit a company to purchase its own shares providing a statutory declaration is given specifying the amount of shares it wishes to buy and that there are no grounds that can be found for the company not to be able to pay its debts.

statutory deductions. The deductions made from a person's gross salary or wage. These deductions are: income tax and national insurance payments. Where necessary an attachment of earnings.

statutory legacy. The right of a surviving spouse of a person who died intestate to receive a sum as fixed by law from the estate of the deceased plus any personal chattels.

statutory meeting. Every company limited by shares or by guarantee and having a share capital shall hold a general meeting of the members of the company between one and three months from the date from the which the company is authorised to commence business. This is known as the statutory meeting.

statutory mortgage. As a special form of charge by way of legal morgage, a mortgage of freehold or leasehold land may be made by a deed expressed to be made by way of statutory mortgage, being in one of the forms set out in the Fourth Schedule to the Law of Property Act 1925, with such variations and additions as the circumstances may require.

statutory owner. A term used to describe a situation where no person can take the property as a life tenant or the land has been settled on a minor so the trustees take the legal fee simple in settled land.

statutory protection. For bankers this is particularly important with regard to conversion. The Bills of Exchange Act 1882 give a paying banker protection by s. 59, which covers a bill as being discharged by payment in due course on behalf of the drawee or acceptor, s. 60 protects the banker if he pays a cheque drawn on him having a forged indorsement or made without authority, providing it was paid in good faith and without negligence in the ordinary course of business, s. 80 protects a banker in paying a crossed cheque providing it was paid in good faith and without negligence and in accordance with the crossing. The Cheques Act 1957 s. 1 covers the lack of an indorsement or an irregular indorsement on cheques and similar instruments that the bank has paid in good faith and without negligence. The Stamp Act provides useful protection for the paying banker when paying 'any draft or order' which bears an unauthorised or forged indorsement. This is useful when paying bankers' drafts. The collecting banker has protection by virtue of s. 4, Cheques Act providing that in good faith and without negligence, (*a*) he receives payment for a customer, (*b*) or receives payment for himself. Then the banker is protected from any claim by the true owner. The banker also has protection for the absence of an indorsement on the instrument. In cases of insolvency, banks receive protection under the doctrine of subrogation, if money is lent for th purpose of paying wages to either sole traders, partnerships or companies. Under the Insolency Act s. 284(5) a bank is protected when it had debited the customer's account and was unaware that a bankruptcy order had been made. A banker also receives protection from the European Communities Act s. 9 and Companies Act 1985, where it is deemed that directors enter into a contract in good faith and that a party (banker) need not make any enquiry as to the capacity of the company or the directors.

statutory receipt. A receipt indorsed on a mortgage deed, when the mortgage has been satisfied, which acts as a reconveyance. The receipt must be indorsed on, written at the foot of, or annexed to, a mortgage for all money secured. It must state the name of the person who pays the money and must be executed by the chargee by way of legal mortgage.

statutory report. By the provisions of the Companies Act, a report must be sent by the directors of the company to all members at least fourteen days before the statutory meeting. This report must also be forwarded to the Registrar of Companies. The report must be signed by at least two directors and approved by the auditors. The report will contain: total number of shares issued, income and expenditure up to seven days prior to the report; names, addresses and description of the directors, auditors, managers and secretaries.

statutory restrictions on company loans. A company may not give any assistance either directly or indirectly to any person wishing to purchase shares in that company. This will include either the giving a loan, the provision of a guarantee to a third party giving the loan, or the provision of any other security. A company is not permitted to make loans to its officers or directors except when such funds are required for the purpose of carrying out duties for the company and approved at a general meeting. Loans may also be given if it is in the ordinary course of business of the company to give loans.

statutory trust for sale. *See* TRUST FOR SALE.

sterling area. *See* SCHEDULED TERRITORIES.

Sterling bonds. Bonds of a foreign country payable in British currency.

Sterling Certificate of Deposit. A certificate issued by a bank or other authorised institution, showing that a sum of money has been deposited with that bank or institution for a fixed period of time at a stated rate of interest. These certificates are issued for periods from one month to five years, exceptionally, a certificate may have a maturity of 7 days, with a minimum deposit of £50 000 per certificate, increasing in multiples of £10 000, with no maximum limit. Interest is paid at maturity of the certificate. The certificates are negotiable instruments and may be sold through the Secondary Market.

sterling M3. *See* MONEY SUPPLY.

sterling securities. Any securities on which dividends are payable, and capital repayable, in sterling.

steward. A person employed to manage the property or affairs of another, especially the paid manager of a large estate; one of the officials superintending the conduct of a public meeting.

stipend. Money paid for a person's services, an annual salary, the provision made for the support of a parish minister.

stipendiary magistrate. A paid magistrate.

stipulation. A definite arrangement, a contract, a specified condition.

stock. Capital, the money or goods invested in trade, manaufacture, banking, etc., the supply of goods a trader has on hand; government securities; a share or shares in a national, municipal or other debt; the capital of a company.

stock appreciation right. It is a right that allows a holder of a stock option to receive a cash payment from the company instead of exercising the option to receive shares or a combination of cash and shares.

stockbroker/jobber. With the 'Big Bang' the distinction between a jobber and a broker has disappeared. The stockbroker or stockbroking firm is still in evidence and will buy or sell stocks and shares on behalf of a client, but the role of the jobber is now in the hands of very large market makers who will act both in the capacity of a broker and a jobber. There are now broker/dealers and market makers.

stock/share certificate. A document issued by a company as evidence that the named person is the owner of the number of shares in that company. On sale of all or part of the shares held, the certificate must be surrendered and returned with the Talisman form to the stockbroker or the company that will amend the register of shareholders. *See also* TAURUS.

stock dividends. The payment of dividends by an additional amount of stock instead of cash. It is a means of allowing a company to retain or increase its cash liquidity, by not paying cash as dividends and at the same time give shareholders the opportunity of increasing their stake in the company without purchasing shares and paying the expenses so incurred. In order to do this, a company must have the proposal passed at its annual general meeting. Any payment of dividends by the issue of increased stock/shares is still subject to income tax.

Stock Exchange. A market situated in London for the purchase and sale of stocks and shares. All deals from the public must be passed through a firm of brokers who will act on their behalf.

The Stock Exchange will provide a daily list of all companies that have a full listing, those on the USM (Unlisted Securities Market) and the Third Market. The daily list will show the movement for the preceeding day.

Stock Exchange daily official list. A Stock Exchange daily publication which quotes all the movements of prices for those companies registered with the Stock Exchange. In addition to the daily publication, there is also a monthly publication which contains the prices of all listed securities. *See also* OFFICIAL LIST.

Stock Exchange indices. *See* FINANCIAL TIMES 30 SHARE INDEX; FINANCIAL TIMES STOCK EXCHANGE 100 INDEX.

stock-in-trade. The raw materials, work in progress and finished goods which are held by a trading organisation for the purpose of selling and making a profit. Such stock is usually valued at cost or realisable value whichever is the lower.

stockpiling. The accumulation of reserves of essential raw materials for an emergency.

stock receipt. A receipt given by the seller of inscribed stocks to the purchaser. It has no value, and is no evidence of title. All inscribed stocks have now been converted into registered stocks.

stock record. A record held by a stockkeeper for each item of stock showing at any given time the amount of stock held. It would also show the minimum and maximum quantities that should be held and the re-order point.

stock-taking. A regular procedure whereby all stocks, i.e. raw materials, work in progress and finished goods are counted and valued. This may be done at a regular date, i.e. at the end of the financial year or on a continuous basis.

stock transfer form. A form used when shares are sold or transferred by the shareholder. The form – now known as a Talisman form – is signed, completed with a description and number of the shares or amount of the stock sold and sent with the share or stock certificate to the broker. On occasions when shares or stock are transferred from one person to another, the form and the share/stock certificate is sent to the company registrar for registration. Where a banker forwards the form with the share certificate it is deemed to have confirmed that the signature of the signatory is genuine. *See* TALISMAN.

stop. To bring to a halt, to obstruct, to check, to suspend.

stop loss order. To limit an eventual loss, an order to sell stock at the best rate obtainable when the price attains or exceeds a given level.

stop order. An instruction from a customer not to pay a cheque that he/she has drawn and issued. A bank would take such instructions by telephone, but would insist that such instructions should be confirmed in writing. The bank would wish to know the following details: the name of the payee; the amount of the cheque; date on the cheque; the cheque number; it would also be useful to the bank to know if a duplicate was going to be issued, so that there should be no confusion. On receipt of an order to countermand payment, a bank official will check that the cheque had not yet been presented and paid. All cashiers will be notified, in case it is presented over the counter, a record is put on the customer's file, so that should it be presented, the computer will reject it. In the event of the payee advising the bank that the cheque has been lost or stolen, then on presentation it will be returned unpaid, but the drawer must expressly request the non-payment of the cheque.

stoppage *in transitu.* The right of the unpaid seller to stop the delivery of the goods to the buyer, while the goods are still in transit. This is only likely to happen if the seller discovers that the buyer has financial difficulties or has become bankrupt.

stopped account. *See* CLAYTON'S CASE.

stopped cheque. A cheque that has been returned unpaid with the answer 'payment countermanded by order of the drawer' or 'payment stopped by order of the drawer'.

storage. A charge for warehousing goods; the space occupied by them.

straddle. On the Stock Exchange, a contract in which a buyer of stock has the privilege of calling for or delivering it, at a pre-determined price. *See also* MARGINAL RISK.

straight. Passing from one point to another by the most direct route; direct, honest.

straight bill of lading. One purporting to consign goods to a specified person.

straight bonds. Bonds having no right or option of conversion into any other form of shares, stock or bonds.

straight debt. A security without rights of conversion into a borrower's common stock.

'straight' deposit. A deposit accepted by a bank without the issue of a Sterling Certificate of Deposit.

straight line method of depreciation. A method of depreciation whereby the annual depreciation is calculated by ascertaining the life of the asset, then deducting the approximate scrap value from the cost and dividing this amount by the number of years in the life of an asset. This amount is either deducted from the asset account or placed to a provision for depreciation account. For example if an asset is purchased for £1100 it is estimated that it has a life of ten years and the scrap value will be £100. Therefore each year for ten years a depcreciation of £100 will be made each year.

striking price. The price at which an option is to be exercised.

sub. Under, below, inferior.

sub-agent. One under the orders of an agent, a deputy agent, an agent's representative.

sub-branch. An office of a bank, that has no national code number of its own, no manager within the office, not necessarily any permanent staff of its own. It is an office that is totally reliant on an independent branch, for all its activities, such as staff, cash in tills, accountancy transactions, lending decisions, etc. A sub-branch is often only open on certain days of the week or just a few hours each day. Many sub-branches are on college campuses and only open during term times to provide deposit and withdraal services. Any other service is usually provided from the main branch. Should the business grow then it is possible for it to have a permanent clerk in charge and perhaps eventually become a full branch.

subject to contract. A phrase used to

prevent a contract to be conclusive. It is used in land, so that until all the formalities have been completed there is no contract. A contract on which action may be taken is when both parties, through their respective solicitors have agreed on the terms and conditions of the contract, signed and exchanged the contract.

subject to survey. Used in the sale of land and property. The contract does not become binding until a survey has been carried out and is satisfactory to the purchaser.

sub judice. Under legal consideration.

sub-lease. A lease that has emerged from another lease. The tenant has assigned all his lease or part of the lease to a third party. Where a banker advances funds for the purchase of a sub-lease, then the deposit of the sub-lease as security should be attached to a certified copy of the head lease.

sub-mortgage. A mortgage of a mortgage. The original lender borrows money against the security of his mortgagor's mortgage. The original mortgagee becomes the sub-mortgagor and the bank (the lender) becomes the sub-mortgagee. The original mortgage becomes the 'head mortgage'. Where the land is registered and a legal mortgage has been registered, then the charge must be sent with the charge certificate to the District Land Registry who will issue a sub-charge certificate. Where the land is unregistered and a first legal charge has been created and the bank has agreed to give a sub-mortgage it will send the District Land Registry the charge certificate, he signed and sealed form of sub-mortgage, with an office copy. The registrar will keep the charge certificate and copy form of the sub-mortgage and issue a certificate of sub-charge containing a reference to the head mortgage.

subordinated loan. In the case of the liquidation of a company, this loan ranks behind all other creditors, but in front of those of the ordinary shareholders. Such a loan may be a bank loan or a loan given by the directors. Such loans are arranged when a business is in its infancy and is intended to reassure the trade and other creditors, so that there is no liquidity problem and credit terms are available.

subpoena. A writ commanding a person's attendance in a court of law under a penalty; to serve with such a writ.

subrogation. The substitution of one person for another, with succession to rights and claims; the standing in the shoes of another.

subscribed capital. That part of the authorised capital which has been issued and taken up.

subscriber. A peron or entity who has agreed – usually in writing – to purchase a stated number of shares in a named company at a stated price.

subscription shares. Shares in a building society, where an investor is allowed to purchase shares by instalments in return for an undertaking to subscribe a fixed sum regularly.

subsidiary account. An account in a ledger keeping a record of transactions of a particular type and the totals of this account are transferred at regular intervals to a more detailed acount.

subisidiary company. A company that is controlled by another company. It may be that the holding company has a - majority of shares and/or has control by having its own directors on its board.

subsidy. Financial aid, a government grant for some purpose such as keeping the cost of living down.

substantial damages. Damages awarded to compensate for actual loss, whether large or small.

sub-total. A sum total of figures which is only part of the numbers to be totalled. To add up part of the sum.

sub-underwriter. An issuing house which is to under-write the whole of a new issue may share out the liability among a number of sub-underwriters, each taking a fraction of the liability.

subvention. *See* SUBSIDY.

sue. To seek justice by taking legal proceedings; to prosecute, to make application, to petition.

suicide. The taking of one's own life. Until 1961 this was a criminal offence and since no criminal can benefit from his/her crime, an insurance policy was void. It is a crime to aid and abet a person to take his/her own life. Any benefit to be paid out due to a suicide in an insurance policy will depend on the terms of that policy.

summary administration. In the case of

a debtor who presents a petition to the court on the grounds of being unable to pay debts, the court, if it thinks fit, may not make a bankruptcy order if the value of debts is small, or if assets are equal to liabilities. However, where the court makes a bankruptcy order, it will issue a certificate for the summary administration of the bankrupt's estate. The appointment of an insolvency practitioner will, as required under s. 273, Insolvency Act, inquire into the affairs of the person and report to the court within the period specified.

summary diligence (*Sc. Law*). A form of diligence available to holders of bonds, bills of exchange, promissory notes and certain other documents, which contain a special clause called 'Consent to registration for preservation and execution'. In these cases the creditor can proceed to use any of the normal forms of diligence without prior application to the court. Bills of exchange have to be dishonoured by non-acceptance or non-payment and must then be protested (*See* PROTEST). The protest is then registered in the books of the Sheriff Court of the county in which the debtor is domiciled. A copy of this registration is extracted for the benefit of the creditor, who can then proceed to the arrest of poinding (*q.v.*) of the debtor's effects. *See* DILIGENCE.

summons. The act of summoning; an authoritative call or citation, especially to appear before a court or a judge.

sum payable. Bills of Exchange Act 1882 s. 9: 'The sum payable by a bill is a sum certain within the meaning of the Act although it is required to be paid (*a*) with interest, (*b*) by stated instalments, (*c*) by stated instalments, with a provision that upon default in payment of any instalment the whole shall become due, (*d*) according to an indicated rate of exchange, or according to a rate of exchange to be ascertained as directed by the bill'.

sumptuary. The regulation of expenditure, one appointed to be responsible for expenditure.

sundry creditors. The various persons and businesses to whom the person or entity owes a debt. The total of all debts due and payable within the following year, would be shown as a liability in the balance sheet under the heading of sundry creditors or merely creditors. The term is used in day-to-day banking by putting an isolated transaction to this account when there is no specific account to which the entry may be put.

sundry debtors. The various persons and businesses that owe money to a person or entity. The total of all these balances are shown as a current asset in the balance sheet, either under the heading sundry debtors or merely debtors. The term is used in day-to-day banking by putting an isolated transaction to this account when there is no specific account to which the entry may be put.

sunset law. *See* ZERO BUDGETING.

superannuation. The payment of a pension to an employee who has been forced to retire due to age, ill health or he/she has been compulsorarily retired due to the fact that his/her services are no longer required.

superannuation payment. A regular contribution to either a pension fund either by a regular payment to an insurance company or by a deduction from a wage or salary, towards that person's pension.

supervision of banks. The failure of the fringe banks in the UK and the resulting rescue operation by the Bank of England and the clearing banks, which came to be known as the 'Lifeboat', raised from 1972 onwards the question of a stricter supervision of banks in a much more acute form. It was thought that the Bank of England, not the Department of Trade, should regulate and supervise the banking system. There was also the question of bringing the UK into line with the system in the other countries of the EEC, who have suggested that banks should be defined by law, licensed, and ought to be made to secure official approval for management and for existing and future plans. A White Paper published in August 1976 described the institutional framework proposed and this was followed by the Banking Act 1979, which divided deposit-taking institutions into two groups which are licensed deposit takers and recognised banks. Although the system worked well, proposals set out in a government White Paper in December 1985, took into account the modifications needed to improve the banking supervision in the treatment of off balance sheet risks, international supervision and the need for regular dialogue with the Bank. The Banking Act 1987 became law on 15 May 1987 and replaces the 1979 Act. The supervision of banks is carried out by a Board of Banking Supervision which meets monthly and consists of the Governor, the Deputy Governor, the Executive Director responsible for banking supervision and six other members. The main objectives of the Act are: 1. to restrict the taking of deposits to those institutions that are authorised by the Bank to take deposits (it abolished the two tier system); 2. to prohibit unauthorised institutions from using a name which indicates that they are banks; 3. to continue the Depositors' Protection Fund as a statutory body; 4. to increase the information that a bank must give to the Bank of England; 5. to regulate those who control the authorised institutions; and 6. to control advertisements inviting the public to make deposits. The Act lays down four criteria for the authorisation of an institution: 1. every director, controller and manager must be a fit and proper person to hold the position; 2. the business must be conducted in a prudent manner – this covers, *inter alia*, adequate capital, liquidity, provisions for bad debts, accounting and other records and internal controls; 3. the business must be carried on with integrity and appropriate professional skills; 4. the minimum paid up capital and reserves must be £1 million (£5 million if called a 'bank'). The Bank must be notified of changes in directors, controllers and managers. Any person who can be classified as a significant shareholder i.e. holding between five and 15 per cent of the voting rights, must notify the Bank. Any person who is proposing to hold more than 15 per cent of the voting rights of an authorised insitution must give advanced notice to the Bank. Failure to do so is a criminal offence. It is also considered a criminal offence if an institution provides false or misleading information to the

Board of Banking Supervision. No institution is permitted to withhold information and, in any case, the Bank has powers under the Act to obtain such information/documents. While information provided is treated as confidential, the Bank may, if necessary, convey such information as it considers necessary to other regulatory bodies and government departments. Any changes in auditors must be notified to the Bank and should any bank auditor wish to qualify the accounts of an institution, it must give notice to the Bank of its intention. Additionally, the Bank may ask auditors to disclose information obtained during the course of an audit, providing that this information is necessary to the Bank for supervision. The Depositors' Protection Scheme now covers 75 per cent of the first £20 000 of sterling deposits. *See* BANKING ACT.

supervisor. A person who has some responsibility in an office, department, factory or site which may be for materials, work procedures or personnel. He/she would be answerable to a manager for his/her area or operations or job specification. In a bank it would be a person who would be responsible for a section of work, e.g. cashiers, accounts, etc., to ensure that the flow of work is in accordance with bank procedures and that each person within the group or section is able to cope with the day-to-day pressures.

supplement. Something added to fill up or supply a deficiency; an appendix, an extra charge.

supplemental instrument. A document that contains additional instructions, provisions and information to the document referred to or attached to. It may be in the form of an alonge, codicil to a will or merely an additional document.

supplementary costs. Those costs of production which are fixed and do not vary with the output, including short-term administrative costs, as opposed to prime costs.

supplementary special deposit. *See* CORSET.

supplier credit. An arrangement whereby an exporter supplies goods to an overseas customer against a cash sum of up to 20 per cent of the contract price, with promissory notes or sterling bills of exchange payable over a period, which are guaranteed by the Export Credits Guarantee Department for the balance. The exporter then sells the instruments without recourse to his or her bank, the latter obtaining a separate guarantee from ECGD. This arrangement is generally found in the case of contracts up to £2 million, the credit period being restricted to five years.

supply. A sufficiency of things required, necessary stores; the amount of a product or commodity which will come on the market.

supply and demand. A phrase used to express the relation between consumption and production; if demand exceeds the supply and prise rises, and *vice versa*.

support. To give aid or assistance to some one or something. A bank will support a customer by offering a wider range of services or by lending money. A country may give support to a weaker country by the provision of expertise, capital equipment, food, loans and lines of credit. A central bank will, where it considers that its currency has been weakened by speculation and other causes, seek to support it and ask other central banks to give it assistance.

support group. *See* LIFEBOAT COMMITTEE.

supra protest. Where a bill of exchange has been dishonoured by non-acceptance it may be accepted for honour, provided it has been protested. This is called an acceptance *supra* protest. Bills of Exchange Act 1882 s. 65(1). 'Where a bill of exchange has been protested for dishonour by non-acceptance, or protested for better security, and is not overdue, any person, not being a party already liable thereon, may, with the consent of the holder, intervene and accept the bill *supra* protest, for the honour of any person liable thereon, or for the honour of the person for whose account the bill is drawn'.

suppression of documents. It is an offence for a person to deliberately or dishonestly to destroy, conceal, deface or destroy any document which can be used, filed or deposited in a court of law or with a government department.

surcharge. An additional charge made due to additional work, weight, load or some other factor.

surety. A person providing some collateral or security. Under the Consumer Credit Act 1974 s. 189(1) this will include any person who has provided security, whether direct or collateral, or an indemnity for the performance of an obligation.

surety bond. An undertaking in writing by a bank or other financial institution that it will pay to the named person a stipulated sum of money if certain conditions are not fulfilled. This bond is to assure the buyer or importer that should the supplier or constructor fail to fulfil the contract then they will suffer no financial loss. *See also* PERFORMANCE BOND; TENDER BOND/GUARANTEE.

surplus. The residue. An amount in excess. When income is in excess of expenditure, the remainder is a surplus. An amount left after all expenses and liabilities have been paid.

surrender. To yield or hand over to the power of another, to deliver up possession of anything upon compulsion, to resign; to appear in court in discharge of bail; the giving up of a lease before the end of its term by a lessee to a lessor by mutual consent.

surrender value. The value of the payment that will be made by an insurance company should the insured or the person/bank to whom the policy has been assigned wish to surrender the policy. Banks will, when taking a life policy ascertain the surrender in order to have an acceptable form of security for a loan given to a customer. Normally a life policy has little or no value for the first three years. The lending bank will make an annual check on the surrender value of the policy.

surviving partner. The survivor in a partnership or the survivor of a joint account. That peron is entitled to the balance of the accounts held in a bank account. On notification of the death, bankruptcy or retirement of a person, a bank will stop the account, so that it will retain a claim on the assets of the retiring or deceased partner's estate.

survivorship. *See* JOINT ACCOUNT.

survivorship policy. A life assurance policy which is payable on the death of the last survivor of joint policy owners.

suspense account. An account where funds are deposited or entries made on a temporary basis until information has been received for the proper identification of the transaction and an entry made in the proper account. Where a bank has a difference in its books, a suspense account may be debited or credited until the error has been revealed or the error has been written off.

suspension of payments. The notification to creditors that a debtor is unable to pay his/her debts. A company may suspend payments by passing a resolution that it will cease trading and will wind-up. An individual may summon a meeting of his/her creditors that he/she is unable to pay the debts, which could lead to bankruptcy or to a voluntary arrangement or the administration of the debtor's affairs.

swap. The exchange of one thing for another. In the foreign exchange market it refers to the purchase/sale in the spot market for a simultaneous purchase/sale in the forward foreign exchange market. These transactions may be performed by central banks, commercial banks or by major international companies.

sweetner. Something extra given to a holder of shares or stock to make it more attractive to sell or buy, e.g. on the issue of a preference share or debenture, it may at maturity have converibility at the holder's option. To induce shareholders to sell their holdings, a predator may offer a price greater than that offered in the open market.

SWIFT. *See* SOCIETY FOR WORLDWIDE INTERBANK FINANCIAL TELECOMMUNICATION.

swing. The movement from one extreme to another. In banking this will refer to the movement of an account from a credit balance to a debit balance in any given period. The fact that a customer has an authority to overdraw the account and that it swings from credit to debit and back again indicates that it is active and trading well, providing there are signs that

there is a gradual reduction of the overdraft. It is only when the swing narrows, the account is less active and the overdrawn balance tends to 'stick', then a banker should take notice and take whatever action is considered necessary.

switching. Changing from one form of investment to another, or from one foreign currency to another, according to the requirements of the time; raising money by issuing certificates of deposit and then on-lending these funds to borrowers on fixed deposits in order to make a turn.

SWOT. Strengths, Weaknesses, Opportunities, Threats. It is a mnemonic word in the consideration of a project or plan that is likely to affect entity.

symbolic delivery. The transfer of ownership of goods by means of delivery of the documents of title (e.g. bills of lading, warehousekeeper's warrant, etc.).

syndic. A legal representative chosen to act as agent for a corporation or company.

syndicate. A group of persons or companies participating in an enterprise or project or joint venture. The objects of the syndicate may be to lend, purchase goods, construct or manufacture.

syndicated loan. A loan arranged by a bank (lead manager) for a borrower who is likely to be a large company, a local authority, government department. The participants are likely to be other banks willing to lend an amount suitable to their own lending policies and in conformity with the directives laid down by the central bank or government. *See also* LEAD MANAGER.

synergy. An occasion when a whole has greater power or value than the sum of its parts. Synergy is frequently the *raison d'être* for the formation of groups of companies by take overs and mergers.

systems analysis. An investigation or enquiry into the efficacy of a procedure or system, to recommend a method or methods to improve standards, procedures to reduce costs or whatever is the terms of reference of the enquiry. *See* OPERATIONAL RESEARCH.

T

TA. *See* TRADING AS.

Table A. A model of Articles of Association which companies may adopt in whole or in part. Each Companies Act since 1862 has had a Table A Schedule, which has been altered on each major enactment. However, companies may if they so desire, write their own articles of association. Companies formed after 1 July 1985 are able to use the regulations as prescribed by the Secretary of State. These may be found in Statutory Regulation 1985 No. 805.

T account. The letter 'T' is used for the rough accountancy entries, at the top of which the name of the account may be put, and on the left-hand side of the perpendicular line the debit entry is put and on the right-hand side the credit entry. This accountancy form is used particularly by students studying accountancy, and illustrates the double entry system of book-keeping.

tacking. Tacking, except by a first mortgagee, was abolished in 1925, but by the terms of the mortgage deed, a first mortgagee can still tack if he/she is obliged to make further advances. Tacking is the right to priority over any subsequent or intermediate mortgage.

take a position. The purchase of shares in a company for the purpose of influencing the conduct of that company, or building up a holding for the possible eventual takeover. Where a holding is of 5 per cent or more, the information must be made known to the Stock Exchange, should the holding reach 29.9 per cent then the Department of Trade should be notified.

takeover bid. An offer made to directors and shareholders of a company by an offeror company to purchase the shares of an offeree company by offering in exchange its own shares, its own shares and cash or a cash offer, cash and shares. Where prior knowledge of a takeover is known, and advantage of this fact is taken, then it is possible that an offence under the Companies Securities (Insider Dealing) Act 1985 may occur.

tally. To keep a reckoning of facts, dates, figures. To keep a score, to keep a record either by labelling or tagging. It is or was a means of keeping an account by scoring notches in a stick. To agree by comparison or identification.

tallyroll. A roll of paper attached to the back or inside of a machine on which is printed itemised accounts, data, figures. This will show a continuous record of entries, but the paper may be torn off at regular intervals for filing or transfer to other persons.

talisman. *See under* TRANSFER.

tally man. The door-to-door salesman who provides occasional clothing, small items of furniture, brooms, brushes, etc., to householders who need the goods but cannot pay immediately. He/she is willing to give credit and will call each week or every two weeks to collect the instalment and possibly make additional sales. Person employed to check the discharge of cargo against the ship's manifest or list.

tally trade. The house-to-house selling of goods on a credit basis.

talon. A slip issued along with the coupons attached to a bearer bond, to be used when further coupons are required.

tangible assets. Property or physical assets belonging to a person, firm or company. Often this may refer to fixed assets as opposed to current assets. In contrast, intangible assets include goodwill, preliminary expenses not written off, patent and trade marks.

tap stock. A system of selling government stock by the Bank of England. This stock is constantly available for sale to the public at large. The Bank of England when it issues such stock will make it available to the investing public, who may or may not buy all the stock on issue. The stock not purchased will be taken up by the Bank of England itself then sold through the Stock Exchange as and when the demand arises. Hence the 'tap' may be turned on or off to ensure that the stock is sold in an orderly manner. *See* LONG TAP; SHORT TAP.

tare. The difference between the gross weight and the net weight of goods. The allowance made for the packaging, wrapping and/or boxing of the goods. When duty or tax is payable on goods, the packaging, etc. may not be included.

tare weight. The weight of an aircraft minus crew and cargo.

target. A mark to aim at; a maximum sum of money aimed at in public subscription, e.g. 'savings target'; the minimum consumption of fuel aimed at in an economy drive, e.g. 'fuel target'.

target company. A company that is the target of a group of individuals or a group of companies acting together to take over a particular company. Where such an activity occurs and the parties acquire sufficient shares to ensure an influence or control, the target company must be notified.

target population. A phrase used to describe a group of people on whom some area of research is going to be undertaken. A group of people to whom some information is going to be conveyed.

tariff. A list of imported and exported goods on which duty is payable.

tariff company. An insurance company having a standard range of premiums.

TAURUS. *See* TRANSFER AND AUTOMATED REGISTRATION OF UNCERTIFICATED STOCK.

tax. A compulsory levy on individuals and companies by the state to meet the expenses of the government. A tax can be direct, e.g. income tax or can be indirect, e.g. Value Added Tax. A local tax is also imposed to meet the cost of local government, the amount payable is based on the valuation of the residential or business property.

taxable income. The income that is left after the deduction of Income Tax from the total income. The amount deducted will depend on the amount of the earned and unearned income and the allowances given.

tax avoidance. The arrangement of the affairs of the person or the company, so that the tax liability is as low as possible within the law.

tax credit scheme. *See* NEGATIVE INCOME TAX.

tax evasion. Where a person or company fails to make a true declaration of income, the payment of the proper tax has been evaded and is therefore illegal.

tax exile. A person who has deliberately chosen to live abroad because his/her tax liability in the foreign country is lower than the UK.

Tax Exempt Special Savings Account (TESSA). This method of savings was introduced in the 1990 budget and became operational in January 1991. Any individual over the age of 18 years, is now able to open this type of account in a bank or building society. The account has an initial life of five years. During these years a total of £9000 may be invested with maximum yearly deposits of £3000 in the first year, in the second, third and fourth year £1800 in each year and only £600 in the fifth year. Interest is paid either quarterly, half-yearly or yearly, depending on the institution, but the interest credited is paid gross and not liable for tax. There is likely to be a penalty for withdrawal of these funds before the account matures.

tax free. Any income received free of tax is regarded by the Inland Revenue as such a sum which, taxed at the basic rate, will leave the amount actually received. The recipient of the sum will also obtain from the payer a certificate in respect of the tax deducted to be submitted with his or her annual return to the Tax Inspector.

tax haven. A place abroad where persons will deposit or invest their funds, or register companies in that place because the tax levy is much lighter than in the UK.

tax liability. The amount that is owed to the Inland Revenue and arises when the amount of profit or income has been agreed. The liability is eliminated when payment has been made.

taxman. The common name for the Inland Revenue.

tax planning. To prepare the financial operations of a business so as to take advantage of any tax concessions and minimise the total tax liability in a legal way.

tax return. A legal obligation on all persons to make an annual return to the Inland Revenue, stating all taxable earned and unearned income, capital gains and any tax allowances that the individual is permitted. Often customers of banks that have complex returns, or for any reason are unable to perform this function themselves, will request the bank's tax department to act on their behalf and regularly submit the annual tax return.

tax-sheltered account. Any account on which the interest is tax-free.

tax tables. Books which are issued by the Inland Revenue to every employer in order to operate the Pay As You Earn method of collecting income tax. By referring to the employee's tax coding number and the cumulative pay to date, it is possible from the book to check how much tax is due to date, the difference is the amount that should be deducted from the gross salary/wage.

tax year. Often called the 'fiscal year'. It commences on 6 April of one year and ends on 5 April the next year. It is over this period that the amount of tax an individual is likely to pay is calculated.

Technical Development Capital, Ltd. (TDC). See VENTURE CAPITAL.

teeming and lading. A fraudulent method of converting the money paid to a bank or creditor to a dishonest employee. Basically, money received from a customer/debtor will be misappropriated by an employee, but before a statement is sent out to that person, funds, misappropriated from another customer, are placed on the first customer's account. As this is a progressive activity, the danger multiplies. The accounts of customers and the handling of cash or cheques, should be maintained by different persons.

telegraphic transfer. A method of transmission of funds by cable, telex or fax. The remitting bank will send an authenticated message to its branch or correspondent abroad, to pay against identification, credit the beneficiary's account or advise and pay the beneficiary. Funds may be either in the remitting bank's currency, the receiving bank's currency or any acceptable international currency. *See also* SOCIETY FOR WORLDWIDE INTERBANK FINANCIAL COMMUNICATIONS; TRANSMISSION OF FUNDS.

teletext. A service offered particularly by the broadcasting authorities which can provide information on either a VDU or a television screen.

telex. A method of remitting a message by a teleprinter which is received almost at the same time as it is being despatched. To a large extent this method of transmission has been overtaken by FAX.

teller. The US name for a cashier, but it is in common use in the UK also for a cashier either at a bank or elsewhere. The name is also used to describe the means of obtaining funds from a machine known as an ATM (Automated Teller Machine). A teller is the officer at an election who is responsible for counting the votes cast. It is also the person in the House of Commons who counts the votes on a division.

teller terminal. See AUTOMATED TELLER MACHINE.

tel quel rate. A rate of exchange that is used for the purchase of a currency bill payable at a foreign centre. The interest that is earned is not taken into account when calculating the rate of exchange.

temporary annuity. An annual payment for a fixed number of years, starting immediately.

tenancy at will. Where a tenant occupies land that is owned by another, with the landlord's consent, and either the tenant or the landlord may terminate the tenancy at any time. While this is rarely created, it arises when someone is given possession of premises for an indefinite period without any reason given. In such cases there is a presumption that he/she is as tenant at will, but the position is basically dependent upon the true intention of the parties.

tenancy in common. A situation where two or more persons have equal shares in the property in which they are all tenants. Should one die, then his/her share passes to the personal representative and not to the surviving tenants. This can occur in the case of a partnership or under the terms of a will where the children are left the land/property equally. *See* JOINT TENANCY.

tenant. A person or entity that has legal possession of an estate. Rent is payable for the property or land occupied.

tenant at sufferance. A person who was a legal tenant of land, but wrongly continues to occupy such land after the agreement has been terminated.

tenant-farmer. One who occupies a farm on payment of rent to a landlord.

tenant for life. Settled Land Act 1925. The person of full age who is for the time being beneficially entitled under a settlement to possession of the land for his/her lifetime. If two or more persons are jointly entitled to possession they both consitute the tenant for life.

tenant right. The legal right of a tenant to occupy property on regular payment of reasonable rent and to receive compensation if the contract is broken by the landlord; any right of the tenant of property, whether expressly stated or implied, such as a right to remove fixtures at the end of the tenancy, or to receive an allowance for seeds or fertiliser put on the land.

tender. To offer for sale. To offer a sum of money. To give a quotation or an estimate. The formal bid for Treasury Bills. The purchase of securities by means of a tender. The offeror will issue a prospectus offering share/stock at a minimum price which he/she is prepared to accept, but will accept tenders from applicants. The highest bidder will succeed. *See also* LEGAL TENDER.

tender bills. *See* TREASURY BILLS.

tender bond/guarantee. When a company submits a tender for an overseas job, the buyer will probably wish to have some guarantee that having awarded the tender, the company will proceed with the work and not change its mind at a later date. The buyer will therefore request that a tender bond will accompany the tender to cover this risk. The tender bond is for about 5 per cent of the contract and is issued by a bank, who will if necessary, request from its customer either a

counter indemnity, cash cover or some other form of security. Also known as a bid bond.

tenement. A large residential property occupied by separate families or individuals (tenants) in separate flats.

tenor. The substance of a document. For bills of exchange this will apply to the content of the bill which includes the length of time to maturity.

tenure. The right and security in holding an office, occupation or property. The conditions and period of holding.

term. A time limit or period for a court sitting, a school or college period. Part of a year. A period of time for the occupation of an estate. A boundary or limitation.

term bill. A bill of exchange payable at some fixed or determinable future time. The term of a bill will be at 'X' days after sight or 'Y' days after date.

term (acceptance) credit. A beneficiary named in an acceptance credit will be able to draw a bill of exchange on the named bank or acceptance house which will either be paid or accepted in the accompanying documents to comply with the terms and conditions of the credit. Once the bill of exchange has been accepted, the beneficiary may, if necessary, discount the bill in the money market.

term days. The days on which the rent falls due.

term deposits. The deposit of funds, usually attracting a slightly higher rate of interest, for a fixed period of time. The capital and interest is repayable at an agreed date. Any early withdrawals would be subject to a penalty.

terminable annuity. An annuity which will stop on a fixed date, or after a certain time, or on the beneficiary's death.

terminal. A machine or device in an office/bank linked to a computer whereby input data is transmitted, output data is received for the various operations of the bank or business.

terminal bonus. A bonus paid when a life assurance policy matures. It is usually in addition to any other bonus stated in the policy.

term loan. A loan given to a borrower for a specific period.

term of a bill. The period of time for which a bill of exchange is drawn.

term of years absolute. A term or lease that is intended to last for a fixed period of time, although there may be conditions whereby the term or lease will expire before that date, e.g. by reentry, operation of the law, etc. Commonly known as a 'leasehold'.

termor. One who has an estate for a term of years, or for life.

term policy. A policy of life assurance which assures a person's life over a certain period. Thus anyone wishing to cover the risk of loss of life through an aircraft crash when about to fly on holiday would take out a term policy for a few weeks. Term policies can, however, last for thirty years or more – all depends on the length of time stipulated by the policyholder. If the policyholder dies during the term his or her heirs get the benefit. If the policyholder survives the term there is no benefit. These are purely protective policies, with no investment element.

term shares. A type of account found in a building society, which is used for the deposit of funds for a fixed period of time and in return the investor has a higher rate of interest.

terms, cash. Payment at time of purchase.

terms of delivery. The agreement between the buyer and seller as to whom is responsible for the payment of all or any delivery and other charges for the goods from the seller's premises to the buyer's premises. In international trade such conditions would be shown in shipping terms as FOB, CIF, etc. See INCOTERMS.

terms of reference. Points for discussion and settlement.

terms of trade. A phrase used to describe the trading situation of a country. Where imports exceed exports then the terms of trade are considered as unfavourable. Where the exports exceed the imports then the terms of trade are considered as favourable.

testament. See WILL.

testamentary capacity. The ability to make a valid will, i.e. a person over the age of 18 years or a younger person in service in HM Armed Forces or the Merchant Navy. The ability to dispose of property.

testator. A person who makes a will.

test case. A case brought before the courts in order to bring to light any misunderstanding in the interpretation of a legal principle. To obtain guidance of the courts on a particular action.

testimonium. The clause at the end of a deed or will which begins 'In witness, etc.' and goes on to certify that the parties have signed the document in witness of what it contains.

theft. Theft Act 1968: 'The act of dishonestly appropriating property belonging to another with the intention of permanently depriving the other of it'.

theory of comparative costs. The theory that even if one country has an absolute advantage in costs of producing all things, the world will still benefit if each country specialises in producing those goods in which it has the greatest relative cost advantage or least disadvantage.

things in action. See CHOSES IN ACTION.

things in possession. See CHOSE IN POSSESSION.

Third Market. A market established by the Stock Exchange in 1986 for the purchase and sale of shares in public limited companies that are not big enough or do not reach the criteria necessary to have a full listing, or a listing on the Unlisted Securities Market.

third of exchange. See BILL IN SET.

third party. A person or party not directly involved in a contract, legal proceedings, or discussions. For a banker a third party would be any person or entity that is not the customer but some other person who may be willing to act as a guarantor, offer collateral, etc.

third party risks. A form of insurance to cover the death or injury to other parties. In motor insurance it is compulsory for cover to be obtained for the death or injury of other persons.

third party security. The security provided by a person or perons other than the borrower. Known as collateral security.

Three Is (3is). A unique private sector company originated in 1945 by the Bank of England and the English and Scottish clearing banks to help meet British industry's long-term capital requirements. 3is is the UKs largest venture capital company with a portfolio of more than £2.3 billion and investments in over 4000 businesses. It invests equity or loan capital on a long-term basis to businesses of all sizes, from management start-ups and management buy-ins, through to major national and international concerns. 3is set no upper or lower limit of investment, from tens of thousands of pounds to £50 million or more. 3is has investment operations in Europe with offices in France, Germany, Spain and Italy and joint ventures in Portugal and Holland. They are also active in the USA, Australia and Japan.

thrift institution. An institution which encourages persons to save and use their money sensibly. Its main sevices are the deposit and withdrawal of funds. The description covers credit unions, building societies, savings banks, loan clubs, etc. These forms of institutions are very popular in the USA. In the UK there are loan clubs, credit unions and a national savings bank, but the major building societies offer a wider range of services other than the basic deposit and withdrawal.

through bill of lading. A bill of lading which covers shipment on more than one vessel or more than one type of transport.

tick. A part of a tenth of 1 per cent indicating a rise or fall in a rate or price.

ticket day. *See* NAME DAY.

tick up. Where an error occurs in the work and it cannot immediately be found by casual observation, then it is necessary to check each individual credit and its corresponding debits and vice versa, so that every transaction is 'ticked' and agreed.

tight market. A situation whereby a stock, share or foreign exchange margin between the buying and selling prices are very narrow or tight.

tied loan. An international loan from one country to another which is conditional that the money lent is spent in buying goods, services and expertise from the lending country.

till. A cabinet containing drawers where a cashier will keep all the notes and coins for the receipts and payments to customers.

till float. Also called cash float. The amount of money that is considered

necessary to enable a cashier to do his/her work efficiently. Where the amount of any coins or notes exceeds the maximum amount permitted, then a transfer is made to the chief cashier for depositing with the branch reserve, or where there is a shortage of money then funds are withdrawn from reserve.

time and motion study. A check on the time taken by an employee to do any particular task in order to see whether it can be done more efficiently.

time bargain. An agreement to contract business at a given time: a term applied to dealings on the Stock Exchange by 'bulls' or 'bears'.

time bill. *See* TERM BILL.

time charter. A charter party whereby the ship is chartered for a specific period.

time deposits. Deposits at a term (including certificates of deposit). *See also* SPECIAL DEPOSITS.

time draft. A bill of exchange which is payable at a stated number of days (30, 60, 90 days) after date, or after acceptance.

time order. An order of the court defined in the Consumer Credit Act 1974 as follows: 1. If it appears to the court to do so (*a*) on an application for an enforcement order, or (*b*) on an application made by a debtor or hirer under this paragraph after service on him or her of a default notice, or (*c*) in an action brought by a creditor or owner to enforce a regulated agreement or any security, or recover possession of any goods or land to which a regulated agreement relates, the court may make an order under this section (a 'time order'). 2. A time order shall provide for one or both of the following, as the court considers just – (*a*) the payment by the debtor or hirer or any surety of any sum owed under a regulated agreement or a security by such instalments, payable at such times as the court, having regard to the means of the debtor or hirer and any surety, considers reasonable; (*b*) the remedying by the debtor or hirer of any breach of a regulated agreement (other than non-payment of money) within such period as the court may specify.

time policy. A marine policy extending cover for a fixed time only.

time value. In a traded options contract it is the amount by which an option premium exceeds its intrinsic value. It also reflects the remaining life of the option.

tithe. The tenth part. Originally it was associated with the giving of one tenth of all crops, fruit, etc. to the church.

title. The designation of a person, office, job or given as recognition of service of distinction. A heading to a report, book, document. Conclusive legal evidence to the right of ownership/possession to land, property or goods.

title deed. A legal instrument giving the evidence of a person's right to property.

token. A reminder, a symbol, a keepsake. A representation. A disc, note, or plastic that can be used instead of money, e.g. the use of a book token to purchase books. A plastic disc exchanged for money that can be used to operate machinery to clean cars. Some item that is exchangeable for goods or services.

token money. Coins where the value of the metal in them is less than the value attached to them by law, such as the cupro-nickel and bronze coins of the UK.

token payment. A deposit given as a token of good faith for the purchase of goods or services. On receipt of the goods or services, the outstanding debt will be paid.

tolerance. The accepted difference between the value, weight or specification of the finished product or contract and the maximum allowance for any differences. Under Uniform Customs and Practice for Documentary Credits, Article 43 states: 'The words "about" "circa" or similar expressions used in connection with the amount of the credit or the quantity or the unit price stated in the credit are to be construed as allowing a difference not to exceed 10% more or 10% less than the amount or the quantity or the unit price to which they refer. Unless a credit stipulates that the quantity of the goods specified must not be exceeded or reduced, a tolerance of 5% more or 5% less will be permissible. The tolerance does not apply when the credit stipulates the quantity in terms of a stated number of packing units or individual items'.

toll. A tax or duty charged for some privilege or service, especially for the use of road, bridge, or tunnel.

tombstone. An advertisement placed in national newspapers giving the names of the underwriters that are involved with a new issue of securities. The names are listed alphabetically in two or three columns so that the appearance of the advertisement gives the appearance of a tombstone. Such an advertisement will appear to advertise the participants to a syndicated loan. It will show the lead manager and co-lead managers plus two or three columns of participating banks.

tontine. An insurance scheme of French origin whereby the contributors pay premiums for a limited period at the end of which the survivors divide the total amount between them. It is named after an Italian banker, Lorenzo Tonti who originated this form of insurance. *See* TONTINE POLICY.

tontine policy. A policy of life assurance which has no surrender value until maturity, so that on the death of the subscriber, no payment is available, nor has the policy a surrender value. It only has value at the end of its life, when the capital sum plus interest is divided between the surviving subscribers. The barren period, when it has no value, is called the 'Tontine' period. *See* TONTINE.

tool of trade. A bankrupt's tools which he/she uses in his trade are not generally available to his/her creditors. Under the Insolvency Act 1986 s. 283(2): '(*a*) such tools, books, vehicles and other items of equipment are necessary to the bankrupt for use personally by him in his employment, business or vocation, (*b*) such clothing, bedding, furniture, household equipment and provisions as are necessary for satisfying the basic domestic needs of the bankrupt and his family'.

'Top Hat' pensions. Very attractive pensions paid to the most senior managers and directors of very large companies. The major contributions to these pension fund is the company itself.

topic. The Stock Exchange view data system which is available to all subscribers. The system carries all current share prices, announcements, analytical details, foreign exchange rates, etc.

topping-up clause. This clause will appear in a charge form when the lending banker and the borrowing customer have agreed that there will be a certain margin between the security deposited and the amount borrowed. Should the security fall in value or the borrowing increases, the lending bank has the right to top up the security to a point where the agreed margin is reached. In the instance where the customer is unable to provide the security, then the loan becomes instantly repayable, so giving the bank if necessary a right of action.

top slicing. Where a person has purchased a bond or a unit-linked single premium policy, then a tax liability will arise if the investment is surrendered or encashed within seven-and-a-half years after the date of purchase. If the holder is a higher rate taxpayer, there will be a tax charge on any gain. This charge will be at the highest rate of tax less the basic rate.

tort. A wrong done to a person which has caused him/her injury or loss to person or property. This will include assault, wrong to reputation, trespass, interference, breach of contract. for a banker the most likely case of tort would be conversion or negligence.

total account. An account where the total amount for any group of accounts is recorded. Often called a control account, e.g. sales ledger control account.

total income. The earned and unearned income of any person.

total price. For the purposes of the Consumer Credit Act 1974, total price means the total sum payable by the debtor under a hire-purchase agreement or a conditional sale agreement, including any sum payable on the exercise of an option to purchase, but excluding any sum payable as a penalty or as compensation or damages for a breach of the agreement.

touch screen. A VDU or screen which is sensitive to the touch of the user which gives a command to the computer or complies with a command given. Used very extensively in the foreign exchange departments of banks, other

areas linked to financial markets, and where there is need for speedy communications.

town clearing. The town clearing is a largely manual low volume, same day value debit paper clearing cheques and other items of £100 000 or more. Only cheques and certain other items which are drawn on and paid into branches of member banks within the limited area of the City of London are eligible. All other cheques drawn on branches of the clearing banks are passed through the General Clearing. The town clearing has since 1984 been substantially replaced by the Clearing House Automated Payments System (CHAPS), which allows payments of £5000 or more to be transmitted by one bank to another via a computer system. The town clearing is part of the CHAPS & Town Clearing Company Limited. *See also* CHAPS & TOWN CLEARING COMPANY LIMITED.

trade. The business of buying and selling, commerce, barter, shopkeeping; occupation (in industry); the purchase or sale of goods or services at home (*domestic trade*) or abroad (*foreign trade*).

trade association. A relationship that exists between persons whose interests are in the same trade and who meet regularly to consider and discuss any legislation, political and economic factors, that has or is likely to affect their trade.

trade balance. *See* BALANCE OF TRADE.

trade bill. A bill of exchange drawn by one commercial enterprise on another commercial enterprise.

trade board. A board of representatives of employers and employees, nominated by the Department of Trade to settle trade disputes, etc.

trade credit. Credit granted by one trader to another who has bought goods from him or her.

trade creditor. A supplier who is owed a sum of money owing to the purchase of goods or services.

trade cycle. A characteristic in business activity that has a tendency to fluctuate between a boom period and a recession. This occurs nationally and internationally. During a recession, employment rises, interest rates rise and there is a tendency for manufacture and production to decrease as well as prices. Bankruptcies and liquidations also increase.

trade debtor. A debt owing to an enterprise by a customer who has purchased goods or services.

trade discount. A rebate on the price of goods given by a manufacturer, wholesaler or retailer. It is usually a deduction from the catalogue price, or a reduction in the unit price when a large quantity is purchased, or merely an unconditional reduction in price to promote sales. No accounting record is necessary in either the books of the seller or buyer.

traded options. These are the rights to buy or sell particular shares on the Stock Exchange, at an agreed price before some specified date in the future. The cost of the option will vary with the life of that option, e.g. three months, six months, nine months. For this right the buyer of the option – the call option – will pay the option seller – the writer – a premium, that is the fee and is forfeited if the buyer does not exercise his right before maturity. Conversely, the right of the seller of an option – the put option – will pay a fee to the option buyer – the writer. For the buyer, the value of the option to buy increases if the price of the shares rise during the life of the option and an active market can develop, not so much in the shares themselves, but in the options to buy the shares. Conversely, the value of an option to sell increases if the price of the shares fall during the life of the option. While companies are prepared to enter the market under favourable conditions, there are position limits based on the market capitalisation of the company. The traded option system allows the investor to sell his/her option or purchase traded options in the same way as stock and shares are purchased and sold. The market consists of 70 equities options and three index products all having both calls and puts. Many other countries, USA, France, Germany, etc. have similar markets.

trade gap. The excess of visible imports over visible exports.

trade investments. An investment in another company – an associate, affiliate or subsidiary company – which will be of some benefit to the investing company, either by obtaining a good profitable return, or to influence that company for the improvement of mutual trading relations.

trade mark. A logo or symbol used by a commercial organisation to be immediately recognisable by the general public. Such a mark is put on the invoices, labels, advertising matter, etc. Such distinguishing marks are registered and to major international companies they have considerable trading value.

trade name. A registered name given by a manufacturer to a proprietary article: a name used among traders and manufacturers for a certain commodity; a name under which an individual or company trades.

trade protection society. An organisation which supplies information as to the credit standing of companies, firms and individuals, primarily those engaged in trade.

traders' credit. An old-fashioned name for a service offered by banks whereby a trader will instruct a bank to pay a number of creditors. At present, all credit transfers from one bank to other banks will be made via BACS Ltd. A customer may deposit with a bank a 'library' of names and periodically request payment of a specific amount to named creditors whose details are known by the bank. The bank will then require the amount to be transmitted and the authority to debit the account with the total amount. Additionally, the customer may arrange with the bank to have a magnetic tape or the availability of a computer terminal direct to BACS for the transfer of funds. This is available to very large companies who pay their creditors and employees direct to a named bank account. At the other end, a small business may list on a bank form, the names of its creditors, the receiving bank's name and address and sorting code number on to a bank form, state the amount each beneficiary should receive and on the due date the remitter's account will be debited with the total amount.

trade terms. The points of a trade contract between buyer and seller that deal with the terms of payment, method of delivery of the goods, transit cost, insurance of goods while in transit, etc.

trade union. A legally constituted organisation of working persons whose objectives is to maintain and improve the working conditions, wages, salaries, safety, etc. of its members. They are usually recognised by government and employers, with whom they are in regular discussion on matters of mutual interest. Property owned by the union is vested in trustees and any banker giving an advance to a union must ensure that it is approved by the union's constitution.

trading account. A part of the final account of a business enterprise that will show how the gross profit or loss has been calculated.

trading as. Shown in banking records as T/A. Where a business or person is trading under a different name, that name must be shown on all records, invoices, cheques, etc., e.g. G. Klein T/A G.K. Tutorial Services.

trading certificate. A certificate issued by the Registrar of Companies to public companies, on receipt of which they are entitled to commence business. The Companies Act 1985 lays down a new procedure for obtaining a trading certificate. Section 117 of the Act provides that a trading certificate will be issued if a statutory declaration, to be made by a director or secretary of the company, certifies that the nominal amount of the issued capital is at least £50 000, and states: 1. the amount paid up on the share capital at the time of application; 2. any actual or estimated preliminary expenses, and by whom paid or payable; 3. details of any promotion expenses. It is an offence for any public company to trade or exercise its borrowing powers in contravention of s. 117 (above), and the penalty for so doing is a fine on the company and on any officer of the company who is in default. However, any transaction entered into by the company before issue of a trading certificate will not be invalid. Instead, if the company fails to meet its obligations under such a transaction within twenty-one days of being asked in writing to do so, the directors of the company will be personally liable for any loss suffered by the other party to the transaction.

trading cheques. Often referred to as 'trade checks'. These are vouchers that can be purchased – usually by instalments – from a shop or representative, and at some future time used to purchase clothing or small household goods from designated shops. The total cost of the voucher is paid off by instalments.

trading company. A properly constituted company, formed by registration with the purpose of carrying on business with a view to profit.

trading down. The sale of an asset at one price and the purchase of a similar asset at a lower price, thereby having cash in hand. *See* TRADING UP.

trading up. The sale of an asset at one price and buying a similar asset at a higher price, thereby improving the standard or efficiency of that type of asset.

trading partnership. The relationship that subsists between two or more persons carrying on business with a view to profit (Partnership Act 1890).

trading profit. Gross profit.

trading stamps. Stamps that are given free by a retailer to a consumer in accordance with the value of goods purchased. These stamps cannot be exchanged for money, but can be used to obtain goods or services from the company supplying the stamps.

tranche. Used in finance to indicate the drawing of part of a loan. Where a large loan has been given either by one bank or a banking syndicate, it is quite likely that the borrower does not require the whole amount at once. Therefore an agreement is made for funds to be drawn at stated intervals, or when notice has been given for the withdrawal of a sum of money.

transaction. The act of carrying through or negotiating a piece of business; an affair, a proceeding; the adjustment of a dispute by mutual concessions.

transaction reporting. *See* CASH MANAGEMENT.

transactions at undervalue. By s. 339, Insolvency Act 1986, a transaction of undervalue has occurred when a person who, before a petition has been presented, carried out a transaction by way of: 1. A gift; or 2. a gift in consideration of marriage; or 3. where no consideration passed or the consideration was significantly less than the value of the transaction. For the trustee to be able to claw back the value of the transaction for the benefit of the creditors, it must be proved that: 1. the transaction at undervalue took place within five years before the presentation of the petition; and 2. the person making the transaction at undervalue was insolvent or become insolvent in consequence of the transaction.

transactions to defraud creditors. These sections of the Insolvency Act (423–425) are similar to the Bankruptcy Acts relating to fraudulent conveyance. Should the court be satisfied that the transaction: (*a*) put the asset/s beyond the reach of person/s making a claim against a debtor; or (*b*) otherwise prejudiced the interests of such a person (creditor) in relation to his or her claim, the court, may (*a*) restore the position to what it would have been; and (*b*) protect the interests of persons who were victims of the transaction.

transfer. The movement of property from one person to another. The conveyance of a title to goods or property either by sale or gift.

transferability of a bill of exchange/cheque. In simple terms a bill of exchange (or cheque) may be passed from one person to another by delivery or by indorsement and delivery. It is purely a physical action, but when dealing with cheques, the term negotiability is included in the meaning of transferability. Where a bill of exchange has been transferred by indorsement and delivery and the transferee received it in good faith, then he/she may get a better title to the instrument than the transferor. A cheque can similarly be transferred, but any holder may restrict the transferability by either crossing the cheque specially or inserting a restrictive endorsement.

transferable. In its widest meaning to convey either ownership or possession or both to another.

transferable credit. Uniform Customs and Practice for Documentary Credits, Article 54 defines a transferable credit as: (*a*) 'a credit under which the beneficiary has the right to request the bank called upon to effect payment or acceptance or any bank entitled to ef-

fect negotiation to make the credit available in whole or in part to one or more other parties (second beneficiaries). (*b*) A credit can be transferred only if it is expressly designated as "transferable" by the issuing bank. Such terms as "divisible", "fractionable", "assignable" and "transmissible" add nothing to the meaning of the term "transferable" and shall not be used. (*d*) Bank charges in respect of transfers are payable by the first beneficiary unless otherwise specified. The transferring bank shall be under no obligation to effect the transfer until such charges are paid. (*e*) A transferable credit can be transferred once only. Fractions of a transferable credit (not exceeding in the aggregate the amount of the credit) can be transferred separately, provided partial shipments are not prohibited. The credit can be transferred only on the terms and conditions specified in the original credit, with the exception of the amount of the credit, or any unit prices stated therein, of the period of validity of the last date for presentation of documents in accordance with Article 47 and the period for shipment, any or all of which may be reduced or curtailed, or the percentage for which insurance cover must be effected. ... Additionally the name of the first beneficiary can be substituted for that of the applicant for the credit. ... (*f*) The first beneficiary has the right to substitute his own invoices (and drafts if the credit stipulates that drafts are to be drawn on the applicant) in exchange for those of the second beneficiary for amounts not in excess of the original amount stipulated in the credit'. *See also* BACK-TO-BACK CREDIT.

transfer accounting lodgment for investors, stock management for jobbers (Talisman). Talisman is a recognised clearing house (RCH) for the Stock Exchange. It is a central pooling system for the purchase and sale of listed securities, incorporating a computerised settlement system for all UK and Irish registered stocks. Stock is delivered by the vendor in advance of settlement and held temporarily by the Stock Exchange nominee company, SEPON (Stock Exchange Pool Nominees), until it is transferred to the new owner.

transfer agent. The office, often a stockbroker, which handles the transfer of shares and the relevant certificates and then despatches certificates to the new holders.

Transfer and automated registration of uncertificated stock. This is a computer based system owned and operated by the Stock Exchange which will record all transfers and registration of shares held in UK companies. It is the intention of the authorities, that once Parliamentary approval has been given, then a pilot scheme will commence in late 1992 and it is expected that only a few companies will change their method of registration of shareholders. Should this pilot scheme prove successful, then all top 100 companies should be in TAURUS by the end of the year. Every company will need to obtain their shareholders approval and this vote will be taken at the annual general meetings. Each company will circulate advance information about the ending of definitive certificates being sent to shareholders. For this purpose, the register of shareholders must be brought up to date as completely as possible beforehand and at this point, all shareholders will be sent a statement giving all the information necessary including the investor and authorisation codes. The investor code will consist of eight characters and the authorisation code will consist of four characters. These must be kept secure. Any changes in shareholder information will have to be notified to the Company Account Controller/Company Registrar, using the investor code. However, to sell shares, both codes must be given. For each company, shareholders will have investor and authorisation codes if they remain within the Company Account. An alternative way of holding stock is through a Commercial Account Controller. This type of account will be run by such organisations as banks, stockbrokers, etc. For clients, only one reference will be required. Holdings will be in individual names and all dividends, annual reports and other circulars will be sent by the company direct to the shareholder.

Once TAURUS is fully operational, it is intended to do away with the 2/3 week account periods and introduce a 'rolling settlement' period. In the initial period this will be on a five-day basis, with the intention of eventually reducing the period to three days. Trading within an account period will no longer be possible. As securities will be loaded into TAURUS on a phased basis, the evolution from a paper based settlement system to an electronic one will take at least 18 months.

transfer certificate. *See* TRANSFER AND AUTOMATED REGISTRATION OF UNCERTIFIED STOCK.

transfer days. Days set aside by companies for registering the transfers of registered stock; the official days at the Bank of England for the transfer of Government stocks.

transfer deed. The instrument transferring the ownership of securities from one person to another, a stock transfer form.

transfer fee. A fee charged by a company upon registration of a change of ownership of shares.

transfer of mortgage. This occurs when the ownership of mortgaged property is conveyed from one person to another. In banking this is likely to occur when (*a*) one banker or building society takes over the security from another banker or building society. In these circumstances, a new mortgage form will be drawn up and signed and the customer will be requested to repay the loan by regular transfers from current account to the loan account. (*b*) A customer who is about to repay the outstanding loan, will request the lending banker not to reconvey the property to him/her but to a third party. The conveyance will be by deed which declares that the mortgage transfers the benefit of the mortgage. The deed will vest all the rights of the transferor to the transferee. The mortgagor will be requested to join in the deed of transfer. Alternatively, a statutory receipt should be drawn up for the sum of money due under the mortgage, which will be indorsed and attached to the form of mortgage, stating the name of the person or company paying the money and executed by the chargee by way of a legal mortgage.

transfer of shares. *See* REGISTER OF TRANS-FERS; SHARE OR STOCK TRANSFER FORM.

transferor by delivery. A person, a holder of a bill of exchange, who without indorsing it merely delivers it to another person, has no liability on the instrument. Bills of Exchange Act 1882 s. 58: 'where the holder of a bill payable to bearer negotiates it by delivery without indorsing it, he is called a transferor by delivery. He warrants to his immediate transferee being a holder for value that the bill is what it purports to be, that he has a right to transfer it, and that at the time of transfer, he is not aware of any fact which renders it valueless'. The transferor is, under these circumstances, not liable on the instrument. While the transferor as above cannot be sued on the bill, he/she can be sued for breach of warranty; for example, the transfer of a forged bill would constitute a breach of warranty. Should a person come into possession of a bill, e.g. finds it, he has no title nor can he give a title. If the bill is not payable to bearer or indorsed in blank, he cannot indorse it in the name of the payee or special indorsee, if he does the bill will become a forgery by virtue of s. 24, Bills of Exchange Act.

transfer order. 1. A request by a customer to a bank to transfer a sum of money to another account in his/her name, or to transfer a sum of money to another person who maintains an account at another branch or bank. 2. An order from a bank to a warehouse-keeper requesting that goods held to the order of the bank should be transferred to the order of the person named in the transfer letter. 3. Under the Consumer Credit Act 1974, it is a court order for the transfer to the debtor of a creditor's title to goods to which an agreement relates and the return to the creditor of the remainder of the goods.

transfer register. *See* REGISTER OF TRANSFERS.

transfer risk. A risk encountered in lending abroad, where although the borrower can repay a loan, his or her country has imposed restrictions because it lacks sufficient foreign exchange for meeting the debt.

transfer stamp. The revenue duty charged on the transfer of shares.

transit trade. *See* RE-EXPORT.

transmission of funds. The method of remitting funds through the banking system. While a customer can send his cheque to a payee, he may instead request his bank to send these funds by (*a*) the automated clearing system (BACS), (*b*) he may pay in a credit for the beneficiary's account at a named bank, (*c*) the customer may arrange payment to be made by the CHAPS clearing, (*d*) funds can be transmitted on a regular basis by establishing a standing order or if the beneficiary is a large company then a direct debit system may be established, (*e*) if funds are going to be transmitted abroad, then this may be done by (*i*) banker's draft (*ii*) mail transfer, (*iii*) telegraphic transfer or where applicable, SWIFT.

travel agent. A retail outlet that will make the travel and the accommodation arrangements for a person or persons wishing to travel from one country to another, whether on business or pleasure. The agent can also arrange for the provision of visas, insurance and frequently for the issue of traveller's cheques. The travel agent will probably be the agent of a number of tour operators and carriage companies.

travel cheques (traveller's cheques). These are cheques issued in round amounts, e.g. £20, £50, £100, etc. or in main international currencies, by banks, building societies, travel agents, travel operators to persons who are going abroad. When issued, the person will be requested to sign the cheque in the space provided, and when it is presented for payment overseas, the holder will be requested to countersign in the place provided in the presence of the paying agent and usually the paying agent will also request as an additional precaution, to see the person's passport to verify the signature and identity. On issue the customer pays for the full amount of the cheques purchased, plus a commission. On payment he/she will receive the local currency equivalent, less a commission. These cheques are usually valid world-wide, and have no maturity date. Should a travel cheque/s be lost or stolen, the owner should in the first instance notify the local police, then notify the local banking correspondent of the issuer of the travel cheque (name shown in a small leaflet given on the issue of the cheques) who will request the holder to sign an indemnity form, then replace the cheques free of charge. It is common practice for travel cheques to be cashed not only at the branches of banks, but in restaurants, hotels, casinos, shops, etc.

treasurer. A person who is responsible for the safety and deployment of funds. For clubs and other non-profit making organisations the treasurer holds an honorary position, is responsible for the receipt and payment of funds and is accountable to the members for his or her stewardship. In a banking situation a treasurer is responsible for placing funds in various markets and ensuring that borrowing and lending, buying and selling of funds, within his or her own portfolio, are matched.

treasure trove. Any money, plate or bullion of unknown ownership found buried in the ground. It becomes the property of the Crown.

Treasury. The government department responsible for the monetary and economic policies of the UK. While the Prime Minister is the First Lord of the Treasury, the political head of the department is the Chancellor of the Exchequer. The Chancellor is responsible for the production of the budget of the country and seeing it become law. The Treasury is then responsible for the collection of revenue via the Inland Revenue and Customs and Excise Departments. The Treasury is responsible for the issue of funds to the various governmental departments and controlling their expenditure. The Treasury, will obtain loans through the Department of National Savings and through the Bank of England who acts as registrar for the issue and eventual repayments of gilts.

Treasury Bill. The Treasury Bill is a bearer government security, representing a charge on the Consolidated Fund of the United Kingdom, payable on or after a certain date and issued at a discount to its face value. Treasury Bills are issued to the public in two ways: 1. By allotment to the highest bidder at a weekly tender and 2. by allotment to the highest bidder in response to an invitation from the Bank to discount houses and clearing banks to bid for Treasury Bills to absorb a money surplus on a particular day. Additionally, they may be issued at any time to government departments and the Issue Department of the Bank. These 'tap bills' are issued at a rate of discount fixed by the Treasury. The Treasury Bills Act 1877, provided for Treasury Bills to be issued for any period not exceeding twelve months but since 1950 they have been offered for a term of 91 days (sometimes for one or two days more or less to take account of public and bank holidays), except for temporary use of shorter-term bills on specific occasions to smooth money market flows. The weekly tender for Treasury Bills is held on Fridays (or the last business day of the week). Each tender must be for an amount of not less than £50 000. Having acquired Treasury Bills, a discount house or bank may hold them until maturity or they may sell all or part of their holdings to another financial institution or to the Bank of England who acts as lender of last resort.

Treaty of Rome (1957). The treaty which established the European Common Market. *See* COMMON MARKET.

trial balance. At the end of a financial period a list of all debit and credit balances is extracted from the books of accounts. Assuming that the double entries have been correctly posted, the total of the debit side should equal the total of the credit side. The trial balance is drawn up prior to the completion of the trading, profit and loss accounts and the balance sheet.

triptique. A document for Customs inspection in connection with cars touring abroad.

trover. The acquisition or appropriation of any goods; an action for the recovery of personal property wrongfully converted by another to his or her own use. The term is also applied to an action for conversion.

true and fair view. The auditor's report of a limited company is required to express an opinion on the truth of the final accounts and balance sheet of the business as at a given date. The directors of a company must, in compliance with the Companies Act 1985 s. 227, prepare such statements and accounts for distribution to its members.

true owner. A person who has in his/her possession a bill of exchange may be different to the person who is the true owner, if the former has obtained it by dishonest means. The true owner of a bill must in the first instance be the drawer, who after drawing it will deliver it to the payee, who in his turn by indorsement and delivery transfer the ownership to an indorser and so on. Where a person takes a bill, in good faith and has all the attributes of a holder in due course, then he/she is the true owner and can sue in his/her own name. In the case of cheques, where a person takes a cheque which is crossed and also bears the words 'not negotiable', then that person cannot be capable of giving a better title to the cheque than that which the person from whom he took it had (Bills of Exchange Act 1882 s. 81).

truncation. To cut off the end. In banking the system of truncation involves the non-delivery of cheques, and other items that are normally sent to the paying banker through the cheque or credit clearing system. Currently, all cheques, credits and other claims on a named bank/branch are presented through the clearing system and the paper will eventually arrive at the branch for final payment or credit. This system of moving paper around the system will take three working days. With the advent of truncation, the movement of paper is curtailed as the item stays with the collecting/remitting banker and the details of the debit/credit are transmitted via the computer terminals to the banker on whom the draft is drawn or for credit to the account of the beneficiary. While the truncation method of settling inter-branch/bank indebtedness seems to be expanding, difficulties arise under the Bills of Exchange Act 1882 as the paying banker will lose its statutory protection, as a cheque is by definition a negotiable instrument. However, by popular description, a cheque also includes instruments that can be drawn not only on a bank but on a building society as well, so that for all legal purposes, such items drawn on a building society do not come within the definition of a cheque. Since the vast majority of cheques are not transferred by the payee, but paid into his/her bank/building society account, it seems that the constituents of negotiability need no longer apply to cheques and therefore some solution needs to be found to withdraw cheques from the family of negotiable instruments. In the Scandinavian countries, truncation works successfully, but in England, with its very large number of banks, the solution is more difficult, but nevertheless it must be found if costs in the movement of paper is to be reduced. Included must be some form of protection for the paying and collecting bankers against fraud and forgery of signatures.

trust. Having faith or confidence in another. Relying on another to perform a function. The owners or shareholders of an enterprise transfer their interests to a board of trustees in exchange for a trust certificate – a business trust. In a charitable sense, it is a body of persons that carry out a function as licensed by the Charities Act 1960. With regard to land this refers to the owner of the property holding and administrating it on behalf of another. also *See* BREACH OF TRUST; CHARITABLE TRUST; CONSTRUCTIVE TRUST; EXPRESS TRUST; FLEXIBLE TRUST; IMPLIED TRUST; INVESTMENT TRUST; MANAGEMENT TRUST; MINISTERIAL TRUST; PRECATORY TRUST; PRIVATE TRUST; PROTECTIVE TRUST; RESULTING TRUST; SPLIT CAPITAL TRUST.

trust certificate. *See* TRUST LETTER.

trust deed. A deed that sets out the terms of a trust. In some US states this takes the place of a mortgage deed.

trustee. A person or persons that have control over property, but are required to deal with such property as specified in the trust deed. A trustee must not (a) profit from the trust; (b) must not delegate the trust except as permitted by the trust deed; (c) must invest the funds in a prudent manner; (d) must distribute any funds to those entitled to receive; (e) deal fairly with all the beneficiaries. *See also* CUSTODIAN TRUSTEE; NAKED TRUSTEE; PUBLIC TRUSTEE.

trustee clause. When a bank wishes to have as its security an equitable charge it will obtain either the title deeds or the land certificate with a memorandum of deposit which will contain a clause to the effect that the bank can request the borrower to complete a legal mortgage of the property if requested so to do. Should the borrower fail to do so, then the bank has an irrevocable power of attorney, appointing a bank official or its trustee to obtain a legal charge prior to sale of the property.

trustee corporation. A corporation authorised under the Public Trustee Rules 1912 to undertake business in England and Wales. This includes the Treasury Solicitor, Official Solicitor and the Public Trustee.

trustee in bankruptcy. A person, in compliance with the Insolvency Act 1986, must be a qualified insolvency practitioner and have been appointed either by (*a*) general meeting of creditors; (*b*) by the Secretary of State under ss. 295(2), 296(2), or 300(6); or (*c*) by the court under s. 297. Where two or more persons hold the position of trustee, provision must be made for circumstances when they act together and when one may act for the others. The appointment of the trustee takes effect from the date specified on his or her certificate of appointment. The official receiver can, in certain circumstances, be appointed as the trustee to the estate.

trustee investments. Investments declared by law to be acceptable for purchasing with monies held on trust.

trust for sale. The intention of the trust deed is that the property established in the trust shall be sold immediately or in the future and the proceeds distributed to the beneficiaries or used on behalf of the beneficiaries.

trust instrument. The document creating the trust, appointing the trustees, powers of the trustees, etc.

trust letter/receipt. Where a produce loan has been given by a banker to his customer, and the goods are held by the bank as security for the loan, then in order to repay the loan, the customer needs to sell the goods. For this purpose a trust letter is signed, making the customer the agent of the bank. This protects the bank from the customer's bankruptcy and any claim from the insolvency practitioner. It requests that the customer protects the goods and on sale transfers the proceeds to the bank. The trust receipt is delivered to the bank who will on receipt give the customer a letter to the warehouse-keeper requesting that the goods be transferred into the name of the customer.

trust officer. An officer of a bank or a subsidiary of a bank who administers the estates, trusts and accounts of customers.

truth in lending. This relates to the Consumer Credit Act 1974 which ensures that the borrower/customer is given all the details relating to the borrowing of funds. The quotation which must be in writing is given or sent by the bank showing the interest rate – which may be shown at the current base rate, plus an additional percentage – the annual percentage rate (APR), arrangement fee, charges for taking security, legal costs and any other charges involved. At this juncture there is no commitment by the prospective borrower to borrow. It merely gives him/her the opportunity of comparing the cost of borrowing with other lenders.

T.T. The abbreviation for a telegraphic transfer.

turn. A word used in the Financial markets indicating the difference between the buying/bid prices and the selling/offer for any security. it is frequently called the spread.

turnover. The gross value of the goods or services, less any trade discounts and Value Added Tax, sold during a stated period of time. Net turnover will indicate the total sales less any returns, while gross turnover will show no deduction for returns.

tutor. In Scotland, the guardian of a pupil, having control of the person and the estates of his or her ward (usually the father, or if there is no father, the mother alone or with tutors appointed by the father during his lifetime, or by the court).

two-tier systems. A service or cost that has differential pricing systems, e.g. where a country has dual exchange rates, one for commercial transactions and the second for foreign visitors. Another two-tier system is that of postal rates. Interest rates may also differ for differing purposes.

types of life policy. *See* POLICY.

U

uberrimae fidie. Of the utmost good faith. A description of a type of contract where one party has in the nature of things information which only he or she can know, but which is vital to the contract. In such a case there is a duty to supply this information truthfully and to make a full disclosure. If this is not done the contract may be voided at the option of the other party. The prime example of this type of contract is the contract of life assurance, where the previous medical history of the assured, and that of his or her family, is clearly of great importance to the question of whether a contract shall be entertained and, if it is, what the premium shall be.

ullage certificate. A certificate which shows the measurement of liquid or semi-liquid extracted from a tanker.

ultimate balance. This is the balance stated in a guarantee form stating the amount due to the bank on the last day of the notice given by the bank to the guarantor. When this occurs, the bank will stop the account, and any subsequent credits and debits will be posted to a new account, which for the time being will have no effect on the final debt due. Eventually, the final balance will be arrived at by a combination of all accounts in the customer's name.

ultimatum. A final warning, demand or notice.

ultimo. The last day of the commercial or *Bourse* month.

ultra vires. This phrase is directly relevant to limited companies. It means 'beyond the powers'. In simple terms any company that commits an act outside the objects of its memorandum of association is void and cannot be ratified. This has in the past caused some hardship not only to banks but any third party dealing with the company. Currently, the European Communities

Act 1972 s. 9(1), has directed that any person dealing with a company is deemed to be dealing within the capacity of the company and that the directors have the powers to bind the company. Additionally, the Companies Act 1985 s. 35 states: 1. 'Any act done by a company which is outside of or beyond its memorandum remains valid and (2) where a dealing is entered into with the company in good faith, the power of the board of directors to bind the company, or authorise others to do so, shall be deemed free of any limitation under the company's constitution'. By these two acts it seems that the '*ultra vires*' principle is a thing of the past.

unable to pay debts. For the purposes of the Insolvency Act 1986 s. 123, a company is deemed unable to pay debts (*a*) if a creditor to whom the company is indebted in a sum exceeding £750 then due, has served on the company (by leaving it at the company's registered office) a written demand, requiring the company to pay the sum so due, and the company has for 3 weeks thereafter neglected to pay the sum or to secure or compound for it to the reasonable satisfaction of the creditor; or (*b*) if in England and Wales, execution or other process issued on a judgment, decree or order of any court in favour of a creditor of the company is returned unsatisfied (in whole or in part); or (*c*) in Scotland, the *induciae* of a charge for payment on an extract decree, or an extract registered bond, or an extract registered protest, have expired without payment being made; or (*d*) if in Northern Ireland, a certificate of unenforceability had been granted in respect of a judgment against the company; or (*e*) if it is proved to the satisfaction of the court that the company is unable to pay its debt as they fall due. By s. 268 of the

Act an individual appears unable to pay debts if (*a*) the petitioning creditor has served a demand in the prescribed form requiring payment of the debt and at least three weeks have elapsed since the demand was served and the demand has not been complied with; or (*b*) execution or other process in respect of the debt on a judgment of any court has not been satisfied.

unauthorised signature. *See* FORGED SIGNATURE.

unbanked. Not having a bank account.

unbundling. A word invented by Sir James Goldsmith, who with others, under the company name of Hoylake, attempted to take over BAT Industries as he considered it too big to be efficient and therefore planned to sell off parts of the group or 'unbundle' the organisation.

uncalled capital. *See* SHARE CAPITAL.

unclaimed balance. *See* DORMANT ACCOUNT.

uncleared effects. The cheques and other items paid in by a customer for the credit of his/her account, for which the collecting banker has not yet received reimbursement. Although these amounts will be shown in the customer's statement, a record of the true balance and balance not cleared is maintained in the books/computer of the bank. While in normal times, a cheque presented for payment through the clearing system will reach its destination, the paying banker three working days later, it is customary for uncleared effects to be held on record for at least five working days, i.e. to ensure that any unpaid items will be received by the collecting banker by that time. Building societies and small non-clearing banks, tend to give additional time to uncleared effects. Whether a customer can draw against uncleared effects will depend on the banker/customer relationship in each case. The bank is under no obligation to pay any cheques drawn against items not yet cleared. Should the bank allow this practice, it can build up a precedent, so that on future occasions it will not be able to withdraw this service.

unconnected depositor. A person who has funds deposited with a bank, but for whom there is no banker/customer relationship. The customer requires none of the basic services, except the repayment of his/her deposit with interest.

undated stock. Gilt-edged security issued by the government on a perpetual basis and having therefore no date by which it will be redeemed.

under bond. Imported goods stored in a Customs bonded warehouse until such time as the duty is paid or they are re-exported.

under-lease. The granting by a lessee of a part of his or her interest in a lease to another person, whether part of the property for any or all of the term, or all the property for part of the term.

under-sheriff. An English sheriff's deputy who performs the execution of writs.

undertaking. A business enterprise; a stipulation, promise or guarantee, given to or by a bank in various connections, e.g. an undertaking to review conditions of service. *See* DEED OF POSTPONEMENT; SOLICITOR'S UNDERTAKING.

under the counter. *See* COUNTER.

underwriter. A person or company whose function it is to cover a risk or part of a risk in such enterprises as insurance and new issues. The underwriter, for a commission will accept the responsibility to purchase any shares or stock that have not been taken up by the public,. While it is feasible for individuals to add their names to syndicates that are underwriting agents at Lloyd's, there is at the other extreme, for example the underwriting of the large privatisation issues, the need for major financial institutions to become underwriters in order to ensure success of the operation.

undischarged bankrupt. Under the Insolvency Act 1986, provision has been made for the automatic discharge of a bankrupt providing certain obligations have been carried out. The legal state of a bankrupt person commences from the date of bankruptcy order is made and continues until discharge which, under a summary administration, may be after two years. Under a criminal bankruptcy, authority of the court is necessary only after a period of five years has elapsed. Should a person be bankrupt for a second time within a period of fifteen years, then an application for discharge may be made to the court after a period of five years has elapsed. In all other cases automatic discharge is given after three years has elapsed. During the period a person is an undischarged bankrupt he or she may not 1. maintain a bank account without the knowledge of trustees or the Department of Trade; 2. either alone or jointly with another obtain credit to the value of £50 or more without disclosing his or her disability; 3. engage in any trade or business under a name different from the one under which he or she was adjudicated bankrupt, without disclosing that name to all with whom business is carried out; 4. act as a company director or take part in the management of any company except by leave of the court. The bankrupt is entitled to a number of *assets* which are as follows: 1. property held by the bankrupt as a trustee; 2. tools, vehicles and other items of business; 3. wearing apparel or furniture, household goods and bedding for himself or herself, spouse or children; 4. personal earnings which are considered necessary for support of himself/herself and family; 5. rights of action for damages for injury to personal credit. Under the Matrimonial Homes Act 1983, the spouse of a bankrupt acquires a right to the occupation of that house which cannot be overriden without a court order. Where the family home is jointly owned by the bankrupt and the spouse, the court will take various factors into consideration before arriving at its decision.

undisclosed principal. Where a person who is an agent of another conceals the fact that he/she is merely a representative, and has authority to contract on behalf of the principal, the third party may if he/she wishes to sue on the contract have the choice of either suing the agent or the principal.

undue influence. Improper pressure on a person by another or others. That person is therefore not free to make a decision on a contract or transaction. where no special relationship exists between the parties, the party seeking to avoid the contract, must prove undue influence as a fact. Where there is a relationship as in doctor–patient, parent–

child, etc., undue influence is presumed unless disproved by the person being sued.

unearned income. For the purposes of tax, income derived from investment.

unearned increment. An increase in the value of an asset due to increased demand rather than to any improvement in the asset carried out by the owner; increased bank profits duie to an increase in the minimum lending rate.

unemployment. No full-time job or work. The statistics for this measurement covers only those who have been sacked from a job or made redundant and have registered as unemployed and are eligible for unemployment benefits the. It does not include self-employed persons who for some reason or other are unable to find suitable work and are not allowed to register, nor does it include persons that have retired, are disabled, etc.

unencumbered. An asset which is free from any claims, covenants and rights granted to another person or persons.

unenforceable contracts. Although a contract may be valid, it cannot be enforced due to some technical difficulty or reason, e.g. lapse of time, impossibility.

unexecuted agreement. This means a document embodying the terms of a prospective regulated agreement, or such of them as it is intended to reduce to writing.

unfitness of a director. The unfitness of a person to act as a director is assessed by the Department of Trade and Industry after receiving a report which contains such details as: name, age and occupation. Position held in the company. The director's conduct giving reasons, if any, why disqualification should be considered. Remuneration and benefits in the previous three years. Other companies where in the previous three years the individual was a director or shadow director. Civil and criminal proceedings being taken against the director. Any other relevant matters such as his/her state of health, personal losses incurred. While the rules under the Company Directors Disqualification Act 1986 are strictly enforced, it is not the aim to take a view on isolated failures, but to form an objective view of the director's conduct.

unfunded debt. Short-term government debt.

uniform customs and practice for documentary credits. A set of rules drawn up by the International Chamber of Commerce and accepted as a standard of practice and conduct by trading nations. These rules cover (*a*) the definition of a documentary credit; (*b*) the responsibilities of the parties; (*c*) the various forms of credits; (*d*) the documents that are acceptable; (*e*) the terms that can be used and their accepted meaning.

uniform eurocheque scheme. A means of accessing one's domestic bank account while travelling in European countries and others bordering the Mediterranean. Eurocheques and the accompanying eurocheque guarantee card differ from the account holder's everyday domestic instruments, but are of standard appearance through all 22 issuing countries and their banks. Eurocheques are encashed in local currency (or in a specified hard currency where the indigenous currency is weak) and the guarantee limit is loosely linked to Swiss francs 300 (350 in France and the UK £100). Eurocheques are encashed in almost all bank branches – more than 200 000 in the specified areas; many guarantee cards are encoded for ATM usage in over 20 000 machines in 14 different countries. Eurocheques are cleared by a streamlined pan-European clearing system which functions much like the UK domestic system, when domiciled back to the UK they are converted into sterling at the current rate of exchange and debited, normally with a small comission/handling charge to the drawer's account.

uniform rules for collection. Issued by the International Chamber of Commerce in order to lay down the standards, provisions and definitions in dealing with clean collections and documentary collections. It specifies (*a*) the definitions of words used; (*b*) the responsibilities of the parties to the collection; (*c*) the method of presentation; (*d*) payment and acceptance of the bill and/or documents; (*e*) matters arising due to non-payment and/or non acceptance; (*f*) expenses and interest.

unilateral. One-sided.

unilateral contract. One which is binding on one of the parties only.

unilateral relief. The relief of double taxation given in the UK for tax paid to an overseas country even when there is no agreement or treaty with that other country. With many countries there is a reciprocal agreement.

unincorporated association. An association of persons that is not a corporation, but meet for a social or non-profit making purposes, e.g. social, sports, music, etc. The membership tends to change from time to time and such groups are governed by a constitution. The association is managed by a committee and officers elected by the members of the society. The bank account is opened in the name of the society and operated by a treasurer and one other officer. As it is not a legal entity, it cannot be sued for the repayment of any advance, so that when an advance is made it is usual to obtain a guarantee from the committee members to be jointly and severally liable for the debt.

unissued stock/shares. *See* SHARE CAPITAL.

unit. A single person, thing or group, regarded as one for the purposes of calculation.

unit assurance. *See* UNIT-LINKED INSURANCE POLICY.

unit bank. A name given to a bank which has only one office. It is independently owned and managed by the owner or majority shareholder. In the UK they are frequently subsidiaries of other enterprises, while in the USA they are separate entities.

unit costing. A method of costing used where manufacture is continuous and units are identical.

United Association for the Protection of Trade. *See* CREDIT RATING.

unitisation. The conversion of an investment trust company into a unit trust.

unit-linked insurance policy. A policy of assurance taken out by the assured, whereby he/she agrees that part of the premium paidis invested in a unit trust. The remainder of the premium is used by the assurance company to provide the benefits under the policy. The income earned by the unit trust investment is retained by the insurance company and shown or paid out as a bonus on the policy. At maturity, or death, the policy-holder will receive the total value of the unit trust holdings, plus any amount including bonuses that have accumulated during the life of the policy.

unit of account. An attribute of money. A unit for measuring values in monetary terms.

unit trust. A method of investment whereby the investor subscribes funds to a 'pool' of money which is invested by the unit trust managers in a variety of different companies. The funds are managed by the managers of the unit trust, but are held by a trustee which is completely separate from the unit trust management. Most unit trusts are 'open-ended', i.e. there is no limit to the amount that can be placed in the fund. The managers will not only sell units in the trust, but will also buy back these units from holders who for some reason wish to sell. The prices are fixed daily with a spread of about 5 per cent between the buying and selling prices. The managers receive an initial fee for setting up the trust and each year are entitled to receive a management fee. The units are not listed on the Stock Exchange, but the prices of all unit trusts are advertised in major national newspapers. Unit trusts are authorised by the Department of Trade only after they are satisfied that the trust deed is in accordance with requirements of the Department. Unit trusts will tend to specialise in different geographical areas, types of businesses, etc., e.g. European, US smaller companies, high income, income and growth, etc. *See also* INVESTMENT TRUST.

unlimited company. A company which is registered with the Registrar of Companies, but is not a limited company. It is unlimited because there is no reference to limited liability in the Memorandum of Association. Members therefore have unlimited liability in the event of the company going into liquidation.

unlimited liability. The debt a person must bear if the business in which he/she is involved goes into liquidation, e.g. sole trader, partnership, unlimited company. There is no separate entity between the business and the owner/s.

Unlisted Securities Market (USM). There are about five hundred companies that require an official quotation but cannot comply with the strict conditions of the prime market. Companies join this market for business development. It allows a company to use its paper for acquisitions and creates a higher profile. The shares of the company can be bought and sold and are an incentive when they are offered as options to the staff.

unpaid seller. A seller who has either not received full settlement for the transaction or has only received partial payment, or where a negotiable instrument has been received as conditional payment and has been dishonoured.

unpaid seller's rights. If the goods are still in the seller's possession, he is entitled to retain them until payment has been made. Should the goods have passed to the buyer, then the seller has a lien for the price and where possible a right of stoppage *in transitu*. If the buyer is insolvent, the seller has the right of resale.

unquoted shares. Shares of a public limited company which has not yet applied, or has not yet applied, for a quotation on the Stock Exchange; and shares of a private limited company. *See also* PRIVATE COMPANY SHARES; UNLISTED SECURITIES MARKET.

unregistered company. A company that is formed without having to register with the Registrar of Companies this will inlcude: 1. A company or corporation registered under an Act of Parliament. 2. Any company not formed for the purpose of carrying on business with a view to profit. 3. Any company that has been granted exemption from registration by the Department of Trade and Industry.

unregistered land. Land that has not been registered under the Land Registration Act 1925. Ownership is evidenced in a set of deeds and documents.

unrestricted-use credit. Any form of credit provided under a regulated consumer credit agreement for which there is no restricted use, e.g. bank overdraft.

unsecured creditor. A person or entity that is owed money but has no security for the debt. His/her only claim is against the general assets of the debtor, but may be a preferential creditor if he/she is classified in Schedule 6, Insolvency Act 1986.

unsecured loan stock. A marketable loan to a company where no security is available.

unwritten law. Any law not originating in Parliament; the common law. *See also* COMMON LAW; EQUITY; GRESHAM'S LAW; INTERNATIONAL LAW.

update. The process whereby the records on a computer file are amended or charged.

upper chamber. In a bicameral legislature, the House that is the more restricted in terms of membership, e.g. the House of Lords, the Senate of the United States of America and some others.

upset price. The lowest fixed price at an auction sale at which, by agreement of the vendor, the property will be in the first instance offered, and at which it will be sold if no better offers are forthcoming.

usance. The period of time allowed for a bill to reach maturity. The usance will depend on where the bill was drawn and where it is payable.

usance bill. A bill of exchange that is drawn in accordance with the custom of the particular trade, e.g. some bills may by custom be drawn 30 days after sight, 30 days date, etc. *See also* BILL BROKER; BILL FOR COLLECTION; BILL FOR NEGOTIATION; TREASURY BILL.

useful life. All assets that have a finite life should be depreciated, the method used and the time taken will vary from asset to asset, but in all cases some form of depreciation must take place over the useful life of the asset. *See* SSAP 12.

usufruct. The right of using and enjoying the produce, benefit or profits of another's property provided that the property remains undamaged.

usury. Statutes relating to usury have been repealed, but the Consumer Credit Act 1974 makes reference to this (ss. 137–140). There is no legal limit to the rate of interest that can be charged, but a court may take into account any exorbitant rate charged in deciding a dispute between parties.

utmost good faith. *See* UBERRIMAI FIDEI.

utter. To put into circulation, e.g. to utter a false cheque, to put forged notes, base coins, etc. into circulation.

V

vacant possession. A term that is applicable to the sale of property where there will be no tenant in residence on completion of the contract. The property must be vacant and unoccupied.

valid. Sound. Legally acceptable and capable of being binding in a contract. Sufficient.

validate. To make valid, to ratify.

validity. Legal force; soundness; power to convince.

valuable consideration. Consideration has been defined as 'some right, interest, profit or benefit accruing to one party, or some forebearance, detriment, loss, or responsibility given suffered or undertaken by another', in other words, quid pro quo. Valuable consideration is not necessary for a contract under seal, but a simple contract must be validated by consideration which must not be past. A benefit given in the past, an antecedent debt is not sufficient in law to support a contract entered into subsequently. For bills of exchange, however, an antecedent debt or liability may constitute a consideration (Bills of Exchange Act 1882 s. 27(1b)), whether the bill is payable on demand or at some future time. In simple contracts there is a presumption that no consideration has been given until proven, but for bills of exchange consideration is presumed until the contrary is proven. Section 30 Bills of Exchange Act: 'Every party whose signature appears on a bill is prima facie deemed to have become a party thereto for value'.

valuation. The act of giving an opinion on the value of some object, idea or property. Often referred to as an appraisal. In banking, any collateral or security offered to the bank by a borrowing customer is evaluated for adequacy against the advance. Real property can be valued either by the branch manager or a professional valuer, depending on the type of property involved. Taking stocks and shares are valued by a comaparison with the prices shown in the *Stock Exchange Daily List* or the *Financial Times*. For life policies, the surrender value is obtainable from the insuarance company. Bank officials can and often break down a company's final accounts and balance sheet, to assess the lending risk.

value. This reflects the monetary equivalent of an asset, liability or transaction. The market price. This may differ, depending on whether the valuer is the buyer or seller. Some items are considered valuable by sentiment and therefore will have no relationship to the market value.

value added tax (VAT). A tax imposed on the sale/purchase of goods by a business enterprise. The current tax imposed on articles is 17½ per cent, but such things as education, insurance, childrens clothing, food taken out of café's or restaurants are either exempt or zero rated. When an enterprise pays VAT to another enterprise it is recorded as 'imputs' and when it sells goods and adds VAT it is recorded as 'outputs'. Each quarter, the business will add up its imputs and outputs and either receive or pay the difference to the Customs and Excise authorities. Every business enterprise that has an annual turnover greater than £38 000 must register for VAT.

value date. The date on which funds are considered as good and cleared and available for use by a customer. This is particularly important to banks that maintain foreign currency accounts abroad, as these funds are utilised by dealers for exchange purposes. Dealers that buy/sell foreign currency to another bank, will customarily deal on a spot basis, but settlement will be made two working days later. The funds therefore will be credited on a particular value date and are considered as good money. Funds which have been credited or paid via CHAPS or the Town clearing are given a same-day valuation.

valued policy. A marine policy having the value of the ship or freight insured stated in the policy.

value in account. A term used in bills of exchange to indicate that there remains a balance in the drawer's favour.

value judgment. An opinion given by a person with some experience or professional knowledge. A bank is frequently requested to give its valued judgment, when responding to status enquiries. A judgment is also made on the viability of a lending proposition.

value received. A phrase often seen on a bill of exchange to indicate that value either in the form of goods, services or money have been received by the drawer of the bill. This has no legal affect on the bill as value is deemed to have been given – *See* VALUABLE CONSIDERATION – by the drawee and/or the payee.

variable costs. The cost in a business or manufacturing enterprise that will vary with production, sales or any other activity within the enterprise.

variance. An accounting term for the difference between a budget, or an estimate and actual performance. *See also* FAVOURABLE VARIANCE.

Vatman. A general description of an official of the Customs and Excise Department who deals in Value Added Tax.

vault. The strong-room in a bank where the cash reserves, valuables and securities are kept. This room is usually below ground level and built to be burglar proof and withstand any damage by flood or fire.

velocity of circulation. The average number of times each unit of money is used in a given time.

vend. To sell, to dispose of by sale.

vendee. The person to whom anything is sold.

vendor. The seller.

venture capital. The funds available for financing the start-up of a business, whether this is due to a management buy-out or any other method of start-up. Funds are available from commercial banks, merchant banks, 3is, business enterprise schemes, etc. Due to the nature of the lending, it is considered as risk capital, but can often be very profitable both to the lenders and the borrowers who may be small businessmen.

vested remainder. An interest which passes eventually to a remainderman if alive; if dead, it passes to his or her estate.

vesting assent. *See* ASSENT.

vesting deed. *See* TRUST INSTRUMENT.

veterinary certificate. A certificate required to indicate live stock as free from specified diseases.

via. By way of.

viable. Capable of having an independent existence. Has a reasonable chance of continuing business. This is very relevant to businesses which appear to be going through a non-profitable period, but is considered as having the ability to break this barrier and trade profitably in the future.

viewdata. A process whereby information is presented on a visual display screen or unit (VDU). Such procedures are used extensively in the larger banks whereby information and data are centralised and can be transmitted to the viewer at a branch or department at the touch of a button or the viewer can request information by inserting his/her identification number and pressing the relevant keys obtain the required information. Such data as customers' files, details of accounts are readily available.

vindictive damages. *See* EXEMPLARY DAMAGES.

virement. Payments by means of a book entry.

Visa. An official endorsement. as on a passport, to show that the document has been examined and found correct; an international credit card scheme.

vis-a-vis. Opposite, over against, towards, in relation to.

visual display units. These visual display terminals are being used more and more frequently by bank staff at branches and departments. They are used by all members of staff, particularly to give customers' balances of accounts, details of entries to the account, standing order and direct debit authorities, etc. Other services such as new issues, investment management, etc. use these services. Obviously, where information is of a confidential nature, then identification numbers must be given to ensure that such information is not available to unauthorised persons. It is also possible to transmit messages and circulars to persons by imputting whatever is necessary and this is picked up with other information at the appropriate time.

void. Destitute of all legal effect.

void ab initio. Of no binding importance at any time from the beginning (of the supposed contract).

voidable. Legal and binding, but capable of being set on one side by one party to the contract at his or her option.

voluntary. Proceeding from choice or free will, unrestrained, spontaneous.

voluntary arrangement. A court may be approached by the debtor who, being in financial difficulties, requests that someone supervise his or her estate. Section 253, Insolvency Act. However, if the debtor is an undischarged bankrupt, then a request to the court may additionally be made by the trustee or official receiver for an arrangement or composition (e.g. 80p in the £) for the benefit of the creditors. The aim of the court in granting an interim order is to protect the debtor's estate from any bankruptcy that may be presented. Thus the debtor is given time to submit to the court, via the supervisor (*a*) the terms of the voluntary arrangement; and (*b*) the assets, liabilities and other items of information that may be required. For a *limited company*, it is a proposal under which the directors have agreed to a composition in satisfaction of its debts or a scheme of arrangement of its affairs. Section 1.

voluntary conveyance. Insolvency Act 1986 s. 207: 'When a company is ordered to be wound up by the Court or passes a resolution for voluntary winding up. A person is deemed to have committed an offence if he, being at the time an officer of the company: (*a*) has made or caused to be made any gift or transfer of, or charge on, or has caused or connived at the levying of any execution against, the company's property, or (*b*) has concealed or removed any part of the company's property since, or within 2 months before, the date of any unsatisfied judgment or order for the payment of money obtained against the company'. For the individual bankruptcy Section 357 of the Act states: 1. 'The bankrupt is guilty of an offence of he makes or causes to be made, or has in the period of 5 years ending with the commencement of the bankruptcy made or caused to be made, any gift or transfer of, or any charge on, his property. 2. The reference to making a transfer of or charge on any property includes causing or conniving at the levying of any execution against that property. 3. The bankrupt is guilty of an offence if he conceals or removes, or has at any time before the commencement of the bankruptcy concealed or removed, any part of his property after, or within 2 months before, the date on which judgment or order for the payment of money has been obtained against him, being a judgment or order which was not satisfied before the commencement of the bankruptcy'.

voluntary insolvency of an individual. Where a debtor simply cannot pay his debts, he may petition the court presenting his statement of affairs, showing his assets and liabilities. If necessary the court will issue a bankruptcy order. Alternatively a bankruptcy order will not be made and instead an administration order will be made.

voluntary liquidation, voluntary winding-up. Where it is proposed to wind-up a company voluntarily, the directors must make a statutory declaration that they have made a full enquiry into the affairs of the company and in their opinion the company can pay its debts in full with any interest due. The resolution must be passed to the registrar of companies wihtin 15 days of passing the resolution. This is called a members voluntary winding-up. For a creditors voluntary winding-up, the company must pass a special resolution that it cannot pay its debts and it would be advisable to wind-up the company. The company must call a meeting of its creditors, giving them at least seven days notice. With a creditors voluntary winding-up, the company must by extraordinary resolution resolve that due to its liabilities it cannot continue to trade, so that it would be necessary for the company to summon a meeting of creditors for a day not later than the 14th day after the date of passing the resolution, s. 98(1). The creditors may nominate their own liquidator, s. 100(1). *See* WINDING-UP OF A COMPANY.

voluntary patient. *See* MENTAL INCAPACITY.

voluntary winding-up. *See* VOLUNTARY LIQUIDATION.

vostro **account.** Banks that maintain accounts, in local currency, for banks abroad – literally, 'your account with us.' *See also* NOSTRO ACCOUNT.

vote. To give an opinion. To give a preference between one person and another or between one item and another. To express an agreement or disagreement on a resolution at a meeting.

voting rights. The rights of a shareholder to vote at a general or extraordinary general meeting. The right of a person to vote at a local or national election.

voucher. A document that confirms or explains an entry in a book of account. A receipt for goods purchased. A document that entails either some verification of a contract or a receipt.

voyage charter. A charter party whereby the ship is chartered for a single voyage.

voyage policy. A marine policy for a particular voyage only.

W

wage. A sum of money paid, usually weekly, by an employer to an employee for work carried out. This can be a cash payment, but often the amount due is paid into the employee's bank account. From the gross amount due, there are deductions such as income tax, national insurance, pension, etc. The sum paid is often referred to as wages, so in popular parlance the singular and plural are interchangeable.

wages/salaries account. While all companies have this type of expense account, it is important for banks, when they feel that a business borrower is in danger of going into liquidation, a separate current account is opened for the purpose of paying wages and salaries. This is done deliberately as the bank can then be classified, for the purposes of the Insolvency Act 1986 Sch. 6, as a preferential creditor. When this is likely to occur, the bank may claim to be a preferential creditor in respect of remuneration paid to employees for a period of 4 months preceding liquidation, for a sum of up to £800 per employee, or such amount as prescribed by order of the Secretary of State. The separate account simplifies the claim that is likely to be made.

waiver. The relinquishing of a claim or right against another party. This act must be made intentionally with the knowledge of the results of such an act, e.g. a holder of a bill of exchange may waive his rights against the acceptor.

waiver clause. A clause in a contract that will permit a party to renounce a condition in certain circumstances.

wallflower. A description of shares that are relatively dormant on the stock exchange as there are few buyers and sellers.

Wall Street. The popular name for the financial district of New York. It is where the New York and American Stock Exchanges are, plus a large number of major US and foreign banks are situated.

ward. Guardianship, control; a pupil, minor or person under guardianship.

ward in chancery. A minor under the protection of the court.

wardship. The office of a guardian; the state of being under a guardian.

warehousekeeper's certificate. A document or receipt from a warehousekeeper that the goods as described on the certificate or receipt are being held in the named warehouse. This document is not a negotiable instrument it is therefore not acceptable by the bank as collateral. Should the bank wish to have the goods so stored as security, it would request the borrowing customer to pledge the goods to the bank and request a certificate to the effect that the goods have in fact been transferred to the bank's name.

warehousekeeper's lien. Where goods have been left for storage with a warehousekeeper, then he/she has the right to retain the goods until payment for storage has been made. From the point of view of a bank, the charge that they may require over the goods, will necessitate the payment of all charges to the warehouse keeper before the goods are released and made available for sale.

warehousekeeper's receipt. See WARE-HOUSEKEEPER'S CERTIFICATE.

warehousekeeper's warrant. A document that is transferable by indorsement and delivery. The ware housekeeper must have the statutory power to issue these warrants. A bank holding a warehousekeeper's warrant for goods registered in its name, will transfer this warrant to a customer only against the signing of a trust receipt, which will then allow the customer to obtain the goods and when sold, remit the proceeds to the bank.

warehouse-to-warehouse clause. This is a clause in an insurance policy that covers the goods from the seller's warehouse until the warehouse of its destination.

war loan. A government stock issued during World War II, with a very low rate of interest and is irredeemable.

warrandice. Chiefly in Scots law, a clause in a deed binding the grantor to make good to the grantee any loss arising out of obligations antecedent to the date of the conveyance; the right conveyed; warranty.

warrant. A document authorising the payment of money. An authority allowing a person to take some action, e.g. enter a person's house, or be brought before a court. A form of cheque issued by a government department. *See also* DOCK WARRANT; WAREHOUSEKEEPER'S WARRANT.

warrant for goods. *See* WAREHOUSE-KEEPER'S WARRANT; WAREHOUSEKEEPER'S CERTIFICATE.

warranty. A form of guaranty that the item in question is of the standard required. An assurance that a thing is as represented or described. A clause in an agreement for the sale of goods, the breach of which will give rise to a claim for damages. In Scotland, a breach of warranty is considered as a failure to perform a material part of a contract.

war risks insurance. A clause in a policy of marine insurance which covers a vessel and the goods on the vessel to cover a state of war between two or more nations, but not necessarily the country in which the vessel is registered. Such acts as hitting a mine, being shelled, etc. would be covered by this clause.

waste. Any material that can no longer be used. Scrap. Any effluent discharge. Damage to land or property that is likely to be a lasting or permanent loss.

wasting asset. Any asset that has a predictable useful life so that it is necessary to make adequate depreciation from annual profits.

waybill. A list of articles or persons carried by a vehicle. Often referred to as a consignment note. *See also* AIRWAY BILL.

wayleave. A right of way granted by a

landowner for some specific purpose in consideration of payment.

ways and means advances. Advances made by the Bank of England to the Treasury to pay for the annual supply services.

weak. A term applied to a currency which has become worth less in terms of another currency.

weak market. A market in which there is very little activity or where there are more sellers than buyers.

wear and tear. The depreciation of an asset by its regular use.

weekly return. The weekly balance sheet of the Bank of England.

weighting. An adjustment on a banking charge in recognition of an exceptional service given to a customer; the giving of a greater importance to certain items in the construction of an index number.

weight note. In trade, a note issued by an independent third party evidencing gross and net weights of goods.

white goods. This description refers to kitchen equipment, which generally is white. This will include, freezers, refrigerators, washing machines, etc.

white knight. The bidder who has received agreement to take over a company to prevent another predator from taking possession of that company.

White Paper. An official statement of government policy on an issue of the day.

whole life policy. A life assurance policy under the terms of which a fixed sum is payable on the death of the life assured, passing into his or her estate for the benefit of the heirs.

wholesale. Sale of goods in bulk to retailers; selling or buying in large quantities; extensive; indiscriminate.

wholesale banking. As opposed to retail banking which deals with the 'man in the street', wholesale banking is the borrowing and lending of funds to other banks, large national and international companies, government departments or agencies, etc. As a general description it will cover activities in the various money markets.

wholesale cost. The cost to the retailer of buying goods in bulk from the producer or wholesaler.

will. A declaration in writing, made by a mature person in a formal manner showing how he would like his/her estate to be distributed after his/her death. The testator's signature must be witnessed by two persons. The will can be revoked, by making out a new one, or changed by adding a codicil.

windbill. An accommodation bill accepted by the drawee to oblige the drawer, without consideration for so doing; a 'kite'.

windfall. An expression used for the unexpected receipt of funds, e.g. the refund of income tax, a premium bond prize, unexpected increase in profits or dividend.

winding-up of a company. The winding-up of a company can be either compulsory – by order of the court – or voluntary by order of the creditors, or by order of the shareholders of the company. The court will order the winding-up of a company if: (*a*) the company has passed a special resolution to that effect; (*b*) the company does not commence business within a year of its incorporation; (*c*) the number of members is reduced to below two; (*d*) the court considers it just and equitable that the company should be wound up; (*e*) the company is unable to pay its debts, (i.e. a debt of £750 or more after due demand remains unsettled for a period exceeding three weeks); (*f*) a company registered as a public company has not been issued with its certificate. By s. 84, Insolvency Act 1986, a company will wind up voluntarily when: (*a*) the period for its duration has been reached, or an event has occurred which was specified in the Articles of Association as an event that would herald the winding-up of the company; (*b*) a special resolution of the company; (*c*) the company by extraordinary resolution cannot continue to trade and wishes to wind up. Where claims of creditors are unlikely to be met, they may appoint a liquidator (under s. 100) to supervise the winding-up.

window dressing. An event that takes place on or near the end of the financial year of a business entity, whereby the balances of various accounts are manipulated to show the state of affairs of the business in a more favourable light. This may be done by the concealment of liabilities, bring forward sales figures. This manipulation of figures may or may not be a fraudulent act. The reversal of these entries will take place soon after the end of the financial year.

WIP. The abbreviation for work in progress or partly finished goods.

wiping. The passing of a plastic card through a card reader to record the information/card details to process the transaction. The card may be used at points of sale (EFTPOS), when the holder's account will be debited within two or three days. Currently the same card can be used for cash withdrawals from an ATM.

wire fate. *See* SPECIAL CLEARANCE.

withdrawal. The act of taking money out of an account at a bank, building society or other financial institution. This may be done by taking cash out of an account, or by the transfer of funds to another person.

withholding tax. A procedure for the deduction of tax on dividends or other sources of income, e.g. interest on bank deposit accounts and building society accounts. Any non-taxpayer may obtain a refund from the Inland Revenue.

without engagement. A term used by banks when they are merely advising another bank or customer of information passed to them by another bank or branch, e.g. on advising a beneficiary of a letter of credit of another bank. A quotation of a price or contract terms which is not meant to be binding on either party.

without prejudice. Without abandoning a claim or right; without impairing any pre-existing right.

without recourse. Can be known as *sans recours*, meaning that a previous party has no responsibility to a previous transaction. In the case of forfaiting a bill of exchange, the forfaitor will agree, that should the bill be dishonoured there will be no recourse to the drawer. A bank will have no recourse to a customer if it is collecting a cheque for itself and not for the customer. With a factoring service, the factor that undertakes the reponsibility for bad debts will have no recourse to the client in the event of a debtor being unable to pay. Buyer credit under an ECGD guarantee, will give the exporter funds without recourse should the overseas buyer be unable to pay. There are many instances where export finance can be available from a bank without recourse to the borrower. A party to a bill of exchange can negate his liability by adding the words *sans recours* after his signature, however the transferability/negotiability will then be somewhat restricted.

without reserve. At an auction, an indication of complete freedom as to bidding and a guarantee that goods will be sold at whatever price is bid.

with particular average (WPA). A clause in a document of insurance which will cover the partial loss or damage to goods while in transit.

'with profits policy'. A policy of life assurance which entitles the assured a share of the annual profits of the company. Such profits are given as bonuses at the end of the financial year. The premiums on this type of policy are usually higher than a non-profits policy or a whole life policy.

with recourse. A right to claim funds from a previous party. A bank will act as agent for collection for a customer and present cheques, dividend warrants, etc., for payment on the understanding that should any item be returned unpaid, then the customer's account may be debited. Any party to a bill of exchange has a right of recourse to the drawer, payee or previous holder should the bill be dishonoured for non-acceptance and/or non-payment. The same conditions apply when a bank discounts a bill for a customer or under a documentary collection remits the financial document and commercial paper to its agent abroad.

witness. A person that provides proof. In a court of law a person who under oath provides evidence. A person who signs his/her name to a document to certify the genuiness of the testator's signature, e.g. a will.

word processor. A piece of electronic equipment which is capable of storing, editing, altering text which has been typed in the first instance on to a screen and then stored into the memory, usually on disks. A word processor is capable of changing the style or thickness of the printing process, underlining, centring and justifying the data. Word processing equipment must include not only the processor, but a disk drive, visual display unit (VDU) and a printer, in order to perform all the necessary functions. Many of the standardised letters sent by banks are maintained on disks and when necessary sent to customers with amendments if and when necessary.

words of severance. Words in a grant or deed which show that tenants will take distinct and separate equal shares of the land and not as joint tenants.

work. The undertaking of some physical or mental activity. It frequently relates to some nature of employment or earning a living, not necessarily to a leisure activity.

work centre. An office, factory, centre, where a person or group of persons go to on a regular basis to perform their particular jobs.

working capital. Often described as circulating capital. The money and other liquid assets available for the day-to-day operations of a business. It is calculated by deducting the current liabilities from the current assets.

working day. For the purposes of the Consumer Credit Act 1974, any day other than 1. Saturday or Sunday; 2. Christmas Day or Good Friday; 3. a bank holiday within the meaning given by s. 1 of the Banking and Financial Dealings Act 1971.

working expenses. All expenses necessarily incurred in the running of a business (e.g. rent, rates, wages, etc.) and entered in the profit and loss account.

working party. A group or committee appointed by a board of directors or some other authority to undertake research or an enquiry within the terms of reference stated and then report their findings to that authority.

work in progress (WIP). Incomplete goods on the production or process line, or a project that has not yet been completed. The value of such an asset is usually valued at cost of materials plus the element of labour. It is brought into the final accounts and balance sheet at the end of each financial period.

works oncost. Production overheads: the cost of the expenses of production.

work study. *See* TIME AND MOTION STUDY.

World Bank. *See* INTERNATIONAL BANK FOR RECONSTRUCTION AND DEVELOPMENT.

writ. An order issued in the name of the Sovereign or from a court ordering some action, e.g. an appearance in court, or an order to refrain from some action.

writ of attachment. *See* ATTACHMENT.

writ of *capias*. A judicial order directing an officer of the court to arrest and imprison a judgment debtor. It is very rarely used nowadays.

writ of *distringas*. *See* DISTRINGAS.

writ of execution. A writ directed to the sheriff, commanding him to take certain compulsory proceedings for the purpose of carrying into effect a judgment of the court.

writ of *fieri facias*. *See also* FIERI FACIAS.

writ of possession. An order directing a sheriff to put a person in possession. The appropriate writ for the recovery of possession of land. It issues against the person in possession and if this person is the tenant he or she is bound to give notice of the writ to the landlord, who may then apply for leave to enter an appearance and defend the action.

writ of sequestration. Where a person fails to perform an act or disobeys an injunction a writ may be issued whereby the sequestrators may take possession of his/her goods or estate until the judgment has been complied with. When a bank hears of a writ issued against a customer, the bank should conduct the account normally until they receive a demand for payment. On receiving such notice, the bank will surrender to the sequestrators such balances, articles, information as demanded. Confidentiality may on this occasion be breached and any attempt by the customer to transfer items from safe custody or balances should be advised to the sequestrators.

writ of summons. The formal document by which a High Court action is commenced.

write down. To reduce the book value of an asset.

write off. To remove entirely from the asset book values, as with a bad debt which it has proved impossible to recover; to cancel; to dismiss from consideration.

writer. The person who executes an opening purchase or sale of a trading option contract. The writer of a put option will be obliged to buy and the writer of a call option is obliged to sell at the agreed price by a specified day. The name given to an insurance underwriter.

write-up. The making of an entry or entries to an account, or the completion of entries onto a statement prior to despatch to a customer.

written law. *See* STATUTE LAW.

wrongful trading. Wrongful trading must be distinguished from fraudulent trading as it is subject to civil proceedings. Wrongful trading is applied to a person if: (*a*) the company has gone into insolvent liquidation; (*b*) at some time before the commencement of the winding-up of the company, that person knew or ought to have concluded that there was no reasonable prospect that the company would avoid going into insolvent liquidation; and (*c*) that person was a director of the company at that time (Section 214, Insolvency Act). The court will not make a declaration if it is satisfied that the person took every step to minimise the potential loss. For the purposes of this Act, the facts which the person ought to have known, or ascertained and the conclusions that ought to have been reached, or the steps which ought to have been taken will be considered in the light of the general knowledge, skill and experience that may be expected of a person carrying out the functions of a director of that company, and the actual general knowledge, skill and experience the director in question has. This section also includes a shadow director. *See* SHADOW DIRECTOR. Should a director be found guilty of wrongful trading, he or she may be ordered to contribute to the assets of the company by way of compensation, the sum being as the court thinks fit.

wrongly delivered. This refers to cheques and other negotiable instruments that have been presented to either the wrong bank or the wrong branch of a bank. The receiving bank must, on the same day, remit the instrument direct to the drawee bank and make the necessary adjustment and claim the amount through the clearing system.

wrong post. The placing of a debit or a credit amount to a wrong account.

X

xd. The abbreviation for ex dividends. *See* EX DIV.

xr. The abbreviation for ex rights.

xw. The abbreviation for ex warrants. This signifies that a stock is trading without warrants attached or to be issued.

Y

yearling bond. *See* LOCAL AUTHORITY BONDS.

yankee bond market. A US dollar bond issued in the USA by non-US banks and corporations when conditions are more favourable than the domestic or Eurobond market.

Yellow Book. The more common name for the 'admission of securities to listing' which is issued by the International Stock Exchange. It sets out the rules and regulations for admission to the Official List.

yearly tenancy. A contract whereby a person has a tenancy on a yearly basis. Notice to quit must be given before the contract expires.

years' purchase. The purchase price of property in terms of a given number of years rent.

yield. The measurement on a profit or return. A measurement of income, usually in percentage terms that a person has received from his/her investment. *See* DIVIDEND YIELD; FLAT (OR RUNNING) YIELD; GROSS YIELD; NET YIELD; REDEMPTION YIELD.

yield curve. A graph showing different interest yields at different times along a scale.

yield gap. The difference between the average yield on long-dated gilts and the approximate yield on shares or property.

York–Antwerp rules. A shipping code drawn up in 1897 amended in 1924 and again in 1974 and refers to the general average in marine insurance.

yours. A word used in the foreign exchange market to indicate that they will sell the currency in question.

yo-yo stock. A description of stocks or shares that are very volatile and whose price rises and falls very quickly.

Z

zero budgeting. It is a concept that in each budget period the costs involved must be justified without any reference to a previous period and without carrying forward any past debt or balance.

zero coupon bonds. These bonds originated in the USA. They are bonds that have been issued by a company in need of funds, but will not pay any annual interest, instead the bonds may be issued at a large discount or at maturity the holder will receive a large premium.

zero rating. For the purposes of Value Added Tax (VAT), certain listed goods will bear no tax charge.

zoning. The division into areas or regions. This may be in geographical areas, commodities, green belt programmes, etc.

zoological certificate. Issued for the benefit of an importer, by a third party in the seller's country indicating whether the hides or foodstuffs are free from disease or contamination. Often called a health certificate.